SALSA TALKS
A Musical Heritage Uncovered
By Mary Kent

Copyright © 2005 by Mary Kent

First Edition
First Printing–2005

Published by Digital Domain
931 N.S.R. 434, Suite 1201-168
Altamonte Springs, FL 32714
(800) 344-4361, (407) 831-0233
www.salsatalks.com

Publisher's Catalog-in-Publication Data
Kent, Mary
     Salsa Talks: A Musical Heritage Uncovered / by Mary Kent.–1st ed.
     Includes bibliographical references, glossary and index
     1. Popular Music—United States–History and criticism   I. Title
     2. Popular Music—Latin America–History and criticism
     3. Salsa Music—Puerto Rico, New York, Latin America—History and Criticism
     4. Salsa Musicians—United States/Afro-Caribbean-interviews
     5. Performing Arts—Salsa (Music)

     781.64 KEN   ML3475 .C35

     Library of Congress Control Number: 2005900309
     ISBN 0-9764990-0-2 Hardcover
     Price $59.95

1 2 3 4 5 6 7 8 9 10

Printed in China

DEDICATED TO

my husband, Bob Katz, for encouraging my every endeavor

and all the Salsa music lovers

Editor
Aurora Flores

Design Concept
José Pacheco

Graphic Design
Book Production
Jeanne Euker

Contributing Editor
Bob Katz

Editorial Assistant
Proofreading
Andrew Hollis

Production Assistant
Rachael Horning

ACKNOWLEDGMENTS

I want to thank some people who generously offered their help so that the final product would be better. Ralph Mercado, who opened many doors in the salsa world for me. Ana Araiz (R.I.P.) for putting me on the Monday night list at SOB's, Maria Martiniello, for the great title for this book and your help in the initial stages of Salsa Talks, Jacques Urrutia, for help with transcriptions; Al Santiago and Joe Cuba for your friendship and unique insight into salsa's cast of characters (as well as being a cast of characters yourselves); Joe Conzo for bringing Tito Puente to my studio; Louie Ramírez for convincing Eddie Palmieri to be interviewed; Victor Gallo of Key Productions, for providing music cassettes of many Fania releases; and Juan Toro, for that secret phone number. To all the artists who granted an interview, you have been so generous. To Polito Vega, for getting me Hector Lavoe's phone number. During his last few months, I'd give Hector a call and talk to him for a few minutes. In a velvet fog, he sensed my presence and he listened contentedly. Then he'd hang up.

Pedro Knight, loving husband of Celia Cruz, talented trumpeter and musician, and Luis Falcón, Celia and Pedro's adoptive son, thank you for your support. Thanks, Edward Palmieri II, for help in clarifying details in Eddie senior's chapter. José Rodríguez, thanks for providing your beautiful photos of Roberto Roena on such short notice; José

Flores for historic Fania photos. Daisy Collado, of Marc Anthony Productions, gracias for your cheery and professional confidence. Edward James Olmos and Andy Garcia, thanks for your support of Latin music and this book.

Thanks to my brother Alexander W. Kent, who funded my first computer so I could start this project; I miss you, Alex. To my dad and mom, for instilling in me the deep love for dancing and this music. My dad, a Cuban-American, was my first dance partner, and he could dance! As a consequence, all my nephews and nieces have developed a love for this music and dancing—Amanda, AJ, Caroline, Jason, James and Christina, this musical tradition will continue to thrive with your help.

I'm not a scholar, I just play the part. In the research part of my work I have met some genuine Latin music scholars who have generously provided their knowledge, among them Vernon Boggs (R.I.P.), Frank Figueroa, and especially René López, Max Salazar, and Dr. Robert Farris Thompson, who have contributed munchy chapter-size bites. And, of course, thanks to all the musicians who are their own enthomusicologists! Finally I thank my husband Bob Katz, audio mastering engineer extraordinaire. So talented and so loving. The many times I got home at 4 AM, after doing research in the clubs, I would hear, without a hint of jealousy, "Did you have a good time, dear?"

SALSA
TALKS!

The slap of a drum, trumpets piercing through walls of rhythms, a piano vamps and swings through layers of music punctuated by the chiseled timing and phrasing of a voice that soars above the musical structure to penetrate our souls, capture our emotions while defining who and where we are. Its rhythms, steeped in African resistance, drive us to our feet to dance in melodic unison.

¡Salsa! Born in a time of change in a life-changing era. The civil rights movement swept the country with strength that only cutting through chains could have. The Black Panthers, The Young Lords, The Last Poets and Nuyorican griots emerged as prophets, saints and callers of the times. Everything Cuban was forbidden while a controversial war waged in Vietnam. Back in New York, AM radio was strong, R&B was king, boogaloo boomed from the projects to the Apollo while Latinos gathered with other revelers of this Afro-Boricua youth movement in Central Park, jamming rumbas and bombas on *barriles* and congas. The heartbeat emitting from the throbbing fusion of flesh and hide wrapped 'round wood was earthshatteringly consuming. Here in the forest of the metropolis, the music that hailed from Africa via the Great Antilles, that began as a form of struggle and solace against oppression, found its spotlight in New York.

¡Salsa Talks! takes us on a personal, photographically illustrated journey through the lives of some of the musicians and insiders who have taken this music around the world. This is not another salsa history book, nor is it an academic thesis turned novel. Rather, it is a testament in photos to the beauty and artistry of salsa and a curious peek into the heart of the people that make this music the soundtrack of our lives.

Since 1988, the red haired Latina from Barranquilla, Colombia criss-crossed concerts and cultures shooting salsa idols with an artistic eye that paralleled the artistry of this musical phenomenon. Cutting an angular figure, camera in hand, on the pulse of the music industry, Mary Kent was a constant on the scene capturing the beauty of a blended music created by racially mixed people who turned the pain of life into glorious musical ecstasy. Her joy for the music and its dance was as deep as salsa's roots and as sincere as the shout of ¡Azucar!

Her passion became the driving force behind the creation of ¡Salsa Talks! After much research on the evolution of this music, Mary took recorder in hand as she shot photos and asked hundreds of questions from which flowed some of the most interesting stories compiled on this music straight from the artists themselves. She conducted and translated all the Spanish language interviews herself providing a most intimate groundwork for the telling of ¡Salsa Talks!

Mary dug deeply beyond the superficial layer of song and dance. Stories of racism, segregation, shady deals and seedy characters emerged to complete the historical picture that is the Latin music world. But there are tender moments as well—such as the time Richie Ray prayed with Jerry Masucci when the salsa producer was sick. Or when Jerry gave him the money to produce his first Christian recording.

The very distinct prisms of reality that these stories are filtered through evoke a variety of emotions while provoking thought on the industry. Cheo Feliciano's daunting tale of redemption crystallizes the pitfalls on the road to fame. Andy González's historical content of the Bronx during his years at Music & Art paint a socially significant scenery that brings the music into direct contact with its R&B neighbors and jazz relations.

On the fringes of a shifted society, musicians of polyrhythmic persuasion mixed music with nationalities. Salsa emerged from *los solares* of the Caribbean to the barrios of Nueva York becoming a form of individual nationality and communal identity.

Salsa has as many definitions as it does colors and cultures. Mary Kent captured the controversy in photos and dialog. Asking each artist their thoughts and definition of the term, Mary encountered a myriad of meanings and reactions as diverse as its exponents.

Looming past the shadows throughout this book are reflexions on Rafael Cortijo y su Combo as well as mastersinger Ismael Rivera. Cortijo's rhythmic innovations mixed Boricua folklore with Cuban dance basics creating a formula that personified Martí's description of Puerto Rico and Cuba as two wings of the same bird. Cortijo's influence appears in the memories of musicians proving that Puerto Rican folk is as much a part of the salsa mix as the Cuban *son*.

Stories of racism and struggle arise in ¡Salsa Talks! Like the time when Louie Ramírez's piano teacher told him that no one will sponsor a Latino kid in classical music. Or his memory of a tour in the South with Tito Rodríguez when the singer was served a steak with a cigarette in it. Eddy Zervigón remembers two Cubas, one white, the other black with separate socials and gatherings for each. While Pete "El Conde" Rodríguez describes a segregated

military that propelled him to embrace his Afro-Boricua heritage with tenacity.

The chapter **Salsa Is Born** puts the music and the business on point. Its historical setting brands New York Latinos with a fever as hot as the fire that swept over Woodstock.

Who really introduced the dynamic duo of Hector LaVoe & Willie Colón to each other? ¡Salsa Talks! has the answer. Other revelations have both Eddie Palmieri and Mon Rivera introducing the trombone sound to New York. Whether Mon or Eddie, only Al Santiago knows for sure.

India speaks on Latin hip-hop and how a professional voice coach saved her life with a powerful technique while Marc Anthony brushes off technique and proper breathing, placing his focus on "feeling."

From the superficial to the sublime, from the proud to the philosophical, "Salsa Talks" raps with the fellas revealing in its absence the lack of women in the industry except for Celia, India and Canelita Medina.

I was thrilled when Mary approached me to edit this book. First I was proud because the book springs from the talents of an upbeat woman, whose sunny disposition radiates warmth and universal blessings. Second, it was a challenge because as a young journalist I grew up in this industry and was personally close to many of the artists that are speaking here in ¡Salsa Talks! Whether you enjoy the redemption of Cheo Feliciano or the swagger of Tito Puente, ¡Salsa Talks! stories will inspire while its photos will take you there.

Aurora Flores *Latin music journalist, historian, producer, musician and bandleader*

foreword

As Eddie Palmieri says, I am here to spread the word of salsa. The artists, producers and educators who speak here have made sizeable contributions to the patrimony of salsa and are in a unique position to share their insights with their peers and audience. Many musicians tell about the frequency with which they have been misquoted. Salsa Talks has made an effort to allow the musicians to tell the story of their lives and to talk about *la música* without any interference; each individual personality shines through, often with a brilliant light.

Writing this book has been a rewarding experience, almost 15 years to gather this oral legacy and mold it into a written structure. In 1989 I started documenting salsa performances as an independent photographer, frequently for the Ralph Mercado organization. The more activities I attended, the more curious I became about the history of this music. Blessed by my proximity to many of salsa's legends, I took on the biggest challenge of my life—to get the story of salsa straight from the protagonists who have determined the course of its history. Little by little, the story came together. I found not one truth, but a multifold dimension of the truth. We learn of their origins, whether humble or privileged, how they got involved in music and how it affected their lives. The picture that they paint is poignant, often charismatic and altogether human, a manifold view of a musical tradition evolving since the beginning of the twentieth century. This story of their lives is their generous gift to us—the stars immerse us in their craft, delivering musical concepts in an enjoyable, easy-going manner.

Some very special musicians are presented in these pages, salsa Superstars. Most have been in the business for over 20 years and have recorded many albums. None is a one hit wonder! The majority of the artists in this book play what is referred to as *salsa gorda* (fat), *salsa brava* (hard-core), the hard-edged salsa that dancers love. Some play *salsa romántica*, a trend that emphasizes the singer fronting the band, with love stories intertwined.

During the book's gestation period, I lost several friends who had poured their hearts out in interviews. The world lost artists Mario Bauzá, Celia Cruz, Hector Lavoe, Tito Puente, Louie Ramírez, and Pete "El Conde" Rodríguez. Producer Al Santiago, promoter Jack Hooke, and impresario Jerry Masucci, are no longer with us. I had an interview opportunity with Hector the last time he performed at SOBs. He was weak and his arms were full of skin lesions; ironically, that was the day I forgot the microphone. But Hector's character speaks through those who knew him, in several chapters. Machito, La Lupe, Ismael Rivera, Rafael Cortijo, and Tito Rodríguez passed away before my New York time. There is a belief that the departed musical giants have formed a big band in heaven. I hope when my day comes, I will get a good seat. I will miss them and the salsa world will always remember them.

The huge controversy surrounding salsa's origins is not over. Cubans, Puerto Ricans and even New Yorkers will be fighting for paternity rights ad infinitum. All parties have made monumental contributions that are intertwined with no clearcut boundary. Larry Harlow reveals how the Cuban revolution directly affected the present form of this music (chapter 13). In chapter 42, Max Salazar showcases salsa, the globetrotter. Home-grown salsa bands are prospering in Japan, Sweden, Germany, Finland, Israel, France and all over the world. Orquesta de la Luz, the hot salsa band from Japan, sold almost a million albums on their first release.

But New York City's hot melting pot percolated and blended the multi-cultural sauce. The spicy beats were broadcast from here—the Palladium mambo, boogaloo, cha cha cha. New York has also been the measure of popularity obtained by the different artists. "If you make it there, you can make it anywhere."

Ferreting my way around this maze has not been easy. Memory is fragile and arbitrary, ten people who lived the same event perceived it differently. But that is how history is written. The busiest musicians were the most difficult to track down, I literally braved a blizzard to get the interview with Roberto Roena! I interviewed Papo Lucca in the dressing room at the new Palladium on 14th street, between performances, amidst the horn section tuning their instruments.

One of the most creative conga players around, Carlos "Patato" Valdés (chapter 38) communicates through his drums. Patato can drop names that bear witness to a varied career—even sex goddess Brigitte Bardot fell under his percussive spell. This Beethoven of the Conga is at his best when his instinctive, intuitive creativity is given free reign. In that impulsive spirit, I grabbed him one day strolling on Manhattan's West Side, convinced Patato to ride the train to my photo studio. I still chuckle at the image of tall Mary and diminutive percussion giant Patato walking arm in arm into the subway.

Larry Harlow quizzed my qualifications, questioned my cause and then generously offered his historical perspective. Larry's creative quest continues in the new millennium with Latin jazz.

The first time I spoke to Joe Cuba, I explained the interview was in my fourth floor walk up photo studio, and that he had to dance for my photo. Recovering from a hip operation, this salsa veteran exclaimed, "You've got to be crazy, Mary!" Finally, he courageously hip-hopped up all four flights to then share a candid, rousing interview and subsequently, danced his heart out for my lens. The rest is—literally—history, expressed in chapter 6.

As a photographer, I have documented the salsa world in its full splendor, from a privileged perspective backstage and in dressing rooms. Thousands of memories are encapsulated in those "decisive moments", like the night when the soneros squared off at Madison Square Garden, or the *Perfect Combination* recording session at Electric Lady Studios.

This book is dedicated to the massive audience that religiously partakes in salsa's rhythmic pleasures. Go to the clubs, demand and support live music, one live band is worth a thousand DJs. Begin your salsa journey by listening to some of the albums mentioned throughout the book. To start off, I recommend the albums *Salsa*, by Larry Harlow, and *Siembra*, by Rubén Blades and Willie Colón. Descarga.com and Latin Beat Magazine are excellent salsa resources. Visit www.salsatalks.com for links to more.

And now, salsa will talk to you, beginning with an insight into the meaning of that elusive word.

Mary Kent *January 27, 2005*

intro

What Is Salsa?

In this preamble, salsa protagonists talk about the origin of the term salsa used for the Afro-Caribbean music rooted in the Cuban *son* and revamped in the barrios of New York. The experts present definitions, characteristics and categories of salsa.

Bandleaders, Musicians, Arrangers, Singers/Soneros, Producers, Promoters, Experts

In the central chapters, superstar salsa musicians, bandleaders and arrangers talk about their lives and their musical contributions to salsa history. We interview the most important salsa lead singers. They tell us their version of the story of salsa and the role they played in its history. We meet the salsa promoters, those who profit from the salsa industry and experts (music historians, writers, record producers).

Salsa Is Born—Three Concerts

Better than a backstage pass, this narration provides a manifold perspective of three concerts that mark salsa history. We travel back in time—through the eyes of the musicians and promoters.

Bandleaders, Musicians, Arrangers, Singers/Soneros, Producers, Promoters, Experts

contents

contents

Salsa Is Born

THREE CONCERTS
from the eyes of the performers

Turn to page 394 for the story of three concerts which were instrumental in spreading salsa all over the world.

¿*What* .*is*

SAL•SA
PRONUNCIATION:
(SÄL'SU; SP. SÄL'SÄ), [KEY] —N.

1. A LIVELY, VIGOROUS TYPE OF CONTEMPORARY LATIN AMERICAN POPULAR MUSIC, BLENDING PREDOMINANTLY CUBAN RHYTHMS WITH ELEMENTS OF JAZZ, ROCK, AND SOUL MUSIC.

2. A BALLROOM DANCE OF PUERTO RICAN ORIGIN, PERFORMED TO THIS MUSIC, SIMILAR TO THE MAMBO, BUT FASTER WITH THE ACCENT ON THE FIRST BEAT INSTEAD OF THE SECOND BEAT OF EACH MEASURE.

3. MEXICAN COOKERY. A SAUCE, ESP. A HOT SAUCE CONTAINING CHILIES.

—V.I. TO DANCE THE SALSA.

"Salsa." Infoplease Dictionary. ©2003 Pearson Education. 19 May. 2003

"It warms your blood"

salsa?

Identifying a salsa tune is not a difficult thing. You listen to it—if the rhythm is cookin' and the bottom of your body starts jumpin' with the urge to dance, there's a good possibility you're listening to salsa music. It's dance music that just happens to be fun! But it's a lot of other things too. Salsa music is an art form rich with tradition, innovation, evolution, and the musical creativity of Afro-Caribbean people.

In the seventies, when salsa rhythms swept the world, the term salsa became part of the international lingo. Several people claim they were the first to use it within a musical context. I was astonished to hear the number of definitions of salsa that came from the lips of my interviewees. Here are some of them...

MARIO BAUZA

On the radio program *Nuestra Salsa en Cuba*, when asked for a definition of salsa a writer responded: "Salsa is an attractive, spunky mulatta. Salsa is the guaguancó's cousin, the mambo's niece and the danzón's sister."

Salsa is nothing. Salsa is all the Cuban genres. I say it was Graciela, Machito's sister, who launched the term. When we were in Puerto Rico in 1966, Paquito Navarro, a radio announcer, asked Graciela: "How are you?" She answered, "I've got more salsa than fish!" a popular saying in Cuba (they even wrote a danzón called *More Salsa Than Fish).*

When he came to New York and landed a radio program, Paquito started using the phrase, "salsa with fish." Well, before long they got rid of the fish and Fania Records kept the salsa.

CELIA CRUZ

Salsa is simply all the Cuban rhythms under one name. I recorded with Pacheco three or four tunes that were previously referred to as guaracha and now are called salsa. If you look at it from my point of view, you will see that I am right. The Puerto Rican folklore is the bomba and the plena. The folklore from Santo Domingo is the merengue. The only thing that sounds like what we play in Cuba is salsa. Tito Puente has played Cuban music all his life. And when Pacheco started his Tumbao, the first tune he recorded was one by the Cuban group Sonora Matancera. When that movement became known as salsa, it took on a broader dimension.

Nobody around here wants to recognize that it is Cuban music, including my maestro Tito Puente, who doesn't like it. He says, "Salsa is a sauce. Salsa is not music." Ok, salsa is not a musical term. Salsa is a name given to this music. But they haven't given that name to the bomba or the plena or the merengue. They have given it to Cuban music. Thanks to this, our music has come back, because in the 60s, when they closed the gates to my country, they used to say here, "Cuban music…old music." They started calling it salsa and it's reached all over the world.

JOHNNY PACHECO

I don't remember exactly when we said, "You know, we should call this salsa and cover the whole thing under one roof." Once we started traveling, people would ask, "What are you playing?" I used to say, this is a *son montuno*, and this is a *son*, this is a *guajira*, this is a *guaracha*. And they were getting confused. They said, "If we put everything under the name salsa, I think it's going to benefit all of us." And so we did.

We are not saying that it's not Cuban music, because I never said it wasn't. We took the Cuban music and since we grew up in New York and had jazz influence, we modernized certain chords. Instead of being tonic and dominant, we made them more flamboyant. And the rhythm section is more pronounced when we perform. For instance in Cuba, the rhythm section used to be in the back. Now we put the rhythm in front, because we figure we're gonna play for dancers, and that's what gives us the percussion sound.

JOE CUBA

What is salsa? It beats the shit out of me. I think salsa is the outgrowth of mambo and guaguancó. Mambo and salsa are different. It's a different flow. Mambo was more tranquil, mambo was on the beat, and salsa is an upbeat type of thing. It's a different feell can't explain.

Arsenio Rodríguez and the charangas that came from Cuba had a tremendous influence. It's really the Cuban roots that started the whole thing, the Cuban sound. They just gave a different name to it and maybe you think you are playing a different feel. I guess after every drink it gets different, it changes.

I always felt that we Latinos, Neoyorquinos were the ones that made the salsa sound. It comes from the barrios, El Barrio, the Bronx, Brooklyn, and Manhattan, but Ricans born here were the ones that really pushed the scene. Even the bandleaders and musicians are mostly Nuyoricans who exploded the mambo and the cha cha cha, now considered salsa. It's not Latinos born outside New York.

CHEO FELICIANO

The expression *salsa*, and what they call mambo, was born in New York. It was a mixture of Cuban rhythms and Puerto Rican musicians. Most of the Latin musicians in New York were Puerto Ricans. We developed a hybrid from jazz which was integrated in what we call mambo, the instrumental part within the arrangement in which the instruments play a riff. Then they started calling the whole creation or the dance, *mambo* which is from New York. So the beginning of salsa is mambo and it's

from New York. Today we call it *salsa*. It had its old names, because it was many different rhythms.

Salsa is a commercial term, the generic name for all of it. It simplified, for the rest of the world, a meaning for all these rhythms. But by using the term salsa we lose definition of the little differences between guaguancó, guaracha, son montuno and cha cha cha. When we call it all salsa, it loses a point in culture, in education, in identification, but it's very commercial. Salsa is easier to say.

JERRY MASUCCI

The music came from Cuba. The roots of the music anyway. Well… Africa by way of Cuba. But, definitely, it was born in New York City. Salsa. Not Latin music, not guaguancó, not cha cha cha. They still do old songs, but they sound different.

It's like having a kid without a name. One day you say, I'm gonna call her Shirley. But Shirley was there all along. Salsa is the name for the old Cuban music revamped by New York Puerto Rican groups in the late '60's, early '70's. It became more hip with a combination of jazz and modern arrangements. They'd take an old Cuban song, do it 20 years later, and it would be totally different. It was still in clave, but technically better, more jazz phrasings, more streamlined.

Before it was called salsa, there were records that to me were salsa, but weren't called salsa. To the best of my recollection, Ismael Quintana used to scream "Salsa!" up on stage. And Izzy Sanabria had a TV show in the early seventies called *Salsa*.

PETE "EL CONDE" RODRIGUEZ

Salsa is the commercial word for Cuban music, the roots come from there. When I played in the sixties, they called it Cuban music; the guaguancó,

son montuno, guaracha, mambo and rumba. We grouped that all together and called it salsa. We added our Puerto Rican style. We pushed that music more than anybody else, because when Castro took power in Cuba, most of that music wasn't reaching the United States and we kept it going. But then we created our own style. You see a Cuban band, they play different from us.

LOUIE RAMIREZ

It's Cuban based, but most people think it's Puerto Rican. People don't give credit to the Cubans, because Cuba was closed because of communism. Salsa is the evolution of mambo. When I write an arrangement for salsa, I'm writing the same thing that we did for mambo, except the definition progresses in time.

It's an infectious rhythm. Americans love it, even if they hear it for the first time. But that also happened when we played mambo.

MARTY SHELLER

Salsa is a name given to music that was basically Cuban. As different generations of *New York* musicians were influenced by different things, the music changed.

The influence of jazz and the Cuban style merged, along with popular music. In the 50s they called it mambo and Latin. As the influences started to change the music, the younger generation needed a way of making it different. The word salsa came about, and

they hooked on to it. A lot of the older musicians rebelled against it. "It's Cuban music and all they did was to put a little jazz on top of it." But it's not as closely aligned to the original Cuban music as it used to be.

LARRY HARLOW

It's a mix of Afro-Cuban music with a little New York know-how. It's the same clave, it's the same form, it's the same swing, maybe a little more flat. Or it's more intense, playing laid back, "Pa'lante y pa' tras."

IZZY SANABRIA

A woman writer from Cuba said the word salsa is used to disguise the fact that salsa is really Cuban music, that we changed it in order not to give credit to Cuba. She's right, but this was not pre-planned. I always said that it was Cuban music. But the young Puerto Ricans kept it alive and developed it. Because of the rhythm of the city, it's now charged with a highly accelerated energy.

This music was from the ghettos, lower class music, but that is where all music comes from. Soul, jazz, it all comes from the lower classes. This music was Negroid. The only dark-skinned salsa artist that the white Cubans exalted was Celia Cruz. The music that white Cubans in this country hear is the charanga

sound played by all white musicians. Orquesta Broadway doesn't want to be categorized as salsa... well it's not. It's very rhythmic, beautiful music. It swings, but it's violin and flute, a softer swing.

I was acknowledged by the American and International Press as having coined the term *salsa*. I didn't coin the phrase so much as I was the first person to start defining this music with the name salsa. As I told a Cuban journalist— Salsa is what gives Latino cooking its flavor. Now, when a band was swinging, people said they were cooking, cocinando. When a group has all the ingredients really clicking, people say they have salsa or sabor, which is relevant to the cooking.

Therefore, salsa was the flavor and spice. It became like Latin soul. Then I applied it to other things. If a flamenco dancer is doing a great thing, this guy has got salsa. I could have said, "He's got jalapeños, or he's got spice." I started using *salsa*. So I defy anyone to find, prior to 1973, which is when I had the television show *Salsa*, or prior to the 1975 Latin New York music awards when this term started hitting the American media, to show me where somebody defines this music as salsa; you'll find the word in an album cover, you'll find the word in songs, you may find the word was said by disc jockeys. But it wasn't defining the music.

Musicians all rejected the term, the top guys fought it. They didn't have the sense of publicity that I had. That defeated the whole public relations campaign to get recognition for this music. Puente's stock answer was, "I'm a musician, I'm not a cook." Machito's answer was, "This is nothing new. This is the same music I've been playing for forty years."

Later Tito Puente told me, "I resisted the term, but now I find my records categorized under *Salsa* all over the world." They don't like categories, but now

salsa, like rhythm and blues or rock n' roll or jazz or disco, has a separate category.

LUIS "PERICO" ORTIZ

As a matter of fact, in the mid 50s there was a record label in New York City called Salsa. The producer was Maisonave and he gave it that name because our music is spicy, sexy and romantic. Then in the seventies, with the movement started by Jerry Masucci and the Fania All Stars, which I was a part of, we made an international effort to bring this music to the world. The mambo era preceded it in the fifties, so they needed a change, a label.

Cuba is responsible for everything we are doing today. But it got to Cuba by way of the enslaved Africans. We Puerto Ricans picked up where Cuba left off, then we put our own flavor and elements from the United States: the jazz influence and the very particular way of playing the clave in New York.

ANDY GONZALEZ

The first time I heard the word used to describe the music we play was on my first trip to Venezuela in 1969 with Ray Barretto. What we call *descargas* New York style, a jam session, like the Alegre All Stars; that was what the Venezuelans called salsa. I did not hear it in New York until a few years later.

MAX SALAZAR

Salsa is that fiery, up-tempo music that warms your blood and makes you feel good inside. It makes you forget about the problems of life, the humdrum pace of life. Especially when I hear a good band with a good pianist doing his montuno.

The first time the word salsa was ever used was in 1929, by Ignacio Piñeiro of El Sexteto Nacional de Cuba. They were in the World's Fair in Spain, where they introduced a tune called *Echale Salsita*. Ever since then, salsa has been used hundreds of

times. Charlie Palmieri recorded an album, *Salsa Na' Ma'* in 1963 for Alegre Records, Joe Cuba recorded *Salsa y Bembé* written by Jimmy Sabater.

It's been used a lot of times. In 1964, Cal Tjader, who's of English and Swedish descent, recorded an album called *Soul Sauce*. The Mexicans adored Cal Tjader, but the Americans couldn't pronounce *Guachi Guara*, written by Chano Pozo and Dizzy Gillespie, so Creed Taylor, who had his own label, said, "Let's give it a different name so the people can understand it. We'll call it *Soul Sauce*."

Because that album was Latin, jazz, and R&B, it got airplay from coast to coast. And the word started filtering from the West, as I remember it. That's what kicked off the salsa thing. Everybody since then has been taking credit for it. Latin music very rarely gets any airplay on a jazz station or an R&B station. But if you listen to *Soul Sauce*, you can understand its appeal to non-Latinos, the same way it happened in Europe. The mambo created the same kind of excitement when it first came out and the cha cha cha did also.

I like the word because it caught on and it started this boom. Tito Puente and a lot of musicians don't like it, even Mario Bauzá. Because salsa is Cuban music, because the most popular dance rhythms are the son montuno, the mambo, the cha cha cha, guajira, danzón, bolero, and I can go on and on. They don't like the New York-bred reinvention. There's a tacit war between Puerto Ricans and Cubans since they got here, and it's called "Who's better?"

Salsa went into space in New York. That's where it took off from, like a rocket ship. Not in Cuba, but here. ∎

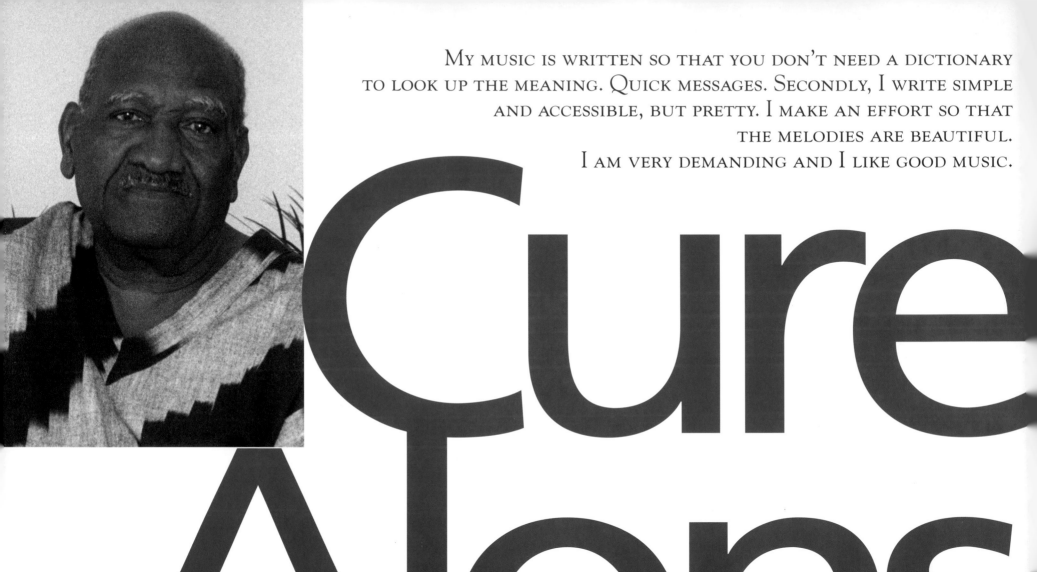

My music is written so that you don't need a dictionary to look up the meaning. Quick messages. Secondly, I write simple and accessible, but pretty. I make an effort so that the melodies are beautiful. I am very demanding and I like good music.

Curet Alonso

Tite

Catalino
"Tite"
Curet Alonso

Born in 1926
in Guayama,
Puerto Rico.
Songwriter,
journalist and
musicologist,
Tite composed
some of
salsa's most
memorable
songs.

b. Feb 12, 1926
d. Aug. 5, 2003

Chapter 1

RAISED IN BARRIO OBRERO

I was born Catalino Curet Alonzo February 12, 1926 in the small town of Guayama, Puerto Rico. I am 71 years old. My parents divorced when I was one and a half years old. My mother brought me from Guayama to San Juan to live. I was raised in the Barrio Obrero, where famous people like Tito Rodríguez were born. I spent my first years at the Alejandro Tapia elementary school. After that I went on to high school and then to college.

But I was raised in El Barrio Obrero. I love it because it is such a nice upbringing, surrounded by many friends. El Barrio is like a university. Those who come from El Barrio Obrero can understand everything in a split glance, because they have grown up in an environment that is equally good and dangerous, yet happy, full of music, bands and singers. I lived close to many of them, so I was immersed in the music. I used to drop in on Tito Enriquez with his guitar. I loved music and I learned a lot from him. I learned a lot from (composer) Pedro Flores also. He lived in El Barrio as well. Rafael Hernandez (composer) lived on la calle doce (12th Street).

From the beginning of my life, I caught the music bug because my father was a musician. He played in Mr. (Hipolito "Pin") Madera's band and in Luis Benjamin's father's band. He played trumpet and trombone. He played the *danzas*, *boleros* (ballads) and *guarachas* of that time. I remember the orchestra was wonderful and sometimes on Sundays, if I went to Guayama, I would see him play with the Municipal Band in the public square. Although he did not want me to be a musician, my father influenced me. My mother was much more opposed because she had been the wife of a musician. But the music was a force in me; such a strong force that nothing could tear me away.

I pursued social studies in college before I decided to join the Post Office. I left my studies because the Post Office offered a steady paycheck every two weeks. I had three sisters that I had to support. I didn't go back to college until later in life when I was married with children. My uncle was a journalist and he used to take me to the newspaper. I saw the printing presses. So I studied and became a journalist. I loved it. I have worked in this field a lot. The lyrics in my songs resemble the news because as in journalism, the adjective is unwelcome. You have to make use of verbs.

I started writing in 1944. I thought I knew how to write until someone in the editing department said to me, "Say, what adjective are you going to use to describe the next character? You already used up all your adjectives."

After finishing my studies, I realized he was right. The journalist uses verbs that describe, not adjectives. It's a narration. But what influences me from journalism is human life, the news. It is a daily occurrence. To say that there is no news today is impossible. The news influenced me greatly in my lyrics. I almost don't use adjectives. I use descriptive verbs.

We humans are always looking for someone to tell us a story. When we are babies, we beg Mommy to tell us a story. And we die with that same desire for someone to tell us a story. Today's generation is being brought up on pre-digested milk. You hardly see newspapers in the normal format; everything is tabloid format because it's quicker. Life is rushing by. All writing has to be quick and to the point.

My tunes are very simple because at times I use repetition since I studied solfege and musical theory. And I know the music. I studied music appreciation, the classics in particular, because that is the music that has all the concepts and cases. When I wrote *La Tirana* for La Lupe, I came prepared with the smarts from journalism to write that song. I write fire to elicit an effect. I study the singer's style: how he sings, if he is good with his vowels or his consonants; the way he pronounces and if he is credible when he sings what I write for him, because if he isn't, he cannot interpret anything with his heart. I always look for that. I am a detective of styles. I have written music for many people, from many countries including Spain, Brazil and Venezuela.

Since I was never allowed to pursue musical studies when I was young, I did it as an adult. I studied theory and solfege with a Colombian gentleman, Don Rubiano, who taught the famous Hermanos Figueroa in Puerto Rico.

Once I started my musical career, this all came in very handy because I was prepared. I had the tools at hand. On the use of language, I had good teachers of Spanish and versification methods. I am no foolhardy writer. I know what I am doing. I have written one act plays for theater and now I am writing for television. I have seven plays to write.

My involvement in Fania came about when Fania hired me as a promoter. When I started writing music, I wrote some tunes for Cheo Feliciano, Santos Colón, and for Bobby Valentin. They began to search me out, wanting more and more tunes. I had to stay home all day writing lyrics and checking the melody with a little toy piano.

From the start, *La Tirana* was a worldwide hit. Before that, I had written a tune for Joe Quijano called *Efectivamente*, which Joe recorded. After that, I didn't write anything until 1968. I was leading a very sad life as an alcoholic and on January 10th, 1965, I quit drinking.

TITE AND CHEO

I met Cheo Feliciano years earlier in New York, when he was with Joe Cuba. But I noticed at that time that Cheo was already a little high on drugs. I scolded him, "What you are singing is nonsense, because you are sidelining the subject matter. The song is about a girl and you are suddenly improvising about the bongo." He understood what I was saying. Then we didn't see each other for some time. When I realized that Joe Cuba was a hit, I was the one in Puerto Rico that talked him up to Alfred D. Herger, the promoter and TV personality who brought the group there. "Fly them down, because I think it will be good." I observed on the jukebox how they played Joe Cuba's music twenty six times. Then they brought Joe Cuba's albums and Joe Cuba to Puerto Rico. When I saw Cheo in bad shape, I told him, "If you need money, I can give you some. I don't like to see you begging in the streets like that. You can't go on that way!" He told me he wanted to feel a sense of accomplishment again. I spoke to Jerry Masucci and told him, "We can record Cheo." He gave Cheo some money and Cheo spent it right away. But then Tommy Olivencia and Silvio Iglesias spoke to him and he checked himself into Hogar Crea (a drug rehabilitation center in Puerto Rico).

> *I write fire to elicit an effect. I study the singer's style: how he sings, if he is good with his vowels or his consonants, the way he pronounces and if he is credible when he sings what I write for him, because if he doesn't, he doesn't truly interpret anything.*

I wrote an album for Cheo Feliciano. The whole format for the LP was ready, but it was never recorded because Cheo was in Hogar Crea. I used to visit him there sometimes. Jerry Masucci asked me, "Do you think we can record him already?" It had been almost two years. He was ready. So Masucci told me, "OK You brought him? You take care of him!" I invited him home for lunch and he came on Sunday. I had written that whole album, including *Anacaona*, in two days. We went to visit Bobby Valentín, the bassist, who had his orchestra and a store for musical instruments. We took all the music and Bobby wrote all the arrangements. When Bobby was done three weeks later, we went to New York. Larry Harlow was rehearsing in one room and the next day, we were recording there. That is why in the album, you see Cheo and me in the studio. I have always been by his side even if I am a bit of a scolder. Cheo likes to drink. He didn't give up drinking. That is the truth.

> *I knew what I wanted to do with Cheo because he was a dual-faceted singer: he is a romantic and a salsero at the same time. And I wrote everything for his voice and for the way he sings.*

Anacaona was such a big hit that it sold about 142 thousand copies. From those revenues, I got myself an apartment in San Juan. That was how I started out with Fania. Afterwards, we did many things with many other artists. They wanted to fire Justo Betancourt, and I said, "Let him do one more LP and let me handle him." Then Justo hit big.

I knew what I wanted to do with Cheo because he is dual-faceted: he is a romantic ballad singer and a salsero at the same time. And I wrote everything for his voice and for the way he sings. When we checked all the tunes, there was one missing. Then I checked my tapes and I found the bolero that was missing which we added to finish the repertoire. That bolero, *Vivir A Tu Lado* became his "rice and beans." And it established Cheo in the bolero format. Cheo and La Lupe were my spearheads because when they hit, the whole world was at my doorstep. Then I started writing for Santos Colon, Tito Puente, and more La Lupe... I wrote for Marco Antonio Muñiz, Ana Belen and many others.

But the Brazilians have given me my best musical schooling. They have been my teachers because they are the sorcerers of the half-tone (medio tono) and of the effective use of words. They don't waste words. And since I was a journalist, I didn't waste words in my boleros either.

I always wrote under pressure. I am basically lazy. I had never heard of *Isadora Duncan*, the tune Celia Cruz sang. Since I didn't see the movie, I asked Nydia Caro to lend me a book called *Primal Moments*, which told the story. I fell in love with that personality. *Isadora Duncan* was like a white La Lupe. I read the story in a couple of days, but I wrote the tune in about half an hour. Celia sang it at the Olympia Theater in Paris. Cheo also sang some of my songs at the Olympia. It fills me with pride, because I never earned a living with my music. I made my living working at the post office and working at the magazine VEA. That gave the impression that I was not interested in making money and sometimes they didn't pay me. The only problem with money is that it's necessary. I don't want to take the record label's money; I just want the money they owe me. They have paid me, but it is my understanding that I am not obligated to mix my royalties with the royalties of the American composers, which goes through a filter earning me less.

I am grateful to Jerry Masucci for launching my career, for supporting me. But he has to pay me what he owes me, because I also produced for him making him a millionaire. I presently work with LEA, the magazine, with the radio station at the university and with the Casa del Artista.

WHAT IS SALSA?

Salsa is the tastiest part of a meal. There is no such thing as Salsa music. There is a word Salsa that is an umbrella term under which the Antillean rhythms fall, and they use that term to commercially sell salsa music. Merengue is included; all of those Antillean rhythms are part of Antillean music. The first Latino musicians that went to New York didn't have a big enough Latino audience to be able to work, so they worked with jazz bands. When the Machito Orchestra got under way in New York, Mario Bauzá, Machito's brother-in-law, had already worked with Duke Ellington, Chic Webb and Cab Calloway. When the Latino audience grew and when it was evident that Latin music was viable, and they had a musical talent pool to draw from, Machito's first arrangements were jazz, but the rhythmic base was Antillean. That is how New York gave birth to a music that is not Cuban, with dance steps that resemble jazz, but with Latin rhythm. The Americans loved it. Latinos got into it. Fidias Danilo Escalona from Venezuela called that music *Salsa* and the term traveled to Santo Domingo and then to New York. But Jerry Masucci was smart. He registered the term and began to make movies about Salsa music and it spread all over the world under that term. But there is no salsa rhythm per se. It is Cuban and Puerto Rican music dressed up with a little jazz and sold under the heading salsa. They call Cuban music salsa.

What they call salsa is fusion music. I have written for all of them: La Lupe, Cheo Feliciano, Celia Cruz, Ray Barretto, Rubén Blades, Willie Colón, Hector Lavoe (*Juanito Alimaña*), Justo Betancourt, Santos Colón, Andy Montañez, Rafael Cortijo, Ismael Rivera, Kako y su Combo, Chivirico Davila, Orquesta Aragón, Tito Rodríguez, Vitín Avilés, Gilberto Santa Rosa and Willie Rosario. There are few I haven't written music for, perhaps the newer ones.

I have contributed two hundred Number One hits. The reward is to have stimulated others, many who looked at my example and started to write. From those, you get five or six that are very good or perhaps better than I. We inspire people. I think I have motivated many people in salsa. I helped Omar Alfano and Rubén Blades, telling them the concepts they should have. That provides a great sense of accomplishment; when others follow in our footsteps and are successful, they are like our children. That comforts my spirit.

MUSICAL STYLE

My music is written so that you don't need a dictionary to look up the meaning. Instant messages. Secondly, my writing is simple and accessible, but pretty. I make an effort so that the melodies are beautiful. I am very demanding and I like good music. I don't have to be thinking. It is all very fast, and everything falls into place where it is supposed to. The melodies come to me out of nowhere.

Tito Puente told me one day, "You shouldn't study any more music, because if you keep on studying music, you'll become rigid and you won't be able to be spontaneous." Maestro Lito Peña and Eddie Palmieri told me the same thing.

Anacaona...

A medium at a spiritualist center asked me to come. She looked at me and said, "You sang to Anacaona, but you didn't sing to Cahonabo, who was her husband. Well, I am going to tell you something: you are a direct descendent son of Anacaona and Cahonabo." Then I wrote *Cahonabo.* ∎

Mario Bauzá

My godfather was a musician, but not full-time. He used to teach in our neighborhood. One day I said, "Godfather, why do your students repeat the same lesson over and over? I already learned the lessons." He asked me to sing one and I did. Then he said, "You are going to be a musician." A week later, I wanted to back down, but he laid down the law: "You are going to be a real musician..."

Mario Bauzá

Born in Havana, Cuba in 1911. Co-Founder of the Machito Orchestra. Musical director of the chick webb orchestra, discovered ella fitzgerald. First example of Afro-Cuban Jazz in 1938.

b. apr. 28, 1911
d. jul. 11, 1993

Chapter 2

CHILDHOOD—THE FORMATIVE YEARS

I was five when my mother died while giving birth to my sister. My godparents lived right next door and they say I used to make eyes at my godmother when she was on the porch. She asked my father about baptizing me, then she asked if they could raise me. So my godmother took my sister and me in.

They took care of me from six months old. My godmother was Spanish and my godfather was part black, but he looked white. He used to tell me, "If you aren't gonna be what we want you to be, you'd better go back to your father. We don't want people to say: '"Those white folks have that black child as an errand boy."' So they didn't let me play ball with my friends. I was always studying and I was pretty unpleasant because they brought me up very rigidly.

My godfather was a musician, but not full-time. He used to teach in our neighborhood. One day I asked, "Godfather, why do your students repeat the same lesson over and over? I already know them." He asked me to sing one and I did. Then he said, "You are going to be a musician." A week later, I wanted to back down, but he laid down the law: "You are going to be a real musician, not a clown." From that day on, I was a prisoner.

I started studying music when I was five. I played bass clarinet in the Philharmonic Orchestra of Havana. Also oboe, but I quit because I didn't like it. Then I studied piano but I stopped because in Cuba, at the time, when a boy played piano he was considered a sissy.

It isn't strange that I studied classical music because what happened in Cuba between the 1600s and 1700s is unique. Cuba produced several world-renowned musicians in the classical field. I won a scholarship to go to La Scala of Milan to perfect my craft, but I didn't go because I didn't think it was profitable. You don't make good money and if you're black, the odds are even worse. My clarinet teacher used to send me tickets to the opera, and to the ballet, but I wanted to play popular music.

Miguelito Valdés was like a brother to me. In Cuba, Miguelito, Machito and I worked at the Dodge car dealership. We were learning to paint cars. After work, I'd go home, get dressed and play music. I'd play all night long, night after night, and then I'd get to the auto shop at 7 AM without sleep. I'd tell them, "I'm sleepy. I'm under a car. Keep an eye out for the boss."

After Miguelito Valdés left Cuba, no one sang Afro-Cuban tunes like *Carabalí, Ariñáñara*, and *Babalú*. His contribution was so meaningful that it revolutionized Cuba and the record industry. As soon as his albums reached the stores, the people wanted them. Miguelito Valdés made Casino de la Playa famous. He started in the Casino de la Playa as the bass player then becoming its conga player and singer. Miguelito was a dancer, a singer, a great conga player, and a man of great influence.

He was a straight-haired black. He was such a powerful figure that the Casino de la Playa hired him and he made the Casino popular. People could not discriminate against Miguelito. He's the first mulatto that didn't lose his color. He never denied his origins and always hung around with his people, but at the same time, he had access to all of the Cuban society. He jumped color lines even in his marriage. When Miguelito got to the U.S., women would offer themselves to him; they'd tear off his shirt. Others would ask for a kiss and leave lipstick on his collar.

Miguelito was a "dandy." Yes, he had some very powerful women. Virginia Gil was the owner of the Flamingo Casino in Las Vegas. The racketeers sent for Miguel and told him, "You leave that woman or die." She was crazy. She used to visit my house with Miguel and say, "See how Miguelito sings *Babalú*? Just like he makes love to me."

Mario Bauzá & The Afro-Cuban Jazz Orchestra play the Music in the Park series in New York City's Central Park.

I first came to New York when I was 16 years old with Orquesta Danzón. People from all over the world visited Harlem… the elegance and those finely dressed ladies, all those white people wearing tuxedos at four o'clock in the morning strolling in Harlem leaving the cabarets. This was paradise on earth. I went back to Cuba determined to come back. When I was 18, I moved there.

The first Cuban orchestra to come to New York, The Don Aspiazu Orchestra, came on the same ship as I did. *El Manicero* (*The Peanut Vendor*) was their hit tune, Machín was their singer. The orchestra returned to Cuba, but Machín stayed in New York and formed a quartet. He was recording for RCA Victor and couldn't find anyone to play trumpet. I told him, "Buy me a trumpet and I'll be playing in no time." The trumpet cost fifteen dollars at a pawn shop and I had fifteen days till the recording. Four days later, I told him, "I've got the embouchure." I blared out a few squeaks, but I reassured him, "Don't worry about it. I'll be ready," …and I kept my word. The day of the recording I decided no more saxophone for me, now I'm a trumpet player. Then I started imitating Louie Armstrong. I fell into a half-assed orchestra at the Savoy.

CHIC WEBB & THE FIRST LADY OF SWING

Chic Webb needed a first trumpet. He called me, but I told him to get someone else. He took me aside and pointed out, "Mario, you have what I need and I have what you need. You're a great musician, you have a good sound, but black music has a message and it escapes you because you were brought up in a white culture. That's why I rehearse you alone." I learned a lot from him. I started listening to him and a year after my debut, they called a rehearsal and he announced, "Gentlemen, starting tomorrow, Mario Bauza will be in charge." I became the Musical Director of the best jazz orchestra in existence in the thirties, The Chic Webb Orchestra. It was a great honor.

And I brought Ella Fitzgerald into Chic Webb's Orchestra. We were playing at the Apollo Theater when there was a contest for singers in the theater next door, the Harlem Open House. An electrician told me, "I wish you could hear the young girl that won." She was in the next show. I got the piano player to accompany her and the girl sang like a dream. I went to the dressing room and said, "Chic, I found a diamond. A young black woman that sings." Chic Webb only loved beautiful women so when he saw Ella, he looked at me with doubt.

That Saturday we were doing two prom dates at Yale University. I said, "We're going to take Ella." He didn't want to take her because he didn't like her looks. I reassured him, "I'll make her look beautiful." The first gown she wore was my wife's. I bought it so she could wear it New Year's Eve, but I gave it to Ella. My wife knew a lot about fixing hair and that evening, Ella looked great.

There were different bands in each ballroom at the university. Within an hour, the word spread and everybody from the other ballrooms crowded around the Chic Webb Orchestra. Ella sang all night long. From that day on, she became the "First Lady of Swing" in the United States. I left the Orchestra in 1938 and she remained with the band until after Chic Webb died. When they dissolved the band, Ella became a solo artist.

DIZZY AND LATIN JAZZ

Dizzy Gillespie got into the Cab Calloway Orchestra because of me. People used to discriminate against Dizzy. The musicians didn't like him. They used to say he was crazy and his playing was insane. I thought, "This man is phenomenal." But he wasn't getting any work, so I told Dizzy, "Tomorrow, I'll call in sick and you show up to work fifteen minutes before we go on. Do your thing but don't overdo it. Hold back." I had him there for three nights. On the fourth

night, Cab asked what was wrong. "I caught cold. How was the guy I sent?" "You know, he ain't bad," Cab answered. Two days later he said, "He's been hired." I told Dizzy to behave because he was kind of crazy. He eventually had a problem with Cab Calloway and left.

Dizzy created the bebop in 1952. Bebop was a musical movement that interested musicians, but not the public. It was too far out. One day they asked Dizzy to fill in at a concert in Carnegie Hall. He asked, "What should I do?" I said, "Why don't you play my music?" He didn't know anything about our rhythms. I told him about an eminent percussionist, Chano Pozo, who had just arrived from Cuba. We went to see him. Chano Pozo began to sing *Manteca* and *Tin Tin Deo* and blew Dizzy away. Dizzy took Chano to that concert. Carnegie Hall came down in applause. The rest is history. That was the beginning of Dizzy's relationship with all the Latin musicians. The United Nations Orchestra is almost entirely Latin musicians.

MACHITO & THE AFRO-CUBANS

I left the Cab Calloway Orchestra to form the Machito Orchestra. The musical innovation of the Machito Orchestra was in the instrumentation and arrangements. In the 1950s, we were doing Cuban music. I wanted to start an orchestra that wouldn't lose the flavor of our music, but with the sound of the American orchestra. That is what I did. I organized the big band sound of American jazz, with five saxophones and lots of brass. However, the bottom, the roots of the band was in the Cuban rhythms.

When I formed the Machito Orchestra, I said, "Macho, when the bongo is played like that, and the timbale is playing like the danzones, they sound like running horses, cloc, cloc, cloc." Macho replied, "Tell the timbalero to play the shell. I'll sing, but the beat of the clave will be doubled up." We introduced that in New York. Macho used to say, "That's out of clave. Fix it. I can't sing if things are out of whack." New York

musicians started learning the clave with our band. Graciela used to play the clave in the band and Macho his maracas.

The music has to be in clave, to conform to the measures of the music. You can't define clave until you feel it. The dancer says, "Those people are not in clave." That's how the dancer marks his steps, that's how they fall with the music.

Then I created Afro-Cuban jazz. It was a marriage rooted in our music, in our Cuban rhythms, the guaguancó, the mambo, with American jazz on top. It is Mario Bauzá's marriage. People didn't think it was possible. Now they have changed its name, everybody calls it Latin Jazz. I wrote the first number, *Tanga Suite*, in 1938 and registered it in 1942. *Tanga* was the first piece written especially for that kind of music.

One day I came up with the melody to the theme *Machito Llegó*. But I couldn't find the Cuban rhythm that would give me what I wanted. I brought in a piano chart of a tune by Gilberto Valdés called *El Botellero* and the pianist started improvising on it. I said, "Keep on playing." Then I started singing my melody and I told the trumpet players, "Do this," and the others, "do that." And I created one heck of a stir, all by ear. Composer Pedro Flores asked the name of the composition. I didn't have one yet. "It's a crazy piece with a crazy rhythmic line." "Call it *Tanga*," Flores answered. "In Africa, it's marijuana." Immediately I said, that's the title... *Tanga*." That is how *Tanga* was born. Chico O'Farrill wrote a concert suite for me. It's the same theme, developed in five different Cuban rhythms.

When I recorded the album *Kenya* in 1957, with Machito's Afro-Cuban Jazz, it was a revolution. At the beginning they wanted me to change the word Afro. I said, "I'm of African descent and the music I play is of African descent. If you don't like the name, don't use the band." Then other bands began using conga players. However, the conga player making all the money was Chano Pozo. Then Patato Valdés came

Mario & Graciela rehearse at Boys Harbor, NYC.

from Cuba to my orchestra. He's a phenomenal dancer and has played conga with all the greats like Herbie Mann and Errol Garner.

Latin bands started to form at El Morocco, the Stork Club and the Rainbow Room. The Musicians Union had a different pay scale for them. At that time they referred to the Latin band as the relief band because the American orchestra was the principal one that played the show. The Latin band was the filler. The musicians of the Latin orchestras were all white. I didn't see one black musician like myself at the Stork Room or the Rainbow Room, and that's why I left Cuba originally.

The musical innovation of the Machito Orchestra came through the instrumentation, the type of arrangement. In the '50's we were doing Cuban music. I wanted to start an orchestra that wouldn't lose the flavor of our music but with the sound of the American orchestra.

When I showed up with our band at La Conga nightclub, the other Latin musicians said, "Those black guys won't be around in 24 hours." They placed bets, especially on me. I was hired at La Conga because the Anselmo Sacasas Orchestra, which normally played, had asked for a two-week vacation. So Jack Harris asked for us because the Jews used to go to Harlem to dance with us. Well, I was the musical and artistic director of La Conga Cabaret for three years and three months.

The Palladium was a ballroom on 53rd street similar to the Arcadia and Roseland. They played the tango and the foxtrot for middle-aged whites. One day, Tommy Martin, the manager at the Palladium, asked me for a favor, "I'm managing a ballroom on Broadway, but in two weeks we're going to have to shut down. We can't compete with the Arcadia and Roseland. Can you give me four weeks after your summer season?"

We opened at the Palladium that Friday and Saturday. The place was packed. All the Jews and Italians were there. But on Sunday, not even two hundred peo-ple showed up and I asked Tommy what happened. Sunday, it turns out, is the day the Jews stay home reading the paper. Then it occurred to me, why don't we give the Latinos an afternoon? They don't have a place to dance downtown. At first Martin said, "Mario, that's a problem. You're creating a racial mix." I said, "Those white folks went to the Savoy when I played with Chic Webb and we never had any problems." They decided to give it a try.

I got my friend Federico Pagani who promoted dances. He said, "We have to create an atmosphere in the club to keep the riff-raff away. We want a classy joint." I used to play a number by Chano Pozo called *Blen Blen*. We asked Chano for permission to use the name, as if an organization was throwing the dance: "The Blen Blen Club Presents." The day we opened, I got dressed early. I showed up at three in the afternoon. The police had barricaded the street. I thought, "Oh God, things went sour." By five o'clock, they had to close the doors because the place was jam-packed. Even the Fire Department was there. Two thousand people were inside the club. Not one more person fit.

The following Sunday, I didn't want to play long hours, so I thought, "Let's give Tito Puente a chance to start a little group." He was playing timbales at the Copacabana with Martin. He didn't have a band, but he got a group together and Federico baptized them *The Picadilly Boys*. Eventually, Tito started his full-time orchestra. Then he started to alternate with me. Tito was the first timbales player in the orchestra. Tito played timbales on the first recording of the Machito Orchestra. But then he got drafted in the Army. When Tito Puente came back, we took the American orchestra out of the Palladium and we brought Tito in full-time. Then we brought in Tito Rodríguez. That's how it all began. ∎

Mario rehearses the orchestra at Boys Harbor.

Blades

Rub

Rubén **Blades**

én

Music and politics are not necessarily related. You can use music to present an idea, or report, comment, or expand on an issue that is political because it's social, because it has an effect in our communities. But you can also use music to relax, to escape reality and everyday pressures, to satisfy erotic urges. I don't think that every act of our lives is a political act.

Rubén Blades

Born in the Republic of Panamá, on July 16, 1948. Composer, singer, actor, attorney, politician, rennaisance man. His lyrics depict a colorful cast of characters laden with humor and pathos.

Chapter 3

ROOTS

I come from a working class family. My father was born in Colombia but at three months old or so he went to Panama to live with my grandma. My mother was a singer, piano player, radio actress; my father was a musician, basketball player, baseball player, and detective. I grew up listening to all kinds of music: from Frankie Lymon and the Teenagers to Jorge Negrete. My roots are in American rock.

I played salsa music with Papi Arosemena and Los Salvajes del Ritmo. It was Afro-Cuban music. I'm still trying to identify the moment when I became aware of the nuances of the Caribbean rhythms. Joe Cuba's music was happy, bouncy, but very urbane, sophisticated. Cheo's (Feliciano) approach to singing was also very suave, elegant, without losing nor compromising its street edge and wit. They were the ones who made me consider singing in Spanish to Caribbean music. The Seis Del Solar composition came as a result of the total absence of non-brass groups from the New York Salsa scene. It made the lyrics stand out even more. It provided room for experimentation, not to have the traditional sound of the other experience.

I left my country because of personal reasons. I couldn't be a lawyer in my country under a military dictatorship. So my decision to become active fulltime as a musician came as an answer to a simple question: What am I to do with my life, professionally, and what do I love the most? The answer was music, and art in general. I didn't "sacrifice" my career in Law for music. There's never a certainty of a "pay-off." One does what one feels one must do and live with the circumstances of our actions.

As for negative stereotypes, I hate them all, whether they're directed at me, at a black, at a Jew, at a woman, gay or handicapped, or at anyone because of their race or cultural origin. My definition of failure is not to try. We Latinos contribute in a great measure to the existence of negative images of ourselves by not participating actively in the defense of our culture and contributions through political participation. Nationalism, jealousy and envy divide us. Until we unite, we'll continue to suffer prejudice.

What is salsa to you?

Salsa is a popular adjective used to describe passion, joy, or liveliness. It has been around for decades in neighborhoods of the working class, from Mexico to South America. Personally, I don't think Salsa accurately describes the range of possibilities, both musical and intellectual, of the Caribbean because it perpetuates a rhythmic approach as the exclusive definition of tropical music. It makes dancing a central reason for the existence of Afro-Cuban music (a much more complex art form than what salsa suggests). It was a phrase utilized by merchants to sell a product, a sexy, vital, sensuous dance, framed by throbbing drums, and all the "exotic" qualities of the mysterious tropics. The fact that salsa did not go the way of the lambada shows how sociologically complex its appeal is, and how real and necessary its existence.

> *Personally, I don't think salsa describes accurately the range of possibilities, both musical and intellectual, of the Caribbean because it perpetuates a rhythmic approach as the exclusive definition of tropical music. It makes dancing a central reason for the existence of Afro-Cuban music (a much more complex art form than what Salsa suggests).*

Luis Enrique and Rubén share the stage at Madison Square Garden.

Why do you think New York provided such an ideal platform for the salsa explosion?

A very smart and shrewd New Yorker, Jerry Masucci, with the help of a very able Dominican musician, Johnny Pacheco, marketed it from there. All of the talent was located in New York. Some were the remnants of the "Golden Age" of Machito, Bauzá, Cugat, Miguelito Valdés and Celia Cruz and La Sonora Matancera. The new talents: Willie Colón, Eddie Palmieri, Ray Barretto, Richie Ray, and Joe Cuba were the result of the New York experience, the fusion of Latin rhythms and Jazz and Rock and Soul (Joe Bataan). It had to be New York. The infrastructure was there, the sophistication and talents were there, the distribution possibilities were there and so was the population whose support, originally, would make it all possible; the Latino immigrant and the hip black youth of the city.

Who came up with the idea of pairing you with Willie Colón?

I first approached Willie in 1969, during his first visit to Panama. I had never seen, nor heard his band before. I was struck by their youth, dynamism and street attitude. They were the youngest Afro-Cuban band that ever visited Panama and they kicked butt. From that moment on, I tried to get us together to work. Only in 1975 did it happen, due to four reasons: 1) I was in New York residing; 2) Willie had split from Hector; 3) Willie got bored and wanted to start a new band with a new direction; and 4) Jerry Masucci smelled gold and allowed me in with Willie.

Masucci likes to tell the world he discovered me. That's bullshit. He knew I had talent, that's why he gave me the opportunity so that he could make money off me. I still, to this day, have to threaten him with lawsuits to get the ridiculous amounts paid to me by his phantom company.

What talents did you and Willie each bring to the picture?

Willie brought his producing talent, his insight into what people like to hear and how, and his arrangement ideas. He had a rudimentary but still effective understanding of a PanAmerican reality; he was short on politics, and didn't really have a grasp on the economic and political background of Latin America. But he was always a businessman, careful not to alienate people because of opinions. I brought in the lyrics, the stories, the understanding of the Latin American from our position, not from the North, but from our perspectives. The combination proved successful and explosive.

Are music and politics related?

A Marxist would tell you they are. In fact, in Cuba, for example, music cannot exist, art cannot exist, outside the revolution and whatever Fidel, or the Communist Party says.

Music and politics are not necessarily related. You can use music to present an idea, comment, report, or expand on an issue that is political because it's social, because it has an effect on our communities. But you can also use music to relax, to escape reality and everyday pressures, to satisfy erotic urges. I don't think that every act of our lives is a political act. I don't see fucking as a political act, provided you don't have a politician on top of you. So my answer is no, music and politics are not necessarily related.

What elements do you include in your music to avoid the "arthritic conformity" of most contemporary salsa?

It is not a matter of merely using different elements so as not to sound like the rest. The song, lyrically, has also to probe something other than *Vente mâmá, vamo' a gozá* (Hey, mama, let's party!). Each song, in a sense, writes itself and provides automatically the type of musical arrangement and melody that suits it best. It helps me that I don't care about selling records or having a hit so that I can have a chance at being exploited in the salsa club of their choice. I write for myself and for the future, not for the instant gratification of name, fame, etc. Most of the musicians I've met fail to understand their obligation to the genre and to its future. They think it's just a party, an occasion for them to fulfill their whims and desires; not all of them, but a lot do think this way. And most of them succumb to drugs, alcoholism, or are exploited mercilessly and die without any money, or without providing security for their loved one. I chose Athens over Sybaris a long time ago, but I still have fun. Only not at the expense of my intelligence.

Do you think it is possible to effect more changes through your music or through politics?

Obviously through the political process. Music merely serves to underscore the importance of being aware of what's going on. However, people must take the responsibility that arises from living in a democracy and accept the obligations it imposes on us. People think they only have rights. You, we, also have duties, responsibilities, obligations; and participating politically is one of them.

What do you consider your most important contribution to Afro-Caribbean music?

My lyrics are the incorporation of stories that deal with the city as a whole and not only of the barrio. Before my songs, most of the subject matter had to do with limited experiences related to the friend that turned Judas, the woman who betrayed love, or sexual innuendos, etc. They only reflected upon a very limited street, very primitive, almost vulgar experience of a corner of the world, as it were. What I did was start writing about the experience of the city in all of its aspects. This is the reason why *Siembra* sold over a million copies in its heyday, the first salsa record to do so; not just the barrio identified with it; everyone did. Old and young, professionals and unemployed, men and women, everyone knew or heard of *Pedro Navaja*, or saw the people depicted in *Plástico*. Throughout Latin America we became truly one nation. It proved my point. Audiences are intelligent and they will support intelligence in music. I also believe my melodies were an important contribution in that they are unusual, and in some cases, very pretty. *Paula C* is a very beautiful melody; *Manuela*, from the album *Maestra Vida*, is a very unusual one; *Canto a la Madre*, *Isabel*, and *Patria*, to name three songs, showed that musicians from the Caribbean are not condemned to create only that which has to sound familiar to be successful. Freedom, and the possibility to create freely is another contribution I leave to all.

Some musicians think music should avoid political content: It is only for enjoyment. How has La Nueva Canción countered that argument?

Some musicians also think that salsa musicians who think music should only exist for enjoyment—should not exist themselves. I'm talking about musicians of classical music for example. They feel that street music is vulgar and its interpreters brutes, with no schooling, formal training or refinement. You'll find arguments 'till Kingdom come! Personally, opinions are that, opinions. I'm not arrogant enough to say, however, what should or shouldn't be included in a song. That's up to freedom of creation, and up to the people at large. If they like it, they'll hear it. Will it be good or bad? It's subjective. The future will determine the impact of what we do today and will judge its quality generations later. I don't waste my time on such bullshit as present tastes.

As for *La Nueva Canción*, my music was not *"de protesta"* (protest), but *"de propuesta"* (proposing new ideas). I never belonged to a political party in my life, only now to "Papa Egoró" in Panamá. Therefore, I didn't follow party lines like Cuban singers, who, whether they admit to it or not, have to in order to play, record and eat. No Cuban singer or writer or artist can do anything artistic or intellectually that may be considered, or construed as an attack or criticism of Fidel Castro and the Revolution. That is not *Nueva Canción* then. That's Communism or the left asphyxiating creativity in the name of political dogma. ∎

Rubén **Blades**

Richie Boni[l]

I GOT INTO THE BUSINESS BECAUSE MY BROTHER WAS
ALREADY PLAYING WITH THE JOE PANAMA BAND. A LOT OF
PEOPLE WERE ASKING ME TO GET THEM LIVE MUSIC FOR
WEDDINGS AND HOUSE PARTIES AT THAT TIME. EVERYBODY
CAME FROM POOR NEIGHBORHOODS. EVEN MY FIRST
DANCES WERE ALL HOUSE PARTIES.

la

RICHIE BONILLA

BORN IN NEW
YORK IN 1937,
RICHIE HAS
WORKED AS
PROMOTER AND
MANAGER OF
MANY OF THE TOP
SALSA ACTS.
ORQUESTA DE
LA LUZ, THE
JAPANESE SALSA
BAND, RECEIVED
ITS FIRST UNITED
STATES EXPOSURE
UNDER RICHIE'S
MANAGEMENT.

CHAPTER 4

THE LATIN MUSIC BUSINESS

I got interested in Latin music in the early fifties as a teenager. Back then, it seemed like all the musicians lived in the Bronx. Everyone was born in the Barrio, but as the years passed they congregated in the Bronx. I was just a fan, but my brother Benny was a timbalero and worked with big band vocalist Vicentico Valdés. So I got to meet all the artists before they got famous.

I was interested in running dances because I was active in sports. So to raise money, we would have house parties and we got a lot of the heavy guys together like Eddie Palmieri and Bobby Valentín, who lived in the Bronx then. Since we were second generation Puerto Ricans, a lot of us didn't speak Spanish too well and we liked American music. At that time, R&B was big, so the parties were a mixture; slow numbers were rhythm 'n blues with up-tempo Latin numbers for dancing.

It was the early fifties when the mambo came in. Machito was big, so was Tito Puente, Tito Rodríguez, Mon Rivera, and La Playa Sextet. Then the cha cha came in super strong in 1955. That's why the Anglos got very interested in Latin music. In the Navy, I had the whole barracks lined up, teaching them the cha cha.

I got into the business because my brother was already playing with the Joe Panama Band. A lot of people were asking me to get them live music for weddings and house parties at that time. Everybody came from poor neighborhoods. Even my first dances were all house parties. At that time, weddings were house parties; even funerals and wakes were done in the homes. So I got the idea to start booking bands.

I got into the business full-time in 1962 and I had all the boogaloo bands. The heaviest ones were Pete Rodríguez, Johnny Colón, King Nando and the TNT band. But that was a terrible period for Latin music because all the lyrics were in English to appeal to the second generation Puerto Ricans. Those lyrics really had no feeling, no story. The Anglos didn't respond to it like they did to the cha cha. It was very chic to dance cha cha. The boogaloo was for the Latino market. It was geared toward the second generation Puerto Ricans that didn't speak Spanish and so it was a Latin melody with English lyrics.

When Pacheco started Fania, the craze was charanga. Everybody was doing charanga. Then Pacheco started a conjunto with two trumpets and playing the little timbales (pailas). I thought he was making a mistake, but that first album did very well, it just hit.

I was very successful before Fania, but Fania eventually put me out of business. I was the first manager for Willie Colón and Hector Lavoe when I opened my agency. My brother told me about them, so I signed them on. Willie Colón was eighteen years old. He had the first album, *Malo*, but he was just another kid struggling out there. To make things worse, the group was riddled with drug addicts. The piano player was great, a beautiful guy, his name was Marc Diamond, but he was a drug addict. So I started helping them by changing their musicians.

I predicted what was going to happen with Willie Colón and Hector Lavoe. They were a perfect combination. Hector sang beautifully, he had such a range. He had personality, warmth and he was super funny. In addition, when you see a little magic

Orquesta de la Luz plays at Madison Square Garden in New York.

happening on the stage, you know it's gonna affect the people. At that time I was getting two hundred and fifty dollars for the band, we had eight guys, twenty five dollars for everybody and fifty dollars for Willie. But my big star was Pete "Boogaloo" Rodríguez. Pete filled a ballroom by himself. Willie was a young kid I was building. Willie was with me for two years before the *Che Che Colé* tune hit. Latin music was becoming popular in the South American countries, but they didn't have any salsa bands. I started bringing music to Venezuela in 1968.

Willie started as a trumpet player in high school. That's where he got his training. One of Willie's embarrassments was that he never finished school. He can talk about it now that he is an adult, but when I traveled with him before he went with Ralph Mercado, that was one of his sore points, that he didn't finish school. But he is an intelligent person. He reads everything he gets his hands on.

Hector Lavoe had the people in the palm of his hands. He told stories and the people hung on to every word. After Hector sang a song, he would get very comfortable. The stage was his living room. He would sit there, smoke a cigarette, sip on a drink, talk to people and the people loved it.

I always liked Willie as a trombone player. He used to move and groove. It was exciting. Willie wasn't considered a good trombone player, but he used to play with a lot of energy and oomph.

WATCHING HECTOR

Hector Lavoe had the people in the palm of his hands. He told stories and the people hung on to every word. After Hector sang a song, he would get very comfortable. The stage was his living room. He would sit there, smoke a cigarette, sip on a drink, talk to people and they loved it. He had such a contagious laugh.

He would always kid with Willie and Willie would just laugh. Willie is a very shy person. His shyness helped his popularity. He sang coro, he was always in the background with his trombone. The people felt warm towards Willie. When he was introduced, he would raise his hands and turn away. He couldn't look the people in the eye. He doesn't let anybody get close to him.

It was Willie's decision to leave the group. He wanted to do something more artistic. I was the manager, I'm telling you. Willie left and Hector stayed with the band and I started booking Hector Lavoe y Su Orquesta without Willie. Hector was loved already and Willie was on his way to being the legend that he is. They were already at the top of their field.

The problem was when Willie left the band, they were starting to put pressure on Hector to go under the Fania umbrella. Ralph Mercado Management started because a lot of people were complaining that Fania had a monopoly. Fania had all the artists, they bought a radio program and they only played Fania artists. They were controlling the airwaves, controlling the artists, throwing all the dances and they started booking the bands, so everybody started screaming. To relieve some of those complaints, Jerry spoke to me about booking the bands. Then the Cheetah started having financial problems, so Ralphy was looking for another avenue. By then, Ralphy already had Eddie Palmieri and Típica '73.

The first contracts Ralphy used were my contracts. I got him his first gig for Eddie Palmieri to go to Curaçao. We used to book all my bands for all his dances. Ralphy opened his agency with Ray Avilés. Willie left, so they started putting pressure on Hector to go with Ralphy, but I had him under contract. Hector asked me to sell his contract to Ralphy as a favor to dissolve his contract and he'd make sure I got what the contract was worth. I sold it to him because of the relationship I had with Hector. And I was doing well, I had a lot of artists.

I always helped unknown bands and I got repaid for my efforts. Pete Rodríguez was an unknown band and they became the hottest thing in the industry. Willie Colón and Hector Lavoe, the same, unknown. I worked with them and they became the hottest thing in the industry. Ray Barretto came into my office after the disappointment of his *Watusi* hit. It had gone to Number One on the charts nationally and then he was working for a hundred and fifty dollars in a club. He was with an agent that didn't work on the career of the artist, he just worked to make commissions. The agent was José Curbello, the godfather of booking agencies. I helped Ray recover.

Back then, nobody wanted anything to do with Ismael Rivera because he had a drug problem. I took him under my wing after he came out of jail. He went to Panama and saw the Black Christ. The people of this religious pilgrimage bathed him in the ocean, and then he carried a heavy cross, like Christ did, with 50 other men around the church. He knelt in front of the cross and he could see the needle marks disappearing from his arms. When he returned to New York, he walked into my office. He looked holy, he was clean shaven and he had that spiritual glow. I started booking the band and he not only showed up on time, but he was packing every place. Within a short time, he was the top band in the industry again. He was always loved.

Eddie Santiago was an unknown band and I heard his tune being played four, five times a day. I feel if he's getting that kind of airplay, he's gonna hit. So I sign him up in Puerto Rico. Nobody knew who he was. They knew the tune *Lluvia*, but nobody knew him. So we made posters with his face and

name and we plastered them all over. Once he played, they knew it was him. I toured with him for three years and he became the hottest thing in the industry.

SALSA FROM JAPAN–ORQUESTA DE LA LUZ

The same thing happened with Orquesta De La Luz. Nora, the lead singer, was in New York on vacation and came into my office. She had a cassette and told me she had a salsa band in Japan. Their dream was to come to New York to play all the major clubs. I played the cassette and loved what I heard. She stood up and started singing and dancing to show me that it was her singing. I was thrilled, so I told her I'd help.

But nobody believed the tape was a Japanese band, because they said you've got to be born with that feeling. They said it must be Latin soldiers stationed in Japan doing the rhythm section. She sent me a video and they were all Japanese. I went with the video from club to club, spoke to some friends, asked for some favors. They said, "You *gotta* be kidding, babe. A Japanese band that plays salsa, with no recordings… and you want to charge the club?" But I was able to get six gigs. A thousand here, twelve hundred there, so I hooked it up for September.

I spoke to Ralph, "Give me the Village Gate and the Palladium." They played at the Village Gate, but Ralphy wasn't there. I asked him about recording and he said, "I'll see them at the Palladium." I never enjoyed myself so much as I did traveling with those kids, just watching the reaction of the people. First the people give very polite applause when they see them because it's cute, but when they start playing, hysteria sets in.

At the Village Gate, they played a number and the jazz artist came out to do the second number. The band was supposed to play and the artist did his thing, because that's his part, but La Luz didn't know the routine. So the jazz artist, a trumpet player, comes out and when he starts playing, the three trumpet players of La Luz step out, go in front and start challenging the jazz man. They started playing back and forth. So the three Asian guys got off the stage. They went down into the audience and started playing by the tables and the people were loving it. The jazz artist is looking at them, because this is his spotlight. Then the people were telling the jazz artist to come down. So the trumpet players get in the middle of the floor and Manny Durán, a Mexican trumpet player, takes out his horn along with another trumpet player and now there are six guys in the middle of the dance floor. Everybody got up off the tables and made a huge circle at the Gate. When they finished, there wasn't one person sitting. It was a night to remember in 1989.

So when they worked the Palladium, Ralph sees them for the first time. And Ralphy has the top attractions. He says that he never saw a crowd react to any artists there as they did to La Luz. Then he wanted to record them. I told them they could trust Ralph and we recorded. Sergio George worked hard with them, polishing the group and helping Nora with her Spanish. Once he got the record, Ralph pushed that band. Now the band is a super hit. ■

Nora dances at Madison Square Garden with Orquesta De La Luz

Richie **Bonilla**

Celia Cruz

While I was in school, my cousin Seraphin told me one day, "On Saturday, get dressed and pretty because I'm going to take you to an amateur radio contest." He took me to Radio García Serra and I sang the tango Nostalgia. I had a pair of claves someone had given me so I sang, "Quiero emborrachar el corazón y ta ta ri ta…" rhythmically, like a bolero in clave and I won the contest.

CELIA CRUZ

BORN IN HAVANA,
CUBA.
THE UNDISPUTED
QUEEN OF SALSA
PERFORMED WITH
LA SONORA
MATANCERA,
TITO PUENTE,
JOHNNY PACHECO,
WILLIE COLÓN,
LARRY HARLOW
AND MANY OTHERS.

B. OCT. 21,1924
D. JUL. 16, 2003

CHAPTER 5

Celia Cruz

Johnny Pacheco, Celia and Louie Ramirez while recording Homenaje a Ismael Rivera at Fania Records.

A STAR IS BORN

I was born in Santo Suarez, a poor neighborhood in Havana, Cuba. I started singing when I was a baby, according to my mother. My first pair of shoes, she told me, were a present from a tourist who heard me sing. I learned many songs. When we had company, mom would ask me to sing. Sometimes I'd sing, sometimes I felt embarrassed.

I began singing at neighborhood parties. Later, I sang with a small neighborhood combo called El Botón de Oro that included a man on marímbula, another on maracas and one on claves. My older sister started as their singer. Because her voice was very thin, they would say she had "throat." My sister did not pursue a singing career. So I became the official singer with El Botón de Oro and we sang at all the parties.

One day, my cousin Seraphin told me, "On Saturday, get all dressed up and pretty. I'm going to take you to an amateur radio contest." He took me to Radio García Serra and I sang the tango *Nostalgia.* I had a pair of claves someone had given me, so I sang it, "*Quiero emborrachar el corazón, ta ta ri ta...*" rhythmically, like a bolero in clave and I won the contest.

At the end of the month, I participated in the finals and I won again. From that day forward, I started going to all the radio contests in Cuba. They were very helpful because those radio programs always had sponsors of products like chocolate, milk or crackers and they would give us bags full of products. My family was very poor so the prize money helped buy my schoolbooks.

I had originally planned to be a schoolteacher until I landed at La Corte Suprema del Arte, the biggest, most prestigious radio amateur contest in Cuba. They paid the best. I didn't win a lot because

I couldn't afford to pay anyone to applaud for me. I won by sheer luck and talent. Thank God I won, with another girl. We got fifty dollars, twenty-five for her and twenty-five for me.

Afterwards, I went to RHC Cadena Azul. I won there too and I made friends with the show's piano player. She told me, "Come to my house and I will prepare some tunes for you." Almost overnight, they made me the starlet of the program. Then the people in the business started getting to know me.

When you go to an amateur radio program, you sing whatever is in vogue. I used to sing tangos, polkas and Mexican rancheras. When the artistic director of one radio station saw me singing tangos, he told me my voice was not suited for that music, that my voice was better suited to sing native Cuban music. The show's pianist agreed and arranged a tune called *Mango Mangüe*, a very pretty pregón. She also prepared *Que Vengan Los Rumberos* and *La Pulpa de Tamarindo*, another pregón.

From then on, I sang Afro-Cuban music. Not the Afro-Cuban bembé, but the Afro music that spoke about the troubles of the slaves. I sang *Noble Soy*. The lyrics said, "Because I am noble, they abuse my goodness, and they make me work without pity. They think I have no soul." I sang many songs in that style because the composers thought my voice was well-suited for it. But they were like a protest, the lament of the slaves and they weren't commercial. That's when I started singing my guarachas.

After becoming active on the radio stations, I was employed by Radio Cadena Suaritos. Amelita Frade was Suaritos's favorite artist. I sang back up once or twice at Suaritos until the owner let me sing alone.

Pedro Knight and Celia Cruz

LA SONORA MATANCERA

One day I had a visitor. As Mirta Silva, the singer with La Sonora Matancera, was leaving for Puerto Rico, Alberto Sotolongo came to ask, "We want La Sonora to continue featuring a female singer."

At the Fausto Theater and at the Canto Theater where I worked, Rodney (Roderico) was the choreographer. I went to see him, "They want me to work with La Sonora Matancera and since you are friends with Rogelio Martínez (founder & director), I want you to introduce him to me." Roderico introduced me to Rogelio.

Rogelio told me to go to Radio Progreso, where they rehearsed on weekday mornings, "and bring your music." But all my arrangements were written for full orchestra and La Sonora was a conjunto. Monday, when I got there, Pedro Knight, the lead trumpet of the band, was rehearsing. Pedro told me, "This arrangement isn't going to sound right for us." The musicians started arriving and, sure enough, when I set up the numbers, they didn't sound right. Rogelio told me, "Leave them, Celia. Severino Ramos will adapt them to La Sonora."

The newspaper started to announce, "La Sonora Matancera has a new singer, Celia Cruz." As soon as Suaritos got wind of it, he fired me. I was desperate for work, but I had to wait two long months. Since Rogelio didn't call, I wondered, "Dear God, could he have forgotten? Did he lose my phone number?" Finally he sent word saying, "Please come. The arrangements are ready." I went and I rehearsed the two numbers. One was *En El Tiempo de la Colonia* and the other *No Queremos Chaperona*. My debut with La Sonora was on August 3, 1950. On the 16th, I traveled with them to Manzanillo.

At first, people started writing letters urging them to get rid of me, insisting I didn't fit in with La Sonora

Matancera—begging for Mirta Silva's return. But I didn't leave. The letters kept coming. I read the ones that were addressed to me and, full of shame, I hid them away or I threw them out. Rogelio never showed me the ones addressed to him. In January 1951, Rogelio recorded me. Mr. Siegel, the owner of Seeco Records, who lived in New York, told Rogelio, "Listen, women don't sell." Rogelio told him, "If she doesn't sell, you don't have to pay her. La Sonora will." We recorded two tunes, *Cao Cao Maní Picao* and *Mata Siguaray* and they sold. Mr. Siegel gave Rogelio his blessing. We recorded eight tunes on the LP and it must have sold well since Mr. Siegel signed me and I was under contract with Seeco and sang with La Sonora Matancera from 1950 to 1965, 15 years!

FROM TICO TO FANIA

I left Cuba in 1960 with La Sonora. We went to Mexico under contract. I had an apartment in Mexico, but I wasn't retired. I was working hard at the Blanquita Theater in Mexico, performing in nightclubs and on television. Jerry Masucci, of Fania Records, kept calling me and I didn't want to come because I was under contract with Tico Records where I recorded with Tito Puente. I thought, "Why is this man calling to offer me work with another record label?" I didn't know him and I didn't know that Masucci and Morris Levy of Tico Records were friends. Since he was Masucci's friend, Morris Levy granted permission for me to perform in *Hommy*, Larry Harlow's opera.

I arrived in New York from Mexico in 1973, and they had scheduled the studio for the following day. They gave me a cassette with the music and I immediately learned it. I recorded it in only one take. Then we performed *Hommy* at Carnegie Hall. It such a success that we discovered after I sang

Gracia Divina, the people started complaining, "Why only one number?" So Masucci asked Bobby Valentín to write an arrangement for *Bemba Colorá* so that I could sing one more song in *Hommy*.

Afterwards, Masucci took *Hommy* to Puerto Rico. On the plane, he kept telling Pedro, "I want Celia…." Finally Pedro told Masucci, "Let's record." And Masucci asked me, "Who do you want to record with?" I wanted to record with Pacheco. Pedro and I told Masucci I was going to record the first album with Pacheco without signing any contract. If we didn't sell, that would be the end of it. Since it sold and it was a super hit, I signed on, until the present.

THE RECORD LABELS

I was never a contract artist with La Sonora. I was an added attraction. The public would request us together because the albums hit so well, but in Cuba I worked with La Sonora only on the radio. At cabarets and other places, I performed with other bands.

At that point, I was no longer recording with Seeco or La Sonora. Leaving Seeco practically meant leaving La Sonora Matancera, because I went to Tico Records. Tico contracted me and Tito Puente was the first person I recorded with; I also recorded with Charlie Palmieri. But our albums weren't selling, so I left Tico. Things went pretty bad because Morris Levy didn't give me the credit I deserved when I sang with Tito, although the recordings were well done.

I found myself in the same situation at Tico as with Seeco: they didn't do any promotion. I recorded *Bemba Colorá* and nothing happened. Then I recorded it with Masucci and it's become my

Finally Pedro told Masucci, "Let's record." And Masucci asked me, "Who do you want to record with?" I wanted to record with Pacheco. Pedro and I told Masucci I was going to record the first album with Pacheco without signing any contract.

signature song. After Masucci took Fania to Africa, then to the Cannes Festival and the Midem Convention, the music reached international proportions. It started to penetrate in the seventies.

WHAT IS SALSA?

I am still singing the same thing I sang with the Sonora Matancera. Nobody is aware of it more than I am. The variation lies in the arrangers. Most of them have been born in Puerto Rico or New York to Puerto Rican parents and they have studied in this country. If it wasn't known as salsa, we could call it Latin jazz, because it has its jazz influence, but with rhythm, clave and bongos. Now, post-salsa, *Bemba Colorá* is ten minutes long. *Bamboleo* is 5:38. When I was with the Sonora Matancera, the tunes were two-and-a-half minutes long. Things have changed, and good thing, because otherwise we would still be in the 40s. But you can be sure that the roots are Cuban.

LA DIOSA DE LA SALSA

I have been improvising ever since I started singing guaracha. To *sonear* is to improvise. Your improvisation is based on what you are singing about. Improvising comes natural to me and it comes natural to all soneros. When I record and I am going to add an improvisation, I write it down so that I won't make mistakes or waste time. But when I am in front of an audience it has to flow. I never take anything written on paper. I give it my all; if I forget a word, I improvise.

Pacheco and I have built a beautiful friendship. Naturally, the music brought us together because the first recording was with him and I like recording with

Pacheco. He is very creative, but even if we never worked again, we would still be friends. Pacheco calls me *Mi Diosa Divina, My Divine Goddess.*

I am a stage artist. I dress dramatically. If I wear pants, they have to be shiny. I took piano lessons twice in my life, but had to quit since I refused to cut my nails. But I regret it today, it would have been easier to speak to the musicians in musical terms than having to sing the tunes to explain how they went. I sometimes lost my voice from singing so much. Fortunately, Pedro rehearses me. And these days Ralphy sends me out with a pick up band.

Pedro Knight is my 50%. I am the one that sings, but he takes care of everything else. When I first laid eyes upon Pedro at Radio Progreso, I was thinking of my work. It never occurred to me that he and I would be husband and wife.

Pedro Knight is my 50%. I am the one that sings, but he takes care of everything else. When I first laid eyes upon Pedro at Radio Progreso, I was thinking of my work. It never occurred to me that he and I would become husband and wife. A deep friendship grew between us and we married in 1962.

Since I was no longer with La Sonora, I had to travel with Tito Puente's orchestra and Pedro started traveling with me. Sonora was one person short. In 1967, Pedro decided to quit La Sonora. He first became my representative, then my artistic director. My career was more promising than the future with La Sonora Matancera.

Not everyone has been as lucky as I in this business. In spite of that, I studied and got my teaching certificate. When I graduated, one of my teachers told me, "Stay with your singing career, because you are going to earn in one day what I earn in one month." And that's how it's been. Y así fue... ■

Celia Cruz in Madison Square Garden at the New York Salsa Festival

Joe Cuba

When you made the Palladium, you knew you'd made it. All the ethnic groups in New York flocked there. If you had a dance in Brooklyn, in a Jewish area, you had Jewish people. If it was an Italian area, you had Italian people. If you did it in a Puerto Rican area or Latin area you had a Latin or Puerto Rican audience. But in the Palladium, they all came together.

JOE CUBA

BORN IN
MANHATTAN
IN 1931,
CONGA PLAYER,
COMPOSER AND
BANDLEADER.
CUBA
INCORPORATED
ENGLISH LYRICS
AND PERCUSSIVE
VIBRAPHONE
INTO LATIN
RHYTHMS.

CHAPTER 6

EL BARRIO, USA

I was born Gilbert Calderón in Manhattan to Puerto Rican parents. I grew up in Spanish Harlem and wanted to study law, but I was a semi-pro baseball player instead. I even tried out for a few of the teams, but I broke my leg. A friend of mine who was going into the army had a conga drum. He knew I was interested in music, so he loaned me his conga drum when I was laid up. I started playing to the records. That's how I began to play my instrument.

Santos Miranda, one of the greatest timbaleros ever, and I used to pal around. We did a few gigs here and there. He played with Alfarona X, the first Puerto Rican band to come to New York and stay.

They had a dynamite group. Sabu Martinez, one of the fanciest and greatest congueros, was their conga player. Sabu got an offer from Hollywood and the same day jumped on a plane and left. So Santos Miranda came around and told me, "Come on. You're playing with me until we get another guy." I went in with Alfarona X and stayed for almost a year because they liked me.

While I was in the neighborhood, Roy Rosa, a good bass player, came around asking, "We've got a group called Joe Panama Quintet and we need a conga player for a couple of weeks." I said okay. Joe Panama was starting out, but fashioned his group after the Joe Loco sound. It was a quintet, no vocals and we played *Tenderly* and all the American type tunes.

Half the places we played at were run by rough and ready guys that didn't want to pay. "Come on. Pack up your band, kid, and blow." But I was a rough and ready guy too that grew up in that neighborhood and I went in and collected. I had to

fight half the time, but I got the money. Only three dollars a man, and they didn't want to pay.

So I became the contractor. I took over collecting the money and getting the contracts so there was no monkey business. After about 6 months, Joe Panama's father fired all of us. He said, "You're not going to collect the money anymore. And the rest of you guys are holding back my son." So I said, "Fine, this way I can go back to study." I wasn't interested in becoming a musician.

About a week later, Roy Rosa came around with the drummer, Jimmy Sabater. And they said, "Joe Panama is going around saying that he's organizing a group, because we stink, according to him." He was badmouthing us. And he'd like to challenge us if we made our own group. I said, beautiful. I love challenges.

So I thought, "Wait a minute. I'm gonna really fix this guy. We're gonna come with a unique sound and blow this guy's head." Orquesta Aragón was one of the most famous charanga groups from Cuba. We loved this music. But you couldn't find violin players in Harlem. The only guys with violin cases packed guns in them. So I tried to find an instrument that was comparable. I had gone to the Apollo Theater to see Joe Loco numerous times. His nephew, Louie Ramirez was playing vibes with Joe Loco and I heard that sound and I dug it. I said, "I'm gonna incorporate that sound." And I was interested in putting English lyrics into the Latin thing. Xavier Cugat used to incorporate American tunes with the Latin rhythm.

Willie Torres spoke perfect English, but when I asked him to join the band he said he'd have to think about it. The original group was The Cha Cha Boys and had no vocalist. It consisted of me, Gilbert

Calderón on congas; Tommy Berrios on vibes; Nick Jimenez on piano; Jimmy Sabater on timbales; Roy Rosa on bass and Victor Pantoja, who was about 15 or 16 years old, was the bongo player. This was the original sextet.

Willie Torres joined the group a week later. We were seven for a while, but because of the liquor license law, employees of a club had to be over 18. So Victor Pantoja had to leave the group. It became the Cha Cha Sextet. And then we went up to Baldies, an after hours club and we kicked Joe Panama's butt with our new sound. Then I began to like it.

I was a firm believer in uniforms, because I used to watch all the big bands and they were always nicely dressed. So we got a set of uniforms.

Federico Pagani was one of the greatest promoters that ever lived. In order to get into the dances, I would help him put out window cards with the names of the attractions and Pagani would give me a pass. I was always begging.

So when I made my group, I told him, "Don't forget, I've got a dynamite group." And I started bugging him. "Don't worry, don't worry," he said, "Call the Park Plaza," It was a very famous club for Latin music and on Sundays he had the Machito Orchestra. Pagani was a slick promoter. He said, "I can't pay you until I hear your group. You play this Sunday. If you're good, I'll put you on another Sunday." So we went and played. Who cared about money at that time? We played opposite the Machito Orchestra. Machito was the greatest.

Then I met Catalino Rolón, another promoter. Catalino Rolón called me up because I was a go-getter. Every day I was hustling for work. So one day, Catalino said, "I've got a job for you. It's a place called the Stardust Ballroom, an American place in the Bronx. You're gonna play for two weeks. Your name is gonna be in the newspaper. Knock 'em dead." Before we played, I looked in the newspaper, and it said: Joe Cuba. It's the first time I saw the name Joe Cuba. So I called up Catalino Rolón and I said, "Who is this clown, Joe Cuba, who took my job? I thought I was working." He said, "That's you. Gilbert Calderón ain't gonna look good in lights, so I invented a name."

But nobody wanted to be Joe Cuba. I didn't want it. I had my own name. In the dance hall, two hundred people came up to ask the same question, "Who is Joe Cuba?" and we'd say, "There is no Joe Cuba." So I got tired of explaining it, and the guys said, "Man, you're Joe Cuba, 'cause I ain't explaining it no more." So I legalized the name. It's very catchy. Gilbert Calderón disappeared, the poor guy.

The first time we worked as the Joe Cuba Band in 1955 at the Stardust Ballroom we stayed two weeks, but the owner said we were playing too fast for those people. So I told the owner, "Give me two weeks to rehash everything and give me another break when I come back." And he told me, "You know, I like your style. You've got two weeks to change." All the big names were coming into that Stardust Ballroom—The Four Aces, Harry James, and Les Elgart....

So I borrowed some money and I bought some magnificent tuxedo tops. Since we were working two days, I bought two sets: white and maroon, and tuxedo pants and bow ties. Then we came back to

> *In the dance hall, two hundred people came up to ask the same question, "Who is Joe Cuba?" and we'd say, "There is no Joe Cuba." So I got tired of explaining it, and the guys said, "Man, you're Joe Cuba, cause I ain't explaining it no more."*

work. Not only that, I cut all the tempos, I got different things going.

The night we showed up with our outfits, the owner was talking to some other guys by the door and when I walked in, he swelled up. He turned around and twirling a big cigar in his hand, he told the other guys, "You see what I mean about my joint? Look at the way they're dressed. And that's the second band." We walked in and we played. Harry James was the other group.

I told my guys, "Come on. We gotta put on a show." So we incorporated dancing. I grabbed a chair, put the drum on the chair and me, Willie Torres and Jimmy Sabater did some cha cha steps. That is how we started dancing. We became famous for dancing while we played. Nobody had a rhythm section that danced in unison. That was the first time I played standing up. And three voice *coros* were coming into the group. Me, Jimmy Sabater and Willie Torres, right out of the sextet, we became like a minor battleship band. We stayed in the Stardust Ballroom for the whole year, every Friday and Saturday night, with all the big names.

One day, on my way to the movies with my girl, I remembered this guy gave me his card. His office was on 51st Street. He was Sid Sayer, an agent I met in the original Roseland Ballroom on Broadway. I went to visit him and I said, "Sid, I have a sextet..." "I can't use your group. It's too big." he answered, but, he added, "Keep coming around." So I got as far as the elevator and all of a sudden his secretary came running out. "Come back here, come back

> *The night we showed up with our outfits, the owner was talking to some other guys by the door and when I walked in, he swelled up. He turned around and twirling a big cigar in his hand, he told the other guys, "You see what I mean about my joint? Look at the way they're dressed. And that's the second band."*

here." Sid was going crazy on the phone, then he slammed the phone down.

Sid had a place in the Catskill Mountains called the Pines Hotel. A very popular trio from Brooklyn called Marty Franklyn played there. It turns out after signing a contract, Marty didn't want to work the Pines and Sid was furious. I sold him the idea that I played conga standing up and we danced. So Sid said, "Listen, this is the money I've got. It's for a trio. If you work it out with your guys, you've got the whole summer. Room, board and the Catskills. But you have to audition first." I'd never heard of the Catskills.

When we auditioned, I put the drum on a chair. He says, "You're not going to put a drum on a chair?" I said, "I've got a stand, but it's being fixed." Baloney. I didn't have any stand, but you've gotta be bold. P.S. We got the job. We went up to the Pines. We were sensational up there, I mean, we exploded up there. When we got on, that place was packed. You couldn't get into the room. And they loved our tempos. When I played some guy said a dead person could dance to it. Add to that the beautiful voice and English lyrics of Willie Torres, and that was it.

And Sid Sayer said, "So where's the stand?" So I say, "Don't worry. I'm going into the city this week." Arsenio Rodriguez's brother who used to make conga drums said, "I make conga drum. No stand." So I said, "If I order the drums, you'll make the stand for them?" He said, "That I'll do." And he made the wildest stand for drums you're ever gonna see in your life.

We were playing a lot of Tito Puente's and Tito Rodriguez's music. Willie Torres did *I've Got You Under My Skin, Stormy Weather, Temptation, I Talk to the Trees* and then we did *Barito*, a very famous tune that Tito Rodriguez recorded. We played mambo, cha cha, merengue and very few boleros.

In 1956 we did our first recording called *Rhythm of Cha Cha Cha* for the Rainbow label. The other side was *Juan José*, our version of a tune Machito did. We added what was called Pudatin, "Put it in, cause I like it," and it was ambiguous. The audience loved it. We stayed in the Pines from 1956 through 1959 and we built quite a repertoire. *Mambo of the Times*, which was originally *Mambo of the Pines*, became a big hit.

At the Pines Hotel, we got room and board. Let's face it, I had never had a full course meal in my house and I never went to restaurants in those days. So when they came out with this little dish of chicken and gizzards, I looked at the guys and I told them in Spanish, "We've been had, man." I turned to the waiter, "Can we have as many of these as we want?" and he said, "Sure." So we had five or six helpings. Then the waiter came over and said, "And what soup do you want…and the main dish…and the dessert?" We all looked at each other in surprise. We were stuffed from that other little thing.

When we auditioned, I put the drum on a chair. He says, "You're not going to put a drum on a chair?" I said, "I've got a stand, but it's being fixed." Baloney. I didn't have any stand, but you've gotta be bold. P.S. We got the job.

CHEO LIGHTS THE ROOM

Around 1957 or 1958, Willie Torres announced he was leaving us. We were a very close group and we loved each other like brothers. Some of us cried. But I was furious at the same time, because here we were, on our way and then one of us wants to leave. So I said, "The hell with it. I don't want no more singers." So the band became a *charanga* style with Jimmy and me singing in unison.

Then Tito Rodriguez came to me one day and said, "Listen, I've got a vocalist for you. You grab this kid, he's my band boy." It was Cheo Feliciano. I said, "Singers are prima donnas and I don't want that crap."

But Cheo was like a light bulb, he used to light up a room. So I gave him a chance. At first, I tried to make him sing Willie's songs, but he couldn't. Let's face it, he can't sing *Stormy Weather*. It's not his style. It wasn't even his key, the poor guy. But then he did a couple of salsa-type tunes and he impressed me. So I said, "What the heck. Let him play bell and he'll join us in the chorus."

When Cheo joined the group, we had three monster albums. I started to let him sing the Tito Rodriguez songs, which he'd eat up like a monster. But up to that point, he hadn't developed at all. He went to the Catskills with us in 1958, but Willie had made such an impact that Cheo didn't impress the people. They didn't understand real salsa music yet. They wanted to hear tunes like *Talk to the Trees* and *Temptation*, but that's not Cheo's thing. Cheo is a salsa and ballad singer.

In 1959 we recorded Cheo. The numbers went well, but he didn't make the impact that he would later. Jimmy Sabater was developing as a vocalist also. Then all of a sudden Cheo's voice opened up with that magnificent vibrato. I didn't know it then, but I was going to wind up with two monsters. They were gonna be two hot 'n heavy guys.

In 1959 we made *Red Hot and Cha Cha*. And in 1961 to 1962, we recorded *Steppin' Out*. It included *To Be With You*, *Como Rien*, and *A Las Seis*. There were twelve tunes on that album, three minutes long and every one of those tunes became a hit single. That album exploded Cheo and Jimmy.

I'm an old doo-wopper. I love doo-wop singing: The Oreoles, The Ravens. *To Be With You* was an old tune Willie Torres sang for years. But when Willie left, I asked Jimmy to cut it. I heard the playback, and said, "Wait a minute, let me add a rhythm 'n blues type chorus." So Nick Jimenez, the writer, put in a chorus and that chorus made a style for Jimmy Sabater. He has that soft Nat King Coleish type of voice, and *To Be With You* became a monster hit.

When I told the owner of the record company Sid Segal I was going to record that tune, he said, "No English lyrics. Latin people won't accept English lyrics. They don't like it and neither do I." He went on vacation, so when I went into the studio I put it on. And he loved it. It became a monster, even among Latinos. Catalino Rolón, the same guy that gave me the name Joe Cuba, got us the record contract. That year, the album exploded in Puerto Rico. So we went to Puerto Rico.

When we landed in Puerto Rico, we looked out the window and saw a multitude of people. And the stewardess said, "Ladies and gentlemen, the people are waiting for the entertainers." We started combing our hair, getting ourselves ready, and in those days, they'd roll up a ladder and you came down the ladder.

So I told the guys, "We'll line up on the ladder and when the photographers come we'll pose and we'll give autographs." There's a ladder in the front of the plane and one in the back. We all lined up on the ladder in the front and all of a sudden they let the throng come. All these people came roaring over and they all ran right past us. I couldn't believe it. We thought they'd come for us. But Perez Prado was on the plane. They came for him. When we got to

Jimmy Sabater

the terminal, we had a few people waiting for us, so we got our egos back.

Cheo is very creative with words. The way Cheo phrases them and sings them were really the whole thing. Most of the singers of the salsa era were imitating Tito Rodriguez. Whenever the phrase finished, he would come in and sing on the beat in the phrase. I call it a train, okay? The singer sings and the chorus answers, the singer sings and the chorus answers.

With Tito Rodriguez it was choo choo chooo. It's like, the train went, the singer sang, the train went, the singer sang, the train went, the singer sang... Ismael Rivera, El Sonero Mayor, the monster, the greatest salsa singer, was unique in his phrasing: the singer sang and pulled the train, the singer sang and pulled the train... "EN DONDE RE BARITO..." before he finished he would say: "EH BARITO...TO EH BARITOTO," he is pulling you, and you're behind him, and it's beautiful. I wanted that rhythm.

This is how I explained it to Cheo one day, "Cheo, coño, stop that. It gets boring because you're just on a train." I said, "Pull us, man," because he was capable of doing it. Boy, when he went into that bag, we exploded.

We exploded all over the world when we went to Tico Records and did *El Pito* (The Whistle). *El Pito* is Tito Puente's melody from *Oye Como Va*. Charlie Palmieri used it as a sign off. When his band was off, he played *Así se goza*. I liked it. So I said, "Charlie, can I use it for my sign-off? We don't play in the same places, anyhow." So I started using it as my sign-off. *El Pito* became the first boogaloo type thing with that vamp.

In 1965, we were working our butts off preparing for an album, and we came in with the tunes. But there was one tune I couldn't stand. Sure enough, we tried to record it and I couldn't get the meat out of the tune. So Teddy Reig, the producer said, "What are you gonna do? We ain't got more studio time. We gotta finish this album now."

So I turned to Nick, "To hell with it, Nick, bring the *Pito* vamp." I was gonna keep playing it over and over. So I got Heny Alvarez, Willie Torres, Jimmy Sabater and the singers doing the *coros* and I said, "Go in the booth and sing the chorus: *Así se goza*. Make all kinds of noise, stomp your feet, clap your hands. This is going to be a party record." I told Jimmy, "I'm sticking that *I'll never go back to Georgia* some place. Keep singing *Asi se goza*." Then Heny Alvarez said, "No, no." He whistles "mi la mi so mi" (*Oye Como Va*). Nick started playing the vamp and whistling and everybody was doing different things and clapping hands and that's how *El Pito* was created. When Nick stopped, Heny came back in with his whistle. Teddy Reig said, "That's the craziest record I ever heard, that's ridiculous." I said, "It goes. We have a record."

He went back and told Morris Levy, the owner of Roulette/Tico Records, "Morris, this guy is crazy!" Morris said, "Good. Bring me three more crazy bastards like him," and he put up a sign in his office, "I want crazy bastards like Joe Cuba."

Nobody realized the tune was going to be what it became because it was a throw in. Normally, record companies put the tune that's gonna be the big hit on Side A, like *Pruébalo*, and then throw some crap on the other side because DJs never turned a record over in those days. WBLS radio was starting to play Latin music and one of the DJs got on and says,

El Pito (The Whistle) was created in the studio. I call it a studio hit. It was done by guys that went impromptu. It's a Frankenstein tune, because all the parts came out of nowhere.

"Man, I'm sick and tired of this *Pruébalo*." And he flipped it over. It was *El Pito*. He said, "My phones never stopped ringing from that moment on." It became a monster hit.

El Pito was created in the studio. I call it a studio hit. It was done by guys that went impromptu. It's a Frankenstein tune, because all the parts came out of nowhere. Heny Alvarez brought out the whistle, the other guys were either stomping their feet or coming through with things. We added *I'll never go back to Georgia*, from Dizzy Gillespie's album. Even the Governor of Georgia called my office in New York to find out what the hell I meant by, "I'll never go back to Georgia." I told him I was referring to a girl and he was happy. The real story is what Dizzy Gillespie said when he sang, "I'll never go back to Georgia;" to hell with that place because it's prejudiced. We put it into *El Pito* for the same reason. I wasn't going to tell the guy in Georgia and blow the sales there.

We always kept doing things over and over till we got what we really wanted, what I call a bastard sound. It wasn't orchestrated by any particular composer or by anybody who was really musically inclined, because we all did it by ear. In other words, we all took all the notes off the top of our heads and put them together and that's where we got that sound from.

One day, we were in the club that became the Cheetah and Jimmy Sabater told me, "Listen, I've got a vamp. These people are going to go crazy." The whole audience used to go, "She freaks aah… She freaks aah… she freaks," while we were playing *El Pito*. But I said, "Why should I put another vamp in there when we've got *El Pito*?" Jimmy answered, "Watch…" and it became *Bang, Bang*.

WHAT IS BOOGALOO?

I said, "This is ridiculous. All we're playing is one vamp over and over." So we put the chorus in. We played a place in New Jersey. We used to go "Pepe ahh Pepe ahh…" and jump up and down. So we came back to New York and we tried that "Pepe ah," but it didn't work with hip people. They weren't going for no "Pepe ahh bullshit." So I brought in, "AHHH BEBE AHHH BEBE." We incorporated it and it became a monster.

I think the first guy that played a true boogaloo was Ricardo Ray. I don't know if *El Pito* was first or wasn't, but *El Pito* wasn't a boogaloo. It fell into that category. You don't go into a rehearsal and say "Hey, let's invent a new sound," or "Let's invent a new dance." They happen. The boogaloo came out of left field. It's the public that creates new dances and different things. The audience invents, the audience relates to what you are doing and then puts their thing into what you are doing.

Boogaloo is a simple Simon rhythm, so to speak. And it's an Americanized sound that you can beat out with your fingers. It's not a Latin feel. In the boogaloo you're playing on the back beat. That was one of the keys to our success. Boogaloo was a sway dance, a feeling dance. You could stand still and do all the gyrations, all the movements without getting tired or killing yourself.

But I still don't completely understand the boogaloo musically, and I was very successful with it. I can play the hell out of it, but there really was no musical aspect in it. It was like a lyric and a flow, a

Boogaloo is a simple Simon rhythm, so to speak. And it's an Americanized sound that you can beat out with your fingers. It's not a Latin feel.

crossover type of feel where the rhythm and blues mixed with Latin rhythms.

It's between a Motown sound like the Temptations or the Four Tops with Latin feelings. The Latin sound, to me, refers to the rhythm and also the phrases and the vamps of the melodic sections. The conga was on a back beat, and the timbales was a combination of the American drum set and the timbales. The bass, of course, is a very integral part of the rhythm section.

A lot of our tunes are not on clave and yet they're big hits. I got away from clave. It was part of the freedom fight sound. This story was told to me about Mario Bauzá. The Machito Orchestra was a monster orchestra. They recorded and when they played it back, if Mario could dance to it, if it felt good to him, that was it. Never mind that this guy is a little off. I felt the same way. If I felt good with it and I felt in a groove, that was it. If there were mistakes in it, and there's a lot of musical mistakes, the hell with it. I ain't going back.

The American born were the proponents of boogaloo. Latin bands couldn't play it as well. You had to have the American influence in order to get into that bag. I'm 'Rican all the way. My bones are 'Rican, my food is 'Rican. But I was born with the American Hit Parade, American songs, and English lyrics. That's why I went into English lyrics. I love the Big Band sound. And most of the Nuyoricans, those Puerto Ricans born in New York, have the same feeling. Boogaloo came in 1965. The Boogaloo era unfortunately came in and went out so fast, three years, four at the most. It was like, hello and then, goodbye.

THE PALLADIUM ACCORDING TO JOE

During the Vaudeville years, when you made the Palace you knew you were a star. When you played to the Apollo audience, that was it. The *creme de la creme*. And the Palladium was like that. When you made the Palladium, you knew you'd made it. All the ethnic groups in New York flocked there. If you had a dance in Brooklyn, in a Jewish area, you had the Jewish people. If it was an Italian area, you had Italian people. If you did it in a Puerto Rican area or Latino area, you had a Puerto Rican or Latino audience. But in the Palladium, they all came together.

The Palladium was awesome, not in size but in feeling. When you went to the Palladium you knew you were in a movement that was happening. You played off your audience and your audience played off you. The Palladium audience were all groovy dancers and groovy people, it was a give 'n take. It was a feeling that went beyond.

Wherever we went, we wanted to knock Tito Puente dead. When we got on that stage we wanted to leave it so hot that when Tito came up he had to perform. We were going after the champion. He's the guy you wanted to try and knock off his pedestal so that the public wouldn't say, "Damn, Tito is a monster, but this guy ain't shit."

We caught Tito and his whole group on an off night at the Embassy Ballroom. We were hot. We kicked butt that night. The next day, we were working the Palladium together, an early matinee. We opened and then Tito came in with his band and he looked fresh. He got his band on that stand and glared at them and when he opened up it was all over, he kicked our butts; I mean, he slammed us into the ground, threw us against the wall as if to say, "You bastards. You'll never get away with that again." He wasn't being vindictive, he wasn't being nasty, he was just saying, "Hey, you caught me on a off night, but now I'm putting you back in your place so that you'll know just where you stand."

I had duals with Eddie Palmieri in the Village Gate too. Eddie is a warrior. His whole band is that way, too. The public is getting dynamite music because we are reacting to each other, the two bands. And man, when that band finishes hot, the next band wants to get up there and work.

We were going to headline the Apollo Theater in New York City when I collapsed with a pinched nerve in my back. I was told I would never walk again. Every time I got up, I fell. And I was rushed to the hospital. My agent called to see if they would take the group with a substitute leader. They answered, "If Joe Cuba doesn't come, it's cancelled and so is the whole tour." A lot of money was involved. I had a manager, a record company, a publicity agent, a PR man, and all kinds of people that were depending on me. We all made a living off the Joe Cuba thing. So they got a specialist who designed a special brace for me. With the brace, I could walk, dance and play. They told the Apollo, "He will make it."

In my act, I used to throw out little whistles for *El Pito*. Even in Carnegie Hall, all the people left their fur coats in their chairs and jumped up for these silly little whistles. People used to kill each other for those whistles. So we went to the Apollo Theater. *Ariñañara* is a nasty tune, very hard physically and they told me to cut that number out. But I threw it in anyhow. I did *Ariñañara* with the twists and jumps and turns and it came out beautiful. We went into *El Pito*, our curtain call tune and I took out the whistles and threw them in the air. I saw a group of kids on my left, I bent over and gave a whistle to a little kid and my brace shifted.

I couldn't get up. I was petrified. I looked up at that whole front row: my manager, Sid Sayer; my attorney, my band boy, my valet, and my PR man, all in shock. I couldn't move until I saw them all get up with that look of consternation, with that look of, "My God, what are we going do if you don't get up?" and they slowly got up. Well, they picked me up with their motion. I was up and I finished the show and they all sat down with a sigh of relief. I promised them, "No more *Ariñañara*, and no more whistles." ∎

Oscar D'León

I have changed musically, physically, and mentally. It was necessary because the road that leads to all good things requires it that way. Everything Oscar d'León does becomes public knowledge immediately, so I have to behave in an exemplary manner. My only eccentricity used to be my flashiness, wearing jewelry, buying cars. Now I am a quiet person. The audience makes or breaks an artist, so I respect that.

Oscar d'León

Born on July 11, 1943 in Caracas, Venezuela. Bass player, band leader, Singer/Sonero. His energetic stage performances electrify audiences.

Chapter 7

THE LION OF SALSA

My parents' families were real party animals and we had lots of parties at home. I am an only child. I got my spankings once in a while for being mischievous. I loved playing cowboy, using a bamboo cane as my horse. I practically didn't have any toys because we were so poor. Aside from the poverty, my house was always spotless and that is how I like it. My mother used to sing, my father played bongos and my uncle played the tres. As a youngster I played the Cuban tres, the bongos and the conga, but not very well. I didn't know I could sing.

I never imagined I'd be a singer. I wanted to be a musician in a famous band. Life presented me with the possibility of becoming a sonero and I jumped into it without even thinking. You never know what path you're going to take. Life opened certain doors for me and I walked right in.

By 1970 I had organized a couple of groups, like the Psychedelics, Oscar y Sus Estrellas and The Golden Stars. The Golden Stars were born from the influence the US has always exerted on Venezuela. At that time, sextets were big in Venezuela. We tried to imitate the sound of the Sexteto Juventud, something I would not recommend to others. With zero organization, I started that group. We performed only once and we earned 5 bolivares each.

In 1971 I was in a quartet that didn't have a name. We worked in only one nightclub. We played cover tunes and did some improving. I got into singing out of necessity. While playing in the house band at the nightclub with no name, they fired our singer. Afraid they would fire us if we didn't have a singer, I pushed myself on the bandstand, scared silly.

My training has been empirical. Nobody taught me. I have guided myself through my logic and it worked. I learned to pluck the strings of the bass by playing along with records and by watching those who knew. I am not a *maestro* like they say, I just try to make my instrument sound coherent.

After I left General Motors, the only job I ever held, I bought some musical instruments: congas, timbales, my bongo, a guitar and I bought a bass for 1,500 bolivares. With the severance pay from GM, I bought myself a taxicab. Then I switched off between driving the cab and playing my music. More music than driving, which led to chaos. But I felt good because I was doing what I loved.

During my taxi-driving years, I enjoyed listening to Eddie Palmieri, Richie Ray, Tito Puente, Celia Cruz, Ray Barretto and the Cuban bands: Orquesta de La Playa and Orquesta Aragón influenced me. Also, Jose Fajardo, Pacheco, and all those great musicians that have been working almost half a century and whom I continue to respect now that I reached their level.

My first jobs with La Dimension Latina were at Tacarigua de Mamporal during Easter. We played all week long and we earned 15 bolivares each. Nobody knew the group. On my first trip to Panama, Richie Ray was there. He was already an evangelist. After Richie Ray left, all the promotion for my arrival proclaimed, "The Salsa God departed, now the Salsa Devil has arrived!" Ever since, they call me the "Salsa Devil."

I don't like strident, discordant percussion. The purpose of the percussion is to accompany. It is a mistake for a player not to be conscious that when the singer is doing his thing it is not the moment to solo on the conga or the bongos. Well, the bongo is always soloing like a curtain. The timbales should

remain within a square rhythm, not doing things that conflict with the singer. I mentioned once that Cubans are excellent musicians, but each one wants to show off his virtuosity. All you get is a cacophony. I try not to do that.

I have fond memories of *La Dimensión Latina*. When the moment arises I will be there to support them. They opened my window of opportunity into this difficult but enticing world. Since then, our relations have been strained. I am a friend, an ally if they need me, but I don't think they feel the same towards me. If we were united, not as their singer, but if a friendship existed, I would gladly help in the production of a song, or even fill in for them at a dance if their singer didn't show. I would gladly go. That is the extent of my support for them. I love them and I'm very grateful to them.

I started playing Upper Manhattan. It was a struggle... sometimes playing for dirt cheap, sometimes for free, sometimes being stiffed. In short, we experienced the common let-downs that occur in this profession of people that take advantage of those that are starting out.

When I started out with Dimensión, and I sensed that I had a golden nugget in my hands, I suggested we travel abroad to make a name for ourselves, to invest in our future. But they didn't pay attention to me. I didn't do anything until I had my own band, La Salsa Mayor. Then I paid for plane tickets, hotels and food on credit in order to bring the product to New York.

I started playing Upper Manhattan. It was a struggle... sometimes playing for dirt cheap, sometimes for free, sometimes being stiffed. In short, we experienced the common let-downs that occur in this profession when people take advantage of those who are starting out. We all go through it. The New York market is a springboard to the world. If you're accepted here you're accepted everywhere. That was my goal and then I started traveling. At that time I invested a lot of money to come to this market. In Venezuela, I used to earn $10,000 in a moment's work. In New York, I couldn't even charge two thousand dollars per show and I lost money. Then "Black Friday" hit Venezuela and I benefited.

My most difficult moments came in 1983 and 1987, when I had problems with the law in Venezuela caused by unscrupulous people that wanted to take my money. I sat with my children and I let them know what was going on. I said, "We have ten phone lines and they aren't ringing. Something is wrong. We need to find a manager," and Oswaldo Ponte appeared.

He produced a global change in my career. My image had declined because of the problems, and since Ponte is into publicity we knew how to combat it and I think we headed in the right direction. This man works even in his sleep, and that has given me a great advantage. We have been working hard with our bodies and our minds in order to support ourselves and we've been successful. It's been very fruitful.

I have changed musically, physically and mentally. It was necessary because the road that leads to all good things requires it that way. Everything Oscar d'León does becomes public knowledge immediately, so I have to behave in an exemplary manner. My only eccentricity used to be my flashiness, for example wearing jewelry and buying fancy cars. Now I am a quiet person. The audience makes or breaks an artist, so I respect that.

Music has provided the best means of support to change my family's life and my own life. I have six children. The most talented one is by my side. He is a talent and he has a great responsibility: to be better than I. The audience is going to ask him to do better than his father and that is going to be a big

problem for him. He improvises, but he sings out of key. I have advised him to study a harmonic instrument: guitar, piano or bass to refine his ear.

I am not composing every minute, recorder in hand, like the great Puerto Rican composer Tite Curet. When I compose, I get flash inspirations. I wrote *El Detalle* in twenty minutes. I never stick to formulas, I'm always changing. I experiment on the fly. My boys are ready… I talk to them in the middle of a coro or during a piano solo, I say, "In this number, let's do this." If we fail, we fail, but I know that on the third try we'll get it.

I want my band to sound different. I try to deviate from the New York sound as well as from the Puerto Rican sound including the El Gran Combo sound, because El Gran Combo is different from everyone else. I try to be on the opposite side of the spectrum. I try not to sound like the New York bands because I want to have my own sound. Nevertheless, anyone who wants to be successful considers New York and Puerto Rico as guides, models.

I am a very sentimental person. I cry at the drop of a hat. I have cried on stage many times, yet I try to bring happiness to the people. I want them to have fun with me. I am Venezuelan by birth, but the world now claims me also. I belong to all Spanish speaking countries now.

MI BAJO Y YO—MY BASS AND ME

Many people get upset when I don't play the bass. The bass, like the song expresses, has always been there for me, supporting me during difficult times. I sing its praises with honor. It looks alive. At times, I set it aside, but it is always with me. I still like it and will continue to play it until my strength fails me. During moments of inspiration you see it happening on stage: Oscar d'León dancing with his bass, and it has become part of the public's taste. But playing the bass all the time during a performance holds me back because I need a lot of mobility. I need to communicate with the audience, to say those things that pop into my mind and with the bass I can't move around as well.

If there are many women in the audience, I behave like a rascal. I show them my chest, because women love a man with hair on his chest. I make them feel like women in front of a man, a macho. I try to display my virility to the people, and it works. Women like the fact that besides being an artist, I am a macho, the macho that makes them vibrate at any given moment.

I will not go back to Cuba unless they solve their political problems because it caused me problems in 1983. We traveled to play music for a people that idolize me, who feel I belong to them, but some people tried to give me a negative image because of it. I haven't been back since then.

I love my work, I am not watching the clock, I don't care about money or anything. When I see an audience that's on fire, euphoric, I just give them more and more. I have participated in many festivals and that has earned me more fans. I think I am the only Venezuelan that participates in Puerto Rican events. I am not trying to usurp, I am only trying to perform with the greatest. ∎

THERE IS A DIFFERENCE BETWEEN A SALSA SINGER AND A SONERO. YOU CAN GO INTO A STUDIO, SING THE LYRICS IN CLAVE AND YOU'RE A SALSA SINGER, BUT YOU'RE NOT A SONERO. A SONERO IS A SALSA SINGER WHO HAS THE ABILITY TO IMPROVISE. SINCE THE BEGINNING, I'VE HAD THAT ABILITY.

El canario

Jo

José Alberto El Canario

é Alberto

José Alberto
El Canario

Bandleader & vocalist, Jose Alberto is one of salsa's best soneros.

Chapter 8

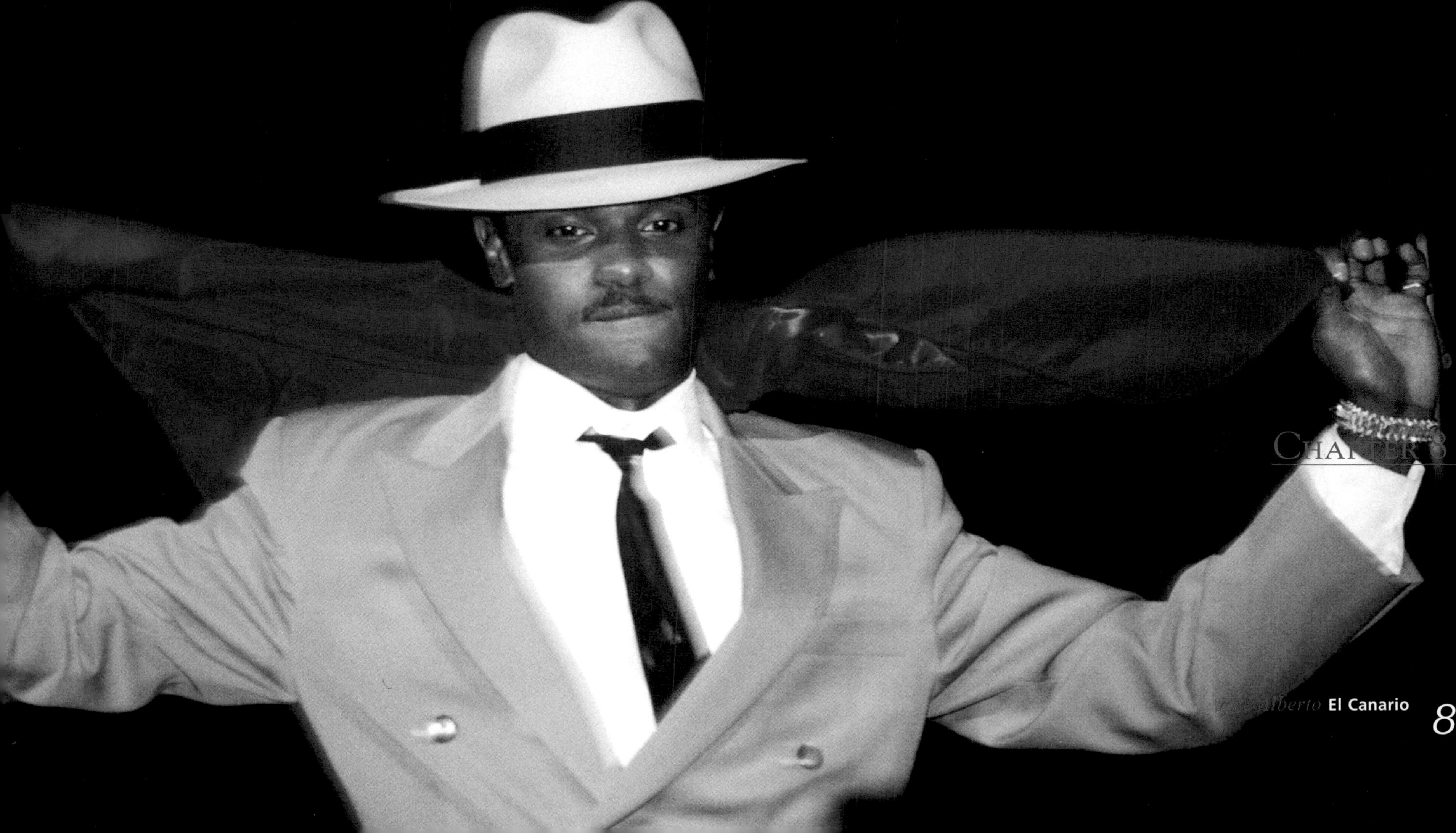

I SAW THEM ALL

I was born in Santo Domingo, Dominican Republic, in a town called Villa Consuelo on December 22nd, 1957. My parents are hard working people. My father was a doorman for the New York Hilton when it opened; my mother was a famous popular dancer for television in the fifties and sixties in Santo Domingo. When I was six my parents took me to Puerto Rico for about two years. I came to New York in 1967/68. Then they took me back to Puerto Rico. That's when I first started getting into the music and I started playing drums at a military academy. My parents brought me back to New York because I felt very lonely in school.

In junior high school, I started getting involved in salsa. I was a kid, but I used to sneak into the clubs wearing a suit and tie. I saw all the orchestras: Pete "El Conde," Justo Betancourt, Johnny Pacheco, Tito Rodriguez, Machito, Tito Puente with La Lupe, Larry Harlow with Ismael Miranda, Barretto with Adalberto Santiago, and Típica '73 when they started in 1973. I got involved in Latin music playing timbales, congas, bongos and trumpet.

I used to play with little groups here and there, but not professionally. When I was in high school, I started singing with Chorolo y su Combo. We played in social clubs with La Sonora Del Caribe. Johnny Ventura produced my first salsa 45-rpm single called *Usted Está Conforme*. Then I met journalist Roberto Gerónimo. He did my first write-up in a newspaper and helped me get into Cesar Nicolas's Orchestra in 1973/74.

Pete "El Conde" was the first guy who gave me an opportunity to come on stage and sing with his group. He was just starting his own band. I was about fourteen, fifteen years old and he told me, "Come up and sing." The first time was in The

El Canario, Tony Vega, Domingo Quiñones, Van Lester, Tito N in New York City.

Hippocampo in the Bronx. I would always go to the club and stand in front of the bands and they'd call me up to sing on stage. El Gran Combo also asked me up to sing with them at El Caborojeño, when Andy Montañez and Pellín were there. At that time, their hit song was *Un Verano en Nueva York*.

I became part of *Típica '73* on October 3, 1977 at El Corso Night Club. I got most of my experience as musical director from working with Típica '73 and from musicians like Johnny Rodriguez, Sonny Bravo, Mario Rivera, Leopoldo Pineda, Nicky Marrero and Alfredo De La Fe. All these cats were in Típica '73. To me, they were the *maestros*. They came from the bands of Tito Rodriguez, Tito Puente,

recording La Combinación Perfecta at Electric Lady Studios

Machito and Fajardo. I recorded five albums in the six years I spent with Típica.

After the band's experience with Adalberto Santiago and Tito Allen, Típica always wanted to have two singers. So I came in the picture with Camilo Azuquita. I recorded my first album with this band and Camilo Azuquita in December 1977. Then he left the band and they brought back Adalberto. Lalo Rodriguez and Rafael De Jesus also sang in Típica with me. I was young compared to those guys. They were superstars when I came into Fania with Típica '73. I wasn't part of the Fania All Stars, but Típica belonged to the Fania label on Inca Records.

In 1980, I did the first romantic salsa album, a production with Louie Ramírez called *Noche Caliente*. Louie called Ray De La Paz, Piro, Tito Allen's brother and me. One of the numbers I picked became its biggest hit, *Estar Enamorado*. I recorded three songs, Ray De La Paz recorded three songs, and the other guy recorded three songs. Louie Ramírez told me he wanted to do an orchestra and needed a singer. I replied, "I'm going on my own."

I went on a trip with Típica and Louie made a deal with Ray De La Paz. They took the voice out of *Estar Enamorado*, gave it to Ray De La Paz and they made an orchestra together. I left Típica on December 31st, 1982. By February 1983, I was recording my first solo album, *Típicamente* under the Sonomax label. I signed with Ralph Mercado Management and my orchestra started June 17, 1983 at Club Broadway. I recorded a second album *Canta Canario*, and a third, *Latino Style* before ending my contract with Sonomax.

I was the first artist signed with RMM. The first album, *Sueño Contigo*, became RMM's first gold record. Then came Tito Nieves, the New York Band and a bunch of other artists. The second album, *Mis Amores*, was released followed by the third one, *Dance With Me*.

I don't believe in salsa erótica. I believe in salsa romántica. I like lyrics that mean something when people listen to them i.e. love, situations that affect us and events that people are involved in. I like lyrics that reflect me as a person, with what I am. And I like danceable music.

There is a difference between a salsa singer and a *sonero*. You can go into a studio, sing the lyrics in clave and you're a salsa singer, but you're not a *sonero*. A *sonero* is a salsa singer who has the ability to improvise. Since the beginning, I've had that ability. On records, I heard guys like Pete "El Conde," Justo Betancourt, Ismael Miranda and Hector Lavoe improvising. I said, "Oh! this is the way!" so I did it. I love what I do. It comes naturally to me. It's a matter of opening with the right tunes to warm up the public. I'm a showman. I work for my public. I joke and play with them, I dance and I sing, I come off stage and dance with them. Yes, I'm an artist when I'm on stage. I have class. I'm an example to those people out there. They have to have a good image of me when they leave the place. But when I'm off stage, I'm a regular human being.

SONERO CATEGORIES

> *There are different types of soneros. I consider myself "un sonero de salon, un sonero de clase" a salon sonero, a sonero with class.*

There are different types of soneros. I consider myself "un sonero de salon, un sonero de clase," in other words, a ballroom sonero, a sonero with class. Marvin Santiago, Hector Lavoe, Ismael Rivera, and Frankie Ruiz are street soneros, savvy and streetwise neighborhood soneros. Oscar d'León is a salon sonero. Gilberto Santa Rosa is a salon sonero. Classic soneros.

I always followed Celia Cruz, Tito Puente, and Rubén Blades. They are role models for me, as Ralph Mercado is on the business end. The first thing you have to respect is your business and your own person, then the others. That is why they are where they are.

It is not easy to maintain a top Latin band in New York City. There is so much competition, but thank God, thanks to my people I'm still there. Tito Puente has been there for a long time because he's been doing things right. Celia Cruz has been there for a very long time because she's done the right thing. I think if I keep on doing the right thing I will be there for as long as I want.

I once had a dream to perform at Madison Square Garden and I have done that. I played Johnny Casanova "El Suavecito" in the movie *The Mambo Kings Play Songs of Love*. I want my music and myself to be recognized as one of the best. In a concert hall when I'm going to perform in front of a big audience, I like to put on a show for the people. In nightclubs, people are talking, drinking and dancing. But in a concert you have to give 100% of yourself.

When I was beginning with my orchestra, I was discriminated against. Now I realize why it happened. It's because you are not hot, you are not happening. They didn't want to give me the opportunity. But opportunities always take time and you've got to work for it. I didn't understand it then, now I understand it. There are no hard feelings. ∎

Felicia

THEY HAD FORTY STUDENTS FOR GUITAR
AND ONLY TWO GUITARS. SO I CHOSE THE TROMBONE. "KEEP ON READING AND
LEARNING BECAUSE WE'RE EXPECTING A DONATION OF ABOUT FORTY TROMBONES," THEY
SAID. I WAS IN SCHOOL FOR TWO YEARS AND STILL THE TROMBONES HADN'T COME.
I LEARNED TO SIGHT READ MUSIC, SING IT, LIP SYNC IT AND LEARNED ABOUT THEORY
AND THE TECHNICALITIES OF MUSIC.
TWO YEARS LATER, THE TROMBONES ARRIVED.

Cheo
no

Cheo Feliciano

Born in Puerto Rico July 3, 1935. Vocalist, sonero & percussionist, Cheo interprets salsa and ballads equally well. His stints with the Joe Cuba Sextet and the Fania All Stars made him a Salsa Superstar.

Chapter 9

MY CHILDHOOD

My father is a carpenter and my mother is a housewife. I was raised in a mixed neighborhood. Middle income families lived on one side of the street while the other side was very poor. We were from the other side. My house was the favorite meeting place of all the guys. It was a small house and the yard was not so big, but we had lots of *quenepa* trees. Quenepa (mamón) is a small green fruit with a big seed. It's sweet, and after you suck it you throw away the big seed. We had about seven trees surrounding the whole property, so we used to climb up on one and travel through the remaining six trees. It was like our big safari adventure. All the kids from the block used to meet in our house. We left from there for the rivers or the beach. I was the center of the action in my barrio.

On Sundays my father liked to cook. He would tell my mother, "Today is your day. Don't cook, go in your room and get pretty." My mother had long hair and on Sundays she would pamper it. My father would go to the market place and buy the stuff he was going to cook, vegetables and meat.

As he started working in the kitchen, he would sing. In those years, there was a mode of romantic music called *contracanto*, or countersinging. I loved it when my father would sing in the kitchen and my mother, while doing her hair in the bedroom, would answer him, countersinging. All week long I would wait for Sunday because I enjoyed it so much. I guess that has a lot to do with what finally happened with me musically.

Later on, I got a group together called *El Combo Las Latas*, The Tin Can Combo's instruments were all *latas*, you know, cans. All sorts of cans, big cans and small cans. We got the group together at Christmas time to do *agüinaldos*, Latino Christmas carols, but the people liked us so much that we kept El Combo Las Latas all year 'round. I was about eight. We wound up with a lot of candies, money and toys.

Then I got very interested in music. I listened to the Trio Los Panchos and I imitated Colombian baritone Carlos Ramírez. I tried to get that sound quality of voice. In junior high school, I started taking music lessons at the first free school of music in Puerto Rico. It was located in a beautiful concert theater in Ponce, the Teatro La Perla. The dressing rooms of the theater were our classrooms.

I wanted to learn to play guitar, but they had forty students for guitar and only two guitars. They suggested I pick a secondary instrument. I chose the trombone. They said, "Keep on reading and learning because we're expecting a donation of about forty trombones." I learned to sight read music, sing it, lip sync it and learned about theory and the technicalities of music. Two years later, the donation of the trombones came.

It was ironic because the day the shipment got in, my father decided that since things were pretty bad in Puerto Rico, we had to relocate to New York. He was willing to do any kind of work, but there was none. I never saw my trombone and that was the end of my music learning years. That was 1952, the year of the famous exodus of Puerto Ricans. A lot of them moved to New York. I was in my second year of high school.

Then I got interested in what today we call salsa. My group of friends, girls and guys, used to hang out in a corner at the Palladium every Friday and Saturday night. It was the best of times for bands like Tito Puente, Tito Rodríguez, Machito and Moncho Leña.

I was a student and didn't have money to pay for admission to any of these places. But I wanted to be there, right in front of the percussion section. So I found the ticket. I became the band boy for all of them. I used to work for Puente, Tito Rodríguez, and Machito just so I could get in. Eventually I became a percussionist.

I did one of my first jobs with Ray Barretto. He still wasn't the renowned Ray Barretto back then. He was working with a black American group uptown at Danny Small's and he invited me, "Cheito, you want to play bongos? I play congas. It's a blues group, but they like Latin." So I started playing bongos with Ray.

SINGING IN PUBLIC FOR THE FIRST TIME

Although I was playing percussion on some dates, mostly I did my band boy gigs. I used to sing at the beach, on rooftops, at Central Park when friends got together, but I had no idea that I was going to sing professionally. They started telling Tito Rodríguez, "Hey, Tito, why don't you give Cheito a break? He sings nice." Tito wondered, "Cheo who?" They said, "Why, Cheo, your band boy." And he asked me, "Cheo, you sing?" I was very fresh at that time. I told him, "I'm the greatest singer in the world." So he gave me the maracas and said, "Go, sing."

He introduced me to the crowd at the Palladium without even knowing whether I sang good or bad. "Our escuelita," as he called his band, "is proud to present its most recent discovery: Cheo Feliciano." I used to imitate Tito Rodríguez to a T. So I sang one of his tunes, *Changó Taveni*, which was popular. I came to the bandstand, counted four, the band came out and I sang. They applauded and asked me for an encore. I sang another of Tito's songs. That was the first time I sang in front of a crowd.

Tito Rodríguez was a perfectionist. He was a very serious guy with his business. I remember the band used to call him "Little Caesar" because he worked with a whip. Everybody had to be ship-shape. He wanted the band to be the best dressed, which it was, the musicians punctual and everything perfect or near perfect. He was a fastidious dresser, a dandy, sharp. He was friendly and a great singer.

It was not easy to get to him because he was very guarded, very much to himself. He was not spontaneous about opening up, but once you knew him, once you established a friendship, Tito was a great guy. When he heard me sing, he told me, "Cheo, you sing very nicely. I would like you to think seriously about singing and being a showman."

One day, he gave me a compliment I will never forget. For him to say a thing like this was close to blasphemy or sacrilege. Tito was a very proud guy. We were at one of our get-togethers with the guys in the Joe Cuba Sextet. Tito Rodríguez was there. Somehow the conversation took a turn towards me. He said, "You know? Cheo sings so good, he sings better than me."

I was shocked that Tito would say something like that, because he was very proud of himself. Nobody could be better than him. And years after, he told me, "I told you, you sing well." That gave me more confidence and I became proud of myself.

Months later, Joe Cuba established a sextet. It was a bunch of kids starting out. There was not much work for the group, but it so happened that when the contracts started to flow, Cuba didn't have a singer. He went by the Musicians Union, by the dances, every place there was music, asking if they knew a guy who could sing. Tito Rodríguez gave me that first break. It was Tito who said, "Cheo sings pretty good. Try him out. I think that's the guy you

need." So Cuba sent Jimmy Sabater, the timbales player and singer from the group, to try me out. I sang the two tunes I did with Tito Rodríguez that they had integrated into his repertoire and I passed the test. That was my start as a singer.

CREATING A SINGING STYLE

I learned everything about singing as I sang, because I was not formally trained. My schooling was on the job. I was a natural, but like a rough diamond that needs to be polished, I got polished as I worked. The first couple of years, I was a copy of Tito, imitating everything he sang, identically. Tito loved to come to our dances just to hear me. "Look at this guy. He sounds just like me."

But the time came when I started to venture on my own, to ad lib. I said, let me improvise and do my own thinking. As I did, I forgot about Tito's style and started putting my own thing in there. It came out naturally. I was a percussionist, so I sang with a bell in my hands. I developed my style of singing and playing the cowbell. I cultivated a keen ear for it. Whenever something was wrong with the rhythm, I knew it right away. I learned from Tito. He was very fastidious about the clave. You could never cross the clave because he could hear it right away.

A couple of bands wanted me to leave Joe Cuba so I could play bell. They admired my bell playing more than my singing. One of them was Cal Tjader, "Cheo, I want you to come with me. Yeah, you'll do some singing, but I want you to play that bell." Mongo Santamaría invited me too. But I was loyal to Joe Cuba and the group. They made me some heavy offers, heavy money, but I couldn't leave the guys. This was family.

I was very proud of myself and kept striving to play a better bell. I used to do a lot of soloing on the

Kako and the guys that I was staying in Puerto Rico. I wanted to make some money by staying a month or two. But that didn't happen.

I did some gigs with other bands but I started rolling down and down until I was not getting any jobs. People were tired of me, of my irresponsibility. They shut the doors in my face. Everybody turned their backs on me. All my friends disappeared. I was alone. I hit the bottom of the barrel, the lowest you can go.

I knew that I had to either get out of it or die. Hitting bottom was the best thing that happened in my life. I disappeared Christmas of 1969. I went into treatment. I was admitted into Hogar Crea in Puerto Rico for two and a half years. Coco, my wife, didn't know where I was for about eight months. She was going crazy. Months later, Coco found me and came to Puerto Rico to visit me. But when Coco showed up, I was working in the backyard of the big house where we lived as residents. I saw that face looking at me. I recognized her and was so ashamed that I ran back and disappeared into the trees. They had to go get me. I couldn't face her.

I had abandoned my family and now they came looking for me. It was very hard at the beginning, but I recognized that I had changed. Since I had made so many promises and failed, I didn't want to make any more promises. I said, "I'm here and I'm glad you came. But you'd better go back." So she went back and kept coming back every month for a couple of days to see me. Meanwhile she became the man and the woman of the house. I admire her so much for that. At the end of two and a half years, I decided I was not going to use drugs anymore.

At the treatment center they didn't want me to go back into show business because they thought the business harmed me. But the business didn't harm me. It was me. I harmed myself.

A mutual friend in New York told me, "When you go back to Puerto Rico, you have a friend called Tite Curet Alonso. He is going to do a lot of things for you. Tite admired me very much. When I met Tite in Puerto Rico, I was still doing drugs in the street. He used to give me all kinds of advice. He'd tell me, "Cheo, get away from that. You've got many things to do, I have many things for you." We established a friendship. He was one of the few people that didn't turn his back on me. He too had personal problems and overcame them, so he told me, "If I did it, you can do it." I said, "Yeah, maybe one of these days."

When I made the decision to get help, one of the guys that influenced me was Tite. When I went into treatment, he visited me every week. Tite would bring me cigarettes or little things I needed. Many of the guys of El Gran Combo visited me as well. Tommy Olivencia and Rafael Ithier of El Gran Combo wanted me to join them, to sing with them, but I was not ready. "You've been here two months, you're ready," they countered. You can't erase fifteen-year-old habits in a couple of months. I needed time.

THE FANIA COURTSHIP

Meanwhile Tite visited me and confided, "Cheo, there is a project on Jerry Masucci's desk called Project Cheo Feliciano. I have written many tunes for you. Masucci wants to sign you to the Fania Company." It was Ray Barretto who told Jerry about me, "You have to sign that guy." After a few months, every time Jerry Masucci went to Puerto Rico, he visited me at Crea, and he would bring the contract. "Are you ready?" "Oh! no, no," I said. "I'm not ready."

> *I did some gigs with other bands but I started rolling down and down until I was not getting any jobs. People were tired of me, of my irresponsibility. They shut the doors on my face. Everybody turned their backs on me. All my friends disappeared. I was alone.*

After two and a half years, I signed with Fania. Tite Curet was witness to our contract. Tite had composed for La Lupe and others and was beginning to get a name. I did my first recording, *Jose Cheo Feliciano*, with *Anacaona*, and all those Tite tunes on the Vaya label, a subsidiary of Fania. Out of ten tunes, one of them was mine. The other nine were Tite's. That was when Tite really came out because each and every tune on that recording was a hit. It still is my biggest album in appreciation and in sales. And Barretto reminded Jerry, "I told you so." We were all happy.

When I came out of rehabilitation, I was not sure that any success was going to come. I was not confident about my comeback because I believed I had left a sour note with my friends. Then I had my first presentation in New York. It was at the Cheetah, with the Fania All Stars. (See the Chapter Salsa Is Born.)

I had to go back and finish my treatment. I kept on doing my recordings and then a lot of jobs came. I started singing and working much more. That was 1972. From then on, Tite's work appeared on my albums. "Yo soy la horma del zapato de Cheo." The perfect fit. Everything Tite has done was to my style, to my understanding and to my liking.

After ten years, I left Fania. Jerry Masucci didn't want me to leave, but I always wanted to have my own label. We were all treated well. Of course, we always wanted more and we thought we deserved a little more money, all of us. But when we traveled, we went first class. Masucci liked to be close to us. In the end, it was good for all of us because we established ourselves around the world. It was great.

I'm essentially a romantic. I never thought I would go into what we call salsa. But it so happened that the world of salsa was here and I fell into it. Nevertheless I feel the bolero very much and it is the future of my music life. Yet, I am very worried that this mode of music and dancing will be lost. I still get the same love from the people and until that dies, I'm not going to, because I know what I'm doing. ∎

Henry Fiol

In Washington Heights there were few Latinos and the ones that came in were treated badly, especially by the Irish. A big Irish gang on the corner was always fighting with the Blacks and the Hispanics. Everybody considered me an Italian because my grandmother would stick her head out the window with the accent, "Junior, come a on. Iza time to eata." And I just went along with the ride.

HENRY FIOL

BORN IN
NEW YORK IN 1947.
COMPOSER, SONERO
PERCUSSIONIST,
VISUAL ARTIST.
HIS RUSTIC STYLE
MUSIC MELDS THE
GUAJIRO—COUNTRY
SOUND WITH THE
CUBAN SON.

CHAPTER 10

Henry Fiol

HALF-O-THIS—HALF-O-THAT

My father, Enrique Fiol, was Puerto Rican and my mother, Celest Alcaro, was Italian. I lived by the Harlem River, a predominantly Irish, blue collar neighborhood. There were Greeks, there were Jews, sort of mixed, not too many Italians. Those were the main groups. The first sprinklings of Latinos were moving uptown. As the years went by, more Latinos moved into the neighborhood. By the end of the 1950s and the beginning of the 60s, the Irish moved away and the Cubans became predominant. By the 1970s, the Dominicans took over.

My father exported potatoes to Puerto Rico. Eventually he became a race horse trainer. My first love was the racetrack and horses. By the time I was six years old I was drawing horses. That's how I got started in art.

As an adolescent, I was interested in the pop music of the day and doo-wop. My father used to play his Spanish 78 RPM records in the house, but I didn't pay much attention. I visited Puerto Rico when I was about fourteen and I saw *Cortijo Y Su Combo* with Ismael Rivera singing live, during their heyday. They played *Quítate de la Via Perico*, *Severa* and those tunes that created so much excitement, it just knocked me out. When I saw that band live, that turned my head around musically and I started to buy Latin records.

Throughout high school, I was collecting Latin records. I was into the charanga sound. Pacheco was a favorite of mine along with José Fajardo and Ray Barretto. When I got old enough, I started going to the clubs. I remember going to the Palladium with phony proof. It was the tail end of the Palladium, after they lost their liquor license. That was also around the time of the boogaloo. I used to go to the Chez José and Colgate Gardens in the Bronx. I was

in the clubs every weekend by my late teens and early twenties. It wasn't just the music, the women in my life were all Latina as well.

I grew up in an Italian home. Now I realize that in the core of my being, I'm a stone guinea. My grandparents on my mother's side lived across the street from me. When I got into Latin music, I rediscovered my other side that I had played down. Anybody that's a half-breed knows the dilemma. You're not one and you're not the other. In my case the Italians didn't accept me because I'm Puerto Rican, and the Puerto Ricans, who are more tolerant than the Italians, accepted me but not 100%. I immersed myself in the Latino culture for decades.

In Washington Heights there were few Latinos and the ones that came in were treated badly, especially by the Irish. A big Irish gang on the corner was always fighting with the blacks and the Hispanics. Everybody considered me an Italian because my grandmother would stick her head out the window with the accent, "Junior, come a on. Iza time to eata." And I just went along with the ride.

I was interested in being a visual artist. I became an art teacher and after I got out of school, I started to get in touch with the galleries and the art scene. I am a very ethnic person. There's accents on both sides. Here I am listening to Italian and my father with his broken English—working class; dealing with these people in these galleries with their fancy attitudes. They never took me seriously. I couldn't relate to that whole artsy-fartsy scene.

They used to play a lot of rumba in Central Park, in the neighborhood, and on the beach. Aside from listening and dancing in the clubs, I started playing conga in the streets in the rumbas and doing the coro, singing the lead. My first gig was with a Latino quintet in the Catskills in the Pines

Hotel. It was a group called *La Placa*. It was an imitation of La Playa Sextet. I was the only Latino in the group. I played congas but they needed somebody to sing. There was nobody else, so I started singing and playing congas.

Then I started playing with groups. The *Orchestra Capri* was a big influence on me. I learned a lot about the conjunto sound, about the simplicity, which is part of my sound to this day. They were Puerto Ricans, but at that time, the Cuban típico sound was very popular. I replaced Ray Castro, who later became the leader of Conjunto Clásico. And I played charanga. I played with different charanga bands, singing coro, playing one conga in the charanga style. Then I started investigating the roots of this music.

SON DE LA LOMA

An interesting experience was a turning point in my musical style. Around 1968, I was working as an art teacher. One day a week I'd go to Tarrytown, NY. On my lunch hour, I went to a bar near the school because there was a Cuban colony that worked in a General Motors factory. All of a sudden, on the juke box I hear a Cuban country music song called *Los Caleteros*, by Guillermo Portabales. It was two guitars, a conga and a voice. Not even a güiro. It was the essence of the mountain country *son*. It was like St. Paul gets hit by lightning. I went over to the jukebox, "What is this? This is funky!" I bought Portabales's records and I started investigating any Cuban *guajiro* country *son* I could find. *Decimas Cubanas, Celina y Reutilio, Ramon Velóz, Joseito Fernández.*

To make a long story short, I got deep into the country *son montuno*, which is very different from the city, urban, Havana conjunto. The thing that distinguishes my sound from the other conjuntos,

from Saoco, is that my sound is more rustic, more country. I fall in the category of salsa, but I'm not really salsa. I'm playing *son*. I'm trying to continue the tradition of the *son* and to create new things. I'm a composer and I'm not interested in doing remakes of the old Cuban tunes. I've done a couple for the fun of it. What I try to do is compose and create songs within the structure of the conjunto and the guajiro sound, to keep the tradition of the *son* alive. I'm more of a *sonero* than a *salsero*. And I'm using the word sonero not to mean a singer. I mean sonero: like zapatero: zapato. Somebody who sings or plays the *son*.

Because of the country element, it seems laid-back. But I'm an American and I was raised with that light sound of doo-wop and R&B. That's why I don't like timbales. I don't like to hear these bells banging away. One bell is enough. That strident abrasive sound of salsa, I find it tacky or corny to my ear. I'm a New Yorker and my ear is a different orientation. My sound has an element of country, an element of jazz, an element of light Brazilian. When I sing, I don't sing loud. I try to be very sparse in my words. I don't try to squeeze fifty words in a four-bar inspiration. I might use just four or five words, but I try to place them in the clave so that they have impact. I'm looking for the understatement.

I was trained as a painter, so when I switched roads from visual art into music, my training as an artist goes with me. I put all those pressures on myself to be creative, not to duplicate somebody else. I'm trying to create art within the context of Latin music or salsa.

> *I was eating lunch at this bar. All of a sudden, on the juke box I hear a Cuban country music song called Los Caleteros, by Guillermo Portabales. It was two guitars, a conga and a voice. Not even a güiro. It was the essence of the mountain country son. It was like St. Paul gets hit by lightning.*

I have a conjunto. Originally I used two trumpets. Then I switched to one trumpet and a tenor sax. Now I use two trumpets and a tenor sax. The tenor is very similar to the human voice. It's also very American and very Brazilian. I'm still learning how to use the tenor more effectively in the arrangements. Now, I'm starting to use the tenor independently doing one line. Also I switched from the tres to a cuatro. One of the things that attracted me to the campesino sound is that they're not using a tres. They're using a *mandola cubana* or a *laud* (Spanish flat-backed lute). The tres goes out of tune constantly. Ever since I switched from the tres, I feel more comfortable singing. It's closer to the sound I was looking for.

The Colombians are into the lyrics. Music is like spiritual food for them, whereas other countries it's the opposite. They don't want anything that is going to make them introspective.

I compose the words and the music and I'm co-arranger. I don't read and write music, but I sing the parts, "The piano does this, this is the bass line, this is the horn lines…" The arranger harmonizes my licks on the horns. The idea is to come up with something that is completely unique, just like an artist creates his style in his paintings.

When I started my label Corazón Records, I didn't realize that the distribution was going to be so difficult, so I lost a lot of my markets that were really good. There was a period of eight or nine years where you couldn't buy a Henry Fiol record. It all fizzled out because they forgot about me. In Colombia I was able to keep it going.

I do happy things, but I also do painful things because I believe that in order to reflect life, it's rainy days and sunny days. I try and balance my records to have major happy with minor sad, with up-tempo, with slow. The Colombians are into the lyrics. Music is like spiritual food for them, whereas other countries it's the opposite. They don't want anything that is

going to make them introspective. "*Yo tengo una gatita, que dice miao, miao…*" (I have a cat that says meow, meow…) Anything that's like, "Yeah, give me a shot of rum and let's escape all of this bullshit." I have tunes that have an emotional message, a spiritual message. I make quasi-political statements.

I've never been cooperative with the powers that be in the music industry. It's a cultural thing, see? The moves that they run on the Latino artists are like *Guinea* moves. What happens with me is that I'm an Italian. The club owners, the promoters, the record guys learned all their moves from Italians. You gonna run an Italian move on a Guinea? I'm more of a Guinea than you are. Are you gonna run that shit on me? I get insulted. They think I'm hostile or negative. So this cultural conflict has hurt me because I'm not playing ball with the people that have the control to give me the presentation that I need. In the US they don't take me seriously. My first records were with Mericana. On my first dealings with Mericana, I had some static with the owners of the company. We went to court, so immediately I got branded a troublemaker. Outside of the U.S., I don't have that problem. The artists are judged more on merit.

I've tried to keep the root of the music alive. Certain artists, when they go on their creative voyage, start out in the trunk of the tree. They want to reach out. That's good and there's an aspect of that in my music, but I'm trying to go to the center of the trunk. My voyage is internal. I think I'm getting closer. Now I'm starting to understand the core real good. I've preserved the root of this music. In other countries, when they hear that, it hits them on a very deep spiritual level. It's almost Jungian. It's like you're giving them something that's in their bloodstream from generations of their ancestors and when they hear it, it's like, "Ah, that's it!" ∎

Andy Gon zález

If you don't achieve commercial success, you don't get respect in the business. When I see bands that don't have half the musicality or the knowledge or the spirit that we have, make commercial successes, I feel hurt. The lack of respect for good musicianship in Latin music hurts me.

Andy González

Born in New York in 1951. Bassist, arranger & musical director. Andy co-founded Manny Oquendo and Libre, formerly known as Conjunto Libre, A Swinging New York style salsa band.

Chapter 11

Andy González 111

THE SOUNDTRACK OF MY CHILDHOOD

My parents are both Puerto Rican. Both my parents were orphaned at a young age due to a severe bout of tuberculosis in Puerto Rico in the 1930s. They got married in 1949. My mother arrived at the age of 14 on a freighter, the cheapest way to get from Puerto Rico to New York in those days.

My brother Jerry was the first of four kids. We grew up in the Bronx in the Edenwald Projects, which was probably the largest low-income housing project in the city.

My father sang Puerto Rican style dance music, *jibaro* music. He was lead vocalist with Auggie Melendez y Su Combo. However, my mother laid down the law, "Either you pursue your career or you raise a family." So my father worked as an electrician, a plumber, and a general contractor to support us and he played with the band on the weekends.

The soundtrack of my childhood was mostly Cortijo y su Combo, Machito, Tito Puente, Tito Rodríguez, Mon Rivera, La Sonora Matancera, and Celia Cruz. There was no umbrella term for salsa music in those days; it was Latin dance music. Later I accepted it as the music I loved.

Spanish was spoken at home, but I didn't speak it. I was a TV kid indoctrinated into the public school system of English and television. My father became a hi-fi buff, so he threw his 78 RPMs away and we used them for flying saucers. We broke many of Machito's records. It wasn't so much a rejection of the music, as going along with my peers who listened to rock n' roll.

We were into doo-wop because that was a big thing in the projects. Everybody sang doo-wop in the hallways. We played together and went to each other's parties. Consequently, Latino people danced rock n' roll and the blacks and whites danced Latin. We taught each other our respective cultures.

I started on the violin in the third grade. For our first presentation, my teacher had us play Duke Ellington's *Solitude*, which was extremely hip, I had no idea how hip it was until years later.

In the fifth grade, one of the bass players in the orchestra moved away. I was the tallest violinist so they asked me if I was willing to try the bass. Since I had good instincts and a good ear, I learned quickly.

Although I started hearing more melodic music playing the violin, when I switched to the bass I realized that the bottom of the harmony intrigued me more. The low frequencies of the bass are the foundation of the music. Everything stems from the bass note. Suddenly it seemed more important to be part of the bottom of the music. It's like a support pillar. Little by little, it dawned on me that this was the instrument I wanted to play.

In junior high school, I met Lew Matthews, a student at the High School of Music and Art. He had started a big band and was intrigued because I could read bass music and my brother could read music for trumpet. On Sundays, we went to his house to play in his big band. We were playing extremely advanced music for our ages. Lew was our first mentor. Lou guided us towards playing quality music and distinguishing what was good about it.

We started listening to the Miles Davis Quintet and the contemporary music of the moment, not just Latin music. We even tried to do free style Latin jazz. We were Latin jazz fanatics from day one.

However, we started going to more parties that were strictly Latino and we went to the Catholic church and heard Spanish mass. We gravitated towards our own culture, so I started going to parties

Andy **González**

and dancing Latin. Then we started playing Latin jazz because that was the music we liked.

When I was a kid, I was afraid to speak Spanish. By the time I was 18, I was playing for a Spanish speaking public and to communicate to this public, I had to speak Spanish. So I broke my mental block.

In the eighth grade, my brother Jerry broke his leg in a few places. Since he couldn't move around, somebody loaned him a conga drum. He started studying and playing congas to Mongo Santamaría, Tito Rodríguez and Cal Tjader records.

I played my first gig at 13 at the Savoy Manor for ten dollars. We formed some Latin jazz groups modeled after *Cal Tjader's* group of vibes, piano, bass, congas and timbales. By then my brother and I realized that we wanted to become serious musicians. I did my first recording session in 1967. I was a sophomore at the High School of Music and Art and one of the bands I worked with was led by Mongo Santamaría's son, Monguito Santamaría Jr. My brother played congas in the band.

However, I didn't start studying the típico approach to the music until I got together with René López. René was our second mentor, a musicologist who has an extensive collection of Afro-Cuban music. I had heard Arsenio Rodríguez play in New York, but I had never heard the records he did in Cuba. They were a revelation. The same was true of Arcaño y sus Maravillas, with Cachao playing bass. Then I realized that the bands in New York were playing second-hand Latin music. They weren't going to the source because that music was not available. You never heard any Cuban music on the radio because of the revolution. All my contemporaries have studied the history of Afro-Cuban music from records. Music doesn't lie. Black

Cuban music was recorded as early as 1909, before authentic jazz was.

Felipe Luciano hosted the original Sunday Salsa Show in 1970-1971. René López and I programmed those first Salsa Shows. It was the first time Cuban music was played on NY radio in twenty years. We started playing Chappottín, Arsenio, Arcaño, La Sonora Matancera, and the great conjuntos.

The most authentic band throughout the history of Latin music in New York was the Machito band. They developed the big band Afro-Cuban sound to a high degree of artistry, beyond what the Cubans were doing. But the Cuban forté in rhythm is where they had an advantage. Luckily, the documents were left behind on 78 RPM records. There were quite a few big bands in Cuba and at the beginning, Machito copied that sound. But then they started getting better musicians, and because of Mario Bauzá's influence in the jazz world, they started using the techniques of the jazz bands from the United States. The Machito band at its height was as good as Count Basie, Duke Ellington or any big band.

The most authentic band throughout the history of Latin music in New York was the Machito band. They developed the big band Afro-Cuban sound to a high degree of artistry, beyond what the Cubans were doing.

MANNY OQUENDO

When I was coming up, the most influential band in New York was Eddie Palmieri's La Perfecta. That's the band that percussionist Manny Oquendo was working with. Manny has been quite influential on the music since the 1940s. He's a contemporary of Tito Puente. He saw the Machito band in its earliest formations because as a kid, his sister used to sneak him in to dances. Then he started playing timbales with bands and several times, after Tito Puente left an orchestra, Manny took his place.

In 1951, Manny joined Tito Puente's band playing bongos, an instrument he studied by

listening to the great bongo players from Cuban records. He is brutally honest and truthful about music, a solid timbalero and a great accompanist. Manny was an influence on me, but I didn't understand how deep the influence was until I started studying the history of the music. I realized that he was also a scholar of the history of the music.

To drive a band, you need a good solid beat. Tito Puente was a superb arranger, an innovator in his solo style on the timbales. His contemporary, Ubaldo Nieto, timbalero with Machito, was a better big band drummer. Uba had a very strong rhythm and timing, like a metronome: defined, secure, authoritative.

In 1969, in my senior year, I started working with Ray Barretto's band. I was starting to play tumbaos influenced by the old Cuban records of the forties and fifties. The model at the time was Bobby Rodríguez, who was the great upright Latin bass player in New York.

That's when I started paying more attention to Cachao. I studied his whole musical career from his records; he recorded his first when he was 17 or 18 years old. Playing the bass is not just reading an arrangement. You're an accompanist and you add to the flavor of the music by knowing where to throw little beats in; little accents that don't interfere with the flow of the rhythm, yet enhance the rhythm.

The Cuban big bands had a timbales with a drum set and a bass drum. The conjuntos never had timbales in Cuba. That tradition happened in New York. The New York bands had a full rhythm section of timbales, congas and bongos. Yet all the bands had timbales in NY, starting with Tito Puente and Tito Rodríguez. That was the major difference. It added to the sound of the city because the New York sound was more aggressive, it had more energy to

114 *Andy* **González**

Manny Oquendo, the great word master, plays at Club Broadway, in NYC.

it, and an urban kind of feel; a little faster, a little stronger. Cuban music reflected a sun and palm tree kind of smoothness, where it originated. Even though there was an urban-ness about it, the music was still more mellow. The aggressive part came from the guaguancó, the drumming, the rumba, but the Cuban dance band was not as aggressive as the New York band due to our urban environment. New York energy.

FANIA—ASSEMBLY LINE STYLE

Fania used the Motown formula of recording music, which was to use the same group of musicians, the same rhythm sections for almost every recording. The same arrangers, the same producers, and the same sounding kind of product. I was aware of it from the beginning because I recorded for Fania sessions; I knew how they did their things.

I got banned from Fania Records early on because I was one of the few that complained. Fania decided to break ranks with the Musicians Union around 1970. Before that they were a legit company. All the checks for recording sessions paid union scale. You got a percentage of sales of your records back in the trust fund at the end of the year.

Around 1970, they made a weird agreement with the Union. They started paying the musicians under-scale, off the books, no trust fund check. If you made any kind of beef about it your services were no longer required by Fania Records. They said, "We'll pay you what you want, but you won't ever record for us again." Quite a few of us were blackballed from Fania Records because we squawked.

So Fania became quite rich for a while. Masucci was driving around in a Rolls Royce with the license plate *Salsa* on it, while ripping off his musicians left and right. They recorded quite a few covers of Cuban songs and never paid any royalties to the composers, crediting as Derechos Reservados. Their excuse was there was no contact with the Cuban record companies. All the singers, all the name artists on the Fania label were getting ripped off through non-payment of royalties. The only ones that successfully settled with Fania Records were Larry Harlow and Rubén Blades. But Rubén Blades is a lawyer and Larry Harlow spent a lot of money trying to get some of his back royalties paid.

SALSA AND DANCE

Culturally, the whole thing behind salsa music is the dance. As a child, I knew the connection between dancing and music, but Latin Jazz took me on a tangent, because that was more music. You could dance to it, but we thought of it in terms of art, the kind of music you sit down and listen to. But playing with Ray Barretto's band brought me back. Then I realized how strong that connection is between the public that goes out dancing and the kind of music they dance to.

Some people dance because of the joy of dancing. But the art of dancing is another level. There is a high level of artistry between the communication the musician sends the dancer on the floor and the dancer returns to the musician on the bandstand through movements. The dancer is as much an artist on the floor as the musician is on stage. It's a sublime communication when you have the best of both worlds.

The clave is the dominant rhythmic pattern that all our music is built on. The music consists of a series of counterpoints against that one figure. Starting with every instrument including the singing, it's all built in counterpoint to the clave figure. When you don't put the music in clave, you're just being lazy, because it takes some thought to create a counterpoint against clave that works. There are a lot of rules involved. You have to know how to make phrases move with the clave. One of my major dislikes in the seventies was Willie Colón's flagrant non-use of the clave.

Clave doesn't have to be played, but it's implied through everything the counterpoint is built on. The minute you hear one phrase you can tell what side of the clave the phrase is being built on, the 2 or the 3. It's a cop out for musicians to say, "It's a jail. Clave keeps you from being creative." They don't have the knowledge you need to create something profound using the clave.

Clave is a key. Once a rhythmic key is established, all counterpoint builds from that key. So if you have this clave "PA PA PA - PA PA," to build a counterpoint, the bell pattern, the rhythm section patterns, the horn lines, the piano, the bass and the singing all correspons with the clave. Every single utterance a vocalist makes pertains to the clave. Everything comes back to the original root: the clave.

When I hear something that is not correctly placed in clave it hits me like somebody screeching chalk on a blackboard. It's something I have taught myself to hear. Anybody that professes to be a Latin musician should study clave as part of their learning process.

There is only one clave and that clave can be inverted, which gives it a different rhythm flow. I'm talking about the 3-2 clave, that is the only clave. The Cubans have clave de son and clave de rumba. The clave de rumba is still the 3-2 clave except the third beat is displaced. It is moved over an 1/8th note of a beat, so instead of going " PA PA PA - PA PA" it goes "PA PA, PA - PA PA." Now that confuses the hell out of a lot of people because they still don't realize that the same rules apply. Nothing changes in the rule.

The counterpoint is built on top of the clave de rumba in the same manner, but that little phrase makes a change in how the rhythm moves. Because of that slight accent "PA PA, PA - PA PA," it moves the music slightly different, it pushes it ahead a little bit. That's one of the nice aspects of that clave. There is a difference in how the feeling of 2-3 clave is as opposed to 3-2 clave. But it's still the same clave, it's a rhythmic feel, like a stream of water. It moves a certain way. If it's moving downstream, it will flow differently.

In the old days, you'd hear the arrangement, the lead singer and you'd hear everybody playing little things, a piano figure here and immediately the listener recognized the player, "Oh, that's so and so playing piano. I could tell by that lick he did there,"or "That's Mongo playing congas because I can tell his style."

Nowadays, the music is recorded so that any musician could have played the music, because there is nothing happening for the musicians, only the singer. The singer is the focus and everything else is a blur. So salsa has become very commercialized, sugary, unmusical because there is not much musical input from the rest of the musicians. Their role is to play the arrangements and back up the singer. The individual expression of musicians is no longer happening.

To me the worst error of Latin music was the boogaloo. Boogaloo was a street expression, in English, played on a backbeat, borrowing from rhythm & blues and attaching Latin rhythms to it. I

Clave is a key. Once a rhythmic key is established, all counterpoint builds from that key. Every single utterance a vocalist makes pertains to the clave. Everything comes back to the original root: the clave.

Andy **González**

give boogaloo credit for being a true street expression and a true sentiment of the streets of that day. What made it to me the worst period in Latin music was the low quality musicians playing the music. I was horrified, because musically it was like listening to kids that could barely play their instruments. Other musicians were forced to play boogaloo because it was the commercial success of the day. If you didn't play boogaloo you weren't gonna play. The last band to record a boogaloo record which they didn't want to record was Eddie Palmieri. He came out with the *African Twist.* Luckily, that was towards the end of the boogaloo era, but Eddie Palmeri was always very true to típico playing. That was his forte, and probably why he was the most influential band of the sixties.

THE SEEDY SIDE OF THE BUSINESS

The manager of a bunch of bands was a drug dealer that owned a string of after-hour clubs. These are clubs where, after the regular dance finishes at 4 AM, the after-hours starts. A particular after hours, above an old theater was kind of an illegal place where all the night people used to hang out. They went there to dance, drink and take drugs. This place was so popular that they started hiring the major bands to play there. The musicians dug it because it was an extra gig. You'd work your regular gig, shoot over to the after-hours and make extra money.

I was working with Ray Barretto's band in an after-hours one night. The dance was packed. Right in the middle of *Hipocresia y Falsedad,* which is one of Barretto's tunes, this guy whips out a gun and blows another guy away right in front of the bandstand. Everybody went flying out one entrance. All you heard were screams and something like

elephants stampeding. The band stopped playing and hid behind their instruments. The floor cleared quickly, they dragged the body out, mopped up the blood and it was business as usual.

Jazz came out of the bordellos of New Orleans. Louis Armstrong's first wife was a hooker. And a lot of good Latin music came out of the same kind of experiences. Tango came out of the bordellos of Buenos Aires. So if truth be told, that's where Latin music developed. There were quite a few Cuban musicians of the thirties, the forties, and the fifties that were pimps. That was part of their income. And yet that didn't take away from their being creative individuals in music. That was part of their life's experience. They didn't call Havana the playground of the Caribbean for nothing. This was a working class music, the lowest denominator of the working class.

It doesn't come as a revelation, it comes as you grow up and as you experience playing music. You notice that these associations exist. It's part of it. The commercial side of the music has distanced the music from those associations, but the associations still exist. This is dance music, and it's a dance music for couples. You can make a lot of associations as to what meanings are behind the body movement. The white establishment put down rock n' roll saying that white kids were imitating the worst aspects of black music.

For the African culture, body movement and sexual things are natural. Nobody makes any moral judgment. The rumba, the guaguancó, the dance where the male pursues the female is supposed to be the rooster pursuing the hen. And the rooster is trying to inject (vacunar) the hen. The vacuna is just part of life, and it's treated as such. The Europeans, who have mistresses on the side disapprove, "That's

Jerry González at the Village Gate, "Salsa Meets Jazz Series"

jungle behavior." It's a matter of looking at life the way life is, with all its warts.

GRUPO EXPERIMENTAL NUEVAYORQUINO

My brother and I started jamming in the basement of my parents' house. We invited musicians like Chocolate Armenteros, Nicky Marrero and drummers like Frankie Rodríguez, Milton Cardona and Gene Golden. Out of that came Grupo Folklórico Experimental. Since we were studying at René López's house and he was on the committee of the Smithsonian Institute, we did the American Folk Live Festival in Washington D.C.

We were all good musicians, so we picked a repertoire of tunes and some original stuff from various contributing members. There was no written music. It was structured, but it was open. We came up with a head arrangement and that's how we performed it. I had a tres (Cuban six stringed) guitar and Nelson González, who was a guitarist, learned to play it in my house. We recorded an album in 1975.

EDDIE PALMIERI—THE GRAND SCHOOL

La Perfecta was the band of the moment in the 1960s, but Eddie Palmieri's next band, the band I was in, was probably the most advanced group in Latin music from 1971 to 1974. We incorporated free form improvisation into Latin music, which no one had ever done before. We were freely improvising, inventing on themes that were running around Eddie's head. We took Eddie Palmieri and pulled him out of his three-piece suit and into Indian shirts, sandals, a beard and long hair. Eddie used to come to my house to listen to records. One day I played him a record of Henry Cowell's music. Henry Cowell wrote cluster music for elbows in the 1920s. Eddie figured out how many notes his elbow hit when he struck the elbow on the keys. Right away, Eddie became a fanatic. He started using his elbows whenever he could. People hated it. So I take blame for the whole thing with elbows on the piano and the clusters.

Eddie liked to use what I call time wasting devices, so he could play the least amount of serious music in an allotted set. He can get away with playing two or three tunes during a whole set by doodling on the piano and letting a conga player take a solo for five minutes while Eddie goes off to have a beer.

When I joined Eddie's band we were all brothers trying to move the music forward. The band was hot and his popularity started building again. We were booked on major tours when I noticed that Eddie was professing brotherhood while getting the superstar treatment. I got pissed off.

Eddie Palmieri was having financial problems. Then he started owing us money. And instead of paying us for a gig, he'd say, "Listen, I owe you money..." We would have to see him during the week to collect our pay. The last six months of my association with Eddie, Manny Oquendo was in the band, my brother was playing congas, and the band was great. In Puerto Rico, Manny warned Eddie, "I won't stand for nonsense. If you mess with me, I'm on the next plane out of here." Nonsense started to happen, so Manny Oquendo went back to New York and half the band went with him. I was part of that half.

LIBRE—FREE AT LAST

During our stay in Puerto Rico, Manny Oquendo and I began talking about playing the music we liked on our own. Back in New York, we started getting

If a singer has the ability, the talent to become a superstar, there is no greater school than ours. He'll learn how to be a great sonero, somebody that improvises.

Libre together. I wrote the first arrangements. We borrowed money from the Musicians Credit Union to buy equipment and we started Libre. Our first gig was October 24th, 1974.

Manny Oquendo is the leader of the band, the ultimate taste decider. I'm the musical director. Manny's quite an idea person and the great word master. He's worked for the best: Benny Moré and Tito Rodríguez. We originally called ourselves *Conjunto Libre*, but we dropped the term conjunto because of its association with other bands of that name. Trumpets, tres guitar, a piano, and rhythm section, that's what a conjunto is. We have four trombones. The first Libre album had one saxophone on one tune, the danzón. On our first album in 1976, we did *Donna Lee*, a Charlie Parker tune as a danzón with jazz solos, the first time that was ever done.

If a singer has the ability, the talent to become a superstar, there is no greater school than ours. He'll learn how to be a great sonero, somebody that improvises. There are few real soneros in Latin music anymore, I can count them on one hand. Ismael Quintana was a favorite singer of mine. But when I started working with him in Eddie Palmieri's band, I noticed that he barely improvised. He sang the same phrases every gig, the same style. I could sing along with him.

Oscar D'León is an improviser, he's one of the few guys I give credit to. Anybody can make a rhyme, but to put two sublime thoughts together, things that make a lot of sense or things that have more than one meaning, or things that have some depth and to rattle them off your brain, that's the true sonero.

Not acknowledging your sources after obtaining commercial success is selling out. Some people can't play a lick and they luck out with a hit record, something that appealed to the public and has nothing to do with their playing abilities or their abilities as musicians. They think, "I had a hit, so I'm a great musician." That's not so.

We are the rebels of the industry and we've had to pay the price for it. Yes rebels, because we don't work for booking agents. I always felt that a booking agent should work for a band and not the band work for the booking agent. We book ourselves. Certain clubs are pressured not to use us because if they use us they don't get the bands from the booking agency. So it's been rough, but fulfilling. We've been on tours of Europe playing major Jazz Festivals. We maintain the original outlook on Latin music, which entails a lot of individual musicianship. Individual voices can be heard in our music, you can hear everybody and you can tell who they are. We want to show the public that some people are concerned with culture more than selling product.

If you don't achieve commercial success, you don't get respect in the business. When I see bands that don't have half the musicality or the knowledge or the spirit that we have, make commercial successes, I feel hurt. The lack of respect for good musicianship in Latin music hurts me.

A new generation of kids coming up today has no idea where the music comes from. They think, "That's the music my parents danced to; that's not my thing." But when kids grow up, they want to know where they come from. That's where we come in. We teach the public about our roots, what kind of music we listen to, why our parents dance to it and the social functions it served earlier generations. ■

Andy **González**

I HAVE ALWAYS WANTED TO DEFEND CUBAN MUSIC AND THE CUBAN FORMS
OF EXPRESSION TO DEMONSTRATE TO THE WORLD THAT CUBAN MUSIC EXIST:
THAT IT IS ALIVE AND THAT IT CONTINUES TO HAVE THE SAME IMPACT AS IN
THE FIRST HALF OF THE TWENTIETH CENTURY.

Juan de

Gonzá

Marcos
lez

JUAN DE MARCOS
GONZÁLEZ

BORN IN CUBA IN
1954. COMPOSER,
ARRANGER,
BANDLEADER,
GUITARIST.
FOUNDER OF THE
AFRO-CUBAN ALL
STARS, SIERRA
MAESTRA, AND
BUENA VISTA
SOCIAL CLUB.

CHAPTER 12

Juan de Marcos González   **123**

DE DONDE SERAN, AY, MAMA

My name is Juan de Marcos González Cardenas. I was born in La Habana in 1954, the son of Marcos González, a Cuban musician of the forties who was actively working until 1953. My mother, Lydia Rosa Cardenas, had nothing to do with the music except that her home town of Matanzas known as the land of the rumberos, or those who play rumba.

My family came from humble origins. My father belonged to that generation of Cubans that didn't allow their wives to work. He was born in Pinar del Rio, the poorest province in Cuba during the first half of the century. My mom had a semi-professional education. She had taken some college-level courses, but she didn't finish because she had ties to the political and social movements of her times. My mother had a high intellectual level. We were poor, but did not live in squalor. We always had the bare essentials: a house, a telephone, a TV and a refrigerator. My father received little education, but was very intelligent and culturally advanced. He wanted us to study and my home was like any typical Latino home. The father strays a little and squabbles with his wife. But in general, it was a positive upbringing.

I was raised in a neighborhood of musicians, and thanks to that, and to my genetic makeup, I have an inclination towards music. I was born on Oquendo Street on the corner of Salud. Compay Segundo (Francisco Repilao) lived on the corner of Salud and Oquendo. My balcony faced his balcony. From the moment I opened my eyes, I was seeing him. The first guitar I had when I started studying music was one my father bought from Compay. One block away from my house was the famous "Solar del Africa," known by that name because only blacks lived there. A solar[1] is a promiscuous neighborhood house that existed, and still exists primarily in Old Havana (the slums). Some of the most important musicians in Cuban music lived or were born at the Solar del Africa. Musicians like Bienvenido Julian Gutierrez, one of Cuba's best composers from the first half of the century; Chano Pozo, who played with Dizzy Gillespie; Papín Abreu of the Los Papines; Eliseo Silveira, one of the best tres players, all came from the Solar del Africa.

They held rumbas there in the sixties and seventies, and I used to sneak out without telling my mother because El Africa was a violent place. It had a reputation of being a bad place, full of delinquency, drugs and so forth. I used to go to El Africa to see the great rumbas where Tio Tom sang and Danielito Ponce played often. We used to hear the rumbas played by the greats, the elders, the people that knew rumba.

Arcaño, the king of the danzones and one of the best flautists of all times, also lived in my neighborhood as did Ignacio Piñeiro, one of the fathers of the Cuban *son* of the twenties. I grew up in that environment. I took my first musical steps there. Not playing the son montuno naturally, but rock 'n roll, like everybody else does at first.

I listened to all kinds of music. The rumba spoke to me because it is the music of my neighborhood, the music I carried in my blood. Although I escaped to El Solar del Africa to see the rumbas, I preferred the rock 'n roll on the radio. In Cuba, rock 'n roll was prohibited at that time. When I was starting my career as a musician, you couldn't buy albums of the Beatles or the Rolling Stones, or any of the bands of the 1960s or 1970s. But Havana is 90 miles from Florida and the southern part of the US.

I learned how to speak English when I was 13 years old in order to sing rock 'n roll. There was a radio station that came from Key West called WQAM and one that came from Little Rock, Arkansas called KAAY. WQAM was a commercial station where they played the Hit Parade. On that station, I was introduced to the well-known American and English bands of those years: King Crimson, Yes, Jethro Tull, the Beatles, Rolling Stones, Credence Clearwater Revival, Steely Dan. KAAY played underground music. We would take all that music, copy it, transcribe it and play it. The first tune I ever wrote followed the type of harmonic sequence done by Jethro Tull and Ian Anderson. It was based on a book written by Bernal Diaz del Castillo, a colonizer who crossed over with Hernan Cortéz. I called the song, *The True Story of the Conquest of the New Spain*. It was my first composition, written in English, because I wrote the lyrics in English and we sang in English.

I studied guitar from the age of 9 to 14 at the Amadeo Roldán Conservatory. Amadeo Roldán was a folkorist who wrote symphonic music ulilizing elements of folk music. I studied at that conservatory until they kicked me out for disciplinary problems. My father was happy with my expulsion because he never wanted me to be a professional musician even though he bought Repilao's guitar. In his eyes, being a musician was not a career. Then he made me go to junior college. Of course I never abandoned the music. So as not to feel guilty, my dad paid for private lessons with two of the most important guitar teachers in Cuba at that time. One was Vicente González Rubiera, known as Guyún, the father of the Cuban harmonic guitar. The other was Leopoldina Nuñez, another great teacher of many of Cuba's important guitarists. I also studied with an old man that came from the old Cuban trova from the beginning of the century named Graciano Gómez.

SIERRA MAESTRA

I went on to college where I studied agronomical engineering. At the university, I started to play music seriously again. In 1976, we founded Sierra Maestra, which was the first group of young Cuban musicians playing the *son*. Some of us knew each other from the conservatory and others were into music and had some musical background.

I was a founding member of Sierra Maestra. The others included: Eduardo Imery, who is still with Sierra Maestra; Carlos Romero Torres, contrabassist, who now lives in Miami and is an electical engineer; the trumpeter Ernesto, who died young; Virgilio Valdes, singer; and Carlos Pizó who played güiro. After the first two years, others joined, like Jose Antonio Rodríguez "Maceo," who has been the singer of Sierra Maestra for years.

Young Cubans weren't atuned to the musicians that played the *son*. It was not fashionable. The Cuban *son* clicked with the young Cubans from the moment in which Sierra Maestra came on the scene, especially from 1978 to 1982. In 1979, Sierra Maestra had two tunes that hit nationally and the *son* became hip in Cuba again. I am referring to Havana. That doesn't mean that the *son* wasn't being played in Cuba. The *son* always had its presence in the eastern region. Musicians like El Guayabero and Eliades Ochoa had always played the *son*. But the *son* was not the mainstay in music. The young intellectuals were listening to music that was happening in the 1970s, the Andean music, which has little to do with Cuba.

Most of us who started Sierra Maestra were rock 'n rollers. I had studied classical guitar and played lead guitar in rock 'n roll bands. I had never held a

I studied guitar from the age of 9 to 14 at the Amadeo Roldán Conservatory. Amadeo Roldán was a folkorist who wrote symphonic music ulilizing elements of folkloric music. I studied at that conservatory until they kicked me out for disciplinary problems.

tres in my hand. When we started the band, we decided that I, who was the lead guitarist, was going to have to play the tres because the tres is the equivalent of the lead guitar in the *son*.

So I began to study the tres and I went to see two great masters. One was Hilario Ariza from Matanzas. The other was a well-known name in Cuban music: Isaac Oviedo. First I went to see Ariza, who was a cranky old man, and he told me, "Listen, there are three basic positions," which are the positions everybody knows. He taught me the positions, the normal first and second inversion. And he told me that he tuned the tres in the second inversion of C major. He didn't want to teach me anything else, although he was proud that I wanted to learn to play the tres being so young.

It was difficult to deal with Ariza, so I went to see Isaac Oviedo. Isaac tuned in D major instead of C major, also in the second inversion, which is tuned A, D, F sustained. He reiterated the same positions and how it would be easy for me because of my musical background to prepare a sequence of chords to do the tumbaos myself even though I had never done a tumbao. Then he sent me to see Iglesias, my first luthier, so he could build me a tres. I remember looking for two albums with Isaac: one by the Septeto Nacional of Ignacio Piñeiros, and the other by the Septeto Habanero that dated to 1926. It had tunes like *Nieve* by Liceo Silveira, *Dulce Habanera* by Gerardo Martinez, and *Tres Lindas Cubanas* by Guillermo Castillo Bustamante. The album by Septeto Nacional had the classic tune *Echale Salsita* by Ignacio Piñeiro.

What did I do with those albums? Well, I sat down with paper and pencil and I literally transcribed all the tunes, everything, even the bongo licks of the bongo player and I came up with our first repertoire. Perhaps that is why Sierra Maestra was

Afro-Cuban All Stars perform in Atlanta with Juan de Marcos and Pedrito Calvo on vocals

126 *Juan de Marcos* **González**

Juan de Marcos relaxes in front of author Mary Kent's Latin music collection

Juan de Marcos **González**

such a hit, because everything was a reproduction. Of course, we added a little bit of swing, but it was basically a carbon copy with the same licks, everything exact. It resembled a group from the twenties with the difference that if you are twenty in 1986, you cannot play the music the way a twenty year old played in 1924 because life was much slower then. In this first phase of Sierra Maestra, we followed the exact patterns, just playing a little faster, which corresponded with the speed of life and time at that moment. By the time we recorded our first album, we had established an identity and we started recording our own compositions. We included classic tunes and combined them with tunes written mostly by me.

When you play the *son* in its traditional form, it has its limits. Nevertheless, even in the *son,* on the breaks, on the bolero part, where there is a little more harmonic freedom, we started interjecting some contemporary elements, but always staying true to the authentic roots. If you make the harmonic sequence too contemporary, it doesn't work. We experimented a lot. With Sierra Maestra, I recorded tunes playing guitar with distortion. We made the first recordings of the septet with a string quartet. We took the basic structure and the essence of the *son* and we extrapolated it to today and added new repertoire. That was the success of Sierra Maestra. At first we played *El Guanajo Relleno*, *Echale Salsita*, and the classic tunes of Cuban music. Then we started playing my compositions and those of contemporary composers of Cuban music. And the lyrics were a bit more ambitious, within the confines of danceable music like the son.

We were criticized. I recorded a version of a song by Arsenio Rodríguez, *Tintorera Ya Llegó*. Arsenio recorded it with a piano solo instead of the tres and used a conjunto with three trumpets. We did it with a septet, but I added a guitar solo with distortion. We recorded tunes by composers of the Nueva Trova, but always within the structure of the *son*, following the patterns of the *son*. In other words, Sierra Maestra always sounded *son*, but black *son* from Havana. There are two Cuban *sons*. You have the Cuban *son* that sounds white, and I don't mean it in a pejorative sense because we had great white bands in Cuba. That is, if we can speak of blacks and whites in Cuba. You can say there are light skinned and dark-skinned people. But there are bands that sound white and bands that sound black, and there are conjuntos that sound macho, strong and there are conjuntos that sound "hembra" or more feminine. A conjunto sounds macho when its sound is compact and energetic, and it sounds hembra when it doesn't sound like that. There are very good conjuntos that sound hembra. To give you an idea: The Arsenio Rodríguez Conjunto sounded macho and the Sonora Matancera sounded hembra. Machito and his Afro-Cubans sounded macho and the Tito Rodríguez big band was hembra. Sierra Maestra was always a macho septet that played black *son* from the city of Havana.

BUENA VISTA SOCIAL CLUB—THE REAL STORY

In 1994, I produced an album for Sierra Maestra called *Dundunbanza*, a tribute to Arsenio Rodríguez, one of the five most important composers of Cuban *son* of the 20th century. I recorded *Dundunbanza* for a record label called World Circuit, located in London. It was a very small label, with only three employees: the record label director, the secretary who did everything and a third man who took care of the computers. Then that album achieved unprecedented success within what people in the first world call World Music. Because there is music:

rock 'n roll; and the rest is World Music. That's how I see it. Within World Music, that album sold 250,000 copies, which was totally abnormal for that market and for Cuban *son*. World Circuit was a very small company, but they had had some success with a couple of albums. They mainly worked with African music and they had put out an album called *Talking Timbuctu* with Ali Farca Touré, a wonderful guitarist from Mali and Ry Cooder. Timbuctu refers to the famous 14th century kingdom in Mali.

While I was visiting London in 1994 promoting our album, my friend Nick Gold (president of World Circuit) and I had a meeting. I suggested the idea of recording a tribute album to the sound of the Cuban big bands of the fifties. I consider the fifties the Golden Age of Cuban music. Cuban music exploded in the twenties. It started to be recognized, but it achieved an expressive maturity in the fifties. The cha cha chá is born; the mambo; a series of elements that define what is Cuban with big bands like Conjunto Casino and Arsenio Rodríguez's Conjunto created a musical and cultural explosion. Great Cuban writers of the fifties like Lezama Lima, the great poets Nicolas Güillen and Alejo Carpentier, reached an expressive maturity.

I wanted to do a tribute to the Cuban music of the fifties. I spoke to Nick and we did the project. "Let's make an album called Big Band," I said. We didn't have a name for that album. But on that recording I wanted to pay tribute to the musicians who were alive that lived in Cuba during that era and who were still able to record. We also agreed to record a second album which would pay tribute to the music from the twenties to the forties, with the

> *I wanted to do a tribute to the Cuban music of the fifties. I spoke to Nick and we did the project. "Let's make an album called Big Band," I said. We didn't have a name for that album. But on that recording I wanted to pay tribute to the musicians who were alive that lived in Cuba during that era and who were still able to record.*

fundamental sound of the oriental Cuban *son*. Nick had "discovered" the Cuban *son*, and he had licensed from Egrem, the Cuban record company, an album called *Adios, Compay Gato* by Ñico Argento. He called it, *Goodbye, Mr. Cat*, to sell it in his market, and the album was relatively popular. Then he licensed a compilation by Guillermo Portabales to Universal. In addition, we went to see a concert by Eliades Ochoa with his quartet at the Queen Elizabeth Hall. And he had listened to some recordings of an album called *Anthology of the Life of Compay Segundo*, released by a subsidiary of Warner Music in Spain called East and West. For that reason, we decided to record an album of Cuban *son* from the twenties to the forties, and to invite three or four musicians to participate.

We also wanted to bring a couple of musicians from Mali because of the desire for fusion that existed in the company. We were going to bring Charlie Madi, an exceptional guitarist from the Super Rego Band and a cora player, a traditional guitar from western Africa, and possibly others. We finally decided to bring only two Africans: Charlie Madi and the cora player. But there is no Cuban Embassy in Mali so they couldn't come due to visa problems.

In 1996, I arrived in Havana to assemble the musicians for the first album, the big band. I gathered some of the best-known musicians from the fifties that could still play, together with some young musicians, many of them friends of mine of exceptional quality who were interested in a fusion of the old with the young. Among the old were Ibrahim Ferrer, Rubén González, Cachaito López, Pio Leiva, Raul Plana, "Puntillita" Manuel Licea and Guillermo Rubalcaba. We went to the studio and recorded, acompanied by young musicians like Julien Oviedo, who was barely 13 years old when he recorded timbales with me on that album, Angá Diaz, one of Cuba's best conga players of the moment, and my brother Carlos González, a bongo player that learned to play from transcribed sheet music of Martino's, the king of the bongos. On brass we had Manuel "Guajiro" Mirabal, Luis Alemañy, Daniel El Gordo, Demetrio Muñiz, Carlitos "Afrocán" Alvarez, and Javier Salva, a bevy of exceptional musicians.

We recorded the first album called Big Band with those musicians. The name was changed to *Afro Cuban All Stars* in March 1996. Then, with those same musicians, I didn't need the brass section to record the album of Cuban *son*, of music from the 1930s and 1940s because they didn't have a brass section in those years. They used one trumpet. So "Guajiro" Mirabal left and we kept Rubén González to play a couple of tunes. We tried to bring the Africans, but we couldn't, we made a special call to Compay Segundo and Eliades Ochoa to record on this album. Using that group, we recorded a second album, originally called *Eastern Album*, because it was music from eastern Cuba.

Ry Cooder was invited by Nick Gold to work on the production of the album because it was a fusion record. The Africans never arrived, but Ry came with Joaquim Cooder, his son, and we started to record the *Eastern Album* with the repertoire I had planned. During the recording, we deleted some tunes and replaced them with other tunes. In the studio, I wrote the arrangements. And right there, we started to record that album known today as *Buena Vista Social Club*. The whole project cost $70,000. Nick couldn't ask the bank for more money because he maxed his credit. When we finished, we had about five thousand dollars left.

Everybody had fallen in love with Rubén González so we decided to record Rubén González with that money. The myth that Rubén suffered from arthritis in his hands is false. Rubén had some sclerosis, but he did not have dementia.

Rubén González's album was slated as Cuban jam sessions based on the piano. So I removed the people I didn't need from the studio. The only thing we needed was a Cuban base: piano, bass, conga, timbales and bongos, and one trumpet to improvise. With that set up, I brought Amadito Valdés and Roberto Garcia into the studio so that they would play timbales and bongos. My brother, who played bongos on the *Buena Vista Social Club* and *Afro-Cuban All Stars* albums, came to play congas. Rubén González on piano, Cachaito López on bass and "Guajiro" Mirabal on trumpet. With that format, we did the first album of Rubén González, which sold almost one million copies, and is paradoxically called, *Introducing Rubén González*. The *Afro Cuban All Stars* and the *Buena Vista Social Club* albums were nominated for a Grammy in 1998. *Buena Vista* won the Grammy and we were all in New York. We held a meeting and decided to record an album for Ibrahim Ferrer.

We never thought we'd be so successful with those recordings. We thought that perhaps we'd sell max 250,000 copies of the *Afro-Cuban All Stars*, maybe a little more of the *Buena Vista Social Club*, because it was a sweet album, and 30,000 copies, if we were lucky, of Rubén González's album. But something extraordinary happened. All of a sudden those albums became a resounding success. We recorded in 1996 and we went on tour in 1997. We all toured under the name *Afro-Cuban All Stars*. We didn't do a presentation of the *Buena Vista Social Club* until late 1998 when we did the only three

Juan de Marcos **González**

presentations ever. The fact that it was such a hit was due to a series of circumstances.

The worldwide success of this set of albums, especially the *Buena Vista Social Club*, can be attributed to economic, political, and social factors, not Ry's presence. In the 1990s, when the Communist Eastern Block fell, the world expected an immediate collapse of communism in Cuba. People started eyeing Cuba closely. The Cuban government started to open its doors to tourism as a source of income. People started traveling to Cuba in 1990. They were mostly European and they started to rediscover Cuba, Cuban culture and Cuban music. But this was the music that they used to hear as children at home. The mambo, the cha cha chá, the son and the danzón were always heard all over the world. While Cuba was under that watchful eye, the subjective conditions were ripe for an explosion of Cuban music around the world. All these conditions determined the success of the Buena Vista Social Club. If another album of the Buena Vista Social Club were recorded now, nothing would happen. And if it had been done in 1980, nothing would have happened either, in spite of the quality of those recordings. Ry Cooder had already been to Cuba and had recorded with Cuban musicians and nothing had happened. Why? Because it wasn't the right moment.

THE MYTH

We used to rehearse at Cachaito's house of the Afro-Cuban All Stars when we began in 1997. World Circuit and Nick Gold, risking even more, invited a set of European journalists to the rehearsals. An excellent English journalist named Nigel Williamson was responsible for creating the myth according to which Ry came to Havana, found the musicians,

wrote the music, took the musicians to a studio, recorded them and recorded an album that led to rediscovering the music. It sounded like the story of Columbus discovering America. The myth was reaffirmed by Wim Wenders, a fine German film director friend of Ry, who Ry worked with on other occasions, since he did the music for *Paris, Texas*. And Wim Wenders went to Havana because Ry was driving him crazy, "The music, the musicians, the old musicians," Ry couldn't stop talking about this project he had participated in. Without much knowledge about how everything happened, Wim Wenders arrived in Havana when we were getting ready to record the album for Ibrahim Ferrer.

We had planned to record Ibrahim Ferrer after the tremendous success we had with Buena Vista. Wim began filming the recording sessions of Ibrahim Ferrer's album, which is the footage that appears in the *Buena Vista Social Club* movie. He started to interview some of the musicians that were participating in the recording, unscripted. Coincidentally, we were booked for the only three presentations we did that year, which included two concerts with all the Buena Vista personnel from the recording at the Amsterdam theater called Le Carre, and one at Carnegie Hall in New York City. We sold out the two nights at Le Carre where we presented the show live for the first time. Those two concerts were filmed by Wim Wenders. Then we came to New York to play at Carnegie Hall and Wim came with us. He shot several scenes of our visit in New York and he filmed the concert. With those three concerts and the interviews, he edited together the *Buena Vista Social Club*, which is undoubtedly a fine film, but doesn't reflect the reality of how the project came about. It is sold as a documentary, but it is a fiction film, no different than *The Matrix*. The film was a

Juan de Marcos **González**

tremendous hit, but it didn't determine the success of the *Buena Vista Social Club*. Wenders's film was the icing on the cake to the success the album already enjoyed, because when the film was shot, we had already sold two million copies. After the film appeared, we were a total hit everywhere. We sold a lot and it was a very positive thing. In the end, credits do not matter. What matters is that Cuban music regained some of the recognition it enjoyed in the first half of the twentieth century in the United States and in Europe.

THE ROOTS OF SALSA

The Cuban *son* has it all. When I use the word *son*, I am including all the different patterns through which the *son* expresses itself. The *son* is the musical complex that defines Cuban-ness. When I use the word *son*, I am referring to the *montuno*, the *cha cha cha*, the *danzon*, the *mambo*. They are all encompassed within the *son* because it has the same alternating structure of the *montuno*; that is, first a *coro*, then switching off between the *coro* and the *sonero*, call and response. The *coro* and the improvisations, which can be executed either by the *sonero* or an instrument, show the African influence in Cuban music.

Salsa is not a musical genre, although they call it salsa. Salsa is a general name that encompasses the exiled Latino, his music and his culture. Salsa music helped preserve the spirit of Cuban-ness throughout the world. Especially in the United States, the most important market. It helped preserve the spirit of Latin-ness, it helped unite the Latinos amongst themselves, because there was a common denominator between the Mexican immigrant, the Colombian, the Venezuelan and the Cuban. There was a common denominator called *salsa*, and up to a certain point, salsa helped preserve the Cuban *son* because it was called salsa.

As of the 1970s and 1980s, in spite of the attempts to make the music a more international language, what was called salsa was ninety five percent Cuban music and five percent elements from the music from other prominent Caribbean regions, such as Puerto Rico or Colombia. If you take a classic album of that time, like *Siembra*, it is Cuban *son*. Tito Puente played completely Cuban music of the fifties, with more modern arrangements. So did Palmieri.

Naturally, some of the elements that were added to those groups identified them with the city where they were playing. It is not the same to write music in New York as in Havana. The speed of New York City is much greater. You can hear the sound of the traffic in the city reflected in the music of Harlow and Palmieri, although it is based on the Cuban *son*. Palmieri started playing with two trombones. That projects the sound of the city, of traffic, of yellow cabs. But it was basically Cuban music. I feel that salsa helped preserve the spirit of Cuban-ness within the taste of certain American sectors, although sadly, salsa never transcended beyond our own people. Salsa was mostly our thing. Certain Americans did go to the salsa concerts, but they were Latinophiles. It never reached the level of the Buena Vista Social Club playing at Carnegie Hall, except for certain stars like Tito Puente, who cannot be considered a salsa artist, but instead a great musician that worked at the Palladium and other important places in New York.

> *Salsa is not a musical genre, although they call it salsa. Salsa is a general name that encompasses the exiled Latino, his music and his culture. Salsa music helped preserve the spirit of Cuban-ness throughout the world.*

Juan de Marcos **González**

135

THE CUBAN LEGACY

Until 1999 I was the bandleader of both bands: Afro-Cuban All Stars and Buena Vista Social Club. Then we divided it. In 1999, we recorded Ibrahim Ferrer's album and Ibrahim started his own orchestra. I started to incorporate youngsters with some of the elders, like Puntillita and Pio Leyva; Eliades Ochoa already had his group and Compay Segundo had his. Barbarito Torres recorded his album and formed his group, and little by little we each did our own projects. The big band became the Afro-Cuban All Stars. I kept the Afro-Cuban All Stars. All the musicians eventually spun off into other bands. We also did a Cuban big band with a saxophone section. Then we did Omara Portuondo's band. I was the A&R man for the company, the one who directed practically everything. Rubén González had his small ensemble.

I believe that in order to preserve the identity of a culture you have to include the young, not the old. The older musicians are the history and respect, but they disappear. If you don't incorporate the young to work with the old at some moments in their lives, they will never understand some of the essentials that are necessary for them to preserve that work, with its form of expression.

The Afro-Cuban All Stars will continue to be a heterogeneous band because I feel there is a certain charm in mixing generations. Its multigenerational nature produces some very nice blends. And we will continue to create Cuban music, adding many more elements from our contemporary music. I have always wanted to defend Cuban music and the Cuban forms of expression to demonstrate to the world that Cuban music exists, that it is alive and that it continues to have the same impact as in the first half of the twentieth century. ∎

Footnote 1:

According to a report titled "The Case of Havana, Cuba" by Mario Coyula and Jill Hamberg, from 2003, "A solar is the popular term to refer to all forms of buildings subdivided into single-room units, usually with shared services. It is essentially a tenement house with single rooms, where poor families live and share bathrooms." Every neighborhood in Havana has solares. Because of the promiscuous nature of the living conditions, many solares are teeming with crime, prostitution, drugs and seedy characters. But according to Juan de Marcos, some solares are characterized by their refined nature and are home to non-marginal, professional individuals. That includes the Solar El Frances, from Oquendo between Jesus Peregrino and Pocitos; and Solar Zanja 100, which is still in existence.

After the abolition of slavery in 1888 in Cuba, the living conditions of the needy remained unchanged: shared services and the promiscuous nature of their old slave quarters carried over into what were now called solares. Although many people think the rumba was born in the solares of Havana and Matanzas, much speculation still surrounds the rumba's origin. The rumba seems to be a rural, not an urban phenomenon. Some forms of the rumba (Yambu, Jiribilla and Columbia) closely resemble their Congo (Bantu) origin and since the majority of the Bantu slave enclaves were located in Matanzas (Union de Reyes, etc.), it has led some to believe that Matanzas could well be the rumba's birthplace.

CHRISTMAS 1955,
I WENT TO HAVANA FOR A VACATION WITH A FEW FRIENDS.
I'D NEVER BEEN ANYWHERE BEFORE AND I SAID, "OH, MY
GOODNESS. LOOK AT THIS!" I GOT INTERESTED IN THE MUSIC.
I STARTED TO LISTEN TO BETTER RECORDS, GOING TO THE
PALLADIUM EVERY WEDNESDAY, LEARNING HOW TO DANCE
AND HANGING OUT WITH HISPANIC WOMEN, WHICH WAS
ONE OF MY BIG TURN-ONS.

Lar

Harlo

Larry **Harlow**

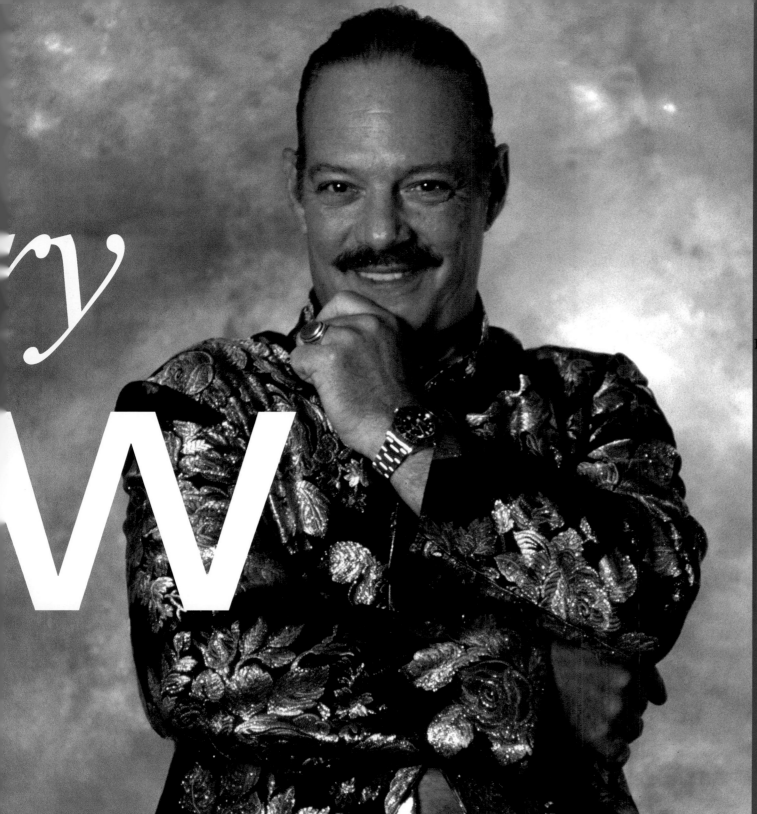

Born in Brooklyn, March 20, 1939. Affectionately known as "El Judio Maravilloso" (the incredible Jew), Larry Harlow zeroed in on the típico sound and ran with it. His vast discography boasts the classic concept recordings of Hommy, the first salsa opera and La Raza Latina.

Chapter 13

Larry Harlow

EL JUDIO MARAVILLOSO

I went to the High School of Music and Art in the middle of the Spanish Barrio on 137th Street. I would hear music coming out of the bodegas. This was the time of *Cherry Pink and Apple Blossom White*; *One, Two, Three*, Jose Curbelo, Al Castellano and René Touzet. These tunes were coming out of the juke boxes and the Spanish radio stations. I was 15 years old and I had never played in a Latin band. I wanted to be a jazz player.

I was a pretty good pianist, classically trained. A guy named Hugo Dickens was putting a band together with no singer. It was like a Latin band. Hugo said, "We're looking for a piano player." They were playing old Cuban stock arrangements such as *Mambo No. 5, Mambo No. 8*, and *Anabacoa*.

I knew how to read music so I read the charts off exactly as written. Then they said, "Okay, piano solo." One chord, a C-7, and I didn't know what to do. I tried to play bebop over it and it sounded ridiculous. So they said "Practice up and come back next week." I went to the store and bought a Joe Loco album, a Noro Morales album and a Jose Curbelo album. I sat down and memorized the solos, those one chord C-7's. I came back the next day and killed everybody. But I didn't understand what I was doing.

In the band was Pete La Rocca who became Pete Sims, Sonny Rollins' drummer, and Phil Newsom, who later became my bongo and timbales player. Joe J. Smith was the conga player. They weren't even Latin guys, they were black guys playing Spanish music and I was the white guy in the band. I think the conga player was Hispanic. We were having fun, but I still wanted to play jazz.

Christmas 1955, I went to Havana for a vacation with a few friends. I'd never been anywhere before

and I said, "Oh, my goodness. Look at this!" I got interested in the music. I started to listen to better records, going to the Palladium every Wednesday, learning how to dance and hanging out with Hispanic women, which was one of my big turn-ons. At the Palladium, all my friends, the Jewish guys were dancers.

In the summer of 1957 I put a little five piece band together called the Al Vega Sextet. There was no Al Vega. All the guys were Italian and Jewish, but we were playing mambo music. Sort of what La Playa Sextet used to play years ago. We had no lead singer. They'd sing the head of the song and from there on it was trumpets and coro, eight or four bars, then the mambo and then a moña, (parts played by the horn section featuring staggered entrances, layered and contrapuntal parts building to a wailing, climactic intensity. Usually introduced during the mambo section, they are generally written, and sometimes improvised.).

We'd work these dances in Philadelphia for fifteen dollars a night, the whole band in one car with all the instruments piled up on top. It took us five hours to get to Philly, play all night, come back, and we'd miss the next day of school.

Harvey Averne's band was working a lot of club dates in New York. I had a book of arrangements, fifty, sixty songs of two trumpets without a lead singer, and he could play all those arrangements with the vibes and I would double on the piano. It was like my band with him up front getting the work. I'd sit at the piano with a cigarette dangling out of my mouth and he'd say, "Play number twenty-one." I'd go, "I don't want to play that song." So he fired me from my own band and took copies of my music.

Harlow plays at Cafe Cristal, in Miami, Florida

But I wasn't satisfied with what I was doing anyway, because it wasn't the real thing. I had already been listening to the Palmieris and the charangas. So I went up to the Catskill Mountains and played again. Mark Weinstein played bass. Mike Kurzman on conga, Paul Serrano, a jazz trumpet player and a Jewish guy named Stewey Fink. We kept playing in the mountains as a Latin band, and we were hip. Most Latin bands were playing *Tea for Two* kind of stuff.

That next Christmas, I went to Havana with these really heavy dancers from Brooklyn who I got friendly with at the Palladium—and I didn't come back. I stayed in Cuba and I went to school at the University of Havana. Cuba was getting kinda hairy. The revolution was starting. This was around 1958.

But there was a band on every corner, a charanga band playing in every restaurant, a sextet over here, people were playing all over the place. I used to follow Benny Moré and Orquesta Riverside. They took me to their homes and I would watch the toques and bembés in their backyards and the rumbas in the streets. I was having a great time.

I was learning the language, the culture, the music. I was carrying a big Webcor tape recorder and I taped everybody. I got friendly with Rafael Lay from Orquesta Aragón. He said, "You want to play?" He knew I was a piano player and I said, "No, I'm not ready to play with you yet," but these were my idols. I left just before Castro marched into Havana on December 28, 1958.

Back in New York I decided to start writing my own stuff. I got together with Heny Alvarez, who was a lyricist, composer and percussionist. I would pick up melodies and say, "Could you put words to this?" or I'd find a word I liked in Spanish, like *náufrago*,

shipwrecked. I said, "Let's write a song about two people getting shipwrecked on an island."

That is how it snowballed into songs. It took me over a year to start thinking about songs I wanted to write. I used to copy a lot of arrangements like *Saca Tu Mujer* and condense them down into this new sound that I wanted to do with trombone and trumpets. So I wrote a whole new library of songs that I liked, a lot of Puente stuff, La Playa songs, a Tito Rodríguez song.

THE HARLOW SOUND

I got married in 1962. That is when I decided to expand my band. I picked the guys I wanted by saying, I'd like to play with this guy, this guy is a good player, I owe this one a favor. And I found a singer named Felo Brito. He was a dancer with Jose Fajardo's band in Cuba. He wasn't a great singer, but I really didn't know too many singers.

I wrote new music and I decided to put trombones with trumpets which had never been done before[1]. Eddie Palmieri had two trombones and a flute, another band had three trumpets and saxes, but there was no band with trombones and trumpets at the time. I didn't have any timbales. I was very *típico*, because I really liked *son montuno* and *guaguancó*. I had bongos, congas, bass, piano, a singer, one trumpet and two trombones. We started working at the Manor. I used to sit in the agents' offices and beg them for work, but you needed a record out.

So I did my first album, four tracks with Felo Brito. All the songs were Heny's and mine. We did one standard bolero. The rest were originals. When I did my first recording, I realized one trumpet doesn't make it, so I switched and put two trumpets. The first singer with my band was also a trumpet player, so we switched him from singing back to the trumpet and added the second trumpet. I added Alfredo "Chocolate" Armenteros to my band because he was a hot soloist. A couple of Jewish guys, a black guy, a Cuban guy, one Puerto Rican guy. These were guys I liked to play with.

Joe Artanis had just opened the Chez José, a club on 77th street and Columbus Avenue that catered to Latinos. It was very classy; no riff-raff, no sneakers, no jeans. It was the opposite of the Hunts Point Palace. Artanis convinced them to use us as a house band every Friday night. We worked cheap. In the beginning, the Chez José ran one night. All of a sudden, two nights. Then two bands, two nights and then three nights. We played the Chez José from 1964 to 1965. We started adding new material and rehearsing twice a week and playing live once a week. Finally the band started making a little noise.

HARLOW SIGNS WITH FANIA

One night, Jerry Masucci was at Chez José. I didn't know who Masucci was. He heard my band and came over, "Listen, I just recorded Johnny Pacheco. I like your band, but I have to send Johnny down to hear you." I knew Pacheco from the Palladium, from the dances. He had just finished the charanga scene with Tico-Alegre and had started the first conjunto with Pete "El Conde" Rodríguez and Monguito was singing with him.

So one night it was stormy and snowing and Pacheco was three hours late. We were all sitting around getting nervous. We were kids. Johnny showed up and liked the music. I was the first artist to sign with Fania Records in 1965 besides Pacheco. I recorded four tracks that summer with Irv Greenbaum. The album came out in late 1965.

Felo Brito was a little erratic, wasn't really a great creative singer and we had our beef. Monguito "El Único" had just left Pacheco's band. He had that voice, that typical Cuban voice that sounded like Miguelito Cuní and I loved that. Monguito was a great maracas player, so I took him in the band and I had a bongo player that doubled on timbales. I was playing a lot of Cuban *son montunos* and writing new *son montunos*.

My second album was called *Bajándote*. I always threw in one or two Cuban songs. We did *Cienfuegos* and a few Arsenio songs, Conjunto Modelo and Estrellas de Chocolate Orchestra tunes, but most of them were originals. The conjuntos were influencing me more than the orchestras and more than the charangas. They had more swing. It was blacker, more *típico*. So my rhythm section was in the back of the band and the horns were in the front, like they used to do in Cuba. The charanga bands always had the percussion in the back.

I understood Latin music when I was still in high school. An Italian trumpet player with Randy Carlos's band sat me down. He explained clave to me, in notes, in time. Once I analyzed the arrangements and saw how the bass was fitting there and why this beat is here, why everybody is playing on certain beats, I realized where it was at. Everything started to make sense to me after that.

The Latinos feel clave naturally. It's not impossible to understand. The American people can't feel it. They'll play as metrically as written, but it's a little hair different. I've had to change a lot of string parts and use funky guys who play out of tune, but they've got the swing.

Joe Artanis had just opened the Chez Jose, a club on 77th street and Columbus Avenue that catered to the Latinos. It was very classy; no riff-raff, no sneakers, no kids. It was the opposite of the Hunts Point Palace. Artanis convinced them to use us as a house band every Friday night.

HARLOW MEETS MIRANDA

I met Ismael Miranda through my brother, Andy. Ismael was singing with my brother's band. He was fifteen or so. He didn't even have hair on his lip. He used to take an eyebrow pencil to draw a moustache.

I was having trouble with Monguito. I knew it wasn't going to last with Monguito because he was too much of a pain in the ass. So I said to Ismael, "Why don't you play maracas and sing coros?" He didn't know how to play maracas, and I never let him sing a lead song at that moment. I said, "Watch Monguito. He's the best maraca player, except for Tito Rodríguez, maybe in the world." And he stood on the side while he learned how to play maracas.

I met Ismael Miranda through my brother, Andy. Ismael was singing with my brother's band. He was fifteen or so. He didn't even have hair on his lip. He used to take an eyebrow pencil to draw a moustache.

Finally we made our first trip to Puerto Rico when the boogaloo was hitting. Everybody wanted us to play boogaloo. I held out as long as I could, but I made an album for Fania with some shingalings and boogaloos and Miranda had four salsa tunes. At that time it was very hard to keep working because a lot of bands started popping up. There was a lot of political shit going on, the pay was small, and it was absolutely horrendous.

I presented an album called *Harlow Presents Miranda*. He wasn't a star yet. He was about seventeen and he was cute and he had a nice rapport with the people. He wasn't a great singer and he was definitely not a musician. I used to take him to my house and throw all the Cuban records on and say, "Listen to this guy, listen to that one." I'd write a song and say, "Put the lyrics to this. I want to talk about this." And he'd do it. I spoke Spanish, but I didn't have a command of the language. I spoke like an eight year old kid.

On the album where I presented Ismael, I decided to use a bigger band and I took Manny Oquendo in. Manny taught me a lot about clave and about Cuban rhythms that I didn't know. He opened my ears to a lot of things I thought were right, but weren't right. He caught a couple of mistakes that I recorded. The only person who said, "Harlow está cruzao." And then, when I really analyzed it, he was right. Nobody knew about it except me and him.

We started working a little bit, but the boom wasn't here yet. Records sold eight, ten thousand units. A big hit was twenty thousand records. We were working three days a week. For Ismael to make one hundred fifty dollars in three days and if I made two or three hundred dollars a week as a leader, that was a lot of money. My apartment cost me eighty-five dollars a month rent in Manhattan on 55th Street. I was driving a big Thunderbird. Then the records and the songs started getting better.

I did the *Tributo a Arsenio Rodríguez* album. That album established my band as a really *típico* band with swing. Arsenio had just died, but he had lived in New York. We worked opposite him a few times in a club called The Bat Cave on 187th Street and Broadway. Arsenio was a marvelous bass player and a great conga player besides playing the tres. . He used to sit in with us at the Corso. So when Arsenio died, nobody had even given a tribute to the man who really created the *mambo diablo*.

Before Arsenio, there were no conjuntos, there were sextets and septets. They used a solo trumpet, a bongo, maracas, two guitarists and a singer. The conjunto meant more than one trumpet. It meant a bass, a piano with rhythm and two trumpets. Arsenio invented what they called *mambo diablo*, *el ritmo diablo* which became the *mambo*. It was black and they had different sections to it. They would have the singer and the *coro*, one trumpet playing a little solo. So they had these instrumental sections, that we call the *mambo*, and then the *moñas*. I'm not talking about the dance, the mambo. I'm talking about the sound, the mambo, which was still the *guaracha* and *guaguancó*. They called it *diablo* because it was more of a get down and dance kind of thing.

The Arsenio album was done in one session. There were six tunes on the album. We did *Tribute to Arsenio* which Miranda and I wrote, and five Arsenio tunes. One song was eight and a half minutes long. They played it on the radio, so I asked a DJ, "How can you play an eight and a half minute cut?" "It gives us time to go to the bathroom," he said, "But it was swinging!"

Before the Cuban Revolution, there wasn't much going on because the Cuban bands would come and play in the Palladium, in all the clubs, in the Catskill Mountains, and at the Raleigh Hotel. The only Cubans in New York were Machito, Belisario López, and José Curbelo. Arsenio came in the late fifties.

The charanga bands got hot in New York when Cuba got shut off because there was no more charanga music coming to New York. Once we got cut off, it was very hard to find Cuban records. That's why the bands popped up. So Pacheco made a charanga, Palmieri made a charanga, Belisario López, Fajardo, Orquesta Broadway. These bands started recording all the Cuban songs around 1960 in the United States.

THE SALSA SOUND

What made up the salsa sound was the addition of modern New York. That's really where it came from. They were doing it in Puerto Rico a little, but New York took it more on the bebop side. Basically,

it was the same thing. There was an intro, the *guía* (verse section of a salsa arrangement), the *montuno*, the *mambo*, the *montuno* again, possibly a second *mambo* (*moña*) and then the *coda*. It's the same song, but the arrangements and the harmonies were different. I used substitute harmonies, substitute chords, made the arrangements hipper, slicker, more modern. I used four, five bar breaks. More intricate and more complicated than the Cuban stuff.

The piano was basically the same. You can't get too far out playing bebop over a Latin thing because it just doesn't work. And except for a bolero or two, there was no mix of strings with horns until later. In 1974, I did the *Salsa* album with *La Cartera*. That was the first time strings were mixed together in a conjunto band. That was another innovation.

At the time, there were 200 clubs in New York City. You could go dancing every night of the week. There were clubs all over the place, plus the Spanish social clubs, the after-hour joints, a lot of jazz rooms, the Tritons, the Savoy Ballroom, the Audubon Ballroom, the Ansonia Hotel, the Riverside.

All the hotels had dances, the churches had dances, the Jewish centers, the Hispanic Policeman's Society, the Hispanic Garbage men. The Spanish had their own little musical mountains in upstate New York called Las Villas. In the summer there were ten villas working three days a week with bands.

In the fifties and early sixties, Latin music was more for Americans due to the Palladium and the Catskills. But when the influx of people started coming from Puerto Rico and Cuba, there was a real big market. The blacks love Latin music too.

It was starting to happen in 1970, but we weren't international yet. New York, Philly, Boston, New

Jersey, and Camden. Maybe we got to Chicago once in a while, but not California or Miami yet.

We did one concert at the Red Garter in 1970. The Red Garter, which is now the Bottom Line, used to have Mondays as Salsa Nights. It was started by Symphony Sid and Jack Hooke. Symphony Sid was a big jazz DJ for many years and then he switched off into a late night Latin thing. He was on six hours every night. He used to play what was happening in salsa and some old Cuban stuff.

At the Red Garter, Jerry Masucci used Charlie Palmieri, Eddie Palmieri, Tito Puente, Joe Cuba, and Jimmy Sabater. These were people that were not with his label. It was an all-star band, but it really wasn't established. The records didn't sell a lot, it wasn't happening yet. When the Red Garter closed, a couple of years later they moved to the Village Gate.

Those were the heavy payola days and there weren't too many Latin record companies around. A couple of small companies, RCA and Tico. There was Seeco, Ansonia, United Artists had Tito Rodríguez, Tico-Alegre was still there. Puente was still with Tico. Pacheco had been gone since about 1965, but a few artists still remained with Tico.

LA RAZA LATINA

I always had free reign with Fania as far as what I wanted to do. Nobody told me what to record, except for that one boogaloo thing. I had pretty unlimited budgets and I always got paid union scale. I kept it very secret.

Then I did *La Raza Latina*, a superb recording which has never been performed live. Besides being a concept album with a symphony orchestra, the songs are all great. It was a huge amount of musicians. People thought *La Raza Latina* was one song into another song. They didn't know it all went together with parts that linked them together again until it was finished. So it was a lot of fun.

I was a big fan of the experimental music from communist Cuba. I really wanted to tell the history of Latin music through music. I had a big band with three girls and three guys singing. I added a few instruments, plus strings, electric guitar, and trap drums. I started out with where the music came from.

The first section, *Africa*, starts with one drum and a guy singing and it goes into a *guaguancó*. Then Rudy Calzado and I wrote a tune called *Suite Part One*. And it goes into "*Ritmo, ritmo, ritmo de Salsa*," a little jazz thing in the middle, a little bridge, a lot of guitar. My favorite musicians for recording, Luis "Perico" Ortiz on solo, John Faddis, Charlie Miller, and Bobby Porcelli all played. It was written in a very modern style. Three people did arrangements on them. The *Suite* wound up being thirty minutes long. I needed some more time, so Johnny Ortiz wrote a song called *La Raza Latina* for me. We put it on as an intro. And we named it *La Raza Latina: Salsa Suite*.

Nestor Sánchez was signed with Rico Records and Rico would only let him sing one song on my album. So I asked Rubén Blades to sing. Rubén wasn't with Willie at that time. He was working at Fania licking stamps, making deliveries to the post office and sitting playing his guitar. He had just finished recording with Barretto. And he said, "Great."

I loved his talent, I loved his head and I loved the way he sang. He was one of the few people who could sing in English without an accent. So he came in and just blew my head away. He was so well prepared and he knew what he was doing. I made a few suggestions here and there, but he really made it go.

After that introduction of *Ritmo, Ritmo de Salsa, Ritmo,* everyone was asking, "What is salsa?" It goes all the way back to the *danzón,* the *danzonete,* the *cha cha cha,* the *son,* the *son montuno,* the *guaracha,* the *guaguancó,* the Afro. There is a section called *The Forties, The Fifties, The Sixties* and *The Future* and the future part was that last piece from *Música Moderna* that was fast with heavy bebop, words in English, great solos and it just swung.

I wanted to pass a little message down to the people: It came from Africa. And Frankie Rodríguez, my conga drummer, who's been dead for a few years, sang a couple of little pieces in the middle of the African stuff.

We did a thing called *The Fifties* which was a take off of the sound of the fifties in the Palladium, and the lyrics went, "*Oiga el mambo de Nueva York,*" but it was the Tito Puente thing. And Rubén would say, "*Oye compadre, vamos pa'l Palladium ahora. Tito Puente, Tito Rodríguez, Miguelito están aquí.*" We didn't say, this is a mambo. I just called it *The Fifties.*

THE LATIN RECORD INDUSTRY

Salsa was probably my biggest album. These ain't real gold albums. These are Spanish gold albums. The *Salsa* album was like a theater. I had four number one hit songs on that album and I knew a woman who owned a little record shop in Panama half the size of this room. I said "How many *Salsa* albums did you sell here?" She said, "Twenty five thousand in this little store." This was a year after it was out and I came back and I got a statement from my record company. All totaled, it said I sold twenty thousand in the world.

You have a contract that says you're supposed to get royalties. You're supposed to get a percentage and you're supposed to get a count on how many records were printed and how many were sold and get paid on that percentage. I don't think my first three albums sold a lot of records, but whatever it was, even if it was five cents, I would like to have known what it was.

So I went and I checked the books and I got accountants and I sued and there was a period of a couple of years where we were killing each other, until I re-signed for another twelve albums and we settled out of court. I did twelve albums in five years for Jerry and after that I said I'd had it. And that is when "*Sube Papo Lucca, Baja Larry Harlow*" (up with Papa Lucca, down with Larry Harlow) started and I was out of the Fania All Stars. When my contract finished in 1980, I was gone.

Meanwhile, I did five or six great albums during that period with Nestor Sanchez, who is a great singer. Jerry would sell enough records to make his costs back, but he wouldn't give me the promotion. He was really keeping a lid on me. And he held one album back.

Rubén wasn't with Willie at that time. He was working at Fania licking stamps, making deliveries to the post office and sitting playing his guitar. He had just finished recording with Barretto. And he said, "Great."

SALSA INFLUENCES HARLOW

What happened with the *soft salsa* thing was good, but they didn't really take it to where it should have been. They should have been writing more important songs, but what they did is take old boleros and turn them into salsa rhythms making the lyrics a little more important.

Where did the Cuban music go when it got cut off from here? They were still playing down in Cuba, but they were playing *mozambique, songo,* be-bop, and more jazz. They went more towards the jazz side. They sort of forgot the rhythm and went more with the be-bop. So it got un-salsafied. Yeah. What Irakere was doing. You call that Salsa? It's more jazz than it is Latin.

We went more on the rhythm side, still with some jazz, but we stayed more *típico* than jazzy. They didn't get jazz from the States so they wanted to play jazz. We didn't get music from Cuba so we wanted to play Afro-Cuban.

Salsa took it up a little more, but what it did more was jazzify and make it heavier, musically. It made it more modern by keeping the form and the clave of Afro-Cuban music, making the lyrics a little more important. It definitely was a New York influence. And a lot of the American guys and jazz guys started playing with the Latin bands, so they gave it their input and their feel. ∎

[1]Editor's note: Actually, Charlie Palmieri did this way before Harlow on a recording called *Tengo Máquina y voy a 60* produced by Al Santiago.

I STARTED WHEN I WAS THREE YEARS OLD.
MY GRANDPA HAD TWO CONGAS AND CUBAN BONGOS.
I WAS ALWAYS PRACTICING. HE BROUGHT ME TO A CLUB CALLED EL FACUNDO FOR
MY DEBUT. THEY TOLD ME, "YOU HAVE TO GO TO SCHOOL." FORGET ABOUT IT.
SO AT THE AGE OF 7, MY GRANDPA AND PUERTO RICAN PERCUSSIONIST MANININ
BROUGHT ME TO TELEMUNDO TO DO A SHOW WITH LUCECITA BENÍTEZ.
AT EIGHT I WAS JAMMING WITH MY FRIENDS IN SCHOOL.
AT 11, I STARTED PLAYING PROFESSIONALLY.

Giovanni Hidalgo

GIOVANNI
HIDALGO

BORN IN PUERTO
RICO IN 1963.
CONGA VIRTUOSO
AND MASTER
PERCUSSIONIST.
KNOWN FOR HIS
PRECISION AND
SPEED, HE IS AT
EASE PLAYING
WITH DIZZY
GILLESPIE, ART
BLAKEY, MICKEY
HART, TITO
PUENTE & EDDIE
PALMIERI.

CHAPTER 14

BORN TO PLAY

I'm from Old San Juan, Puerto Rico. My biological mother, Celenia died when I was about one year old. She's still in my heart. My father's name is José Manuel Hidalgo, nicknamed Mañengue. He played in groups like the Tito Rodríguez Orchestra and Orquesta Metropolitana in San Juan. Then he went with Barbó Jiménez, a trumpet player from Puerto Rico who played with Richie Ray & Bobby Cruz and the Puerto Rico All Stars from 1970 to 1975 during the Fania years. Richie Ray and Bobby Cruz were another style of salsa, although hot salsa, like Eddie Palmieri's. Now my Dad is playing with my group and he has a little quintet in Puerto Rico.

As a kid, I used to listen to records all day long: Ray Barretto, Mongo Santamaría, Patato, Cándido Camero, Tata Güines, Francisco Aguabella, Armando Peraza, Cal Tjader, Willie Bobo, Tito Puente, and Tito Rodríguez. Every Saturday my aunt cleaned the house and played Joe Bataan, Pete Rodríguez, Ernie Agosto y la Conspiración, Frankie Dante & Orquesta Flamboyan, Lebron Brothers, Joe Cuba, La Lupe and many more. I was also listening to jazz: Dizzy, Count Basie, and the Jazz Messengers. But I also remember Tom Jones, Englebert Humperdink, Sandro, Raphael and Pérez Prado.

I started playing the conga and bongo drums when I was three years old because everybody in my family was a musician—my grandma, my grandpa, my father and Tura, my father's girlfriend. I grew up in the middle of jam sessions. My grandpa had two congas and Cuban bongos. I was always practicing on them. He brought me to a club called El Facundo for my debut. They would tell me,

I started playing the conga and bongo drums when I was three years old, because everybody in my family was a musician—my grandma, my grandpa, my father and Julia, my father's girlfriend. I grew up in the middle of jam sessions.

"Forget about it. You have to go to school." So at the age of 7, my grandpa and Puerto Rican percussionist Manínín brought me to Telemundo to do a show with Lucecita Benítez. At eight I was jamming with my friends in school. By 11, I started playing professionally with the Puerto Rico All Stars, still wearing my school uniform. At that time it was Papo Lucca on piano, Tony Sanchez on drums, Polito Huerta on bass, and my father on congas. I was the mascot. I played one or two tunes, my father was on the congas and I played the quinto, doing a little show. Then I played with Mario Ortiz the trumpet player and with Luigi Teixidor, the singer of La Sonora Penceña. I began working with Charlie Palmieri at 14 and stayed until I was 17 while playing with Batacumbelé at the same time.

Charlie was a great teacher and a great director. I had been listening to his style and his music before I ever joined his group, those great piano *guageos* and *montunos*. So I continued with the same metronome when I started with him. He would laugh because I knew just when to hit him in the right spot. But I was always learning so I was quiet and humble.

Then I left Charlie and joined Batacumbelé. That group still holds an important place in my heart. I played a year with Zaperoco, the late Frankie Rodríguez's group. I played a short stint with Batacumbelé again, before I joined Eddie Palmieri. Palmieri helped me and I appreciate it. While working with Eddie, I got to play alongside Dave Valentín, Paquito D'Rivera and Art Blakey and the Jazz Messengers. Eddie plays salsa, but he plays Latin jazz like Cal Tjader. Yet, Eddie has a unique style, and his own montuno. You are not going to find a piano player like him for many years.

I started playing bongos with Eddie. With Charlie, it was the opposite. I learned to play with feeling, with passion. I played with my heart. However, Eddie was a challenge so I was quiet and when the first tune came, I followed him the right way.

THE DIZZY CONNECTION

In 1988, thanks to Paquito D'Rivera, I started working with Dizzy Gillespie and stayed with him for four and a half years. With Dizzy, I developed another branch of my knowledge in music on the conga drums. I also developed a personality, the way to perform on stage: when to talk to other musicians; when to follow the arrangements…the silence. To be at peace with myself. After the gig, we can relax and drink a beer.

It was a great experience to work with Dizzy and the United Nations Band. I didn't expect to go with him to so many countries. That experience developed my ego nicely. Other people use the ego with an attitude. That's wrong, because the ego is astral, it is spiritual. In those years, I was the only Puerto Rican in the band. Later on they added Danilo Perez, David Sánchez and Charlie Sepúlveda.

Musically, my experience with Dizzy and the United Nations Band was a gift from God. It was like a flashback, as if I were listening to the radio when I was small in my grandmother's house. Back then, the radio programs played everything: jazz, Deodato (Brazilian), everything.

The academic thing is important because we have to read music. I started reading music at the age of eight. By ten, I took piano lessons with Rafael Angulo, piano player from the Xavier Cugat band. I missed one lesson and he threw me out. But I kept going. I went to the conservatory with Pablito Rosario, one of the founders of Batacumbelé. At the conservatory, I developed with Freddy Santiago. At home, I read books and played along with records. I listened and followed the old conga players like Tommy López and Manny Oquendo, but at 45 RPM, not at 33. It was a challenge. You'll get tired, but the record player won't. That's why I did that. When I am 60 years old, I still want to play fast, in peace.

Changuito (one of the world's leading percussionists) helped me to develop another side of the position. I added the rudiments. You learn a lot about style when you find a person that explains something that makes sense to you about where to put the hand and the arm in order to be flexible and hard.

A MUSICAL TRADITION

For me salsa is a sauce. The son montuno is a style, a tradition. You are dealing with different atmospheres and vibrations. You can combine it but they are going to sound dissonant. In the thirties, the Latin style was different.

Jazz has recognition now. Although abstract, jazz is always there. Salsa is more for dancing. There is a big audience for salsa and jazz now. It's an era of combinations. To do a combination you have to analyze it simply.

I have to play like I do because it is the legacy that will remain here on earth. I am not the best nor the biggest. God has sent me to this earth with this talent, and I do it with all of my love and as best as is humanly possible. I have to be born at least 12 more times in order to understand the essence of the human being and music. Nevertheless, here I am and what I do is entertain the people, which is why music gives our spirit a sense of peace, harmony and well-being. ∎

For me salsa is a sauce. The son montuno is a style, a tradition. You are dealing with different atmospheres and vibrations. You can combine it but they are going to sound dissonant. In the thirties, the Latin style was different.

All star percussion line up from left to right: José Claussell, Richie Flores,
Giovanni Hidalgo and Jimmy Delgado playing with the Eddie Palmieri Orchestra

Giovanni **Hidalgo**

My name is Linda Bell Caballero. The name that became an instant hit with me as a newborn was India, I-N-D-I-A. Because of my skin color being so brown, my dark hair, dark eyes, my family instantly saw me as "una India," little Indian. When I signed with Jellybean Records in the 1980s, producer John Jellybean Benitez asked me to submit my artist name for my first contract.

So I said, "I hate to say this, but my grandmother calls me La India, India," and he goes, "That's it! That's the name you're gonna go by!" I trademarked it. Nobody had the name India in the music industry. It stuck by me to this day. Nobody calls me Linda. Everybody calls me India, La India.

India

India

Born in Puerto Rico. Transitioned from Latin hip hop to salsa. India has worked with Eddie Palmieri, Tito Puente and Celia Cruz. She achieved diva status with Vivir Lo Nuestro, the duet recorded with Marc Anthony.

Chapter 15

India

IT'S SPELLED I-N-D-I-A

My name is Linda Bell Caballero. The name that became an instant hit with me as a newborn was India, I-N-D-I-A. Because of my skin color being so brown, my dark hair, dark eyes, my family instantly saw me as "una India," little Indian. My grandmother used to call me La India. It stayed with me through my teenage years, a stage at which I was not so happy about her calling me India! I didn't think it was cool. I would say, "Grandma, please don't call me that in front of my friends. I don't want them to know!" And she always replied, "Sweetheart, you never know if that name will bring you fortune one day." Later on, when I was asked to submit my artist name for my first contract my grandmother's name for me came up. I had signed with Jellybean Records in the 1980s, a label started by John "Jelly-bean" Benítez during his popularity with Madonna and as a DJ, mixer, and producer. He didn't like the name Linda. So I said, "I hate to say this, but my grandmother calls me La India, India," and he goes, "That's it! That's the name you're gonna go by!" I trademarked it. Nobody had the name India in the music industry. It stuck by me to this day. Nobody calls me Linda. Everybody calls me India, La India.

I was born in San Juan, Puerto Rico, in 1969, after my parents lost my nine-month-old brother. They were still mourning the loss of my brother when my mother became pregnant with me. They were hoping that I would be a male! But I turned out to be a female, and it caused a lot of controversy. They were young and rebellious and they didn't know how to make things happen, but they had the help of my grandfather. He was able to buy them a little house. So they depended on my grandpa for survival. Later on, they sold the house and with the money they moved to the Bronx, New York, about 1972.

I was an island girl. Even though I was living in the Bronx, I always warmed for the islands and we would go every summer and every Christmas to be with our family in San Juan. I was much more an island girl than a city girl. But I didn't mind being brought up in the Bronx. I had great experiences. I listened to every kind of music, from salsa to romantic Latin music, rhythm and blues, jazz, pop, rock 'n roll, funk, rap, bebop, disco. My mother and father were into having a good time, singing and listening to music. We were always watching all those music programs on television: American Bandstand, Soul Train, all the dance competitions, Dance Fever, Star Search. We were into anything that had to do with music. And we knew every artist, from country to rock to jazz to pop.

My mother was a high-spirited, happy person. We used to go to sleep with music. Most parents tuck you into bed and say, "You have to go to sleep now." They turn off the light and close the door. My mother would put on the radio, put the music on very lightly, and then she would tuck us into bed, kiss us, turn off the light, and leave. So I used to go to sleep with music and wake up with music.

My parents separated and my mother was left with my older sister and me. She tried to get a job to keep things going. She had to send me to Pennsylvania to stay with my grandmother, and I had an incredible time. My grandmother was a gospel singer for the church and she used to sing all the time. And the ladies from the church would go up to her house and they would read, pray to the Lord, and then sing and practice all the beautiful voices. My grandmother was an amazing opera singer, she really sang her butt off. So I was three or four and my grandmother used to tuck me into bed and she always said she would find me singing and humming little melodies and trying to remember the gospel songs that they were singing. My grandmother recalls that she saw me singing in my crib and she knew that I would be a singer. She commented it to my mother, but they laughed it off and didn't think anything of it.

When I was a child it was hard to get all the syllables together, but by five years old I could sing a whole song. We sang gospel and Latin music to the Lord. I always sang in a high-pitched voice, so when I was singing in the church you could hear my voice over everybody. Everybody would laugh because they were amazed that I was little and I could hold my own in church. I could really sing.

MY VOCAL INSTRUCTIONS

The only training we had was standing next to the piano and trying to learn voices for harmonies. As I got older, there were singing programs at school and we would practice. But it wasn't until my teenage years that I was practicing opera and gospel, singing today's popular music, and studying artists and their voices and the kind of melodies that were beautiful. They were great for training.

Then I met a man named Don Lawrence who is an amazing vocal instructor in New York who has worked with the best artists in the world. Recently he's worked with Christina Aguilera and Bono from U2.

He taught me to use my voice as an instrument. He said, "Most musicians play, then they put their instrument away and they rest up for the morning because they have another show to do. But singers can't do that. Singers have to learn a technique." How you place these notes by using your diaphragm, and doing exercises according to your range, starting from low chest notes all the way to soprano notes, will allow you to use your voice, expand, and have more air control. High notes require a lot of energy. Don saved my life, he showed me how not to be afraid of the note. If I saw the note, I easily broke into the technique, the control, and I would hit it and it was there.

I learned many other things with him; like when they're recording an artist a lot of producers will say, "We're keeping that because it has a lot of feeling, even though it's off key. It has a lot of emotion so we're gonna keep it." That's a poor excuse, because you can hit the correct note and it'll be from the heart and soul with as much feeling or more. That's what makes me today—I consider myself a singer that has grown a lot, and I am never afraid to learn how to use my voice. A lot of it has to do with my motivation to learn.

Don has been in my life since my late teenage years all the way up to my late 20s. I still go back to him to tune up before recording projects and when I do, we have amazing conversations about today's singers and why Pro Tools has given a career to a lot of singers today. Pro Tools is a machine that allows a person that's off key to be on key. It's a machine that fixes messed up voices. You don't have a lot of singers who go in there and sing from the heart and soul without Pro Tools. A teacher teaches you how to sing without Pro Tools. If Pro Tools is the last resort, some people prefer that.

I'm a perfectionist. I know that my voice is very high pitched, so I make sure that I sing on key and I fix everything that I have to fix without using Pro Tools. When you mix my voice you just get the raw emotion, the notes, the phrasing and everything else. I think a lot of it has to do with being involved

He taught me to use my voice as an instrument. He said, "Most musicians play, then they put their instrument away and they rest up for the morning because they have another show to do. But singers can't do that. Singers have to learn a technique."

India

in the production, the writing and also the mixing process of your product. I'm getting into co-producing, producing my projects and opening myself more to songwriting. We have amazing songwriters and I've been very lucky to have a lot of great songwriters submit songs that I've turned into hits in the tropical market. But I feel that I have a lot to give, and for the last ten years I've been working hard to develop myself into a more serious songwriter.

I wrote the number one song we put out in 2002, *Seduceme*. We've had a lot of interesting hits, but that one meant a lot to me because I felt like songwriting is something I'd like to do for the rest of my life. It makes you feel good, too. "This is my baby, I created this."

DANCE MUSIC

Latin hip-hop is dance music. They wanted to create that movement right after disco took a wrong turn, when it got overexposed and died out. But dance music in the clubs continued to play a lot of dance classics like James Brown and Lolita Holloway. So there was a sound that was emerging through drum machines when the Latin Rascals were really hot, after WKTU went down and Paco went to jail. This was in the mid 1980s. The old 92 WKTU and Paco Navarro was the hottest thing on the air. Around that time he had given the opportunity to two young Latino editors by the name of the Latin Rascals—Albert Cabrera and Tony Moran. And there was a time when they were creating and editing a lot of music, dance music, and new drum machines were coming out. Mantronix, Sleeping Bag Records, Mick Mack Records, and other affiliated labels were signing artists and putting them out. A lot of them were

Latinas. I was one of them, Judy Torres was another, Naomi was another one, Lisa Lisa too. A lot of artists were emerging around that time.

I came in through a collaboration with my friend Little Louie Vega. Hector Lavoe was Little Louie's uncle. Louie helped me break into the music industry because he knew that I could sing. Everyone knew I could sing. A lot of my friends would ask me to sing for them. We would be at my house or in the car on our way to the club and our favorite song would pop on the radio and they would say "India, sing this," and I would sing. Everybody would be surprised that I was singing to them and they liked it. I would get a lot of compliments, "You really have a pretty voice." It was encouraging to know that people were noticing. I started working with Little Louie Vega when he became a disc jockey. He had an opportunity to work with Jellybean Benítez, who was very popular at the time and who was Madonna's boyfriend when Madonna was becoming huge. It was a whole new time and hip-hop was becoming really big.

THE LATIN HIP-HOP ERA

Latin hip-hop is a mixture of rap, hip-hop, dance and disco. I think a lot of the sound had to do with the Latin Rascals. A lot of it was all studio work, drum machines, samples, and a vocalist, some background singers, some great edits and a great mix.

Little Louie wanted to make me the new addition to a group called TKA; it was Tony, Kayel, Aby, and Spider. They wanted a girl, so they held an audition at a club called the Devil's Nest in the Bronx that today is called Rumba. The day before the audition I went to the group's manager's house, Joey Gardener. I auditioned and he loved my voice.

The night of the audition they didn't listen to any of the singers because they had already chosen the girl. Andy Panda went up on stage and said "Ladies and gentlemen. We found the girl who is going to be the first female in TKA. That person is Linda." They said Linda because the guy said India was too "street." Well, whatever. People were still calling me India when they went to see me sing. It was a good opportunity for me to get in.

So I was in TKA doing dance routines and singing backgrounds, but I never took lead because they had their lead singers. A year later, with the help of Louie Vega I signed to Jellybean's label and went solo. There were some interesting artists signed to that label—Jocelyn Brown and Anthony Malloy. So it was a good time. I went in there like a diamond in the rough—I was raw, I needed a lot of experience. I became a local sensation because I had a good show. I had my sister with me, a keyboard player who was real pretty, another female that was playing the guitar and dancers. My dancers were voguing way before Madonna. Serious! And we had a fabulous time, but it wasn't what I wanted to do.

I was young and I felt that I could sing a little bit of rumba. I felt that I could do a little bit of salsa, I felt that I could do a little jazz, and I wished that I could do everything. And so Latin hip-hop was a great opportunity for me to create a base and allow people to hear me and hear of me.

I wanted to sing Latin. My first attempt to do Latin was not so good even though it was a club hit—*Dancing on the Fire*, a Spanish version called *Bailando en el Fuego* and I felt it was horrible because instead of saying amor with an "r" I wrote it

> *I wanted to sing Latin. My first attempt to do Latin was not so good. I did Dancing on the Fire, a Spanish version called* Bailando en el Fuego *and I felt it was horrible because instead of saying amor with an "r" I wrote it with an "l", because I was so inexperienced.*

with an "l" because I was so inexperienced. But it made a lot of noise, and in Puerto Rico we went to do the Latin hip-hop concert at Roberto Clemente Stadium. It was sold out and the young Puerto Rican generation wanted to see, "Who's this India girl?" I remember I got up looking like a hooker! With little high boots and a mini skirt. My dad asked, "What are you thinking?!" And I said, "It's me," all rebellious, "this is who I am." Today I look back at it, oh my God, I would never have come out of my house looking that way. But when you're a teenager you don't think that way. You think that being rebellious is cool. It was a great experience and I grew.

I met Marc Anthony when he was about sixteen and I was fourteen. I recall he used to sing with his sister—he was aspiring to be a singer and an actor. Louie Vega wanted to do a project with him and that's when I was called in to do songwriting and backgrounds.

The collaboration came out on Atlantic Records in the late 80s. So Marc and I go back a long time. We have always known and respected each other. I knew he was the guy who wasn't really that great looking, but had a golden voice, so I knew that something great was going to come. It was a time when Latin hip-hop was dying out, the sound was overrated, there were a lot of singers that weren't that good and it lost its prestige. Not many Latin hip-hop hits play today.

ONE TAKE TITO

I was married to Louie Vega, an extremely innovative DJ. He used to travel a lot, so he knew what was happening in Europe, and it was a great time for us to get into more underground and tribal dance songs. That was when we did *Love and Happiness* with Tito Puente. Tito came in and he was very innovative. This man did not ask any questions, didn't care if it was musically rough. What he cared about was that we were young people trying to make some noise and that even if it wasn't musically correct, it had something interesting, which is called *la calle*, the street. He said, "They call me one-take Tito," and he did one take of timbales, mixing Afro-Cuban and African-American meets Latino, and it worked. Then we added some chants from the Afro-Cuban Santería where they're singing to the saints and I took certain phrases that are very hard to sing and I just held my note. I improvised my feelings on the *Yemaya* and *Santa* and the *Caridad del Cobre* and it became a number one Billboard Dance hit. And it made Tito Puente feel proud because he was part of the collaboration, working with two young Latino kids that he felt were promoting a new generation of Latin music. He loved seeing us growing little by little.

Dave Maldonado was representing Marc Anthony at the time and was working very close with us. He and concert promoter Ralph Mercado were forming this record company called RMM Discos, and then it really took off. Ralphy had become famous booking artists throughout the years, José Alberto "El Canario," Tito Puente, Celia, Oscar D'Leon, Marc, Ray Sepulveda, Guayacán, a lot of people.

LLEGO LA INDIA

Ralphy had Thursday Nights at the Palladium in which a dance track artist would open up the show for the salsa band that came after. And he was hearing a lot about the good time people have at my concerts, so he hired me. I know how to make people scream. I always have a good relationship with the crowd—if I ask them to scream, they scream. That's just a street way of communicating with your friends and having a good time.

Then they were looking for someone for RMM Records. They were working with Orquesta de la Luz, and Nora, who at the time was called the Salsa Princess. A Japanese band was a great novelty, but people were complaining that she wasn't Latin and they felt that that gap was still open, and that's when I came into the picture. That's when I collaborated with Eddie Palmieri and we did the salsa album *Llegó La India*.

My background is in salsa. My mother was a huge salsera, she grew up on Fania. We knew everyone—Celia, Tito, El Gran Combo, Oscar D'León…. We knew Hector Lavoe because he was family through Louie Vega, so we followed up on all his success. And don't forget, the Bronx is the salsa county. At Christmas parties I would tell my mother, "Mom, we've heard twenty salsa records. Could you please let us play some English dance music? Let us play rap music," and she'd say, "Ok, one rap music and then ten salsas." So we were salseros, what they refer to in Puerto Rico as *cocolos*.

WORKING WITH EDDIE

I hooked up with Eddie Palmieri through Little Louie Vega's experimental project, and we clicked from the very beginning. Eddie smoked cigars and I smoked cigars at the time. It was fabulous. He was listening to all my background arrangements. He loved the fact that I was a Latina and was able to collaborate so well with African-American gospel singers, and he said, "You're soulful! Let's do a project together, but let's do it in Spanish. Have you ever worked on a Latin project?" "No," I said, "I love Latin music, but I think I feel more downbeat than upbeat, clave.

English music, R&B, funk music, soul music is on the downbeat. And Latin music is totally the opposite, it's upbeat, and it has clave. So I told him it's going to take a little time for me to make that transition, but I would be interested in working with him. So, we wrote the songs and recorded. I also had a very good friend by the name of Tom Domastro, who is my business manager and is married to Louie Vega's sister. He was able to work with us and we did *Llegó La India Via Eddie Palmieri*. And it was my very first collaboration, which got good and bad reviews, but at the end of the day, years later, I'm still singing the same old songs, and people like them.

The good thing that they said was, "Wow, a powerful new singer, with Palmieri." They were used to his singer Lalo Rodríguez and Eddie had all these affiliated singers that later on joined his Grammy-winning projects. But it was the first time that he was working with a Latina singer. The album that he was supposed to do with Celia didn't happen. And so he was blown away by my range, and he knew that I could hit these high notes. Eddie said, "I want to go crazy with this girl, I want to make her hit notes that nobody hit before in salsa." And I come out of nowhere and I'm singing really high, piercing, powerful notes. Trumpet notes; people were like, "Who is this girl?"

Other people criticized me saying that they felt that I screamed too much and that I was not suited for *la música*," that I wasn't going anywhere. All kinds of criticism—the songs were too high for me, they felt that I was screeching. But it's like I said, I'm still singing the songs and I'm still singing them in the same key. So maybe I was young—and let's face it, I wasn't an ugly looking girl. Also, a lot of people

were shocked to learn that "La India, the hip-hop singer, is India!" I was excited.

I also did something courageous and different. I was the first one to cross over from English into Spanish. Gloria Estefan did Spanish into English, but it just hadn't been done. And when I took that step everyone else followed, Marc Anthony, Chrissy I-eece—unfortunately she wasn't successful. Then came the Brenda K Stars and George Lamonts and everyone else, because in this business it's monkey see monkey do. But if one person doesn't take that initial step, no one dares to do it. But I don't think that way. I believe that if it's in my heart and soul and it is something that I am going to do to the best of my ability, I will do it. I felt that salsa is something that's in my blood. I love salsa, tropical music, and I just had to make downbeat meet upbeat in my mind and make it work. And that's what my style is today, downbeat meets upbeat in an unpredictable way because the rhythm in which I decide to sing is in clave. But the way I come in is different than the other soneros. And they have not been able to map just what is it that I do. I think it's just growing up in New York, studying dance music, jazz, rap, rock 'n roll, blues, country. America has some amazing musical journeys and I was lucky.

My experience with Eddie was incredible because he is a very eccentric, dark, yet witty scientist who pushes the boundaries and the buttons and irks every nerve he can of everyone if he has to, just to get it right. Even when it's right, he still thinks you can do it better. And so I learned a lot from him. He was very demanding with his own piano performance.

> *My experience with Eddie Palmieri was incredible because he is a very eccentric, dark, yet witty scientist who pushes the boundaries and the buttons and irks every nerve he can of everyone if he has to, just to get it right. Even when it's right, he still thinks you can do it better.*

He helped because he was critical with me. He was never the type to kiss my ass, he was the type to say, "Hey do it again." And he goes, "Listen to the clave." He would sing the clave in my chest, and in my shoulder. He would do the clave with his hands and make me do it with my hands too. At first, I would mess up, having the insecurity of downbeat in English music. But as I went along, I started letting myself go and I discovered that I had ideas locked up inside. Palmieri helped me unlock those ideas by being critical and by hammering me. He helped me get rid of the fears so I am very grateful to him. He was there to bring out the best in me.

AFTER THE FIRST LATIN ALBUM

I went back and sang more English songs, and I had a second number one, *I Can't Get No Sleep*. And we had fun, we traveled Europe. Louie would be DJing at three o'clock in the morning and I would be his act. It was a great era. Then the *Perfect Combination* album came along and RMM wanted to do duets between different artists. They placed me with Marc Anthony because he was also from the new generation. I opened up with *Llegó La India*. And it was wonderful putting his voice and my voice together. He's a great singer, and I was able to be a good listener, to blend with his voice and to deliver a hit. *Vivir Lo Nuestro* was the song that shocked everybody because nobody really believed in that song. Only the producer, Sergio George said, "This is going to be the song that's gonna sell the album." And it did; the song made me a superstar.

People that had criticized me suddenly loved me, Marc Anthony became a household name. Marc then came out with an album which is called *La Otra Nota*, which made everyone aware that a new generation of talent was crossing into this music. That huge hit opened up a lot of doors. We went in with Sergio George and did a whole new different sound, mixing hip-hop, salsa, R&B, gospel, jazz, everything. And we came out with *Dicen Que Soy*, the biggest selling album in my tropical music career. There were eight songs on that album and the bonus track was *Vivir Lo Nuestro*. Every song on that album was a hit. It went Quadruple platinum! And it was collecting gold and platinum albums everywhere—Colombia, Puerto Rico, Santo Domingo, Venezuela, Peru, Spain, Mexico. This album was huge.

No one else can be Celia Cruz. I had to make my own path; when I came in with this sentimental, high pitched, powerful voice, singing about women's issues, I became an advocate, a voice for women. And that's who I am today. Today I'm known not as a sex symbol. I'm known as a powerful singer with a lot to say, a message and a voice that touches a generation of people that are intrigued by the music. And I think that's why I'm still around.

If you put on the radio you are going to listen to all the legends; Celia, Tito, but now India's a part of that history. I think a lot of it has to do with my willingness to collaborate with these legends in a loving, non-threatening way. They did not see me as a rival, but as a friend, a student with open ears and an open mind.

The word sonera is someone that can carry a band and has something to say. What is the difference between a sonera and an improviser? A sonera can sing her *son* with flavor. And an improviser is someone that every other line has to rhyme and makes things up on the spot. So, I consider myself a little bit of both.

COLLABORATING WITH TITO PUENTE AND THE COUNT BASIE ORCHESTRA

Tito Puente and India, it's called *Jazzin'*, with the Count Basie Orchestra as the special guest. We had the amazing arrangements of Hilton Ruiz, an incredible latino jazz pianist who was very close to Tito Puente. Tito loved him a lot and worked really hard at making sure that these arrangements hit home. We wanted an album that was really hard and in your face. My vocals were very Arturo Sandoval (trumpeter). He plays in a very high pitched tone and he blows everybody away. We wanted to do the same for me as a singer.

On this album we had flutist Dave Valentín, and saxophonist Mario Rivera. Tito was in tip-top shape. He sat next to the piano and wrote a lot of the arrangements for the huge Orchestra and mixed Latino, African-American, and Afro-Caribbean all together reflecting how New York interprets this music. *What a Difference a Day Makes* was done very fast. It reminds me of Ricky Ricardo in a way, but then it's Tito Puente all the way because there are a lot of fast phrases in Spanish, "*Cuando esté a tu lado, y esté solo contigo. Las cosas que te digo, no repitas jamas...*" And everything's so quick, you don't have time to breathe. You had to be aggressive.

A lot of these tunes were done in high keys. What I did with *Wave* was give a very high piercing horn sound to the vocals, but at the same time I wanted it to be very jazzy, Broadway, Latin and dramatic. I would say that it describes who we are—Tito Puente and La India—everybody knows that it's two New Yorkers coming together and delivering the goods. And yes a lot of people were overwhelmed, but there were a lot of people that loved it too. We had a great time. It went gold, we won Best Latin Jazz project by a Duo for Billboard. We were excited. Tito grabbed the award and never gave it to me! He said, "Give me that. This is mine!" I don't know what happened to the award, but I'm glad that it made him happy.

I've recorded over ten albums. In 2002 the album *Latin Songbird: Mi Alma Y Corazón* went gold, and crossed over to tropical and Latin pop too, which is amazing, so we were hitting the national charts and tropical charts at the same time. As of 2004, I will be a free agent, and I will continue to put out my music.

Pop music has a lot of great artists. I'm sure they wouldn't mind hearing me, but the Latinos are so protective with their artists, I wouldn't want to ever abandon them. It's a big commitment, and I feel like I just have to keep coming out with great music and they'll be there with me.

REFLECTING ON THOSE WE HAVE LOST

Celia and Tito have been my only influences. In 2000, we lost Tito Puente, who is primarily the one who kept it going, maintaining visibility by taking our music worldwide and saying, "Hey, this is Latin music and this is what it's all about." We had Celia, so we were holding on to her and we were having a great time because she was taking us on a lot of fun musical journeys, teaching us that age is just a number, and that people are going to love your music no matter how old you are. And she fed us that incredible youthful energy. She's no longer with us, so right now we're going through a rough time. With Celia and Tito it was like I was part of them. I could walk by and be in Hollywood and walk by their stars on the Walk of Fame and say, "There goes my hero!" "There goes Tito Puente, man. That's my dog! Ha!"

There are very few artists doing what Celia did and doing it tastefully. It didn't matter that she was a woman. She represented men, women, children of all ages.

So right now it's interesting to see what's going to happen with the music. Are we going to have new artists come in with authentic talent? Ralphy had the best company in the industry. When RMM went down, Sony tried to hold on to it, but it's not like the way it was in the past. And I think it's gonna take some time. I know I'll be doing something, and I do hope and pray that tropical music is safe and that we continue to push for and strive for excellence.

I'm glad to be a part of the whole New York tropical salsa scene. And I'm very proud to have had that opportunity and been at the right place at the right time, and collaborate with these incredible legends of our music.

> *Singing salsa to me is spiritual, it's powerful. You feel the rhythm, you just orbit into another space, the whole rhythm section goes into my heart and soul and to my feet, and it travels my whole body.*

Latin music is my spirituality, my fountain, my stability. Dance music is my hobby. Singing salsa to me is spiritual, it's powerful. You feel the rhythm, you just orbit into another space, the whole rhythm section goes into my heart and soul and to my feet, and it travels my whole body. And the people give you love. Latin people are so responsive to the music. Dance music is sort of like, "If I'm not singing at a gay club, I'm not happy." The gay community supports my dance music, and they're the best screamers of all. They appreciate a great show. I can move that crowd, I can get close to my gay friends through my dance music. They're the ones that make me go number one on the Billboard dance charts!

Latin music is incomparable. Nothing comes close to it. Latin music is challenging. I've got to be in top shape and I have to work around that clave. Make sure that I dominate clave, clave doesn't dominate me. It's like riding a horse! You better ride on or you'll fall off! Nothing beats the excitement or the challenge that Latin music provides for me. ∎

Chucho Vald

Although people used to say I played well, I felt dissatisfied with my piano technique. When I was seventeen, I started studying a new technique with Rosario Franco, a student of Claudio Arrau who studied at Julliard. Then, I became the pianist at the Martí Theater under the direction of Emilio Peñalver. Soon after, I started at the Hotel Havana Riviera. From the Riviera, I went to the Teatro Musical de La Habana.

In 1963, I started the group Chucho Valdés Y Su Combo.

és

CHUCHO VALDÉS

BORN 1941,
CHUCHO VALDÉS
IS ONE OF CUBA'S
PRODIGIOUS
MUSICAL
GENIUSES.
ARRANGER,
COMPOSER, PIANIST
AND BANDLEADER.
IN 1973, HE
FORMED IRAKERE,
THE LEGENDARY
GROUP THAT
TRANSFORMED
POPULAR CUBAN
MUSIC.

CHAPTER 16

Chucho Valdés 173

A MUSICAL LEGACY

My name is Dionisio Jesús Valdés Rodríguez. They've called me Chucho since I was a boy. I'm the son of Ramón Emilio Valdés Amaro, better known as Bebo Valdés, and Pilar Rodríguez. I was born in Quivicán, south of Havana on October 9, 1941, the same day as my dad, who was born in 1918.

My dad is a pianist and my mother is too, but she was a singer more than a pianist. I was always surrounded by pianos. According to Bebo, I played at the age of three without taking one lesson. One day, I sat at the piano and started playing melodies with one finger. Bebo was shocked. At four, I was playing things I heard on the radio. When I was five, I started taking lessons from a composer who wrote many tunes for Celia Cruz and La Sonora Matancera, like *Tongo Le Dio a Borondongo (Burundanga)*. He taught theory, solfege and piano.

I started at the music conservatory when I was eight and I finished my training in piano, solfeggio, theory, harmony, counterpoint, fugue and some orchestration at the age of fifteen. When I was sixteen, my father started a band called Sabor de Cuba because he wanted me to learn how to orchestrate and to work as a bandleader, and he thought that someday he would leave me that band. The singers in that band were Rolando La Serie, Fernando Alvarez and Pio Leiva. On trumpet we had El Negro Vivar, Chocolate Armenteros, Platanito and Corbacho. The saxophone section had the Peñalver brothers, Emilio, Osvaldo and Santiago. On percussion we had Oscar Valdés Sr., Roberto García, Bor, el Negro Vivar's brother, on bass, Blasito Egües on Cuban timbale, and Emilio Del Monte on güiro. I started my first jazz trio with Carlos Emilio, who is still with me and the bassist Luis Pellejo Rodríguez from that band.

Although people used to say I played well, I felt dissatisfied with my piano technique. When I was seventeen, I started studying a new technique with Rosario Franco, a student of Claudio Arrau who studied at Julliard. Then, I became the pianist at the Martí Theater under the direction of Emilio Peñalver. Soon after, I started at the Hotel Havana Riviera. From the Riviera, I went to the Teatro Musical de La Havana. In 1963, I started the group Chucho Valdés Y Su Combo.

In 1964, we recorded our first album with a vocalist called Amado Borcelá, who was known as Guapachá. That group stayed together until 1966, when Guapachá passed away. Aside from the group with Guapachá, I also had trios and quartets.

But I was still dissatisfied with the technique I had studied. I lacked certain knowledge, so for the third time, I started to study piano with José María Romero from ground zero.

Each technique had its advantages. The first technique was very good for the fingers. The second technique concentrated on sound, a strengthening of the wrist. Arrau's technique of gravity emphasized the fall of the shoulders, the body over the keyboard, which made me stronger and more relaxed, but it didn't give me the speed. I needed to be able to do anything that popped into my head. Lastly I studied with Zenaida Romeu, the teacher that hit the nail on the head with regards to my needs, because she played popular music as well as classical. She is Antonio María Romeu's niece. Romeu performed the first piano solo in *Tres Lindas Cubanas*.

Till that moment, my teachers had been strictly classically trained. They didn't understand how I wanted to apply the classical techniques to popular music. But Zenaida taught me how to apply the classical techniques to popular Cuban music,

Flautist Mauricio Smith, Chucho Valdés, Johnny Pacheco, Carlos "Patato" Valdés and pianist arranger Oscar Hernández

without losing the flavor and without sounding foreign. That was the most interesting point in my life and I believe I was her best student. I worked with her for a long time. She instilled in me the self-confidence I lacked and she taught me what I needed to learn. After Zenaida Romeu, I realized I had attained a good part of what I wanted.

After studying with Zenaida, everything started to sound better on the keyboard. And it occurred to me that I should distill the best of all those techniques. Since I started out playing by ear, I incorporated the useful things from my natural technique as well. I always preferred popular music, in particular the music that allowed me to create and improvise, to put part of myself into it. I also liked classical music, but it was not my favorite fare.

This all happened in the forties, when the Feeling Movement was born in Cuba. Elena Burke, Omara Portuondo, Portillo de la Luz, José Antonio Méndez, all of them used to go to my home to sing to my dad the new tunes they composed. I had contact with a wealth of musicians.

My father was one of the most important arrangers of the Feeling Era. At the same time, he worked in the orchestra at the Tropicana Cabaret, a favorite with American jazz musicians. Those that visited included Woody Herman, Buddy Rich, Dizzy Gillespie, Lionel Hampton, Milt Jackson, and as a consequence, there was a tremendous jazz influence among the best Cuban musicians like Peruchín, Lecuona and Lily Martínez. I used to hear them play in my home or I would go to the dances where they were playing.

When Guapachá passed away, my combo continued but we switched to instrumental music. The last instrumental recording I made of that group was in January 1967. In February, things got under way to organize an all-star group. They hired the best musician for each instrument, and I was chosen for the piano. That was the end of the Chucho Valdés combos. I started working with the Modern Music Orchestra.

By coincidence, they also contacted Paquito D'Rivera, because Paquito was in Guapachá's combo. They called Carlos Emilio (Morales, guitar), Carlos Del Puerto (bass), Enrique Pla (drums); and suddenly we realized that Chucho's whole group was in that orchestra. So we decided to continue our work on the side. I was 25, Paquito was 17, Carlos Emilio was 27.

We were the newest generation. We pursued our work from a more creative perspective. Don't take me wrong, other musicians also improvised. They were outstanding, but their work consisted mostly in accompanying singers at song festivals. Most of the time, our group was playing music I composed. So we decided to invest more of our energies in the group and take it on as a professional pursuit. Then we added Jorge Barona (trumpet), Arturo Sandoval (trumpet) and Carlos Averoff (saxophone). That is how the idea for Irakere was born. Irakere comes from the Nigerian word that means forest, pony tail, cannonball.

BREAKING THE MOLD IN DANCE MUSIC

At that moment the danceable music scene was practically at a standstill. Neither folkloric nor African instruments were being used in popular dance music nor in concert music. We started acquiring the instruments and learning the languages of the Yoruba religion so as to incorporate them into the danceable and concert music. We recorded two landmark tunes, one a danceable tune called *Bacalao Con Pan*, which was a resounding hit.

In *Bacalao Con Pan* we broke with the traditional mold of dance music. The tune was slated as an instrumental and the voice part grew out of the instrumental. The orchestra began a phrase and the voice finished the phrase, which was split into two parts. We also introduced the pentatonic scale, which had not been used in dance music. And we incorporated electronic elements such as the pedals with the bass guitar, the electric guitar, the organ with wa-wa. Little by little we created a contemporary sound. We added the *bata* drums and the *shekeres* which were not used in dance music, and we came up with a combination we called *batumbatá*, a combination of five congas played with a heavy wooden stick (masa) and two cowbells circling the congas. It was a rhythmic combination between the drum and the percussion. The conga and the drum had their combination with the bass and the piano. That was *Bacalao*. It was a resounding hit and it marked a break with the past. The orchestrations, the work on the brass section that I did also broke the inertia. That was in 1973.

Irakere is music. We don't classify it as dance music nor concert music nor recital music. We do it all. When we do dance music, it is danceable. We have a Latin jazz repertoire, an Afro-Cuban jazz repertoire and an Irakere repertoire for symphonic orchestra. That's what kept the boredom away. You see, the musicians were too good. I couldn't have the musicians only playing dance music because their abilities went beyond that. By playing concert music, they could develop and I could write things that broke with the limiting concept of the dancer.

When you write for the dancer, you can't include deconstructed times, you can't do strange harmonies or endings, otherwise the people won't dance. In our concert music, we cut loose, we wrote longer blocks for the brass section, even though the brass sections in the dance music were pretty sizeable, like in *Xiomara Mayoral*, which has become a classic.

This is how I was able to do both things. I simply couldn't support a Latin Jazz group for a small audience without being popular with the many people that liked to dance. We won over the dance audience and pulled them into Latin jazz. So whenever we gave a concert, Irakere's dance music fans became fans of Latin jazz and Afro jazz.

On October 12, 1978, we gave a concert that was called *Leo Brower and Irakere*. At that concert, Leo Brower played classical guitar with us. We played *Concierto de Aranjuez, Los Preludios* by Villalobos, *Misa Negra*, Mozart's *Adagio*. That concert was filled with Irakere fans and people who loved classical music. The theater held 5000 people. We sold out all three days and many people couldn't get in. The dancers remarked that they'd never heard Irakere play that kind of music, but that they liked it. And the people that liked classical music said, "Irakere's popular music is very good, too." From then on, dance or concert, Irakere pulled all the audience in.

The most important event was our performance at the Newport Jazz Festival in Carnegie Hall. We won the Grammy with the album *Misa Negra*, partially recorded that night at Carnegie Hall and finished at the Montreux Jazz Festival in Switzerland. In 1979 we recorded the second album called *Irakere Dos*, which was also nominated for a Grammy, for Columbia Records.

We play popular dance music for enjoyment. It is always going to be tops on our list. The Cuban *son* is the only music you can perform in a stadium.

> *When you write for the dancer, you can't include deconstructed times, you can't do strange harmonies or endings, otherwise the people won't dance. In our concert music, we cut loose.*

Irakere was not the only group that developed it. Other groups like El Ritmo Oriental, Los Van Van, and La Original de Manzanillo also contributed.

The sixties was the decade with the greatest proliferation of rhythms in Cuba, a period of tremendous evolution. It all began with Juanito Márquez with his Pa'ca rhythm. The most popular rhythm was Pello El Afrokán's Mozambique, Pacho Alonso had el Pilón, Repeché rhythm. Each band had its own rhythm and its own identity. The seventies was a decade of perfecting danceable music. There was also lots of Nueva Trova, but we have an audience for every taste.

When we were starting out, we barely filled the Cultural House at a national jazz festival. Nowadays, we hold the jazz festival in ten different venues because the audience is so large. The jazz audience in Cuba is enormous now.

NEW YORK FROM A CUBAN'S PERSPECTIVE

We were always aware of what was happening in New York. I remember Eddie Palmieri, Ray Barretto, all of them. Many people in Cuba used to say that it sounded like the music that was being done in the fifties. The sixties was the rhythmic revolution, the drum revolution. In the sixties, we considered the bands that played in fifties style antiquated. In the seventies, it was even worse. They were considered even older.

Now, that doesn't mean that we considered the New York bands old-sounding. The New York bands contributed greatly to the harmonic aspect, to the structure, the arrangements, which are very good. I consider Palmieri a genius, Papo Lucca another genius. Rubén Blades is a good salsa singer, Oscar

D'León is very good and Celia... the queen. She is the Benny Moré of women. And who can call Celia antiquated? A phenomenon like Celia will not repeat itself this century nor the next. It doesn't mean we consider that music passé.

Rubén Blades's literary contributions... We recognized the value in that music. And we called it good music. But it was different from the music we were doing. Now, what must be said is that it is Cuban music. It is rooted in the Cuban *son*, and no one can deny it, because otherwise let's go to the discography. It developed in another direction, with a personal dedication, with creativity and with talent. Nobody can deny that. And a very good style developed which in turn helped Cuban music grow. In addition, our music was kept alive by these interpreters.

Just as everybody receives influences, Cuban music has received influences from everyone. Otherwise, fusion wouldn't exist. Dominican Republic, Puerto Rico and Cuba are three islands with the same roots. Therefore, that music must be related. Nobody has taken it from anybody else. Each one works with his roots and produces music. I believe that salsa and the Cuban *son* are Caribbean genres that belong to the Dominicans, the Puerto Ricans as well as the Cubans. I believe we are part of a formation that comes from the Spaniards and the Africans, and some Indian. That is the source of a music that represents us. We cannot divide it into two or three parts.

Modestly speaking, Irakere never did things in order to come up with something new. Things just happened. Irakere doesn't resemble any previous orchestra because it created music with a signature, with an arranging style, a thematic style and a perspective that hadn't been used before, and yet it was Cuban music. Our contribution consisted in taking the African roots and developing them more, in taking jazz elements, and I consider myself an heir to the jazz legacy, although I don't live in the United States. Jazz music has its roots in Africa and my music has its roots in Africa. What I won't do is take elements of music and rhythms that have nothing to do, that don't interplay with what I do. We have taken from jazz, classical, the Caribbean, reggae, and rock and we have come up with something that is not a hybrid. I believe our true contribution was our originality. ■

Israel Cach Lo

PEOPLE USED TO DANCE JAZZ EVERYWHERE IN CUBA, BUT IT WAS ON THE DECLINE. THEN CUBAN BANDS FORMED AND STARTED TO PLAY CUBAN MUSIC, THE DANZÓN AND THE MAMBO, AND TO SING. THEY DIDN'T HAVE ANY OTHER CHOICE BECAUSE THE PEOPLE DIDN'T ACCEPT JAZZ ANYMORE. OCCASIONALLY THEY'D PLAY A JAZZ TUNE, BUT THEY HAD TO CUT IT SHORT BECAUSE THE PEOPLE DIDN'T WANT TO DANCE THAT. THE PEOPLE WANTED TO DANCE THE DANZÓN MAMBO.

Israel "Cachao" **López**

ao
pez

ISRAEL "CACHAO"
LOPEZ

BORN IN HAVANA,
CUBA IN 1918.
COMPOSER,
ARRANGER,
BANDLEADER,
BASSIST. CACHAO
AND HIS BROTHER
ORESTES ARE
CREDITED WITH
WRITING THE FIRST
MAMBO IN 1939.

CHAPTER 17

CONTRIBUTION TO THE MUSIC

Cachao is my family name. My great-grandfather was from Andalusia, my grandfather from Cuba. Everybody calls me Cachao, it's a nickname. I am better known as Cachao than Israel López.

From an early age I made a lot of sacrifices for the music simply to preserve our roots. In Antonio Arcaño's Orchestra, my brother Orestes and I wrote 3,000 danzones. Arcaño's entire book and another one that has never been heard remained in Cuba. We did it to create the orchestra, but since my brother and I went in another direction, we didn't continue. All that music is lost. There is still music of mine in Cuba and some that made it to different countries.

One day Arcaño said, "Cachao, they stole the charts." Whoever took them didn't understand what he had taken. "We have to redo them," I said. Then at a wicked pace of 28 danzones a week, we were able to reconstruct the book between the two of us. My brother Orestes and I both did 14 a week. Hurrying to finish the book, I'd work through the night 'till daylight. I'd be wandering through the streets writing, writing, and writing till one day, I sat down somewhere and I didn't get up again. They took me to the hospital. My health failed because I didn't sleep.

I was a popular musician before I ever became a symphonic one. I started playing the bongos, then the tres guitar, the trumpet, the bass and the piano, but I stuck with the bass. It was my instrument. In 1930 or 1931, I joined the Philharmonic Orchestra and I was playing both kinds of music. I played concerts and afterwards I'd go play popular music at a dance. I was good in both genres. I'd leave the concert wearing a swallow-tailed coat to head towards a dance. I had to change from the tails and put on my band clothes. I played everything; jazz, tango, a variety.

The popular musician is born into his music. He is not made because he is not obligated to study music. But he is obligated by nature to express himself in a *típico* style, with feeling and gusto. He reads music. Many musicians read and still have gusto. But the classical musician, the symphonic one, isn't made in the street. He is made by the music. He studies, he plays and reads. He plays the music of Beethoven or others, but he doesn't create. In popular music, we can do creations, as I have done.

When Miguel Faílde invented the *danzón* in 1879, he debuted his music in a township called Simpson Heights in the Matanzas Province in Cuba. That New Year's Eve, he got everyone dancing, the governor, the mayor and all the authorities. Right away, the white society embraced the danzón. That didn't happen with the *son*.

The *son* suffered a social decline in Cuba. The people who played the *son* were not socially accepted. The blacks accepted the *son*. Nobody wanted to own up to the *son*. "Is so-and-so a *sonero*?" Neither the middle class people, much less the people from the upper classes, wanted anything to do with the *son*. It was the music of the lower classes. In 1925 General Gerardo Machado Morales, the President of the Cuban Republic, contracted the Sexteto Habanero to play at the Presidential Palace

> *I was a popular musician before I ever became a symphonic one. I started playing the bongos, then the tres guitar, the trumpet, the bass and the piano, but I stuck with the bass. It was my instrument.*

Cachao rehearses with Nestor Torres on flute at Lincoln Center in New York City before a performance

Israel "Cachao" **López**

and he made them wear swallow-tailed coats. Since the President accepted the *son*, everyone embraced it from then on. Until then, no one had dared. Everyone feared being criticized. Machado had the guts to say, "Why not? It's music." From that day forward, the *son* took its place socially. Then everyone was set free.

A NEW RHYTHM

We are musicians from the period before the mambo, when we played the *típico* music of Cuba. We wrote danzones from that period, but in 1938 we decided to vary the format. We created what they referred to in Cuba as a new rhythm. We did the modern danzón, different from the old danzón, but still a danzón. It expressed innovation and was well received, but the reaction from the public came too late.

The people didn't understand that type of music because of its new rhythm. We didn't work for six months. The music was ahead of its time and people perceived it as strange until they listened and listened. Then they realized that this music could carry on the rhythm of the typicity of our music. Today music is played in the same exact way. It marks a time.

We included the mambo in the danzón. Then we did it all alone, and a típico orchestra as well as a jazz orchestra could play it. You can hear small variations in Pérez Prado's mambos, but essentially, the format is ours. The mambo of the típico orchestras was played with flute and violins and Pérez Prado's mambos were played with a jazz orchestra.

When Pérez Prado played the mambo in the 1950s, there was confusion. They called him the Mambo King, and we don't deny it, Pérez Prado was the Mambo King. Thanks to Pérez Prado, the mambo was heard all over the world. Just as Jazz King Paul Whiteman didn't invent jazz, Prado did not invent mambo. People used to dance jazz everywhere in Cuba, but it was on the decline. Then Cuban bands formed and started to play Cuban music, the danzón and the mambo, and to sing. They didn't have any other choice because the people rejected jazz. Occasionally they'd play a jazz tune, but they had to cut it short because people wanted to dance the danzón mambo.

The *danzón* is generally made up of three parts: The flute part is first replacing the clarinet of the past. The second part is romantic, and the third part is the swinging section for dancing. In that section, you danced with moderation. When we included the syncopation and the mambo in the last section, the people started to loosen up, to dance. It had an impact. At first they didn't want to dance, but then they realized, "You know, this is good stuff." Well, they loosened up and the problem was over.

A *descarga* is similar to a jam session. Those that don't know better think it is a jam session. It is not. We did not play jazz. It was done in *típico* style in Cuba and it had an amusing origin. I thought of it one afternoon and that evening I notified the musicians. They were all working in different nightclubs. When they finished at 4 o'clock in the morning, we went to the studio and recorded the *descargas*. From 4 AM till 10 in the morning we played 12 *descargas*. We were improvising, without papers, without writing anything, without knowing anything would happen. In Cuba, nothing happened with the *descargas*, but in the United States they had a tremendous impact. I decided to continue doing *descargas*.

THE CUBAN PATRIMONY

The bands in New York that play our music have innovated. Based on what we did, they made innovations that do not detract anything from the music itself. On the contrary, they enrich and strengthen it. A musician comes up with an idea, he executes it and another one follows him and creates something from that. But within the variation, it doesn't stop being Cuban music.

In my country where the African influence was very pronounced, I produced Afro-Cuban music, but we also did *tipico* Cuban music, which was not influenced by the music from Africa. People think all music born in Cuba is of African origin. In the beginning it was, they even sang in *Lucumí* language. But then the format changed. Then came the music of today, which has nothing African about it. My music and the one from that era was done *típico* style, without thinking of Africa.

My interest was always to do our *típico* things, purely Cuban things. For example, the mariachi is typically Mexican. The Puerto Ricans have the *bomba* and the *plena* which no one can play like they do. And they do not have African influence. But there is always something in the composer that, yes, the African in him comes out. Our first settlers after the Native American Indians were the Africans. That generation became ingrained in the brains of all Cubans. And that is the reason for the influence called *Africa Viva*, with African origins.

The *clave* is one of the bases of our music. It guides the rhythmic instruments, the singer and the dancer too. The dancer is very important. The *merengue* is an easy dance, anybody can dance it. You dance it as if it were a rapid foxtrot or *paso doble*. But the *danzón* is another matter, because you have to know how to turn to the left, to the right. That's why it didn't have such great impact.

WORKING WITH TITO RODRIGUEZ

Tito Rodríguez was a very disciplined individual. He liked everybody to be on time. The band-boy would set up everythingand when we sat down to play the charts were open and ready. There was no excuse because even the sets were organized and laid out. We didn't have to ask what number was next. But Tito had a bad temper because he was very jealous of his work and his band, in terms of discipline. He wasn't a bad person, but he was a stickler. And very romantic.

We went to play in Sacramento, California. The charts we took were sensational. Really good ballads. We got there, and the people only danced polka. We started off with a hot set and nobody even budged. "What's going on?" asked Tito. And the chief of police, a threatening woman with a gun asks, "Do you play the *Beer Barrel Polka*?" And so all night long, we played the *Beer Barrel Polka*. Tito didn't even sing, he sat down for the entire night.

I was playing for some senators and representatives at a political dance in Cuba. One representative was soused and started looking at me with one eye through his drunken stupor. He told me, "What is that, a large guitar?" I say, "No, no. A bass." He threatened, "I don't like it." He pulled out a pistol, BANG! And he shot my bass. The bullet entered and exited, making a small hole from side to side. It went through the bass in a vacuum, so it didn't crack. His secretary said,

> *People think music born in Cuba is of African origin. In the beginning it was, they even sang in lucumi language. But then the format changed. Then came the music of today, which has nothing African about it. My music and the one from that era was done typical style, without thinking of Africa.*

"Look what you did, doctor," He said, "Don't worry about it," and he handed me a thousand dollars, "So you can repair it." I repaired the bass for $40.00. Months went by. I went to another party with the same people and the same man was there. I stood in front of him, brandishing the bass before his eyes, tempting him. But he wasn't drunk and he'd left the pistol at home and home. ■

Israel "Cachao" **López**

Alexis

Loza
no

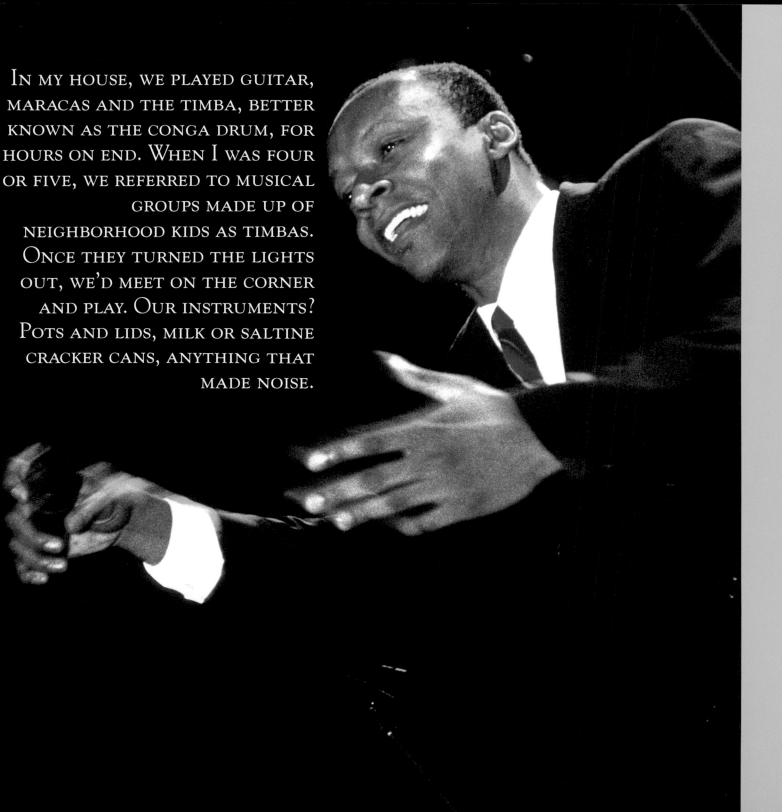

In my house, we played guitar, maracas and the timba, better known as the conga drum, for hours on end. When I was four or five, we referred to musical groups made up of neighborhood kids as timbas. Once they turned the lights out, we'd meet on the corner and play. Our instruments? Pots and lids, milk or saltine cracker cans, anything that made noise.

Alexis Lozano

Band director of Guayacan, arranger, producer, trombonist, guitarist, tres and güiro player.

Chapter 18

Alexis **Lozano** 189

ALEXIS JOVEN

I was born in Quibdó, Chocó on the Pacific coast of Colombia on July 10, 1958. Chocó's geographic location borders on Panamá. On its northern side, it has a piece of the Atlantic Ocean. In El Chocó, everybody sings, dances and writes poems—they are all artists by nature.

In El Chocó, you'd hear the music of Argentina, Mexico and Cuba. We used to listen to Matamoros, Sexteto La Playa, Habanero, Casino de la Playa, Chappottín, Arsenio, Cachao and Orquesta Aragón. I listened to Sonora Matancera, Mon Rivera, and the rhythms of *plenas, bombas* and *son*. The old-timers referred to it as Antillean music. I think the word Afro-Antillean is more precise. From Colombia, I heard the music of the northern coast, like Los Corraleros del Majagual, La Sonora del Caribe, Pedro Laza y sus Pelayeros, Alejandro Murán and the beats of vallenato music.

I founded Grupo Niche with Jairo Varela around 1979. Jairo was the composer, I was the director, arranger, musician and producer. Jairo said, "I have the name, Grupo Niche." Niche was an affectionate term for black.

The generation that started recording in the eighties listened to the music produced in New York by Fania and its maestros, such as Johnny Pacheco, Cheo Feliciano and Roberto Roena.

I am the youngest of seven brothers. In my house, we played guitar, maracas and the timba, better known as the conga drum, for hours on end. When I was four or five, we referred to musical groups made up of neighborhood kids as timbas. Once they turned the lights out, we'd meet on the corner and play. Our instruments? Pots and lids, milk or saltine cracker cans, anything that made noise. Then we'd sing from store to store, and the store-owners would give us confetti and small change to buy candies.

Father Isaac wanted to teach us to be musicians to serve the church. He taught us solfege, how to play wind instruments and notions of harmony. We also joined the band of San Francisco de Quibdó in our hometown. That band played both at religious occasions and rumbas. When Father Isaac heard us play secular music he'd get upset. Sometimes we'd get to church drunk because the night before we had played a rumba.

Then I moved to Bogotá where I joined the musicians of the Presidential Battalion. I also attended the conservatory at the National University in Bogotá for two years, but the conservatory didn't teach popular music so I left.

I founded Grupo Niche with Jairo Varela around 1979. Jairo was the composer; I was the director, arranger, musician, and producer. Jairo said, "I have the name, *Grupo Niche*." Niche was an affectionate term for black. I got myself a trombone and started teaching myself how to play. We recorded the first album that I arranged, directed, produced and played the trombone on.

Grupo Niche recorded four albums with me. But there were things I didn't like, conceptually, stylistically and in terms of human behavior, I dislike conflict. We finished the fourth LP at a recording studio in New York, so I told Jairo, "Mission accomplished. Give me my share and I'm off to Colombia. I'm starting my own band."

After leaving the group, Jairo called on me several times to fill in and to direct the group. I was always willing to cooperate, but once Guayacán got on its feet and started to make waves, it didn't sit well with him.

I told the owner of a bar that I was starting a band to play on weekends. He said, "I don't know what your band sounds like, but I believe in you." I went to Chocó and brought some kids to Bogotá to give them a musical foundation. After rehearsing for two months we played at La Tejada Corrida in Bogota from 1983 to 1985.

People remarked, "Alexis is crazy. He quit a band that was generating big bucks in order to work in a bar with some kids from Chocó."

GUAYACAN, A COMMERCIAL PRODUCT

We recorded a four-song demo and took it around to several record labels. My music was more aggressive sounding, not like the newer trend that was catching on. I knocked on practically every door of the record labels in Colombia and they said, "It sounds good, but it's not commercial."

In 1985 or 86, Julio Segundo Villa, A&R director for Sonolux, heard the demo and liked it. I told him, "Let's record without a contract. If my record sells, you pay me. If my record doesn't sell, you don't pay me." He got scared, because they don't like to work like that, but they opened their doors to me. The first LP, *Llegó La Hora De La Verdad*, sold 25,000 copies.

The second album included forceful, really nice tunes, but it was music for those in the know, for the cognoscenti of Antillean music. Your average Joe is not interested in the ideological or linguistic content of exquisite music or poetic language:

When in the nets of my hammock I surrender
The weariness of my daily toil
Soothed by the breeze from the sea
A black chant comes to me
It invades with profound emotion
My crimson lucumí blood
If far away Africa, cradle of my race
The gods of my elders Yemayé and Changó
That at the beat of the drums my blood rushes
It's 'cause my cradle was rocked to the beat of
a drum

Most musicians would love to play to the masses, to compose a catchy tune that everyone can sing, but writing commercial music is not easy. Nino Caicedo, our head composer, urged us to produce more elemental music without sacrificing the force or the flavorful rhythm and still retaining the fiery quality. Nino said, "Let's compose words for the heart and rhythm for the feet." That was the key. Guayacán started making its mark in 1989.

When we recorded *Oiga, Mire y Vea*, our sixth LP that includes *Invierno en Primavera*, Guayacán was a smash. In 1991, we won in the Cali Festival. In 1992, we re-recorded *Torero* and were awarded the Hit of the Cali Festival and a gold record for *Oiga Mire y Vea* and *Torero*.

In Colombia, Guayacán's music was known, but we didn't have the promotional infrastructure to help people associate the tune with our band. We made seven LPs before people started realizing all that music was Guayacán's.

I have made good use of my knowledge of Colombian folklore in order to provide Guayacán with an identity. Let it sound like salsa, yes, let's play in clave, yes, but with a more Colombian national identity. To fuse things with elements of the *cumbia*, of the *currulao* from the Pacific, with elements of the *vallenato* from the northern coast, with linguistic elements from the folklore of Colombia. That is one of the contributions Guayacán is making to today's music. When romantic salsa arrived with all its fury, Guayacán continued producing its strong rhythm, romantic lyrics, and its folkloric *típico* music.

They criticized us a lot and said Guayacán was nothing more than street musicians because our style of playing was very *típico*. Afterwards, reports started surfacing from Venezuela and Europe that Guayacán was doing folk salsa. They proclaimed, "Alexis Lozano, creator of folk salsa."

What is salsa, who plays that music? A mulatto born in Cuba. A mulatto is the child of a Caucasian and a black person. What did the whites contribute? The techniques, the instrumentation, the trumpets, the trombones, the pianos, the violins and the harmonization aspect. What did the blacks contribute? With their drums, they brought the essence, the rhythm, the fury, the spice.

Salsa is a mixture of everything. The *son* and the *guaguancó* are no longer being played in their primitive state. Nowadays, when a band is playing, it is no longer clear whether it is a *rumba*, a *guaguancó* or a *bomba*. All the elements are scrambled. Salsa means a mixture of all that is Latin and non-Latin.

When the *son* arrived with its clave rhythm to Puerto Rico, the Puerto Ricans played it with a Puerto Rican flavor, with native *bomba* and *plena* influences. When that *son* rhythm reached New York, the New York musicians, children of Latinos and Americans or Nuyoricans, gave this rhythm the jazz influence.

Guayacán is consciously giving a more Colombian identity to the one, two, three; one, two; giving the clave beat a *vallenato*, a *cumbia*, *currulao* identity, a touch of folklore from Chocó, from the Pacific.

In the production that includes *Torero*, we did a fusion with the *vallenato*. In the past, many orchestras played the *charanga* with an accordion. But it's one thing to have an accordion playing in a *charanga*. To preserve the pattern of the *vallenato* within a salsa rhythm and to integrate it is another. I am preserving a musical pattern and marrying it with another.

In Cali, Colombia, salsa penetrated through the lower class neighborhoods. Who lives in lower class neighborhoods? The blacks. This delicious music that can condemn you to hell has a unifying effect when white students and professionals start to realize how enjoyable it is and start partying with the blacks.

In places like Bogotá, it penetrated through the upper classes. Rubén Blades delves into the social themes by playing a content meant for intellectuals to the rhythm of salsa. When the intellectuals embrace it, they are dancing to the lyrics, not necessarily to the rhythm. They are interested in Rubén Blades's message. He touches upon interesting social concerns and he conquers an audience that was otherwise undecided: the intellectuals. He baits his audience and they eat it. They become salsa aficionados.

Similar to jazz, salsa is a cultural-historical movement. The Peruvians play salsa, the Venezuelans play salsa, the Panamanians play salsa, the Dominicans, the Cubans, the Puerto Ricans, the Colombians, the Mexicans....

Salsa is no longer the rhythm that was born in Cuba and stayed in the Antilles, Cuba, Puerto Rico and the Dominican Republic. I believe that this rhythm has been instrumental in communicating with the masses. First it united the Latinos, then the non-Latinos. That young mulatto is leaving his mark. ■

Papo Lucca

THE JAZZ INFLUENCE IS VERY EVIDENT IN OUR MUSIC. I WOULD SAY IT IS PRESENT IN ALMOST ALL THE BANDS THAT PLAY THESE RHYTHMS. YOU CAN SENSE IT IN THE BRASS PHRASING, IN THE SOLOS. THE ARRANGERS IN PARTICULAR HAVE THE DUTY TO DRESS UP THE NUMBERS MAKING IT INEVITABLE TO HEAR A PHRASE IN SALSA THAT YOU HAVEN'T NECESSARILY HEARD IN JAZZ, BUT SOUNDS LIKE IT ORIGINATED THERE DUE TO OUR INFLUENCES.

a

Papo Lucca

Born in Puerto Rico April 2, 1946. Bandleader of the Sonora Ponceña, pianist, arranger, composer, Fania All Star.

Chapter 19

Papo Lucca
195

A MUSICAL GALLERY

My father is the bandleader and business manager of La Sonora Ponceña. He founded the group in 1954 and he was originally the guitarist of the band. I was born in Ponce, Puerto Rico. My first steps in music were at rehearsals of La Sonora Ponceña when I was 5 years old. I played congas and would mess around during rehearsals. By age 7, I entered the Escuela Libre de Música in Ponce where I studied piano. I began playing piano with La Sonora Ponceña at 11.

My early influences were El Gran Combo's Rafael Ithier, Lilí Martinez from Cuba, Peruchín, and Rubén González, pianist of the Orquesta Jorrín. Then I started to listen to jazz. I heard Bud Powell, McCoy Tyner, Oscar Peterson, Bill Evans, and Chick Corea. Now I listen to some of the new generation from Cuba: Emiliano Salvador, Gonzalo Rubalcaba, Chucho Valdés and other orchestras. I have been influenced by all those people.

In the beginning, La Sonora was a band that covered tunes of the more popular bands from Cuba, Puerto Rico and the United States such as La Sonora Matancera and Cortijo. We copied a lot of things by Orlando Marín, a New York based band for many years, Mon Rivera, and Moncho Leña's Orchestra. We would take from their records. That is how I got started doing arrangements, by copying from recordings. That prepared me for my future work doing original arrangements, an opportunity which I got around 1968. I am eternally grateful to Mr. Tommy Olivencia for introducing me to the owners of Inca Records. At that moment, I started to write original music, and from then on, La Sonora Ponceña developed a more defined style and its own music.

La Sonora Ponceña always plays tunes that showcase the singer, then the orchestra, then the conguero, then a tune that showcases my piano playing. We do not limit ourselves to just showcasing the singer. Most of all, we have the dancer in mind, that is our main focus. One tune might require a certain structure and another can require a different format. When you are working with lyrics that talk of love, your response has to be pretty. You cannot answer back with violent phrasing because it will seem out of context.

I write some music, but La Sonora has never recorded anything of mine, well, maybe one or two. We generally use composers like Francisco Alvarado, Tite Curet Alonso, Roberto Anglero, Joe Torres and Adalberto Alvarez from Cuba. Tite Curet is one of the most prolific writers we have on the Island, the one who has written the most for everybody out there—Eddie Palmieri, La Lupe, Tito Puente... everybody.

FANIA—WHERE IT'S BEEN, WHERE IT'S GOING

This salsa phenomenon was created by Jerry Masucci. In fact, he was the one that started calling the Caribbean rhythms salsa. Originally, he did it to market the genre. Both Puerto Rico and New York made it happen, not just New York. Rafael Cortijo with his Combo was definitely the school.
I don't think any musician can deny that Cortijo influenced our Puerto Rican music in some way or another. This is music of and by poor people, the lower classes, with some middle class involvement. It is now reaching other people because of its widespread dissemination by way of radio and television. But there are places where salsa is still discriminated against. We have played for Presidents of countries. We play for the Governor of Puerto Rico

very often and he loves salsa. So I think salsa doesn't attract a particular social class. I believe salsa delivers and is accepted across the board.

I don't think Fania has declined. I think they have sat back to recover some of their investments in all the worldwide promotion they did for salsa. They are no longer investing in promotion. I have traveled throughout Europe with La Sonora Ponceña and I can always find my albums there. Oddly enough, there are bands that are signed with bigger, more powerful companies, and for some reason, their albums are not distributed there.

Initially, I was recording with Inca, a Miami based Cuban label. Then Fania bought that label. I don't know how, but they paid for La Sonora Ponceña's contract and Lito Peña's contract along with Willie Rosario's Orchestra and Tommy Olivencia. The four orchestras were signed on that label. We became part of Fania Records in 1972. Then in 1976 when Harlow had a problem with them and left the company, I started playing with Celia and Pacheco, then with the Fania All Stars. I lived in Puerto Rico, but I traveled to New York to record.

Masucci and Pacheco first called me in to play on Celia's album *Químbara*. When they had problems, I started arranging for the solo artists on the label, like Ismael Quintana, Cheo Feliciano and Pete "El Conde" Rodríguez. Then I started officially as the Fania All Stars pianist in 1976 and have remained to this day. We recently signed a three-and-a-half year contract. When the All Stars have something, we play together. There isn't too much opportunity because all the guys have their own orchestras and it's very difficult to schedule.

> *La Sonora Ponceña is on a subsidiary label of Fania. The instrumentation was originally one trumpet, three guitars, bongos and a singer. It was like a sextet. Then they added another trumpet and the congas. I joined the group when there were three trumpets.*

IS THERE A DIFFERENCE BETWEEN NEW YORK SALSA AND PUERTO RICAN SALSA?

There is a difference in the concepts, but basically the salsa is the same. There are good musicians in Puerto Rico and in New York. I think the difference is in the way they play things, the way they do the arrangements. But the audience doesn't perceive such a big difference.

It is something that we the musicians notice. But basically, there is no difference in the music, except in the names.

To me, salsa is a combination of the Caribbean rhythms: the bomba, plena, the guaguancó, and also the merengue. It has its clave, not the same one, but it has its clave.

The clave is made up of two measures that define the salsa rhythm, or let us say the Caribbean rhythms: guaguancó, guaracha, danzón, the plena, and the bomba. So the clave is incorporated into the Cuban rhythms.

This salsa phenomenon was created by Jerry Masucci. In fact, he was the one that started calling the Caribbean rhythms salsa. Originally, he did it so as to market the genre. Both Puerto Rico and New York made it happen, not just New York.

In salsa you either have the 3-2 or 2-3 clave. In the bomba it's different, but the bomba has nothing to do with the salsa clave because it has its own clave. These Caribbean rhythms were grouped under one name to make them more commercial. We included all of them in one genre, salsa, but they have their differences in the clave. The slaves who brought this rhythm to Cuba and Puerto Rico came from different regions of Africa, that is why there is a difference in the clave of the two rhythms.

What is being done lately is really a variation within the salsa theme. The subject matter in salsa used to be a simpler motive about the people, full of sayings, joyous. Then Rubén Blades brought in some more complicated subject matter. Later the musicians started using ballads, which they have turned into salsa. But I think it has all been good for the progress of our music.

THE RHYTHMS OF SALSA

The rhythmic base of salsa is practically the same as it was in its beginnings in Cuba. They have made some changes, but these changes have come about as a result of the influence of rock on Cuban music, in spite of the blockade. I visited Cuba in 1977 and there was a discothèque where they played nothing but Michael Jackson and James Brown. The Cuban musicians are studying the styles of Coltrane and other American musicians, and they play like them. The salsa which we know as salsa, the one we play sounds more like what people like Chappottín, Arsenio Rodríguez and Benny Moré played in the 1950s. Naturally, it has been improved with the ideas and influences acquired by musicians in New York.

I am always trying to explore, always striving for innovations, to sound different within that style without drifting to another style. I'll start an intro with the brass and piano, the bass, or answering a question with the bass and brass or percussion, or a chorus, instead of with the conga. In other words, always experimenting, but within a style.

The jazz influence is very evident in our music. I would say it is present in almost all the bands that play these rhythms. You can sense it in the brass phrasing, in the solos. The arrangers in particular have the duty to dress up the numbers making it inevitable to hear a phrase in salsa that you haven't necessarily heard in jazz, but sounds like it originated there due to our influences.

And the music has to be danceable. We musicians can play different kinds of rhythms,

Papo plays at Club Broadway, in NYC.

Papo **Lucca**

different kinds of timing, 3/4, 6/8, but you cannot give a dancer a 3/4 in the middle of a guaracha or a guaguancó, because what can he do? He is going to stop because he doesn't know how to dance the 3/4. That is music to listen to, not music to dance to. Danceable music has to be simple without being old fashioned, always maintaining a contemporary perspective without loosing the danceable element.

The guaguancó is a rhythm that can be played by an orchestra, but the original guaguancó only uses voices and rhythm, or drums, that's all. The guaracha was conceived with an orchestra in mind. And there is a big difference in the theme. The theme of the guaracha is more playful than the guaguancó. The guaguancó is sometimes more philosophical. I am referring to the guaguancó in Cuba, with the drumming that includes some social criticism, that touches upon the problems in the barrios. The son montuno has its little romantic things in the lyrics, but then it has the *guapeo*.

You have to be thinking of the specific genre. You can't hear much of a difference between the guaguancó and the guaracha if you are playing in a dance band. You will notice the difference in the guaguancó in tunes where the percussion is playing one way. Guaguancó, guaracha, son montuno, bolero, and danzón—nowadays people don't even know how to dance these rhythms. But when I was starting out with La Sonora Ponceña I played all

kinds of rhythms. I played danzas, merengues, bomba, plena, guaracha, guaguancó, and bolero. Now if after playing three salsas you then play a bolero, people boo you. Now you have to play what people like because they are the ones who are paying you to play so they can dance.

La Sonora Ponceña is on a subsidiary label of Fania. The instrumentation was originally one trumpet, three guitars, bongos and a singer. It was like a sextet. Then they added another trumpet and the congas. When I joined the group there were three trumpets. Then we had four trumpets and one singer. At the time, there was one singer and we were experimenting with new ideas, "Let's have two singers." Now we have four. Improvisation is when something is happening at the moment and your singer takes advantage of it. He is the sonero. We have two that are particularly good: Danny and Luisito. There are many soneros out there, but to me, mine are the best. The nucleus has been growing, always trying to improve the quality and the things we do. A small group can't do the same things that a group of 14 musicians can do.

We play certain music that is classified as romantic, but doesn't cross over into the erotic. We always maintain a more serious approach. We don't think you have to use certain phrases in order to sell. That is my conviction. ∎

Papo Lucca at Club Broadway, New York City circa 1994

Marc Anthony

I'VE BEEN SINGING SINCE I WAS THREE. I THINK I KNEW HOW TO SING BEFORE I KNEW HOW TO TALK, SO I FELT TOTALLY COMFORTABLE EXPRESSING MYSELF THAT WAY. I STARTED SINGING AT HOME WITH MY DAD. HE WOULD WRITE HIS OWN SONGS AND SING ALL NIGHT. I WOULD SING FIRST VOICE AND HE WOULD SING SECOND AND WE'D HAVE A LITTLE SHOW AT THE HOUSE ON WEEKENDS.

MARC ANTHONY

BORN IN NYC ON
SEPTEMBER 16,
1968. ONE OF
THE HOTTEST
STARS IN SALSA
AND POP. SINGER,
SONGWRITER,
AND ACTOR,
MARC STARTED
OUT IN FREESTYLE
MUSIC BEFORE
MIGRATING TO
SALSA AND
BRANCHING OUT
INTO MAINSTREAM
POP.

CHAPTER 20

Marc **Anthony** 203

BARRIO BOY

My name is Marco Antonio Muñiz and I was born in East Harlem, a.k.a. El Barrio, Spanish Harlem in Mt. Sinai Hospital on 99th and 5th Avenue. I was raised on 101st between 1st and 2nd Avenues. My dad was a hard working father. He worked in a factory, motels, hospitals, and in the kitchen. He was a manual laborer and a musician who had to settle for those jobs in order to provide for his family. There were eight of us to feed and he did a hell of a job supporting us. It's not 'till you get older that you realize what it takes to raise a family. My mom was a housewife. We didn't know we were poor. We thought everybody lived that way. My dad made us speak Spanish while he spoke English. That was the rule, and I'm glad we did. If I didn't speak Spanish, my life wouldn't be the way it is now.

It wasn't until I traveled for the first time that I realized that other people had more options than we did. But my dad surrounded us with music, culture and our language. We listened to all kinds of music, from *rancheras* to *boleros* of the 20s, 30s and 40s. My dad would sing them when his friends came over and it became a jam session every Saturday. Salsa would be blaring out of my two brothers' rooms; boleros out of my mom's radio and eight track.

Being in New York, whenever I would leave my house, I was listening to totally different music. There was disco, R&B, the Motown sound and Barry White. I was exposed to two totally different music worlds and they're both what I appreciate.

Growing up in that world, I thought everybody was Puerto Rican. My world was my block. Now looking back, I can appreciate the eclectic nature of how I was brought up musically. After I matured and moved out I could look back and romanticize how my musical influences came about.

I never studied music or voice. I tried it once, but they tried to change my style. The two times I went were for basic voice lessons. I remember one teacher used to train Bon Jovi and a couple of Opera singers. I didn't subscribe to that philosophy that you have to be the perfect technical singer in order to get your point across. I realized that emphasis on my technique was tapping into how I interpreted the song so I quit. I stuck with my gut that if you feel it, if that's what you put into it, then that's what you get out of it.

I've been singing since I was three. I think I knew how to sing before I knew how to talk, so I felt totally comfortable expressing myself that way. I started singing at home with my dad. He played boleros. He would write his own songs and sing all night. I would sing first voice and he would sing second and we'd have a little show at the house on weekends. Because I was surrounded by it, I was never intimidated by it.

WORKING IN THE STUDIO

I was part of an after-school program when I was 11 to 12 years old. The director, David Harris, used to be a singer in the 70s. He heard me and my sister singing the Mickey Mouse Club song in harmony. Apparently he really liked it. He was doing demos, and he introduced me to the studio for the first time. I started out doing background vocals and jingles making twenty bucks here and there. Dave Harris really invested in my sister and me and taught me a lot about the studio and techniques.

Back then, there was this movement we call freestyle music. A couple of clubs became really popular: the Devil's Nest and Heartthrob. I frequented these clubs. In freestyle, the name was the producer, not necessarily the artist. At that time, there were a lot of producers in the studio, because they were mini idol-makers. They'd walk up to you in a club and say "Do you sing? Well don't worry about it. I'm going to give you a record deal."

I had quite a bit of experience by the time I was 18, 19 in the recording studio. I acquired all that experience in the studio, in freestyle. What freestyle did was it freed me up to use my experience in a more commercial way. I've done over 300 records in 5 years in freestyle and house music.

I met Louie Vega in my teens in the club scene. He was the producer and I met the Latin Rascals and Carlos Rodgers, and it was studio heaven. It was 24 hours a day in the studio making the next hit, making the next hit, making the next hit. Louie found out that I was a vocalist and he tried me on a couple of records and used me for backgrounds. Then after becoming friends over the years, he got a deal with Atlantic records as a producer and he didn't have a singer. One day, he came to pick me up at my house and I remember he was really nervous, and he said, "Would you want to sing on my album as my vocalist?" "Oh absolutely, no question." And it changed my life forever.

Tito Puente and Eddie Palmieri played on *Ride on the Rhythm*, my first album with Little Louie. That's the first time I wet my feet. I knew Eddie Palmieri because he wanted to use me as a singer.

That *Ride On The Rhythm* album was a great experience all around. But that's when I first realized that I suffer from stage fright. Yeah, massive stage fright. I felt really uncomfortable. It was just me, Louie and two other people on stage. Back then, they played the track, but I would sing live. I always had a little quirk that I cannot for the life of me lip sync. Everything I've ever done is live. So I was deathly afraid. The album came out and we started getting work at clubs and I couldn't perform. I never felt comfortable performing during the Little Louie Vega days, and it has nothing to do with Little Louie or anybody else who was on stage. During the *Ride On The Rhythm* days, I didn't doubt my vocal ability, but I definitely doubted my being an entertainer. I remember my manager, Dave Maldonado at the time, telling me, "Marc, when you find your personality on stage, your life is going to change," because he knew me personally and I'm funny and so damn silly. I'm a clown, a prankster always doing something silly. But when I was on stage, he would worry about me because I was so serious and so miserable.

> Back then, there was this movement we call freestyle music. In freestyle, the name was the producer, not necessarily the artist. At that time, there were a lot of producers in the studio, because they were mini idol-makers.

THE SONG THAT CHANGED MY LIFE

Dave Maldonado truly believed in me in the beginning and made everything possible for me. He used to manage Willie Colón and Rubén Blades, who was my absolute all time idol. Dave took me under his wing for many years and taught me the ropes. He truly became my father. He was managing me since I was 15, 16. I've never given him this credit before because I never wanted to talk about him because of how our relationship ended. But now that I'm older, I can honestly say that he helped shape me as a man, as an artist, as a thinker. I saw a lot of things with him for the first time. I traveled for the first time, to do showcases. And then the freestyle thing happened and he was managing me through that. He's the one that suggested I do salsa.

I was stuck in horrible traffic with Little Louie's sister. We were right in front of Madison Square Garden and she said, "Listen to this song." She puts on *Hasta Que Te Conocí*, by Juan Gabriel and just like that, it changed my life. I jumped out of the car and I called David from a pay phone, "I'm so excited! Dave, I just heard the most amazing song of my life." And he says "Marc, Juan Gabriel already sang it." And I said, "I have to sing this song." And he said, "The only way is if you do it in salsa format." Up to that point, it had never crossed my mind to sing salsa. And I was like, "I'll sing salsa."

DMM was Dave Maldonado Management and RMM, Ralph Mercado Management. They weren't partners then, but they were close friends and allies. David called Ralph and sold him on it. Right after I heard the song, within two weeks, I was in the recording studio, signed as an artist, with Sergio George cutting my first record. Sergio George was the absolute hit-maker back then. I knew Sergio from the freestyle days, from the hip hop days. He was a guy from the projects just like me, who played the piano. He played with all the salsa bands and I would see him coming and going. So we had a great rapport. From the beginning, we were just two freestyle kids figuring it out. He'd play me songs and ask, "What do you think about this?"

FINDING MY SINGING STYLE

Ralph Mercado sent me about 200 CDs, the history of salsa from Benny Moré to everybody you can imagine. He sent me these CDs with a message to, "learn the music," and I refused. Not while I was recording the album. I said, "No, I'm gonna sing this my way and if it doesn't work, it doesn't work." I was afraid that if I heard hours and hours of salsa music, that at some point I'd start mimicking. I wanted it to be fresh. I just sang. I said, "Look, Sergio will do the tracks and I'll sing with my style of interpretation."

I had no idea how to make a salsa record, so the first one was extremely experimental. I found my style in the studio drawing from my deep R&B influences. We experimented a lot in the studio and we figured out my singing style and my style of salsa as well.

The first day I got to sing salsa live with my own band was at the Roxy. I had no time to be afraid. I flew in from Miami and got there 15 minutes before I went on stage. I didn't even have a shirt to wear. I borrowed somebody's vest with a red parrot on it. I went on stage and I spoke to my musical director, "What am I going to sing?" And he goes, "Just relax. We call it as it is." I was not nervous at all because I looked back and there were twelve guys. I knew they weren't going to let anything happen to me. It changed my life. I think that it was by far the best show I've ever done. I was so naïve. I felt like I was brand new out of the box. And from that day forward, I felt comfortable on stage. The Roxy show solidified my belief that I had something to offer as an entertainer. And I realized that's where I wanted to be, that's where I wanted to live: on stage.

In order for me to feel comfortable, I had to stand for something. The first thing I told my band was, "You do not have to wear a uniform." I don't know of one salsa band that never wore a uniform, before I came along. I didn't like it. It's just a part of my comfort. I didn't idolize anybody that wore a suit, the gold chains, the hairy chest, and the pinky ring. That was the stereotypical salsa look and I just couldn't relate. If I was going to bring anything to the table, the only thing I could do was be me. Early on, I remember we'd show up in jeans and t-shirts and baseball hats and they'd say, "Sorry there's a dress code." I'd say, "But I'm performing tonight." "I'm sorry, I don't know who you are, but you can't perform like that." I went home the first couple of times and then people started showing up to see me

and they said, "Don't stop him at the door anymore because the people get upset." And it stuck, and I felt even more comfortable on stage. Then it became the norm. Nobody wears uniforms anymore. But it wasn't easy. You'd hear all kinds of shit in the beginning. "Oh you'll never make it. You're going against the grain." I stuck with it and I think that's why we've been able to make all the changes we have in Latin music.

GETTING EDUCATED

The RMM artists that I was exposed to on a daily basis were Tito Nieves, Celia Cruz, and Tito Puente. The first time I traveled the world was with *La Combinación Perfecta* with RMM. We went to Colombia, Argentina and Panama touring with Celia, Tito Puente, Tito Nieves, Oscar d'León and José Alberto El Canario. That's when I became a student. I would open up the show, then I had two hours of sitting on the side and watching the masters. I was receptive to everything; anything and everything they would tell me was gold. I was the baby on the tour. I remember Celia keeping an eye out for me, saying that I was one of the good ones, and that the musicians better not ruin me. And she would always tell me not to hang out with the musicians and go straight to bed after the show, and she always kept me on the straight and narrow.

To be a sonero is an art form, but it's an art form that's unfortunately dying. It's almost like freestyle rapping. And not everybody can be a Jay-Z off the top of their head. It's like you have this innate talent to do it because you dominate the language, you dominate the music, you understand it, you understand the history of it, and that's not where I

I knew that I was a singer and not a sonero, nor would I want to be. I'm extremely comfortable with who I am and what I've offered Latin music.

came from. I grew up with salsa on the periphery of my life. So right off the bat, I knew that I was a singer and not a sonero, nor would I want to be. I'm extremely comfortable with who I am and what I've offered Latin music.

I spearheaded a lot of change in the salsa world. For instance, my sidemen. I was always close to the sidemen. I never saw them as just my musicians. I remember the norm was 90 bucks a gig; you get it however you want it. Back in those days, you could get it in cocaine if you're a cokehead, a bar tab, or cash under the table. I stepped into this world, "What the hell is this, man?" I sat down with my accountant and I said, "How can we clean this up?" and I came up with a plan. "Listen, you guys are gonna get paid once a week by check, and you're gonna pay taxes on it." It was the revolt of all revolts. They all quit on me, "No, this is a cash business!" until I told them, "But I'm gonna pay you three hundred dollars, not ninety." I was very keen on that. Even though they resisted in the beginning, it became the norm.

Today, my musicians, most of who are still with me minus two or three, have houses and several cars. They have credit. But the one thing I told them, "I'm going to pay you more than three times what you get paid a night, but when I start making money, I don't want to hear anything about a raise." So, I changed a lot that way.

I changed people's perception of salsa. Especially the younger generation. There was a time when my generation had nobody to look up to in Latin music. And it wasn't until the kids started thinking it was cool, and you could walk down the street and hear one of my albums blaring out of a car with three teenagers in it, that it took on a whole new life; the whole demographic changed. And I

Marc **Anthony**

think it's because I was just like them, that kid from East Harlem. I'm passionate about it, I just loved what I was doing and it translated. So, I've been a champion for Latin music for years. I'm not a big fan of salsa with a kick and a snare. I've always said, keep it in its purest form.

I think what has made it different is the sensitivity. That is my style. *The Bed* was a salsa track from Sergio George. I was in my early twenties then. It was almost like salsa seen through the eyes of a new generation. So, if you took a hip-hopper, or an R&B artist and gave him an R&B track, how would they sing it? That's how it ended up.

LATIN VS. POP

When I was going to sing in Spanish, I thought, "oh my God, what do I do?" Of course José Feliciano and *La Copa Rota* and Odilio González, Felipe Rodríguez, and everything I ever heard came into play because you tap into that. All I could do at that time was trust my taste in music and trust that I could do the job. But José Feliciano is one of my all time favorite vocalists. I grew up on him, and studied him even for my freestyle stuff. I was standing in the middle of this melting pot of music that I felt was normal, and now I thank God that I was exposed to so many influences. But, if you hear any bit of José Feliciano in my style, that's because he's just a part of my musical life.

Performing pop music and performing Latin music are two totally different energies. But there is no difference, as far as me interpreting. Both are just as fulfilling to me. I have one voice, my voice. I don't have two compartments in my heart. I sing the song because I feel it. Every song I ever sang has been fulfilling. But, I'll tell you one thing, man, performing Latin music is totally different. I hear those congas

and those timbales come in and *la campana* (the cowbell) and I can't breathe.

I've turned down covers on Time Magazine because it was going to be the stereotypical interview. They were going to sell the package like it was Latin music and they didn't want to hear what I had to say about Latin music, which is Afro-Cuban music, salsa, tropical music, as I know it. They wanted to sell *I Need To Know* as Latin music. It's not fucking Latin music, man. And I turned a lot of things down because of that, because I was not interested in misrepresenting my music, like "oh my God, now is the time, it's really cool to be in." Get out of my face. I've been Latin all my life, and I've been in it all along. I was always passionate about that. I almost felt like it was exhausting traveling the world setting that record straight.

Please stop selling, *If You Had My Love*, Jennifer López's R&B song, as Latin music. Europe was more open to hearing the history of Latin music and seeing the difference; that this was just a ploy by the record company to create record sales. But it was definitely not Latin music. It's just pop music. It doesn't deserve the title of Latin simply because I'm Latin. And I feel very strong about that. *You Sang To Me* is not Latin. *She's All I Ever Had*, by Ricky Martin is not Latin music. Oh, this Latin pop boom, Latin boom? And I'm like, "Latin boom?" "Oh, Latin music is being accepted…" No it's not. It was me and Enrique, Jennifer, and Ricky, singing pop music. Jennifer doing R&B, nothing Latin about it. Maybe one or two Latin influenced tracks, but it's not Latin pop. It's annoying because the only reason they put Latin in it is because we're Latinos.

I've produced my last four albums. It's 100 percent me. I choose every single song because I'm adamant about my taste in music, and it's my style. I mean if it's not broken don't fix it. And I created this filter in me for what I like and what's my style and what's not.

With RMM, the relationship ran its course and I felt like I outgrew them. I wanted bigger things, and I gave them every opportunity to be involved but they were not equipped to do an English album, to expand their horizons.

Tommy Mottola became a mentor for me, he took my case personally. And he's the CEO who has 40,000 employees taking an personal interest in me as a human being, as an artist. He said, "Marc, you're not a one hit wonder, you're a boxed set kind of artist. We'll have a relationship for many years. Not everything has to be a hit, but express yourself in the studio. Hand in albums that mean something to you, and you'll see twenty years from now, we'll be able to put a box set together."

That's his goal for me. He sees me like a young Frank Sinatra. He took me under his wing and taught me a lot. I had a lot of questions in the beginning, because the pop world is absolutely different than the salsa and it took a lot of adjustment. And he walked me through each and every step. Taught me not to be afraid.

Performing pop music and performing Latin music are two totally different energies. But there is no difference, as far as me interpreting. Both are just as fulfilling to me. I have one voice, my voice. I don't have two compartments in my heart.

THE MOVIES AND CELEBRITY

Music was my priority for many years, but I'm just as passionate about movies. Rubén Blades had a movie agent called David Lewis that I became friendly with. And whenever I was with Rubén, I was a bit of a clown, a personality, and David asked me one day, "Would you consider doing movies?" He sent me on my first audition and I got my first film. And on my second audition I got my second film.

I've done seven films and seven albums. I've been able to do both simultaneously. I did my first movie when I put out my first album. My second movie with my second recording. It's almost parallel careers. And I'm just as passionate about acting. I haven't had the time lately because of music. I must have turned down 25 movies because of time constraints. When I'm recording, I don't do anything else. Not being in the public eye for a few months doesn't dilute the experience for me. When I go to the studio I have to be complete. Because that's what going to end up on that record. So when I'm in the studio, I allocate three months and that's all I'm gonna do. I become a studio bum.

Celebrity has nothing to do with it at all. I don't subscribe to that. I'm still in shock when anybody recognizes me. I'm going to tell you something interesting about the Latino community. I know lounge singers that are the most successful people because that was their dream, they accomplished it, and they sleep well at night. That's success to me. There's something about being successful and doing things your way, and believing in a dream and seeing the whole story come to life. If I didn't think that for a second, I wouldn't have made it, I would have quit. That's what gets you past that one day you want to quit, when you can't take it anymore, and you miss your family.

But I doubt it would mean as much if I was just American. I would be one of thousands of people who had a dream that came true in America. Every one of my accomplishments is an accomplishment for Latino people. When you break down doors, when you break barriers, it means something to your people. Because it's not just me, I'm one of them, they're all of me. ∎

Eddy Zervi gón

I wasn't a musician in Cuba. I was a meteorologist. When I came here, I liked the music scene because of the women, as a hobby, but I didn't like living off the music. But when I got here, the good jobs in my field were few and with my language barrier, I had to dedicate myself to the music completely. I speak English with the flute.

Eddy Zervigón

Born in Güines, Cuba July 7, 1940. Flutist and bandleader, Eddy founded Orquesta Broadway in 1962. Broadway's hit, Isla del Encanto, became a second anthem for the Puerto Ricans.

Chapter 21

Eddy Zervigón

213

CHARANGA DEFINES BROADWAY

Sometimes at a dance someone says, "Play me a salsa, please." And I answer, "What is salsa?" To me, salsa is like a good condiment. Now if we're talking music, you can play a *guaracha* with a típico orchestra just as easily as with a brass band. It's the same *guaracha* they play in Cuba, only that people here don't know that it's the same music and call it something else. It sounds different because you are using brass instruments, like the trumpet, saxophone and trombone. But it's the same music.

I began to study the flute when I was 15 years old. I used to listen to the flute masters Richard Egües and José Fajardo. They inspired me to take up the flute because I used to be a trumpet player in a band. After listening to Orquesta Aragón, Orquesta Fajardo and others, I decided that I wanted to learn the instrument. I studied music and flute with Richard's father in Havana. Usually when people start studying an instrument, you tend to want to imitate them, but then you have to go your own way. I wasn't a musician in Cuba. I was a meteorologist. When I came here, the music scene was my hobby because of the women, but I didn't like living off the music. It was difficult to live off of it. The good jobs in my field were few when I got here and with my language barrier, I had no choice but to dedicate myself to the music completely. My flute became my translator.

The sound of the *charanga* is very enjoyable for dancing and is very different. It isn't a scandalous sound, it's a sound that requires improvisation and a lot of thought to speak through the flute for that long. Free improvisation is what makes the music what it is. If there is no improvisation, people get tired of listening to the tune. The most important elements are spontaneity and the *gusto* you put into that improvisation. You put a good groove into that improv and you don't have a problem. That's when the tune becomes more danceable.

> *Frankly, the Cuban is not a dancer, especially the white Cuban. The ones that have supported the charanga since 1962 have been the Puerto Ricans. If I had had to depend on the Cubans, I would have died of hunger.*

NEW YORK PUERTO RICANS SUPPORT THE CUBAN SOUND

When I arrived from Cuba, my first job was performing at a cabaret in Miami for two months. I never liked Miami because there was little work, mostly in cabarets. Then I moved to New York. It was during those years that Johnny Pacheco had his charanga orchestra. At that moment, Pacheco was recovering from a throat operation, so I was asked to fill in for him. I played for about two to three months with Lou Pérez and Alfredo Valdés. The charanga was going strong from 1962 to '64.

I founded Orquesta Broadway in 1962 on Broadway and 135th Street together with my brothers Ruddy and Kelvin, plus the pianist Abraham Norman and singer Roberto Torres. Broadway has always worked a lot because our sound is different. Ever since I got to New York, it has been like a wave that goes up and down. Sometimes the conjuntos are very popular and the charangas are doing poorly and vice versa.

In 1977, the whole orchestra decided to move to Miami. We stayed for one year, but there was no work. Miami was going through difficult economic times and there were only one or two dances a week. One promoter who hired only two bands was booking those dances. Ours wasn't one of them. So we were stuck again playing in cabarets, something I don't relish—you're always playing for the same set of drunks. Since we felt so limited, we came back to New York.

Puerto Ricans have supported the charanga since 1962. If I had had to depend on the Cuban dances and parties in New York, I would have died of hunger. I would be down to skin and bones. Cubans in New York were always saving their money to move to Miami to be closer to their homeland. They went dancing on December 31st and February 14th. They didn't go dancing unless they were divorced, widowed, or single and out on the prowl. So we packed our bags and headed back to New York.

Back in the Cuban province where I am from, they had dances for the society of whites and the society of blacks. These were private social and cultural organizations whose members paid a monthly fee. Both were proud of their societies, but they were segregated. The society of blacks was not allowed at parties of the society of whites and vice-versa. This was good for the musicians because it meant there was more work. The charanga mostly played at the society of blacks before 1952-3, before the cha cha cha hit. The whites hired bands like Orquesta Riverside. At the white parties, the music was more diverse: *paso dobles*, *merengue*, Glen Miller's music. Naturally, I preferred to play and party at the society of blacks, because that is where they really knew how to dance and have fun. At the black parties, you did not hear *paso dobles*. Just pure swing: *son montuno*, *danzón*, and *guaracha*. The charangas were the orchestras of the societies of color. Once the cha cha cha hit, the Orquesta América and Orquesta Aragón started playing at parties for both societies. In Havana, the segregation was less evident. I think blacks and whites partied together more.

Roberto Torres and I are from Güines. He's a born singer with a commanding presence on stage and he makes you feel what he is singing. He is willing to give his all for the audience when he's up on that bandstand. He used to work with Rafael Sori's Swing Casino in Güines before he came to the U.S. in 1961. When I arrived in the States, we decided to organize Orquesta Broadway. Roberto joined the U.S. Army to invade Cuba after the Bay of Pigs invasion. For three months he wasn't in the band, but when he returned he joined the band again.

Well, even the best marriages split up and it's a pity. Who wouldn't miss a good singer? But although the singer is very important in a charanga, the flute is the one that handles all the improvisational work. Can you imagine a charanga without a flute? After leaving, Roberto joined the Sonora Matancera for a while before forming his own conjunto.

BOOGALOO FROM BROADWAY

We were recording a boogaloo called *Black is Black* with Al Santiago producing the album for Musicor. So we started changing the original lyrics, from, "I want my baby back," to "I want my jeva back," but with such a heavy accent that everybody started laughing at what we were doing. Al said, "Let's leave the laughter in there." He was a genius. Although he had some rather strange ideas, it worked because everybody loved that tune. It was a huge hit.

In 1972 or '73, we went to play at the wedding of the daughter of the President of the Ivory Coast in Africa. We were there for three weeks. We even played at football stadiums. Then we went to Dakar, Senegal, but since they couldn't pay us in our currency, we turned back. At the airport, 5,000 people were waiting for us with the press and radio stations. But we didn't play. They wanted to pay us in

So we started changing the original lyrics, from, "I want my baby back," to "I want my jeva back," but with such a heavy accent that everybody started laughing at what we were doing. Al said, "Let's leave the laughter in there." He was a genius.

African Francs. What are we going to do with African Francs? At that time, one of our tunes, *La Quinta Guajira* was a big hit there and was like a hymn for them. It starts like Beethoven's *Fifth Symphony*. Two months later, we went back. We got our money up front. We always need our money up front, with round trip tickets. Otherwise, you don't get paid. They'll even leave you stranded.

Ever since 1974 we were busy and didn't stop playing until 1984/85. Thank God we have always had work. On Fridays, we used to play two or three dances; Saturdays we'd play four or five dances, from one club to the next. We'd start playing at eight p.m. and sometimes we'd finish playing at ten or eleven the next morning. Meanwhile, our album *Pasaporte* had a number one hit with *Isla del Encanto* in tribute to Puerto Rico. *Arrepiéntete* followed, also reaching number one, then *Barrio El Pilar* went uno, then *Presentimiento* hit too, four or five tunes hit number one.

In *Barrio Del Pilar* we do the montuno section as a play on words on the composer, Felo Barrios, who now lives in Miami. We tried to recreate the sounds as if it were a neighborhood (barrio)party, a *rumba*. An engineer recorded the noise in the street on 52nd and Eighth Avenue for eight hours. We couldn't get the sound of a bullet so we had to bang a can, and, POW! it sounded like a bullet.

At that time we were working like crazy. We had to include a trumpet in the band because I couldn't handle all the work. I had a hernia in the esophagus. The trumpet changed the quality of the sound, not only the type of sound but also the inspiration. Roberto Rodríguez used to sing the charanga and he knew the style and how to play trumpet for that kind of charanga. He was the only one that could play with us. And he was also a singer, so we got two-for-one.

Very few people are recording nowadays, because of bootlegging. There is too much theft. Musicians spend $15,000 to $20,000 on a recording and then when one of the tunes on their album finally hits, it's bootlegged and sold by street vendors. I don't know how they do it, but suddenly the albums are selling for $1.50. Bootlegging is destroying this business. Not only in the U.S., but everywhere.

To me the simpler you play a tune, the more groove it has. In certain music like erotic salsa, they do not use the fundamental chords. That is why the music doesn't swing. I listen to it and ask myself, when is he going to make it come together? It doesn't have the swing of the older music like Eddie Palmieri, Machito and the other legends. It is missing the fundamental chords, what we call the roots of the music. ∎

José Fajardo, Johnny Pacheco and Eddy Zervigón
jam at S.O.B.'s, New York City

Eddy **Zervigón**

I HAVE NO FORMAL MUSICAL STUDIES, NOT EVEN VOICE STUDIES. I LEARNED EVERYTHING I KNOW FROM THE SCHOOL OF HARD KNOCKS. WHEN YOU HAVE LIMITATIONS LIKE THAT, EVERYTHING IS DIFFICULT.

Canelita
Medin

Canelita **Medina**

a

Canelita Medina

Born in Venezuela. Sonera has recorded over 20 albums. Was offered a recording contract by Johnny Pacheco in the 1970s, but her record label turned it down claiming she had a jealous husband.

Chapter 22

A VENEZUELAN SONERA

My name is Rogelia Medina. I was born in La Guaira, Venezuela on March 6, 1939. My musical career began at a young age, because I have always loved to sing. At home when I had doll parties I loved singing. Then, when I was fourteen or fifteen, my friends got me excited about going on an amateur radio contest. The band that accompanied the amateurs was La Sonora Caracas, a very well-known group in Venezuela. The band liked my voice, my style, and from that day forward I became a professional singer with La Sonora Caracas. I was fifteen; I sang with La Sonora Caracas for nine years.

La Sonora Caracas was the top conjunto in Venezuela at the time, instrumentally similar to La Sonora Matancera—it had four trumpets, percussion and the singers. I traveled with them a lot. They are no longer in existence.

There is always rivalry between groups and when a singer hits, they try to steal you away. A similar conjunto called Los Megatones de Lucho offered me more money than what La Sonora Caracas was paying me, so I left. I worked with Los Megatones de Lucho for three years. Then I went on to Victor Piñero's orchestra where I remained for three years. Then I didn't perform for four or five years because there was no musical work and I went to work for a private company for a time.

For a brief time I worked with Las Estrellas Latinas de La Guaira. That's when I had the opportunity to share the stage with Johnny Pacheco's group and he spoke to me about recording an album with him. He was very interested but nothing further was said.

I really came back on the scene in 1972, when Federico y Su Combo Latino called me. With Federico I had the opportunity to alternate with the Fania All Stars and with all the Puerto Rican groups: La Sonora Ponceña, Los Hermanos Lebrón, El Gran Combo and many others. I was on Fonográfica del Caribe Records, Foca Records, who signed me as a soloist/headliner. I recorded my first four albums with them. My first album *Rosas Rojas* was a big hit. I also hit with the album *Sones y Guajiras*. I traveled with the promoter for the record label as a soloist. I went to Peru, Panama, Costa Rica, Cuba and the Dominican Republic. And I visited New York.

PACHECO AND THE LOST OPPORTUNITY

Pacheco's official offer to record an album for Fania came around 1975. I got a call from a Venezuelan business man named Alejandro González, who was a good friend of Johnny Pacheco's. In New York, Johnny had asked Alejandro, "Who is the most popular singer in Venezuela right now?" Alejandro told him it was Canelita Medina and then Johnny calle me. I gave him the record label's phone number so that he could talk to Alvaro Tovar, but Mr. Tovar did not give me permission to record. I had a five year contract and I had three years to go. The opportunity to record with Fania escaped from my hands.

Johnny Pacheco talks about Canelita— "The first time I saw her, I was visiting Venezuela. We were in La Guaira, in the Catia La Mar area. I went to do a concert in Venezuela as a soloist. They had a band that had the same instrumentation as the Fania All Stars. They had arranged some of the numbers by Celia Cruz, like *Quimbara* and *Toro Mata*. They had about four tunes and they asked me to conduct. When Canelita started to sing, she shocked the hell out of me because she sounded terrific. When I heard her, I approached her. I was interested in doing something with her because Celia was already traveling on her own. So I figured this was something I could add to my group, El Tumbao. I wanted to do a recording of some those tunes that I did with Celia, with her. But she couldn't leave Venezuela.

She has that timbre like Celia, more or less; that powerful voice. She had that flavor that I like. Especially her inspirations, they were very well done. She did a hell of a job *soneando*. At first she did some of Celia's inspirations, but then she went on her own. I could see that she had the initiative to ad lib, which is the most important thing in a singer.

I didn't pursue it because the record company told me that Canelita's husband was jealous and he wouldn't let her travel. I thought it was going to be a problem. Time passed and I never heard from her again. Until one day when I was working at a Colombian festival and I ran into her. We reminisced about Caracas, but we never talked business. But it's never too late."

THE MUSIC BUSINESS

I don't know for sure what Tovar told Pacheco, but for him to have mentioned my husband was a lie because at that time, I was no longer with my husband. I got married when I was twenty and we stayed together only four years. From Foca Records I signed with CBS and I never contacted Pacheco again.

Things were not easy for me because I have no formal musical studies, not even voice studies. I learned everything I know from the school of hard knocks. When you have limitations like that, everything is difficult. Most of the time I was a singer with an orchestra and they did not demand very much from us except that we have a good voice, work and sing like a maniac, and be a slave on a bandstand! For that reason, it was very difficult for me to record as a solo artist. In order to record as a headliner, I had to spend ten years in an orchestra as the singer in the band. Now I have my own band and I am always working. After being under contract with CBS, with Combo Records, I am with Foca Records once again. I have a four year contract. I have never been a free agent. I have always had the opportunity to record.

The problem with royalties is serious here. You hear the album being played everywhere, everyone says they have bought the album, but when it's time to settle up, the record label claims they have only sold a small quantity. You can never hope to live from the royalties.

The problem with royalties is serious here. You hear the album being played everywhere, everyone says they have bought the album, but when it's time to settle up, the record label claims they have only sold a small quantity. You can never hope to live from the royalties. I record so that people will know that I'm still around, so that they play my music on the radio, but not because I think that someday I'll be rich, unless it's an international hit.

When I started to sing my inspiration was Celia Cruz, I started out singing her tunes. I had the opportunity to share the stage with her while working with La Sonora Caracas. The first carnival where I performed with her, I had to sit out the whole night, because all of my repertoire was the same as Celia's. For sure I wasn't going to sing her tunes better than she was, so the following year, I tried to bring new songs that were not sung by Celia, then I came up with a totally different repertoire.

It's not only Celia's voice. It's the flavor she has, the swing, her phrasing. It reaches me. But the people knew me as, "She sounds like Celia." I realized that I couldn't live my whole life in the shadow of another person, "Canelita, you have to make a name for yourself. Let them know that you are Canelita." Nowadays, people know me as Canelita, someone that has her own style. And so far I have recorded 19 LPs.

Ninety-nine percent of my music are tunes by Miguel Matamoros and Rafael Hernández. I love the Cuban music of 1936-1940. We have made new arrangements for them and adapted them to today.

I have been very successful with that. The company selects the music and I also suggest tunes that I like. In this last album, we included several original numbers. I also have an album with five compositions by my daughter Trina, my own exclusive in-house composer!

In the beginning I met up with many difficulties, including the fact that the music I sing, which is popular music, Caribbean dance music, was poorly compensated. I had to sing with a dance band for six hours, from 10 pm to 4 am and sweat like crazy and finish completely exhausted. And at the end of the party I would collect pittance. I had the sole responsibility of my daughter since my husband and I separated before I gave birth. Then things got even tougher for me. Sometimes there was no work. I lived hand to mouth, and I didn't want my daughter to go through that.

So at first I didn't want her to sing. I wanted her to study a career. She heeded my advice, she studied business and then started to sing. I have taught her discipline and respect for her audience, but her accomplishments are her own. But she has also struggled a lot. I think it was helpful for her to be Canelita's daughter when she wanted to get into the business. But aside from that, she's a talented singer.

I still sing and I sing my tunes that I recorded twenty years ago in the same key. Music is a means of communicating. I feel like I am doing something for my country.

■

In the sixties, we used to promote people like James Brown, Aretha Franklin, the Temptations, Gladys Knight. But in 1971 I came back to salsa. What brought me back was the business. What I was doing with the soul music was changing too fast. On one of those tours I lost one hundred thousand dollars, so I said, "Let me come back to salsa for a while." That's when I got involved in the Cheetah.

Ralph Merca

do

RALPH MERCADO

MANAGED CELIA
CRUZ, TITO
PUENTE, AND
SCORES OF SALSA
ARTISTS. IN
1992, HE
CREATED RMM
RECORDS, AND
WENT ON TO
SIGN OVER 140
ARTISTS AND
LAUNCH THE
CAREERS OF
MARC ANTHONY
AND INDIA.

CHAPTER 23

PROMOTER, MANAGER AND RECORD EXEC

My name is Ralph Mercado and in Puerto Rico I use Ralph Mercado Prieto, my mother's maiden name. I was born in Brooklyn on September 29, 1941. People used to ask me, "Ralphy what are you?" and I'd say "I'm the only Puerto Rican-Dominican that speaks like a Cuban, looks like a nigger, and thinks like a Jew."

My father worked on the docks. My mother worked in the Brillo Manufacturing Company for many years. We weren't wealthy but we weren't considered poor either. I was brought up in downtown Brooklyn around what they now call Cobble Hill, by the courts downtown.

I was brought up on salsa music. As a kid, I would hear the records of Tito Rodríguez, Tito Puente, and Joe Loco… the people of that time. During the 1950s and 60s, Americans were very involved in this music. The Catskill Mountains were full of Jews and Italians and this music. The bands used to spend the whole summer in the different hotels. One hotel had Tito Puente all summer, the other had Joe Cuba, Machito, and Tito Rodríguez. They danced mambo and they loved bands like La Playa Sextet. There were two or three stray Latinos, but it was mostly Americans. Maybe they didn't understand the words but they understood the rhythm.

I've been in the business since I was about 15 or 16 years old. I started off in Brooklyn doing what they used to call waistline dances. You know, measuring the girls and charging them two cents an inch, and doing these dances down in a basement on Pacific Street in Brooklyn. From there we grew into the Three in One Club which was a loft on Flatbush Avenue in Brooklyn in the early 60s. We also held a lot of functions at the Fraternal Clubhouse in Manhattan, the Manhattan Center, the St. George Hotel, the Towers Hotel in the Heights, and the Granada Hotel in Brooklyn.

I was a promoter before I became a manager and a record person. I promoted dances and parties. At the Three in One Club every Friday night we always had a big name band running. That was in the early and middle 60s. That's where guys like Richie Ray and Bobby Cruz got started. Tito Puente played one Friday and Eddie Palmeri the next and Joe Cuba the following. Charlie Palmeri, Ray Barretto, all the guys used to play down there. But in those days, we could get the top bands for $250 to $400.

Later on I realized that our club was a death trap because the entrance was also the exit. We would pack 400 people on a Friday. Later on, when these tragedies started happening I thought, "Thank God nothing happened back then." Those are things you learn as you go along, it's part of the growing process.

On the radio, besides the Latin stations, Symphony Sid used to play this kind of music every night, five or six days a week, from 11 PM to 4 AM. So he would hook the people. This helped Jerry Masucci a lot because when Symphony Sid was in full swing, Fania started to grow.

In the sixties I was involved with black music. I would do soul productions. We would promote people like James Brown, Aretha Franklin, The Temptations, and Gladys Knight. But in 1971 I came back to salsa. The business brought me back. Soul music was changing too fast. I lost one hundred thousand dollars on one of those tours, so I said, "Let me come back to salsa for a while." That's when I got involved in The Cheetah, before I became part owner of that club.

When Fania got started with Mr. Jerry Masucci and Pacheco, they rehearsed a group they wanted to film in my Three in One club in Brooklyn. I knew

Jerry, and I worked with the Fania people, but I'd never managed their artists. Jerry was always after me to manage and book their artists, but at that time I was a promoter.

In 1973, I started Ralph Mercado Management, the agency for artist management. The first artists I handled were Eddie Palmieri and Ray Barretto. I was in love with Eddie's music, we were friends and we started doing things. Then came Joe Cuba, then eventually all the other artists. I used to run a lot of shows at the Manhattan Center, the Audubon Ballroom, Hunts Point Palace and the St. George Hotel in Brooklyn. We produced the biggest shows and dances and I always used Eddie Palmieri. He was recording with Harvey Averne of Coco Records, and Harvey said, "The only person that can manage Eddie is you." We were managing and booking the top stars of the era.

I started managing because I used to produce all these shows and I helped a lot of artists along. When I broke up my partnership at the Cheetah in 1974, I started working with Fania because of Ray Aviles, my partner. He came out of Fania. That's when we got Celia Cruz, Willie Colón, Hector Lavóe, Rubén Blades and the guys that came from that Fania label. Eventually I got Tito Puente and everybody else. The only one that we didn't manage totally was Johnny Pacheco, but we worked with him. Johnny was a very big star at the time, He had just made Celia Cruz very famous. I managed Celia Cruz for about 26 years of her life on a handshake—it went a long way.

The filming of *Our Latin Thing* at The Cheetah in August 1971 caused salsa to explode worldwide. This is where we started. Before that, salsa was Latin American music, but there are twenty different Latin musics. Each country has its music.

SALSA BUSINESS IN THE NINETIES

RMM is similar to Fania, but we have younger artists, although there are a few who were with Fania before. When I started RMM, I was looking more for singers because that's where the business has gone. Ninety five percent of the contracts of our company are singers. You can start with a very good musician, but the singer is always up front.

This is a business of singers nowadays. Things changed dramatically for musicians like Barretto and Eddie Palmieri because their singers left and all that music changed. Eddie Palmieri can play all the same tunes, but it's not the same if Ismael Quintana (his previous singer) doesn't sing them, or the numbers Lalo Rodríguez made famous with him. Those are the ones people remember.

When Rubén Blades started with Willie Colón, the friction was there. It came from the one who wanted to stand out: Willie Colón. Willie was already a star with a name, but Rubén was quickly becoming one also. He was starting out, but he was the one writing the lyrics. When the two of them came together, it exploded. *Siembra* was one of the biggest selling salsa LPs of all time.

I think it is more difficult for a musician to hit with a band than for an independent singer. Whenever a singer hits, we immediately organize a band for him or her. Then you hire a musical director and you're set.

STAR QUALITY

The most important thing we sell is the quality of the voice. Looks come second. Some guys are not very good looking, they are big, they are small, but if

Fabricated talent doesn't last. I think truly talented people last. Our strength as promoters and producers comes from what we are selling, because we don't play, we don't sing. If my artists are good, I'm set. If they are bad, I'm screwed.

they have the type of voice people like, we prepare them physically, within our possibilities. You mold it the best you can. Then comes the professionalism of the person and other considerations, but talent comes first.

Fabricated talent doesn't last. I think truly talented people last. Our strength as promoters and producers comes from what we are selling, because we don't play and we don't sing. If my artists are good, I'm set. If they are bad, I'm screwed. Some artists take longer to develop than others. When Luis Enrique started out, he was playing congas with Oscar D'Leon before he started to sing a little. His first LP didn't go anywhere; the second one exploded. Some artists have recorded several LPs and nothing's happened and other artists don't get the necessary promotion. Timing is very important in a person's success. Preparation meets opportunity.

A *sonero* is like a scat singer in jazz, making rhythmic sounds with his mouth or improvising like Oscar D'Leon, Jose Alberto "El Canario" or Cheo Feliciano. The best soneros are Oscar D'Leon, Andy Montañez and Cheo Feliciano. They invent while they are singing. They improvise. The term sonero became famous with Ismael Rivera who was called El Sonero Mayor (the Master Singer), Benny Moré and other artists back then.

The sonero has to improvise on the fly and say things that make sense. I love to put soneros together to improvise one after the other to see which one puts out more. They all say they're the best, that they're the ones to contend with. Well, if they're so hot, let's get them to sing and kill each other.

I am always thinking about the future. When we are recording, we are planning the shows with the artists, just like they do in the American market. The challenge is at Madison Square Garden pleasing twenty thousand people.

The music from Cuba has been influential. I think that when Castro came into power in 1959 the *guaguancó* and the mambo came to an end. Ten years later, salsa was born, but I think it is more or less the same thing. The arrangements are better, bigger, and more sophisticated. You have more breaks in the musical arrangements now. Things were simpler, more *típico* before.

There are people that love this music and the rhythm but don't understand the lyrics. Lots of young Latinos are into house music, dance music and they pay more attention to a song in salsa rhythm if it is in English than if it's in Spanish. I am trying to get all my singers to sing at least one cut in English and up to now, it has worked. I think that when we start composing in English and bilingually, a more serious explosion can occur.

Salsa unites everybody. It is a common language that people understand and a rhythm that brings everyone together. More so in Europe, because Latinos that move there bring their music with them. Colombians move to England and they take their Joe Arroyo, their Niche albums with them and little by little they infiltrate. They have radio programs and they are producing specials with the BBC. During our Salsa Festival at Madison Square Garden you see cameras and people from all over the world.

Lalo Rodríguez's *Devórame Otra Vez* sold one hundred thousand copies in Spain, then Azúcar Moreno doubled that number with the same song, so something's happening. Sales are growing daily. That means the market is growing.

In our company we listen to everything before it leaves. We have a couple of main producers, and together with the artists we choose the tunes. We pre-select thirty to forty tunes, then we narrow it down and try to produce the best possible record.

I don't believe in rushing things because records last forever. That's one of the reasons why I had a record label, because I did many concerts that were not recorded, filmed or documented. Many of the albums I am producing become shows. For example, Tito Puente's 100th album is a concert. I am always thinking about the future. When we are recording, we are planning the shows with the artists, just like they do in the American market. The challenge at Madison Square Garden is pleasing and dealing with the masses, twenty thousand of them. Everything has to have a reason. Things don't happen by accident. Only babies are born by accident.

ROLE OF THE PROMOTER

In my experience with the artists, I've had to be a psychiatrist, brother, father, many things. I have seen many things, sad things. I have seen people destroy themselves; people that are loved by the public. Drugs are always the problem. Ninety nine percent of the problems are drug related. That's why it hurts. Some people don't know how to control their thing. They become addicts. One tries to help and cure them, but they always go back.

Artists are like your children. You scold them, you may spank them, and you scold them again. You get mad, but you keep trying to help. But you can disown them, where you can't disown your kid, but we have seen guys who just don't want to do it by themselves. I walk away from people like that. When a person doesn't respect himself, what the hell can I do?

I wear a lot of different hats. I'm not only a promoter of shows or a producer of records, but I'm also a manager of artists, and that's where my management arm comes in. If I can't manage them, they're no good on my shows, they don't get on the records, they're not good for anybody. So as management, we try to get involved in family things. Everybody tells me their problems, and I try to solve everybody's problems, one way or another. But who solves my problems? Who do I talk to? I'd like to find somebody to manage me!

LIFE AFTER 9/11

From 1991 to 2001 salsa music did ok. I believe in the old saying in Spanish, "No hay mal que por bien no venga." (Roughly—every cloud has a silver lining). I got out of the record business not in the way I wanted, but at the right time as history shows. I sold RMM to Universal Records three months before 9/11 in 2001.

After 9/11, everything changed. Besides the whole world, the music business changed. I think a lot of the groups have out-priced themselves for the club scene. The younger generation perhaps isn't dancing as much salsa as the generation before. There are still people that dance salsa, but you don't feel the fever of the 70s and 80s. Record sales have dipped. The record business is in bad shape. Maybe it's starting to come back a little now.

A lot of people tell me that ever since I sold RMM Records, the whole salsa thing has gone down because there's no one waving the banner. Celia Cruz and Tito Puente and others that were the spearheads of the salsa world died. Jerry Masucci died, big stars like Marc Anthony wanted to do crossover things that up to now haven't worked. And now we're in a new phase with a new generation that's into hip-hop and reggaeton. And salsa's hanging on, like merengue, like tropical music. I don't see the emerging stars of the future. We have Gilberto Santa Rosa and Victor

But who solves my problems? Who do I talk to? I'd like to find somebody to manage me!

Manuelle, and a couple of guys still hanging in there like Tito Nieves and José Alberto and a few others, but I don't see the young stars, the 18 to 20 year old guys that are going to be super stars of the future.

But the music is always going to be there because the artists are always going to produce good music, There are still plenty of good bands like El Gran Combo and Sonora Ponceña, but it's not the same torch shining. You see it in the clubs in New York where DJs are more popular than live music. They play salsa music but it's not live performances like it used to be. I remember in New York when there was live music every night. You had the Village Gate, the Palladium, the Ipanema, and the Casablanca. You had all kinds of clubs that don't exist today.

AN ERA COMES TO AN END

I sold RMM Records because of a lawsuit that I lost in Puerto Rico over a song. I feel like RMM Records and Ralph Mercado got raped because of the decision they gave to Glenn Monroig, over a song that Gilberto Santa Rosa and Cheo Feliciano did of his called *Yo Soy*. The soneros changed the lyrics and did a couple of the inspirations. We sold maybe 40,000 copies in the whole world of that record. It was one cut of 10 on the record and they awarded him over 8 million dollars. Since I couldn't come up with the 8 million in cash to cover it, I had to go into Chapter 11. By the time the lawsuit finished we owed the guy almost 12 million dollars with interest. We paid him off and I had to sell the company. I had to get out. I was frustrated.

I had also used the tune in a movie that I did called *Del Son A La Salsa*. We had to pull the movie, take out the song, and change the soundtrack. The movie was filmed in Puerto Rico, New York, and Cuba and it was done by a Cuban director who just

threw the song in there without getting it cleared, and we made the mistake of putting it out. But we never thought that a ridiculous judgement like this was going to be handed down. It was totally out of place. But like I said, "No hay mal que por bien no venga". If I had stayed in the record business, I probably would have been hurting big time now. But those are the ups and downs of this business and life. It took a lot out of me. One works so hard to accomplish something and in a minute it's gone. I felt resentment. To this day I'm still in litigation with a lot of these things. We're still trying to collect money that is owed to me from the sale of the records and from the sale of the company. My lawyer's bills are tremendous.

But aside from that, we had a lot of great hits at RMM Records. We had a lot of great artists, we did a lot of great albums. We maintained Celia on top during her entire career with us along with Tito Puente, guys like Oscar de Leon and Tito Nieves, La India, Manny Manuel, Domingo Quiñones, and of course Marc Anthony. All these great artists came out of this movement.

I still have a couple of my publishing companies and I'm still producing shows at Madison Square Garden, Radio City, and Carnegie Hall in New York. I do an occasional show in Puerto Rico and Miami. And I'm into the nightclub and restaurant business now. I have a couple of restaurants.

The New LQ, which is short for Latin Quarter, that we moved to 48th Street and Lexington has only one night a week of salsa—Wednesday night, so that's the only thing we're booking. Saturday nights we do an Anglo crowd and on Friday nights we do a mixture of Latin music playing reggaeton, house music, salsa, hip-hop and everything else. Many of the top groups are asking for a lot of money

Ralph Mercado, Celia Cruz, Johnny Pacheco, Tito Puente, and Pedro Knight

to play some of these places. It gets very expensive to promote them.

Now I don't have to get up as early in the morning. I start working after 12:00 so I go out at night, I get home and I'm able to rest and I get up and by 1 or 2 in the afternoon I'm at work. And if I go to a club at night or one of the restaurants I can hang out for a while. I don't have anything else to do. It's something to keep me busy and not get too bored while still keeping my hand in the fire.

My contribution to salsa music—wow! I've been involved in it since I was a kid. I still love it. I gave my whole life to this music to try to develop it, to carry it. We opened up a lot of doors throughout the world with this music. I've created a lot of artists, a lot of great shows. I've produced hundreds of shows at Madison Square Garden and all over the world. So I think I've put my cultural hand in it. ■

Ismael Miranda

WITHIN HIS STYLE OF MUSIC, LARRY WAS THE ONE THAT BEST PLAYED THE SON MONTUNO, AND I BECAME ONE OF ITS BEST INTERPRETERS. I'M REFERRING TO THE ARSENIO RODRÍGUEZ STYLE, WHICH IS MY VEIN OF MUSIC. WE GOT ALONG VERY WELL BECAUSE LARRY PLAYED THE KIND OF MUSIC I LOVED AND I SANG THE KIND OF MUSIC HE LOVED TO PLAY.

ISMAEL MIRANDA

COMPOSER, SONERO, BANDLEADER, FANIA ALL STAR. HIS COLLABORATION WITH PIANIST LARRY HARLOW, EL JUDIO MARAVILLOSO HAS BEEN CALLED "THE PERFECT COMBINATION."

CHAPTER 24

Ismael Miranda

PA' BRAVO YO

I grew up surrounded by drugs and gangs and I had my temper. Those mafia movies rub off on us, but I've never been a *Mafioso*. I get along with everybody as long as they get along with me and don't cause me problems. I behave 100% so that others will behave 100% with me. But I can be quick with my fists. Yes, I can be a little violent. I don't put up with anything from anyone. *Pa' bravo yo.* I composed that tune for Justo Betancourt, so you better watch out!

One time we were rehearsing for Fania and I got there late. Johnny Pacheco said, "Well, well, here comes the *Pretty Boy*." Since I was always well dressed and kinda cute, the name stuck. Everyone started calling me "*El Niño Bonito de la Fania,*" To this day they call me "El Niño Lindo." Not that I'm the eighth wonder of the world, it's just how that crap started.

I was born in Aguada, Puerto Rico on February 20, 1950. At the age of four my parents brought me to New York. We lived in the basement of a very small two family home in Long Island, until I was about six years old. Then we moved to Tenth Street in Manhattan. My childhood was very normal. We were raised in a Spanish neighborhood, and we did every normal thing that Spanish kids do: eat rice and beans, listen to Spanish music, play dice, play cards, and gamble... you know what I mean? We hustled to get ahead.

I have worked since I was eight years old. I worked at the *Marqueta*, a food market, in a fruit stand and a pet shop. Everybody had to work, my mother, my father, my brother and me, My mother worked in a factory sewing sleeves, my father planted trees along the highway that leads to Kennedy Airport.

If my parents could only afford four dollars for a pair of $10 pants, it was up to me to come up with the additional six dollars. None of that, "Papi will get it all." Monday nights we played cards. We had like a gambling casino in our house.

I studied at Junior High School 60. Miss Anita Shapolsky, my teacher, would take us to her house. She used to help keep us out of trouble because we were young and liked getting into trouble. Most of us were Latinos. We lived on the same block, we were in the same gang. I was in the Persian Knights. We used to get into fights to defend our territory. That was our main activity. It was very violent. Out of that group of friends, only five of us are alive.

I started taking singing lessons when I was eight. At the age of 11 or 12 I sang at the first Muscular Dystrophy fundraisers with Jerry Lewis, Frank Sinatra, Andy Williams and Tony Bennett, "*Lover please, please come back. Don't take the train coming down the track*" and "*I'm a traveling man, made a lot of stops, all over the world.*" When I was thirteen, I toured with Troy Donahue when he did *Palm Springs Weekend* and came to Nueva York. I formed a group called Little Junior and the Classmates. I had a manager who got me wedding gigs.

I started playing the conga and getting interested in Latin music. I spoke and sang in English, but the Latin thing was always there.
I started with a little group called Pipo and his Combo. And I worked with Andy Harlow and Joey Pastrana. I started buying a lot of Cuban music by Benny Moré, Chappottín, Arsenio, Roberto Faz, Conjunto Casino, and Los Papines. Then, I began to improvise. That's when I became a *sonero*. I began to *sonear* (improvise) and to write some tunes and little by little, I acquired a unique knack for the music.

I used to rehearse at the Three In One Club around 1965. I played the congas and I sang. One day, while Andy was rehearsing he asked, "Why don't you try out?" I started to play and to sing. He liked it and I started with him. One night, we were playing at a club and Joey Pastrana asked me, "Do you want to record with me?" I did my first recording with Joey when I was 17 years old. It hit in Puerto Rico and played on the radio in New York. The Joe Cuba Sextet, Eddie Palmieri, Mario Ortiz in Puerto Rico, Orlando Marín, Joe Quijano, and Tito Puente were the hot groups then.

THE PERFECT COMBINATION

Shortly thereafter, the Harlow Orchestra began.
I loved that band, with singers Felo Brito and Vicky. Then Monguito started with them. I listened to the music and became very interested in it. Since I felt capable of singing it, I started pursuing work with them. It wasn't too difficult, since I had worked with Andy Harlow. Then Larry called me and I went to audition for him. Ismael Rivera was auditioning also. Ismael told Larry, "This kid has potential. You should stick with him. You'll run into problems with me because I'm an old fox." So that's how I ended up with Larry, at the age of 18.

I worked in a dry cleaners by day. I started as an errand boy and became manager. I would stay up until all hours of the night singing with Larry Harlow. I got home at 4 AM from my gigs and had to be at work two and a half hours later. I'd get to work and I'd fall asleep on top of the clothes. One time, Justo Betancourt called me to do *coro* and play maracas for his record. He said, "It'll only take fifteen minutes." I

Then Larry called me and I went to audition for him. Ismael Rivera was auditioning also. Ismael told Larry, "This kid has potential. You should stick with him."

left the laundry at twelve and got back at five. I was fired. That was my last official job. After that, thank God, I have lived from the fruits of my music.

The combination of Larry Harlow and Ismael Miranda was a perfect one. Within his style of music, Larry was the one that best played the *son montuno*, and I became one of its best interpreters. I'm referring to the Arsenio Rodríguez style, which is my vein of music. We got along very well because Larry played the kind of music I loved and I sang the kind of music he loved to play. We were the perfect pair, made for each other. We used to get down heavy, *bien típico*. Larry has tremendous knowledge of Latin music, of the musical roots: *son montuno, guaguancó* and I learned a lot from him. I learned the rest by listening to the music and hanging around the older people. I started to hang out with Tito Puente, Santos Colón, and they accepted me very quickly. This gave me an opportunity to learn from them. I was the baby of the group. I never let an opportunity go by.

During my years with Harlow, he asked me to write some songs and I said I'd try. *El Exigente, Las Luces, Me Voy Para Borinquen, Guasasa, La Revolución, Mi Mami Me Quiere, Tu Me Abandonaste, Abandonada Fue*, I wrote a whole slew of hits. We did about 7 LP's. I'd say 75% of the songs I recorded with Harlow were my compositions: *Arsenio, Señor Sereno, Abran Paso, La Contraria*, etc. Later I composed *Así Se Compone Un Son, Ahora Sí, Borinquen Tiene Montuno*, and more hits.

When it was my turn, I was out to bust everybody's chops. When it was Cheo's turn, he was after the same thing. But when we had to let someone else exhibit their talent, we did. We each had a huge following and when they put us all together, it was a feeling of euphoria.

On the bandstand, we were very competitive. Larry always wanted to be the star and I also wanted to be the star, so he tried to outdo me, and I tried to outdo him. As a result, we put on quite a show. But it was a healthy competition. He called me Junior and we wore some pretty wild outfits. Larry was the first one to start using the electric keyboard. When he started, he drove me crazy, because I wasn't used to it. I liked the real piano, the acoustic one.

Then we started to have differences. But we always remained friends. I decided to go out on my own because I had the talent and I wanted to do a lot of things differently from Larry. Larry was disappointed with the industry and wanted to switch over to rock. In fact, he quit for one year and I kept his band, then he came back. Since Larry couldn't make up his mind, I didn't have any stability and so I decided to form my own band. In 1972, I formed the Orquesta Revelación and we recorded the LP *Así Se Compone Un Son*. I dissolved the band when I left for Puerto Rico to become a soloist.

I sang the night of the big concert at Yankee Stadium. After the concert we'd had a few drinks. Justo Betancourt said, "Ismael, why don't you go to Puerto Rico? You're one hell of a singer with three sets of balls. You're the best improviser, you come across strong, you're good looking, and you dance well. You have to make your move." I told Justo, "I just bought a house, my wife is pregnant, and I can't leave." He said, "Forget it. I'll pay your plane ticket and we'll go together."

I got home at four in the morning, packed my bags and told my wife, "I'm leaving for Puerto Rico. I'll send

Ismael Miranda rehearses at Boy's Harbor in New York's El Barrio, with Domingo Quiñones (singer), front, Bobby Allende (conga) middle, Ray Colon (bongo), Ruben Rodriguez (bass), Bobby Franceschini (sax), Angel Lebrón (trombone) upper left, Sergio George (piano) behind bongo, Barry Danielian (trumpet) black hat back right, Pablo Nuñez (timbales), Luchito Cabarcas (vocalist) white cap, Victor Vazquez (trombone) white jacket back & Mac Gollehan (Trumpet) back row right

for you." I left for Puerto Rico and that same weekend, I started earning money, and I'm talking real money. In New York, I cleared about eighty to one hundred dollars a dance. In Puerto Rico, I started making five hundred dollars an hour. A typical week-end, I made $1,500. Sometimes I'd earn $5,000 a week-end. When I saw all that dough, I decided to stay. For about ten years, I was the hottest act in Puerto Rico.

FANIA ALL STARS

The Fania All Stars was the group that gave Latin music its biggest push. We traveled around the world and wherever we went, thousands of people flooded the stadiums to see us. We had the opportunity to share in a tremendous brotherhood. When it was my turn, I was out to bust everybody's chops. When it was Cheo Feliciano's turn, he was after the same thing. But when we had to let someone else exhibit their talent, we did. We each had a huge following and when they put us all together, it was a feeling of euphoria.

Hector and I wore the same size and when I stayed in the Bronx, I wore his clothes and when he stayed in Manhattan, he wore mine. One night I went to play at the Hunts Point Palace. I see him walking in with a beautiful suit and tie and I say to myself, "Damn, that suit sure looks familiar."

When the Fania All Stars went to Panama, Rubén Blades was starting to make a name for himself and gave me the tune *Cipriano Armenteros*. Rubén used to go see us with his guitar and he'd sing us his songs. One day, he sang *Cipriano Armenteros for me*. He hadn't wanted to give it to anybody because he wanted to record it himself. We became good friends and I told him, "Give me that song." He made an exception because he was sort of a fan of mine. It was a song about a man who earned the respect of the people, a Panamanian Pancho Villa. He could have been a Puerto Rican. You can find a *Cipriano Armenteros*

anywhere. Well, Rubén gave me that tune and it was a hit. When he moved to New York, he continued composing for me.

Hector Lavoe was a great friend of mine as well. We met during the Willie Colón period since we worked in the same places. As a matter of fact, he used to spend the night in my home. My mom was crazy about him. When Hector didn't go to the dances, I would sing for him because a lot of times, he'd be sleeping and I had to start singing until he got there. He was always the king of timeliness.

One time in London I bought a really fine brown suit with four buttons in the front, a tie and a really sharp shirt. I was saving it for a special occasion. Hector and I wore the same size and when I stayed in the Bronx, I wore his clothes and when he stayed in Manhattan, he wore mine. One night I went to play at the Hunts Point Palace. I saw him walking in with a beautiful suit and tie and I said to myself, "Damn, that suit sure looks familiar." As he comes towards the bandstand I announce, "Here's Hector Lavoe." Everybody was applauding, he picked up the two microphones and brought them up to his mouth, "Mi gente ZZZZZZZZZZ…" and he got electrocuted. He fell on the floor and started knocking down the timbales and the congas. Everything was all over the place and he totally ripped my suit. I kicked the mike until I managed to tear it out of his hand. Forget about the suit, I saved his life. Then I yelled, "I'm gonna kill you."

When I'm on the bandstand, I take command. That platform is mine. I control the musicians, and I control the people. I don't let the people control me with their emotions. I'm the boss when I'm performing. ■

Andy Montañez

WHEN I SAY I DON'T CONSIDER MYSELF A
SONERO, IT'S BECAUSE I THINK THERE ARE
OTHERS THAT ARE BETTER AT IT THAN I,
FOR EXAMPLE ISMAEL RIVERA. I'M A GOOD
SONERO BECAUSE I IMPROVISE. I DON'T
WRITE THE WORDS OUT, THEY COME TO ME.
THAT'S THE DEFINITION OF A SONERO.

ANDY
MONTAÑEZ

BORN IN
SANTURCE,
PUERTO RICO
ON MAY 7,
1942. SONERO,
PERFORMED
WITH EL GRAN
COMBO AND LA
DIMENSION
LATINA BEFORE
GOING SOLO.

CHAPTER 25

EL NIÑO DE TRASTALLERES—SONERO

When I say I don't consider myself a sonero, it's because I think there are others that improvise in that style much better than I can, for example Ismael Rivera. I'm a good sonero because I improvise. I don't write the words out, they come to me. That's the definition of a sonero, improvisation. They give you a chorus and you improvise over that chorus. If you are blessed with the ability to improvise and you have a pleasant voice, you've got two things in your favor.

Trastalleres is a neighborhood in Santurce, Puerto Rico where the built houses behind some mechanics shops where they fixed the train. That's the origin of the name Trastalleres—Behind the Mechanics Shops. Daniel Santos, El Inquieto Anacobero, was born there, so was Herminio Avilés, the first Puerto Rican vocalist of Trio Los Panchos. Sammy Ayala who sang with Ismael Rivera was born there, I was born there.

Aside from making 17 children, my father liked to sing and he still serenades my mother. I attribute my musical bent to him. My mother used to take me to sing on an amateur radio program when I was 12 years old, and with some neighbors we started a trio for serenades. That's how I started.

My school was at bus stop 18 and the musicians played at bus stop 12, at a radio program where they aired live radio with an audience. I'd change my school shirt so they couldn't identify me and I'd go watch Ismael Rivera sing. I used to skip school to see Rafael Ithier, Martin Quiñones, all those guys. But I never imagined that one day I would sing that kind of music.

I went to an audition at a nightclub called El Esquife. Noro Morales's brother Luis was performing with his band and he heard me. On that day, as if straight out of a movie, the singer didn't show. Luis told me I could do the ballads (boleros). I sang boleros with them for about six months.

One day, Rafael Ithier went to the alley in Lali where I lived looking for me. It seems someone told him I sang. I knew a tune by Vicentico Valdés that says, "*If I had a million, I would love you.*" He tested my sense of rhythm and my ability to sing in tune. I have never studied, but I believe that in order to sing, you have to have clave, rhythm and intonation. I wouldn't say I have a privileged voice, but I have the rhythm and intonation. I thought I was going to sing ballads, but Rafael started to teach me how to sing dance music. He tried me out for six months, then I joined El Gran Combo.

One of the people responsible for the strength of my voice is Rafael Ithier. I knew nothing about music. Without my realizing it, he slowly started raising my pitch. Around the fourth year, I noticed I was singing more strained, and he revealed, "I have been raising your pitch without telling you." By the time he was done, he'd raised my pitch an octave and half. He says the vocal chords are like a muscle. If you exercise them, you develop strength.

LA DIMENSION LATINA IN VENEZUELA

I was pampered in El Gran Combo and I was Rafael Ithier's pal. I was earning good money with them, but I wanted to test myself. Dimensión Latina offered me the possibility to go to Venezuela. If not with them, I would have gone off alone or with somebody else. I wanted to see if I could make it without El Gran Combo. And I think it worked. Those years were necessary. If I hadn't lived through those years, my sons wouldn't be performing with me, we wouldn't be discussing Andy Montañez. I'd be working for El Gran Combo, proudly, but I'd be a singer with El Gran Combo.

My departure was sad for Rafael. There were songs in which they called me "*Scorpion! Nothing's happened here.*" I sang back, "*Why do you call me scorpion?*" But I don't think they were angry, they were sad because I left. It's always been hard for me to leave Puerto Rico and it was even more traumatic to leave for an indefinite period of time. Quitting El Gran Combo was like walking in the dark. Many people thought Andy Montañez would disappear. It crossed my mind, but I risked it all.

La Dimensión Latina was a popular group, but never like El Gran Combo. I had economic security, but the economic thing wears off. After four years, I felt homesick. I was away from my children, had divorced my wife and it was time for me to go back. So I returned and formed my own band.

I've never been a bandleader. I've always delegated that task because I don't have the strength to boss people around. I don't like to scold people. The ego is there. Everybody has that ego that delights when they applaud you, that rejoices when they love you. I have felt that. And I've managed to do the songs I've wanted to do, I've managed to perform with my two sons, to hug them, to have the audience applaud the three of us; for my kids to hug me when we have triumphed, to feel sad when there's been a setback.

It's a privilege to be a singer. I'm thrilled and have been blessed by God. I have gone from little league to the big leagues, with a little jump. I leaped from a small group to El Gran Combo, and six months later started traveling to Panama, Venezuela, Colombia.

People bring me tunes. I like romantic tunes, not erotic ones. I try to put myself in the

> *One of the people responsible for the strength of my voice is Rafael Ithier. I knew nothing about music. Without my realizing it, he slowly started raising my pitch. Around the fourth year, I noticed I was singing more strained, and he revealed, "I have been raising your pitch without telling you."*

Andy and Celia sing at the Salsa Festival at Madison Square Garden in New York City. Luis Falcón, Celia's son, reports that Andy called Celia during her last days on this earth to tell her from his heart, "Puerto Rico te quiere. Yo te quiero." Celia's deep love for Puerto Rico made her feel as Puerto Rican as she was Cuban.

composer's place, to think about how he felt at that moment. Since I used to sing boleros, I think my way of singing salsa is emotive, expressive. It's not just singing, it's all about singing with feeling, as if it were happening to me. That's part of the secret to my success. People believe in me, they believe what I'm telling them because I believe in me. I respect the audience, I respect my mother, I respect my friends.

THE FANIA TEMPTATION

I was never signed with El Gran Combo. No musician ever signed a contract with El Gran Combo. During the Fania years, Ray Avilés, Jerry Masucci, my brother Johnny Pacheco, even Ralph Mercado approached me, with napkins, with blank pieces of paper, "Sign with Fania," but I was never interested. Fania was very big, but there were times when Cheo would be at the top of the charts, and you wouldn't hear Ismael Miranda for two years. The following years, Ismael Miranda would be on top, but Cheo stayed behind. I don't think it was possible to get individual attention.

During the Fania years, I did not exist as a singer, I was in El Gran Combo. El Gran Combo was so beloved by its audience that we were constantly traveling, independent of Fania, to Venezuela, Colombia. El Gran Combo was never influenced by any group because Rafael Ithier always did the arranging. The Nuyoricans who were born here were influenced by Cortijo before El Gran Combo, but they also were jazz influenced by Machito. All those mixtures created this type of salsa that I play now.

Andy at Salsa Festival at Madison Square Garden with sons Andy Jr. and Harold singing chorus

Andy **Montañez**

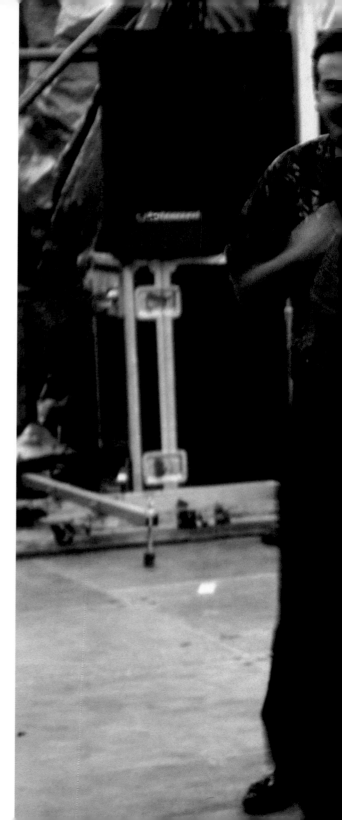

WHAT IS SALSA

The word salsa doesn't signify any rhythm. It is a common denominator to refer to certain rhythms like *guaracha, guaguancó* and *son montuno*. I used to sing a tune called *Changó Tavení*. I recorded it with El Gran Combo when it was not called salsa. In the LP, it is referred to as *guaguancó*. Before that, Machito recorded it and it wasn't salsa and Benny Moré recorded it and it wasn't salsa. Now, the same arrangement I did with El Gran Combo is called salsa. The name salsa caught on and it signifies this type of music. It is a way of expressing a type of music, a type of feeling of the villages that stop being villages to become cities. It is a way for the people to express themselves.

My sons have their path laid out for them. They have the two indispensable elements for singing: clave and intonation. Maybe they will never be accepted by the people, but they can sing. Living in my shadow may be bad for them.

On every LP I have recorded, at least one tune has hit. I have seen people that rise like foam and three years later they have disappeared. That is sadder and hurts more. When you're on top, you can start thinking you're God.

I have never reached the top and I have never hit rock bottom as an artist. I have remained at a level in which people accept me and I work. One time I didn't record for three years and yet I worked every single weekend. I am very satisfied with what God has given me and I don't care about top billing, it's all the same to me. But one thing's for sure—when I'm on the bandstand, I'm gonna give it my all! ■

Andy and sons Andy Jr. and Harold

Andy **Montañez**

Luis Perico Or

I'M NOT A 100% COMMERCIAL ARTIST.
AND I NEVER WILL BE. COMMERCIAL, TO ME, HAS A BUNCH OF
LIMITATIONS, BECAUSE YOU HAVE TO CREATE A MUSICAL
LANGUAGE THAT PEOPLE CAN UNDERSTAND AND DANCE TO. WHEN
PEOPLE GO TO DANCE, THEY DON'T DANCE TO A SINGER, THEY
DON'T DANCE TO MY TRUMPET.
THEY DANCE TO RHYTHM.

otiz

Luis "Perico" Ortiz

Born in December 26, 1949 Santurce, Puerto Rico. Trumpeter, producer, arranger, composer. Worked for Tito Puente, Machito, Mongo Santamaría, Tito Rodríguez, Fania All Stars, Johnny Pacheco.

Chapter 26

Luis "Perico" **Ortiz** *249*

PAINTER OF EMOTIONS

My background is in classical music. I studied in a special program on the island consisting of a half day of music and a half day academic study called Escuela Libre de Música.

I started to play trumpet in La Escuela Libre when I was 10. The first song I learned by ear was a monstrous hit named *Quítate de la Via Perico*, by Cortijo y Su Combo, vocalized by Ismael Rivera. I played it day and night. There was a little playground where the kids used to play baseball and there was a beautiful mango tree three stories high. On my break, I would climb up the tree to eat and play so nobody would bother me. The kids called me, "Perico, Perico." The name stuck. I also have a big, crooked nose that looks like a parrot's.

I knew I was bound to represent this music at some point in time. In the fifties, the radio stations were playing Cesar Concepción and his Orchestra, Moncho Usera, Orquesta Panamericana, Mario Ortiz and Cortijo y su Combo. I used to listen to the radio at noon. I would take two cracker boxes, turn them around and play music on top of the boxes. At that point, I realized I had that love in my veins. I would go to church and put clave to hymns like the *Ave Maria*. That seems disrespectful, but really I'm a newborn Christian. I go to church. And I feel it that way. I feel it in clave.

From there, I went into the Conservatory of Music. I majored in music education with a concentration in trumpet. When I was fourteen, I worked under the direction of Pablo Casals with the Puerto Rico Symphonic Orchestra. My vocal teacher was Zubin Mehta and my trumpet teacher was Henry Novak, considered one of the top ten Baroque trumpet players in the world. My format was classical music for many years.

From that point on, I went into the pop market. I had the pleasure of working with Sammy Davis Jr., Tony Bennett, Paul Anka, Ann-Margaret, The Supremes, Trini López, and Engelbert Humperdinck. I was working the main hotels on the island and was on the staff of all the bands on the TV programs. I used to work thirty-seven TV shows a week and played on all the jingles. I was active from 9 AM till 2 AM every day, including Saturdays and some Sundays. I consider myself a workaholic.

The money came, but that wasn't the priority. The priority was to make as much music as I could. I worked with these people and understood what they were doing. I developed a knowledge of what popular American music is all about. My music today has all those elements. The Afro rhythm comes from Africa, and I have influences in the field of jazz and popular American music.

IF YOU CAN MAKE IT THERE...

I was doing a chart for Yolandita Monge. In front of my house there was a lake, very inspiring for writing and I was listening to Maynard Ferguson. While listening to his music, I said, "This island is getting small for me. I have to leave my country and develop myself. And if Ferguson made it, I can make it." The issue was not money, because it's very hard to make it in this country. But if you make it in New York, you make it anywhere.

Then I started to create what is my style today. People that have followed my career for the past 20 years representing Caribbean music, what they call salsa, hear one note and immediately say, "That's Perico." I have a style that I put together and produced. I didn't create it, I put different pieces together and the structure is how I play. In me, all that influence is represented in a very intricate music called salsa.

I never was a street-wise type. My life was my trumpet, a little cassette to hear the sports and church. I was afraid to get involved with the people's music because at that time in Puerto Rico every dance ended with knives and bottles. From the island, I was doing arrangements for groups that were signed to Fania, like Roberto Roena, Ismael Miranda, and Tommy Olivencia who I produced for five years. They knew who I was.

When El Gran Combo needed a trumpet player in the late sixties, Rafael Ithier and Andy Montañez went to see me at a hotel where I was playing and asked me to be their lead. I was scared to death. Richie Ray went to Puerto Rico and had offered me a similar position and I turned him down.

I came to New York for the first time in 1968. I came from Puerto Rico with Orquesta Panamericana who I played with for five or six years. Though a Puerto Rican artist, I don't play the Puerto Rican forms bomba and plena. We played guaracha, guaguancó, son montuno, and mambo, the commercial element of the Cuban music that is salsa. It's how we interpret the music transported to us from Cuba.

YANKEE STADIUM CONCERT WITH MONGO

I went into Latin jazz from pop music as a member of Mongo Santamaría's band. I was with them for three years until I came to New York to live in 1973. We were in California on tour with Cal Tjader and Dizzy Gillespie when Mongo told us, "When we stop in New York, we're gonna do a movie and a live album at Yankee Stadium for a new label called Fania." That day, they filmed the *Salsa* movie with Jerry.

The energy of the Latinos in New York City immediately hit me. I went into Yankee Stadium I scared to death because our people are very rowdy. And New York is the most difficult arena. I was a rookie, a newcomer. My participation was with Mongo, so we already knew what we had to do.

In Mongo Santamaría's band, the only Puerto Ricans were the timbales player and me. In Mongo's band, I used to play timbales, trumpet, flugelhorn and flute. So when we were playing, Mongo announced, "On trumpet, flugelhorn, flute and timbales, from Puerto Rico..." And when he said Puerto Rico, my God, my ego exploded. It feels like someone grabbing something out of your insides when 50,000 people cheer you on. That moment was one of the turning points in my decision to stay in New York.

So we did our show. Mongo, as always, was a superstar. The Fania All Stars went on. Close to the end of their show, the people couldn't resist getting close to the stage in the center of the field. They started going onto the turf and a riot started. You saw timbales flying, it was like the Beatles. Yes, that was the biggest concert ever in Latin history.

So that was the end of the show. When we finished our performance I met Jerry Masucci and Johnny Pacheco backstage. And Johnny comes to me and says, "Louie, tremendous job. We're very impressed with your work and we'd like to have a talk with you." Pacheco invited me to go to France as a guest with Fania. They wanted to talk business with me.

> *When we were playing, Mongo announced, "On trumpet, flugelhorn, flute and timbales, from Puerto Rico..." And when he said Puerto Rico, my God, my ego exploded. It feels like someone grabbing something out of your insides when 50,000 people cheer you on.*

Luis "Perico" **Ortiz**

...YOU CAN MAKE IT ANYWHERE

After Europe, I received an offer from Jerry and Johnny to be a staff arranger, producer and musician for the Fania label. That's when I started. I never saw marijuana or cocaine until I came to New York. When I went to a recording session here, they introduced me as Perico, from Puerto Rico. The guys started, "Hey Pericoooo, let's go to the bathroom." Later on I saw the white powder and they told me, "That's Perico. Perico is cocaine." I immediately grabbed a hook, Luis "Perico" and featured a bird, a Brazilian Guacamayo, on all my albums. I'm not into drugs, but people that don't know my background think that I am a heavy-duty user because of my nickname.

I was one of Rubén Blades' first producers. Rubén and I did *Pablo Pueblo*. That was the first time I ever included tuba with trombones in the production, and I wrote a classical interlude in place of a mambo (which is a repetition of the first four or eight bars, four times). I remember being thrown out of the Fania office by Jerry Masucci. He said, "You crazy? How are we gonna put this out? First, Rubén comes in with a testament of three million pages of lyrics, and then you come in with classical music. These people you're playing for work 9 to 5. They are not here to analyze your music." Tito Puente was at the office then and said, "Either these guys are gonna do something in music or they're crazy. Let's give it a chance." Masucci released *Pablo Pueblo* as a twelve inch only, and the rest is history. I did *Pedro Navaja, Plástico*, and all those hits.

I was part of the turning point of the music in the seventies in New York. Everyone started to look for me. I had the pleasure of producing, arranging or performing in records for Celia Cruz, Tito Puente, Machito, Cheo Feliciano and many others. We were in the studio every day and night, arranging, recording, and playing. We did close to 435 albums. I did all of Ismael Quintana's catalogue, all of Ricardo Ray's catalogue with Fania, and most of Tito Puente's recordings. I also worked on the music for Celia Cruz, Johnny Pacheco, Willie Colón with Hector Lavoe. Our schedule ran from 12 to 6 with Rubén Blades, and then from 7 to 2 AM with Celia Cruz. The next day there was another artist. It was a factory, but it was a factory of love. We would rehearse in the studio and then record that first rendition that you hear in all this music. Everything was recorded live except the voice. That was the only thing that was overdubbed.

PACHECO'S MUSICAL DIRECTOR

One day Johnny Pacheco told me, "I don't want to be performing every night. I want you to be the musical director." I did it for four years. I got really in tune with New York because I was directing one of the hottest bands on the scene at the time. People used to see Johnny Pacheco, but the guy that was conducting, arranging and producing the show was Perico. So people started to relate to me.

As a writer, composer and arranger, I never studied Cuban music per se. I respect it very much, but I tried to create my own unique style. I received the green light from Johnny. He would bring me cassettes of Cuban and Mexican music. Then he'd say, "Now I want you to put yourself into the group." And we had the hottest band that Pacheco ever led.

I was twenty-something with a new vision. I started to put notches into the music from a different perspective. I consider myself an artist for people that are more musically inclined. It's very hard to pave the way, but it's been my choice and it will be until the day I die. I started to use a lot of American influence in the structure of basic Cuban music. I changed core structures, inserted counterpoint melodic lines, like subliminal messages behind the lyrics. The result was a richer harmony. Before that time, everything was: "trumpet, you play now. You keep quiet now. Now the singer sings." Everything was done by taking turns.

I received offers from Velvet of Venezuela and Oscar D'León to be his band's musical director. I was content with what I was doing and I was working towards my next step, but I wasn't forcing it. So I did my first album, *Julian Del Valle*, in Puerto Rico, which was my first hit.

After that hit, all the club owners started to request my services as band leader, separate from Johnny Pacheco. I was in Venezuela with Johnny during the carnival. I expressed to Johnny that I wanted to see what it is like to have a band in New York, as a native Puerto Rican.

PERICO THE BANDLEADER

I had never wanted to be a band leader in this music. Organizing my own orchestra was an accident. I did an album in 1978 called *My Own Image* for Latin Percussion, Martin Cohen's label. We had top quality musicians like Jon Faddis on trumpet, the Brecker Brothers, Lew Soloff, and Patato. When I received my second offer, I said, "I'm gonna make a dance album." That first salsa album, *Super Salsa*, was my first gold record.

My orchestra began at the right time. It was needed in New York, because the Tito Puente, Machito and Tito Rodríguez era was fading. There were a lot of bands that didn't have the enthusiasm people expected. My band was energetic, young, and well dressed. We brought back the classiness of stage presence for the artist.

I'm not a 100% commercial artist, and I never will be. Commercial, to me, has a bunch of limitations, because you have to create a musical language and lyrics that people can understand and dance to. When people go to dance, they don't dance to a singer, they don't dance to my trumpet. They dance to rhythm. So the music has to be very rhythmically oriented, not too heavy in the charts, and the lyrics have to be people's thoughts of what is current.

In the seventies, I made a difference in what salsa is today due to my creativity. These people allowed me to be creative. They would give me a record from Cuba and I would listen to the Cuban record, but when I sat down to start writing, I kept only the text, the lyrics. Then I wrote what I felt.

INNOVATION

In my case, innovation has to do with the musical elements; how I incorporate the jazz elements, the jazz harmonies, how I perceive different background vocals. One thing I respect is the integrity of the rhythm of the *guaguancó, son montuno, and mambo*. We're talking about Cuban music. That's very important because that's what makes the people move their feet. It's the strength of the rhythm attached to the colors of the brass, the arrangement, the set of lyrics, and how you produce and mix all that to make that rice and beans with *tostones*. That's how you dress it. But I don't invent with it. I have too much respect for it.

After being away, I'm back as a public entertainer to set an example. A presentation is equal to culture and that is what we are representing: our socio-political culture. When I

perform, it's not party time. I have tremendous respect for our music. My objective is to present the value of a gift that I received when I was born, which is music. My name is Luis Ortiz. I'd like the world to know who I am, not because of Luis Ortiz, but because of what I represent. I want the American people to see Luis Ortiz representing and being accepted as a Caribbean artist. I'm very proud of what I am and where I come from.

CLASSICAL TRAINING VS. STREET EMOTIONS

I think it's very important for instrumentalists to have a classical background, because it teaches you how to play correctly, technically and how to start developing emotions. From the moment you start working with Bach, Beethoven, Vivaldi, the first things that you get from your conductor are emotions. It's not the note you play, it's how you play that note. That is missing in salsa because there is no College of Salsa, so all we get are street emotions.

When I play, I sing with my trumpet. I might play one note, but that note is the one that's going to get to you. I'm not going out there for this trumpet player to see how high I can go or to play three hundred million notes on a trumpet. It's a very private thing I have within me, and if you get it, Amen. ∎

I USED TO PLAY THE MERENGUE ACCORDION. MY CAREER STARTED BECAUSE A GUY CALLED ME UP AND SAYS, "YOU STILL PLAY ACCORDION? WE'RE GOING TO PLAY IN VILLA PÉREZ. WE'LL GIVE YOU NINETY-FIVE DOLLARS FOR THE WEEKEND, PLUS ROOM AND BOARD." THAT SOUNDED GOOD. I TOOK THE ACCORDION, PUT AWAY MY TOOLS AND I BECAME A MUSICIAN UNTIL THIS DAY.

Pacheco

Joh

256 *Johnny* **Pacheco**

California together. At the Hollywood Palladium, we packed them in.

Everybody went to the Palladium to dance. The non-dancers used to stand around watching people dance. Then they would go to the corners and practice. When Tito or Machito played, everybody danced. The boys and girls all had routines.

THE PACHANGA

I started the pachanga dance and the charanga craze. That's why I was number one. The charanga is a type of band. If you don't have violins it's not a charanga. You don't dance a charanga, you dance with a charanga band. The pachanga was the dance. You dance it with the hop, with the hankie.

We completely changed the sound of music because the charanga is played with flute and violins, two voices in unison and the rhythm section: timbales, güiro and tumbadora or conga. That's the typical Cuban sound and I started it in 1959. My opportunity came in 1960. It's ironic because I was trying to get the group recorded, but nobody wanted it. They said, "That crap is going to die, forget about it." But I never gave up. I went in a studio and did a demo with *El Güiro de Macorina* and *Oyeme Mulata* and went over to a guy who loved charanga, Rafael Font, and said, "*Coño*, can you play this for me?"

He heard it and said, "This is going to be a hit." That Sunday, Al Santiago, founder of Alegre Records, dropped in and asked, "You want to record, kid? I'll give you a contract." I had no idea what was going on. I didn't know they had flooded the radio station trying to find out where to get the record. It became an instant hit and since Al had a record store, the people went over on Saturday and said, "I want to buy that thing on the radio, *El Güiro de Macorina.*" "Who the hell is *Güiro the Macori?*" he

asked. Nobody knew who recorded this thing. It was just a demo.

So I signed a contract with Alegre Records. The contract wasn't worth the paper it was written on, but since I shook hands on it, to me that was my bond. The tune was a tremendous hit. If I had known it was so hot, I would have done it myself, but I had no idea. I recorded it again and then I did the first album with Al Santiago and Irv Greenbaum. I stayed with Alegre until 1963.

FANIA COMES TO LIFE

Towards the end of 1963, I left Alegre and started Fania Records. I met Jerry Masucci. We became very good friends and when I learned he was a lawyer I utilized his services as my own personal attorney. He had been to Cuba a few times and he loved the music and the *charanga* sound.

I said to Masucci, "I'm gonna start my own record company." Jerry asked, "Do you need any legal advice?" I said, "Yeah, I'm gonna need a lawyer to get the papers together and I'm gonna need some money, because I don't have any." We borrowed twenty-five hundred dollars and went into a studio to record.

I had all the music written, I did all the arrangements and we did the first album. At that time, I switched the band from *charanga* to *conjunto*, replacing the flutes with horns and called it Pacheco y su Tumbao. One of the reasons I switched to the conjunto was that there were no good Latino violin players in New York anymore. All the decent Latino violin players wanted to play classical music.

The first album we did was *Cañonazo* and the catalog number of the album was 325. I recorded it

> *I was making a conga and he was working on a project for the Air Force. He had a piece of metal lying there. I picked it up and hit it with a wrench. It had a ring to it and I said, "Jesus Christ, I've gotta make a cowbell."*

on my birthday, March 25th. We started getting calls from guys that wanted to record and we went after some of them, like Barretto. Some groups didn't make it. But then we started getting all the salsa players. The one concert at the Red Garter, however, didn't have all of the Fania All Stars yet.

We were the ones who started salsa because the boogaloo that came before salsa had died. What was beautiful about salsa was its glamour. We had class: openings with Rolls Royces, big stretch limousines, big parties and shit like that. The office we had was fantastic. And the people were proud to see Latinos on a par with Americans. When we showed the movie *Our Latin Thing*, we had a big opening at one of the theaters on Broadway.

JUST CALL IT SALSA

I don't remember exactly when we said, "You know, we should call this salsa and cover the whole thing under one roof." Once we started traveling, people would ask, "What are you playing?" I would say, *son montuno*, or *son*, a *guajira*, and this is a *guaracha*. And they would get confused. Someone suggested, "If we put everything under the name salsa, I think it's going to benefit all of us." And so we did.

We are not saying that it's not Cuban music, because I never said it wasn't. We took the Cuban music and since we grew up in New York and had jazz influences, we modernized certain chords. Instead of being tonic and dominant, we made them more flamboyant. And the rhythm section is more pronounced when we perform. For instance in Cuba, the rhythm section used to be in the back. Now we do the opposite and put the rhythm in front. We play for dancers, and that's what gives us the percussion sound.

HECTOR, WILLIE, AND RUBEN

Hector Lavoe was one of the greatest. He was nuts, crazy, but he was one of the most loveable guys I knew. He was like my son. He used to come up and I would let him sing. But I already had Pete El Conde. Then I found out I was recording Willie Colón. Willie told me that the kid that was singing with him died of leukemia. Right there I said, I have to get these two guys together. Two young kids, forget it. That's got to be a great combination.

Rubén Blades started working with us when he came from Panama. I remember the first time I heard him sing—*Bilongo*, you know with that coro, *"quiquiribo mandinga,"* and he looked so funny to me, because he folded his arms behind his back while singing like that. I said, "What a strange guy." He always liked my band and we became very good friends, but he was looking for work. He had just moved to New York and we got him a job working in the mailroom at Fania Records and then I saw him writing lyrics. He started singing with little groups. That's when Willie split with Hector Lavoe. I said, man, this guy would be perfect with Willie.

BIRTH OF A SALSA TUNE

Every tune starts with an introduction. Then comes the body, the idea of the tune. That's where you put the lyrics. After that you've got the montuno that either starts with a coro or with the instrumentation. When you get into the montuno, you are restricted to either four or eight bars of repeated music so the singers can ad-lib and the coro can come in. As they used to call it in Cuba, the estribillo (ad-libs) is the same melody that the coro is going to sing. If the instruments play the estribillo, then the singer starts. Usually if the coro initiates it, then the lead singers do the ad-libs. Sometimes they

Johnny Pacheco y su Tumbao Añejo play at the First Hispanic Festival of New York City in 1992

do the estribillo and then they do the coro. After that, you bring in a soloist. If you're gonna have an instrument solo, like a piano, tres or any instrument taking a solo, it should be in that spot, because after the solo comes the mambo.

Then you want to add some excitement and that is when you bring in the brass: what we call the mambo section. And if you want to get more exciting, then you bring in the *moña*, the blast. That's what keeps the thing going. In the *moña*, you can have the brass and continue the coro. I usually change the coro to a half-coro that is punchier to finish. The moña is a phrase that is supposed to build the excitement more. Actually the moña is like a second mambo. I've been calling it moña for so long, I don't know where I got the *moña* from... una moñita. It's the hot part, the hottest part before going out, before terminating the tune, before going into what we call the coda. Coda means the end.

WHAT IS CLAVE

The clave is what keeps the music intact so it won't fall apart. It's very important. When you write a figure you've got to make sure it's on clave before you write it. Clave is a measurement that you use in order to do an arrangement. People think that the clave is a pair of sticks, but those sticks are playing a two bar figure that you have to use to write the music. If you don't use that, you will be out of rhythm. And if you cross the clave it throws the arrangement right off. There are a lot of recordings where the clave jumps.

The clave is the scale to write music from. When you write an arrangement you use either two, three clave (clave de rumba): "PA PA — PA PA PA" over two bars, or you use the three, two clave (clave de son) which is the opposite. But when you start the song in two three, you've got to go from top to bottom. That's the scale. It's like a mason putting up a building and you need the level. That level guides you to have everything square.

There is no limit to what you can write as long as you do it in clave. Let's say you have a piece of cloth and you're making a dress. If you're going to change it, make sure that the design on the seam is right because otherwise it's gonna look terrible. You've got to continue the same idea throughout and develop what you're writing in order to be in clave. Clave is just a measure to keep everything together. Some ears can't tell. I have heard a lot of stuff that sounds bad because it comes in in the wrong spot. It's because they are not following the pattern of the clave.

Sometimes a lot of people do arrangements and they go a little out of clave, and since the clave is two bars, everything has got to be even: you've got four bars, eight bars, sixteen bars, thirty two bars. Once you see five, seven, any odd number, the arrangement has got to be wrong. It has to be wrong because there have to be two bars to a measure. That's the clave. If you have three it's out of clave.

Some guys want to add a riff in the middle of a tune and they'll go out of clave. So they either take out a bar or add one if it's wrong. If it's fifteen, they must make it sixteen or fourteen, but you can't have fifteen bars because the chain doesn't end. It comes up short.

MAMBO AND SALSA—THE DIFFERENCE

The mambo I danced growing up was flashier and included more hand movements. We got that from all the dancers that used to mambo, especially Cuban

The clave is what keeps the music intact so it won't fall apart. It's very important. When you write a figure you've got to make sure it's on clave before you write it.

Pete and Américo. When we performed with the Fania All Stars, Anibal Vázquez did all the stuff he used to do years ago with the mambo. But in salsa, the couples dance together more than in the mambo. In the mambo, you could be dancing with anybody, nobody knew. There wasn't that much physical contact only when you did pirouettes (turns).

The difference to me between the mambo and salsa is that the mambo was more staccato, more pronounced. Mambo was a stable thing, like a machine. That's what I hear in my head. If you hear the records you can notice the mambo was a choppy kind of sound to go with the percussion. There was a lot of hand and leg movement in the mambo. You could stay in one spot and they'd applaud you.

Salsa is more melodic. It's more sustained than in the Mambo Era. The percussion we do with salsa is more of a rhythm pattern for dancing; it's a flowing thing, easier to dance. The tempo is the speed of whatever you're doing. You can have a mambo in the same tempo as a salsa. What is different is that the rhythm is stricter. The mambo flows, but it's stricter than the salsa. Salsa flows more.

I want to be remembered because of the basic formula for salsa that I created with El Tumbao. I also want to be remembered because of what I did with the All Stars which is still alive. It was a very prestigious thing. To be the organizer and have the top musicians follow my leadership... it was like a family. We had a thing and we still have it, which is *compañerismo*. You've got to be companions. This is why Pacheco y Su Tumbao has been around for so many years. One thing I believe is that once you have a formula, you don't change it. First it was Pacheco y su Nuevo Tumbao, then it was Pacheco y su Tumbao, now it's called Pacheco y Su Tumbao Añejo. Añejo means aged, like a good bottle of wine. ∎

Maestros Johnny Pacheco and José Fajardo dueling flutes at the World Trade Center, Battery Park City in New York City

Johnny **Pacheco**

One of my main influences was the Stan Kenton Orchestra, which had a big brass sound. I love that brassy sound. And I was listening to Duke Ellington, Count Basie, the Tommy Dorsey Orchestra, Charley Barnett, Benny Goodman… the big jazz orchestras, swing orchestras. Gene Krupa was my idol, because I am a percussion man. That American influence was very much into my head, plus the Latin. So that's a good combination.

Puen

266 *Tito* **Puente**

Tito te

TITO PUENTE

BORN IN NEW
YORK CITY.
BANDLEADER,
COMPOSER,
ARRANGER,
PERCUSSIONIST,
VIRTUOSO
TIMBALES PLAYER,
MULTI-
INSTRUMENTALIST,
SHOWMAN
EXTRAORDINAIRE,
TITO RECORDED
OVER 100
ALBUMS.

B. APRIL 20, 1923
D. MAY 31, 2000

CHAPTER 28

MY INSPIRATIONS

I consider myself a Puerto Rican because my parents were born in Puerto Rico and my Spanish Harlem neighborhood where I was brought up is Puerto Rican. But what's the difference between American and Puerto Rican? Puerto Rico belongs to the U.S. I served in the war three years, as a veteran for the USA. I feel like a Chinese, Japanese—I go all over the world.

Spanish Harlem, *El Barrio,* was a very poor neighborhood. We grew up with all kinds of Latino and jazz people. There were a lot of bandleaders around the neighborhood, but my influence came from Cuba. In the thirties, we used to get records of Arsenio, Conjunto Rumbavana and Conjunto Kubavana. Casino de la Playa got me into the big band sound. I gained my experience working with the bands I grew up with—Machito, Noro Morales, Orquesta Siboney, Pupi Campos, and José Curbelo.

I played with Machito when I was 13 years old. Macho and Mario Bauzá were great influences on Latin music in this country as far as Latin jazz or modern jazz. They were my mentors. We heard other bands, but I grew up with them more because I was in the neighborhood and part of the band for a long time. I was writing arrangements for them in the forties and fifties, but as the years went by, I experienced more and we got it all together. Everybody reads the books, but you learn the music in the streets—playing with people, jamming out.

One of my main influences was the Stan Kenton Orchestra, which had a big brass sound. I love that brassy sound. And I was listening to Duke Ellington, Count Basie, the Tommy Dorsey Orchestra, Charley Barnett, and Benny Goodman… the big jazz orchestras, the swing orchestras. Gene Krupa was my idol, because I am a percussion man. That American influence was very much in my head, plus the Latin. So that's a good combination. People that really knew the music—Mongo Santamaría, Chano Pozo, Cándido—the great conga players and Cuban musicians that lived in the neighborhood all surrounded me.

We had a lot of Latin jazz going on, but the people responsible for putting the jazz and the Latin together in this country were Dizzy Gillespie with Chano Pozo. They started that influence with *Manteca* and *Tin Tin Deo*. From there, the tradition kept going. Machito did it and Noro Morales was playing it.

Pérez Prado was recording for RCA Victor and he was called the Mambo King. I was playing at the Palladium and swinging like crazy, people were nuts about me. Somebody told them at RCA, "This little guy is hurting our sales. We'd better get rid of him." So they signed me and put me away on a shelf—to stop the competition, to help sell Pérez Prado albums like *Mambo Nº 5, Nº 10, Nº 6… Patricia,* which were all very good. That's the way RCA used to work in them days.

Every week I would go up there, "When are you going to record me?" Then I came in with my boys from uptown, "You'd better record me." And they got scared. They gave me a title, "Here comes Little Caesar." All I know is that I'm here in 1996. They're still putting those albums out. I must be good, huh? There you go, baby, they were too hip. I was playing the good music.

They flipped out in Cuba at a carnival when they heard us. And my piano player was Jewish! Prado's music had a lot of interesting tonalities with the trumpets doing unison highs. The music that I played was more danceable and still is. I cater mostly to good Cuban and Latin dance music.

THE TICO YEARS

I was a Tico artist from the beginning. Most of my albums are on Tico, which had the greatest and still has the greatest catalogue of Latin music. I was a composer, with Morris Levy's publishing and so I introduced Morris Levy to the Tico people. We had our friendship because I played Birdland and a lot of jazz clubs. It was difficult to play in them days because Morris either owned the clubs or the artists, the big jazz artists. I'm talking about Basie, Duke Ellington, guys like that. But my music was so good in the Palladium that he had me playing at Birdland, the Roulette Club and BeBop City—a lot of different places. That's how we got involved.

I don't want to say that I got Morris involved with Latin music, but I was partly responsible for him acknowledging more of the Latin music. That's why he bought Tico Records from George Goldner. Then we went with Morris, who loved Latin music.

I was a king, one of Tico Records' major artists. Many of our artists from Tico were competitors of Fania at the time. Then Fania bought the Tico Records catalogue, the heads of the company got together and my contract was passed over to Fania. I got a nice check to keep my mouth shut, but I was happy with Fania because they were popular.

I didn't record much for Fania, but I recorded some creative albums and they were happy with me. We got along, but I wasn't their top artist. I was one of the boys. They tried to eliminate me and push their artists more. But it doesn't make any difference because you can't supercede a talent. And I was a talented man. I still am. They couldn't keep me down. So I did what I had to do for them—good albums.

At the presentations at Madison Square Garden, they had their Fania All Stars. I wasn't one of them because I felt that I was bigger than the Fania All Stars, but the relationship was good. They paid me well. When the contract was up, I was ready to leave, because I wasn't very happy there either. In Tico Records, I was free to record Lupe or Celia or Ismael Rivera or the big artists that we had. Fania was a young company.

La Lupe was an eccentric individual. There's nobody that sang like her. She was versatile. She sang boleros, guaguancó, guaracha, and joropos from Venezuela, waltzes from Peru, rumbas, bembés. A lot of people have tried to imitate her. It will never happen because I knew her personally. I knew where her talents were. I'm talking as an artist, an arranger, and a composer—her boss. I created that monster and believe me, she was a monster. She was great.

I get asked all the time, "Tito-o-o-o, what do you think about crossover?" I tell 'em, "Crossover? I'm on my way back." Hey, if it's good music, you don't call it crossover. You accept it because it's good, whether it's German, Italian or French. Latin music has always been good. Non-Latinos love it. A lot of young people ask, "Did you just record this?" Nah—That was recorded in the fifties. That's how far advanced I was. Now that the masses are getting hipper and they're opening their ears, they're listening to our music.

Our Latin American music comes from the Caribbean area. Brazil has the samba, Cuba has the guaguancó—all the beautiful rhythms; Puerto Rico has the bomba and the plena, the Dominican Republic has merengue. Haiti has its rhythms; Jamaica has its reggae sound. All that comes from the Caribbean area and is considered Latin music. So it's a combination.

I play Caribbean music—Cuban music, Puerto Rican, Dominican—I play the mambo, the cha cha

cha, and the guaguancó. When I was growing up, my band was playing Cuban music, but I developed a more modern harmonic concept. I always try to base my music on Cuban music because of the clave and the way we play the percussion instruments. I introduce that into all the jazz harmonies. Machito used to do that, too. I was brought up in that era.

Salsa is a condiment of food. It's not even music. That's a word that they use, a terminology for that type of music. I always call it salsa de tomate. Salsa de espaguetti. But the word salsa means sauce.

The Latin American instrumentalists have been getting recognition in the last ten or fifteen years. We're no longer considered street musicians. Our Latino people considered us street musicians, because if you played a percussion instrument like the conga or a bongo or a timbale or a güiro or maracas, you weren't a studied musician. You grew up in a neighborhood and you learned how to play these percussion instruments. I received honorary doctorate degrees from Hunter College, Yale University, and Fordham. They are giving recognition to the percussion, which is very important in our music because that's what people dance to.

Even if you don't understand Spanish, you listen to the rhythm and you get up and dance. The percussive beat is what makes that music danceable.

After professional drummers learn jazz, rock 'n roll or commercial Latin pop music, many find out there's a deeper level to the music. They're not interested in Santería (the African belief system based on nature) because they don't know what those rhythms represent. They're interested in playing 6/8 rhythms. Some travel to Cuba or listen to records and get interested in the syncopation. They want to involve themselves in something more percussive and complicated, particularly the good jazz drummers. But very few people play the cultural tradition of the religion and the roots.

Anybody that plays batá drums, congas or any percussion instrument is involved in the religion. Each rhythm revolves around a saint. The 6/8 rhythms are a deep and beautiful music. You need a lifetime of studying to play those types of instruments. I have a knack for it—I believe in it.

THE TIMBALES SCHOOL

In the old days and in Cuba, the percussion section of the band always played behind everyone. The congas and the bongos were all in the back. The saxophones, trumpets and singer were in the front. I was the first one that started standing up in front of the band. Nobody had done it before. I didn't do it purposely. It happened by accident. I was sitting in the back with the congas and the musicians had to turn around to catch cues. So one of my trumpet players, Jimmy Frisaura, who was my right hand man for forty years, suggested, "Why don't you go up front, Tito? Bring up the timbales and play standing up," and it was easier to give the cues to the band. After I did it, all the other bands started putting the percussion rhythm in the front of the bands. I did it by accident and it kept going.

THE LATIN JAZZ CONNECTION

I am a jazzman and a damned good one because I know jazz. I know the influence and I grew up with the big people in jazz. I was involved and

Salsa is a condiment of food. It's not even music. That's a word that they use, a terminology for that type of music. I always call it salsa de tomate. Salsa de espaguetti. But the word salsa is like a sauce—más salsa que pescao.

played in jazz clubs, but I'm a Latino. I'm a Latin jazz musician.

Throughout the years all the jazz orchestras have tried to play with some Latin feeling in their music. Stan Kenton, Woody Herman, and Duke Ellington all have some tune in their repertoire with a Latin influence. Jazz has a progressive harmonic and melodic concept. But we have the rhythm and the syncopation that makes for the excitement. Latin bands are exciting when they play well together and the rhythm section is there.

All the percussion has contributed to the excitement of jazz. Latino musicians have contributed a lot of our percussive drumming from the culture and the roots of our rhythms. And the marriage, like Dizzy Gillespie used to say, is a very important thing. We have contributed the Latin feeling into jazz music. The jazz musicians can't play Latin the way we play jazz. How do you like that?

Jazz has contributed the modern aspect of harmony and its modern melodic compositions to Latin music. They have a lot of jazz progressive things, maybe more modern than our Latino harmonies. However, the combination of our Latin rhythms with their jazz themes (which people relate to in jazz), causes more excitement in the music.

Any time I work the masses I give my utmost. There may be a young person coming up in the future that can do the same thing I do or better, but I've done it for a long time, and that's why I've built up my reputation.

Everybody thinks, "Oh, I'm gonna put him away." Not a chance. First of all, just by seeing me, they get nervous. It's not that I'm bragging. I'm in a position now that if it happens, I can deal with it. But, when I go on the stage, I don't want people to say, "Ah—because he's Tito Puente, the people

accept him." No. I work hard, I play hard, and I'm laying it down.

Mr. Willy Bobo, my bongo player who passed away, taught me a word—TCOB. Taking Care of Business, okay? When I'm up on the bandstand, I take care of business! I try to give the most that I can creatively to the people so that they can feel my vibrations. I don't fool around up there. Neither do my musicians. They respect me for that, and I respect them because I always have good musicians behind me. And being that I inspire them, they give out the most of their talents and I try to give the most of mine.

The secret to my success is that I try to keep my music *típico* as best as I can, without losing my excitement of the roots and the cultural rhythmic patterns of our music. I give it new harmonies, exciting brass breaks, mambo riffs on the saxophones, thrilling trumpet players, and good dance music that excites the people to really feel it. That's why I always ask, "Did you feel it?" And they scream. That's important, to keep it happy.

I stay up to date. I stay with the young people. I'm a role model to them. There are a lot of progressive bands coming out of Cuba with jazz and Cuban music together. I don't see much in this country. They're playing the same kind of music we've been doing for years, a little better recording technically. Musically, the only record that I heard recently is the Puerto Rican All Stars CD done in Puerto Rico. Excellent arranging, excellent vocals. Other than that, this is mostly a singer's world. You have to be a pretty boy and sing in Spanish. You get a hit record, they play it on the radio, and you last about a year. After that, you're not around anymore.

Tito Puente and trumpet virtuoso Arturo Sandova ham it up and exchange instruments during rehearsal

Tito **Puente**

STAY HIP IN THE CLAVE

When you play the típico music, you can feel it, you can dance it. But if you evolve too much in Latin music, you get away from the roots and culture of it. When you get into the harmonic aspect in progressive music, you lose the authenticity of the music that comes from the bottom—because you are involved with harmonies and dissonance. That doesn't go with our típico music. I'm not talking about corny music. I'm talking about the good Latin dance music, a good rumba, cha cha cha, and son montuno, any of those wonderful Latin dance musics. If you get too modern you get away from our rhythmic roots, the clave, which is very important. If you're not into that you're going to lose that feeling. You have to maintain the montuno tonic with dominant changes to make it Latin.

I'm a dancer. I love dancing. We do not have a lot of young people that know how to dance anymore. They love the music, but they don't know how to dance it the authentic way. If they did, they would love it. When I met my wife, she came up to the Palladium to hear some other band playing. All her friends were good dancers and they used to come up and dance to my music. but she wasn't much of a dancer. So I told her, "Baby, you don't know how to dance because you're not hooked on my music." She learned.

So far, I have 102 albums, but I don't want to stop there. My original albums were recorded so well that on CD they sound even better. After playing for so many years I get great personal satisfaction from knowing that people love our Latin music and it's getting more recognition.

I always advise young people, if you're studying an instrument—trumpet, saxophone, piano, vocals or dancing—stay in the conservatory of music, because we need you to maintain our music at a high level, like the rest of the musics around the world. Just stay hip in the clave. ∎

Tito and Celia Cruz perform at the JVC Jazz Festival in 1996

Louie Ramírez

WHEN I WAS EIGHTEEN OR
NINETEEN I STARTED PLAYING
PROFESSIONALLY WITH JOE
LOCO. HE WAS A BIG NAME,
MORE THAN PUENTE AND ALL
THESE GUYS AND HE DIDN'T
EVEN USE SINGERS. HIS FIRST
BIG HIT WAS *TENDERLY*. THAT
THING SOLD SO MUCH, THE
COMPANY GAVE HIM A
CADILLAC—AND THEY WERE
GANGSTERS. THEY NEVER GIVE
YOU CADILLACS.

Louie **Ramírez**

Louie Ramírez

Louie Ramírez is credited with being the mastermind of Salsa Romántica. Percussionist, bandleader and one of salsa's premier arrangers, he was a bona-fide hit-maker.

b. feb. 24, 1936
d. june 7, 1993

Chapter 29

STARTING OUT

My father was Cuban, but I never really saw him, except in the candy store that he owned. He threw me out. He didn't know me and I was crushed because that was my father. What a drag that was. My Puerto Rican mother beat him up because he wouldn't recognize me.

I studied classical piano as a kid, but according to the teacher, "No one will sponsor a Latino kid in classical music." So I took up orchestration. Most Latin musicians I talk to, and I'm talking big names, say the same thing. At one time or another, they wished they'd gotten into some other kind of music. Especially the guys born here. I've said it myself; I should have been a rhythm & blues or rock musician, where there is a lot of bread. Ours is a minority music so the field is very small making many of us think, "On my level now, if I were an American, I'd be a billionaire."

When I was eighteen or nineteen, I started playing professionally with Joe Loco. He was a big name then, more than Tito Puente and all these guys and he didn't even use singers. His first big hit was *Tenderly*. That thing sold so much the company gave him a Cadillac—and they were gangsters. They never give you Cadillacs.

We toured the United States, five guys, no singing. We played anything on the American scene with just vibes, piano and rhythm. We did an album with Joe Loco playing the classics. We played Chopin in clave, and then we played all the other classical composers in clave. Joe was kind of crooked. He would put "Composer: Chopin and Joe Loco." I mean, when did they ever collaborate? He wanted to do *The Lord's Prayer* and sign it off as Joe Loco and Jesus Christ. That is when I knew, "This guy is really loco. Let me get my money and split."

I became the musical director of the Tito Rodríguez band five years before he died. He was just starting the company TR Records when I recorded with him. It was flattering for me because he put us both on the cover, which he would never do with anyone.

They said he had leukemia, but Tito denied it. On New Year's Eve in the Cheetah Club, he bought us all a drink and made a toast to the New Year. I'm always kidding around and answered, "You know, Tito? I'll toast to the old year, because that's the year I didn't die." I saw his eyes tearing. That's when I knew he was sick.

He was the classiest guy I've ever seen. He was in the car on his way to a gig wearing a blue mohair suit. In the back I saw a pair of pants. He explained, "That's in case these wrinkle." He inspected the shoes of the whole band, and if something wasn't right he'd say, "Oye. What are you, a bum?" His orchestra was precision in motion. I never saw women flopping all over a guy like this guy. He sang boleros and they were crying and screaming. He was dark, kind of Indian-looking. He told me once that down south, the band went into a restaurant and when they served him his steak, they stuck a cigarette in it. He gave the guy a five dollar tip, took his band and left. Everything he did was super-classy.

Shrewd, smart, talented and business-wise, I learned everything from him. He was the first to tell me, "Write your music simple." And his belief was, "I don't want the best band," even though it was, "I want the most popular band."

Louie **Ramírez**

Before Fania, there was a label called Alegre that was formed by this crazy guy named Alberto Santiago (see Ch. 35). But he was so much fun. He paid you a hundred dollars with a check and he'd say, "Lend me fifty," he'd rip the check in half and take half. I played a concert he was promoting, *Juvenile Delinquency versus Latin Music*, and he brought in strippers. We started playing and all these girls came out.

His sessions had no written music, not like the Fania All Stars. They were improvised. After everybody's gig, musicians would come play and that's why they had that spontaneity, that sound. We recorded the Alegre All Stars that way.

Johnny Pacheco was the hit band at Alegre. I wrote a thing called *El Güiro de Macorina*. Johnny recorded it, it hit and we made all kinds of money. I wrote an arrangement for a charanga band. That type of music was coming on strong. Then Pacheco got tired of all this Alegre nonsense and he formed the Fania company with Jerry Masucci.

The All Stars stuff came from Al Santiago. A lot of the things Al did at the beginning were good sound business. But Jerry took it a step further. If it weren't for Jerry Masucci, Ralphy Mercado wouldn't have learned his techniques.

Johnny Pacheco did about three productions a year; I used to do about fourteen or fifteen and was working up to eighteen hours a day. I had a hit tune with Rubén Blades, *Paula C,* and I wanted to go out on the road and have some fun with the Fania All Stars. They wanted to keep me in the studio producing, so Jerry told the promoters I was afraid to fly. I thought it was a joke. Then it really pissed me off and I confronted them, "How did I do all those productions in Puerto Rico? I didn't swim there."

Latin artists weren't used to making much money. I don't remember anyone getting royalties. You got a flat rate. These guys didn't understand that if you're not going to get royalties, you have to make a deal with what you're not going to get, so I said, "Jerry, instead of giving me royalties..." which they couldn't admit they weren't going to do, "...give me a flat rate." So they had to work it that way, under that guise. The other guys didn't do that. But they all became big names and made some money.

At the beginning, there was a conference room where we all met and decided on the music. Pacheco, Jerry, myself and whoever else was producing at that time. We'd sit down with the artists and decide what was best for them. Jerry Masucci was not a musician, but he came up with great concepts. When they got big, the artists themselves decided. After a while, they were making a lot of money and nobody cared. The conference room was for the girls. It was like Rome, it got decadent. Yeah, it got wild. Pacheco would say, "This empire will never fall," with a girl on his lap. You think it will never end, but you're wrong. Everything falls.

ROMANTIC SALSA

We invented romantic salsa. Let me tell you how it started. Joannie Figuerez from K-Tel Records called from California one day, and asked Tito Puente, "I'm tired of people putting women down. Is there any way to convert the romantic songs of the composers of ballads to salsa?" Tito didn't want to accept the work and told her it couldn't be done because of clave. But you can take Beethoven and

> *I had a hit record with Rubén Blades, Paula C, and I wanted to go out on the road and have some fun with the Fania All Stars. They wanted to keep me in the studio producing, so Jerry was telling the promoters I was afraid to fly.*

adapt the clave to it, so I took the job. They said, "You're a genius."

We started singing all those Julio Iglesias tunes, *Todo Se Derrumbó* in salsa. That was us. I met the president of Venezuela through that tune. *Estar Enamorado*, that's us. That's my band, our production. Ray de la Paz sang it. When it took off, everybody got on the bandwagon. We weren't putting women down anymore. Now you told them how much you loved them, how beautiful they are. Forget it, sales went uuuup!

I was the first one to do it, so I make sure it gets written about. I look at it as a business. I didn't think of it, the producer thought of it. I just put it together for her and I got the credit because it's my name and Ray's. I recorded on K-Tel with Ray De La Paz, Jose Alberto "El Canario" and another guy named Piro Allen, who is an evangelist now.

Although a guy who doesn't know music can create a sound in his head and hire an arranger, singers aren't musicians, they don't create. The singers are only worried about their lyrics. A musician is somebody who knows music.

That romantic trend was a big success because women bought it. The ballad singers came out with great lyrics, so the singers gained more stature. They're the leaders of the industry now. But once something hits, everybody copies it. The music is becoming formulaic because the bandleaders are singers. Although a guy who doesn't know music can create a sound in his head and hire an arranger, singers aren't musicians, they don't create. The singers are only worried about their lyrics. A musician is somebody who knows music.

If I'm not working with the band, I'm writing. If I'm not writing, I'm composing. If I'm not composing, I'm producing. When I was with Ray de la Paz, he figured, "I'm doing the singing, so I must be selling the records." When we split, I kept selling

more records. Then he started wondering how come that happened. It was simple. I'm used to producing and picking better tunes, I know my way around radio stations and I'm more political.

I don't understand people that don't want to change. Tradition is laziness. Why should a guy born in the U.S. play the way a guy plays in Cuba? Here we have the influence of jazz drummers, rock drummers, and rhythm 'n blues. There is no way it's gonna be the same. And the music will die if that happens. When musicians say, "Play this way!" I say, "No, no. You play that way."

WHAT YOU WANT? RESPECT!

There comes a time when you've got to take it to a certain level with people in New York. Most people that come here learn two things, "Meee" and "Fuck you!" That's it. When it comes down to it, I don't get messed around with because I take it to that level. Then they cool it, you know, "Louie's crazy. Leave him alone." In Fania, if an artist brought an arrangement and I wanted to change it, I called the arranger. That's the proper way to do it. But you don't offend musicians by stepping on their toes or pulling them out.

Ralph Mercado was using one arranger and giving him too much leeway, so I told Ralphy, "When I record, don't touch my arrangements." His answer was, "I've made a lot of money with that kid. You have to respect the fact that he's my A&R man." My answer was, "He doesn't know that I've forgotten more than he knows." I have seventy-three productions, eighty something bonafide hits. This kid just started.

The best prophet of the future is the past. I've seen all this before. We're not rock 'n rollers, we don't have a Rolls Royce waiting outside for us. So

Vocalist Ray de la Paz at the Palladium in New York City

where does all this ego from? Even the guys that are selling drugs. The guys that look at it as a business are successful. The guys that look at it as an ego thing, the gold chains—they're in jail. It's a business.

MUSICALLY SPEAKING

My band is an aggressive band. I can't play that fluffy stuff because I go to sleep—and we invented it. Aggressive salsa is something else. The musicians that don't know clave and don't feel clave are against it. But the art to this music is to write in clave. That's the skeleton of the music; without your skeleton, you're a blob of meat. You'll just fall. What makes it swing is the clave. Bands like Puente and Eddie Palmieri know it and every time they go somewhere they swing because they know. The guys that don't know won't survive. They make a big splash, then eventually disappear.

When I write an arrangement for salsa, I'm writing mambo. This is the evolution of mambo. All the arrangers write the same way we did it for mambo, except it's the present. Mambo was started by a guy named Arcaño in Cuba, who coined the phrase before Pérez Prado. Then they all started to say, "I invented it, I invented it."

Salsa has definitely become a certain style of music. It's Cuban based. Some Puerto Rican musicians say, "But salsa is ours." I say, bomba and plena are ours, not salsa. That's Cuban, we're playing Cuban music from the fifties. Some musicians don't even know that the basis is Cuban. You've got to remind them. One time an engineer asked me, "When you write an arrangement, is it still mambo or is it salsa?" Let's go back further, is it still *guaguancó* and *guaracha*?

IS SALSA JUST COMMERCIAL MUSIC?

As opposed to being an art form? No, it's an art form. It's valid music and it's good music because the arrangers have kept it that way, because we have a musical competition going. And we really care about what we write. So it's a high type of art.

So, forget about ego, ego is the killer. This is a business. If you can't beat them, join them. Voodoo won't work. They want to say, Louie Ramírez, "El Genio de Salsa," those are the guys with the stickers who stick them on the walls, but I don't believe it. It's strictly a business to me. I'm still living with the money I made with Fania, because I invested it, and that was over sixteen years ago. I don't have to play, I don't have to perform, and I don't have to write. I do it because I like it. ∎

Salsa has definitely become a certain style of music. It's Cuban based. Some Puerto Rican musicians say, "But salsa is ours." I say, bomba and plena are ours, not salsa. That's Cuban, we're playing Cuban music from the fifties.

Louie **Ramírez**

FROM THE TIME MY BROTHER RAY AND I WERE KIDS, WE WERE RELATING MUSICALLY TO BOBBY CRUZ. MY INVOLVEMENT IN THE MUSIC WAS MOTIVATED BY MY DAD'S DESIRE FOR US TO STUDY.... BOBBY WAS BORN FEBRUARY 2, 1938, IN HORMIGUEROS, IN THE MAYAGÜEZ AREA OF PUERTO RICO. FOR A TIME, HIS MOM AND MY MOM WORKED TOGETHER IN A FACTORY SEWING LIFE PRESERVERS.

Richie Ray

&

Richie **Ray**
Bobby **Cruz**

Bobby Cruz

AFTER NEARLY A
DECADE OF
UNPARALLELED
MUSICAL
POPULARITY, THE
DYNAMIC DUO
RICHIE RAY AND
BOBBY CRUZ GAVE
IT ALL UP TO FIND
GOD AND RELIGION.

CHAPTER 30

MUSICAL CHOPS

My full name is Richard Maldonado Morales. I was born in Brooklyn, NY on February 15th, 1945. My mom was from a town called Orocovis, Puerto Rico. She was a housewife, but she also worked very hard as a cleaning lady. My dad is from Manatí, Puerto Rico and he worked almost all of his life for a luggage company cutting the cloth that goes inside of luggage.

They came to New York in the late 1930s or early 1940s, that generation of Puerto Ricans that came looking for a better life and to give their kids a good education. Their whole life was dedicated to children and family.

My dad played the guitar with groups that played at weddings and get-togethers. He never studied, although he had great rhythm. He was a real flashy player and a lot of people liked the way he played. He was not a womanizer, but women liked him, which used to concern my mom. I remember one day he wrote a date on the guitar case with a piece of chalk and it went into a closet forever. He gave it up for her and he dedicated himself to educating us.

In the house there were always rehearsals and records. My dad liked jazz, bebop and Brazilian music. Early on, he got the idea that whatever he could not accomplish, he wanted his sons to accomplish.

My brother's name was Raymond Maldonado. He was a very famous trumpeter and he played with Mongo Santamaría, Ray Barretto, and just about everybody. A friend just gave me a tape where he played with Hector Lavoe. He died an early death at around 33 because of drug use and general self-destruction.

At one point my dad sat us kids down. He asked us if we were interested in music. I was very young so I don't know what possessed me to say, "I would like to study piano." And my brother jumped up and said, "Trumpet." For my seventh birthday, a spanking brand new Wurlitzer Spinet showed up at the house and I think it was a Selmer or a Bach trumpet for my brother on his birthday. Along with the piano came an old Italian gentleman that used to come on Wednesday afternoons to give me piano lessons.

We lived in a brownstone in Brooklyn. While we were asleep, my dad bathe us in Brahms, Beethoven and Mozart through some big speakers. I often think that those months of listening formed my musical head.

Thanks to my dad, we went to a school called Bromley School of Music in Brooklyn, where I learned classical with an introduction to popular music, chords and chord symbols, how to read sheet music and play songs. They had a dance band and we used to sit in with people and play. Then I went to the Brooklyn Conservatory of Music. They had a choir and recitals and I got some good training there. We also attended our regular public school. I went to the High School of the Performing Arts, where they based that series called *Fame*. After that, I spent over a year at Juilliard School of Music.

My entire preparation was as a concert pianist. I had been very protected up to that point. I never played baseball or any sports because early on I knew that I had to protect my fingers. A couple of times I had a spat in school, broke a finger and I had to play the next day. Well, my dad was very strict about us practicing, starting us with half an hour, then an hour, then an hour and a half. By the time I was in college, for a time I was practicing eight hours a day. If we didn't practice we were beaten, either with a belt or with an electric wire. This was the old school, "They'll live through it." We did, although I did spend a lot of years with some difficulties because of this. When I decided I didn't want to be a concert pianist, it didn't go too well. But we're buddies now. He's 85 and we get along well.

I loved Juilliard and I had full academic and music programs. But I felt overpowered by it, a little over my head socially. I got the idea that to be a concert pianist, you have to be weird. You also have to devote so much of your life, you have to pay such a high price to reach that level, that I said, "let me look on the other side." It wasn't because it was easier, because I love practicing, I love the music. "But," I thought, "does that mean that if I want to be on top, I have to be like them?"

THE LATIN SIDE OF THINGS

When I was about 16 I worked with a group called Kako y Su Combo. Kako (Francisco Bastar) was a great timbalero, on the level of Tito Puente. He needed a piano player that could stay right on the beat while he was doing all these wild things on his solo. I had no problem with that, so he liked me. Everything Kako did for his 16-piece band was made up on the spur of the moment, right in front of everybody. And he was great at it. He would call it "El Truco" (the trick). That was great training.

I'm the type of guy that will take somebody aside and pick their brain. So I talked to these musicians more about life than about music. If I thought the classical world was wild, this one was REALLY wild. I asked about women, drinking, about drugs, about everything, all while I was getting some musical experience. After that, my brother was playing with the Sexteto La Playa, so I did a few gigs with them. That was a smaller group, but much better organized.

My two gods were Eddie and Charlie Palmieri. Charlie was the more accomplished pianist, but Eddie had that original thing. I can say, when we were doing the Richie Ray Band, I was always trying to have the rhythm like El Gran Combo, which I really admired. For ideas, I looked towards Eddie Palmieri. Wow, when those guys played... people today have no idea what salsa is. Afterwards, I left the university and bounced around a bit.

ALONG COMES BOBBY CRUZ

From the time my brother Ray and I were kids, we were relating musically to Bobby Cruz. My involvement in the music was motivated by my dad's desire for us to study. Bobby's situation is more what you see every day. His mom and dad got divorced in Puerto Rico, so he, his mother and sister came to the States. They had to deal with the whole welfare situation—the single mother with kids. So Bobby ended up breaking heads on the streets with the gangs. But he was a natural talent, never studied. Born February 2, 1938, in Hormigueros, in the Mayagüez area of Puerto Rico. For a time, his mom and my mom worked together in a factory sewing life preservers. Bobby tells the story that I played a song at school in assembly. I was about 9. He goes home and tells his mom, "This kid at school played some tremendous music." His mom said, "Oh, that's Cristina's son."

Bobby had "Un grupo de segunda," a group that would alternate with the big names. He'd play Latin top forty; the latest hit merengues, cha cha cha, or mambos, so my brother and I would do the transcriptions for him. Since I had studied, he would give me a record and say, "Give me this arrangement." I would hear it and give him the bass part, the guitar part, the trumpet part and then I ended up playing with him, and my brother would end up playing the trumpet.

Bobby tells the story that I played a song at school in assembly. I was about 9. He goes home and tells his mom, "This kid at school played some tremendous music." His mom said, "Oh, that's Cristina's son."

THE BIRTH OF A MUSICAL FORCE

I started working with Bobby when I was about 12, but a lot of life went by before we got together to make the band. After I had been at Juilliard for a couple of years, I bumped into Bobby and then we got together.

My folks had told him, "Richie has gotten away from his classical music and is getting wild on us." Bobby was in a crossroads. He was a talented jeweler and he'd become a partner, but he had all this music inside. So we started talking for days on end and something came over us. We talked so much that all those thoughts became our foundation. We talked about a group that would be not too big, that we'd be able to book easily. I remember Bobby said, "Listen Richie, I've been bouncing around a lot. I've had to break heads on the streets; I've learned a lot about life. With what you know about music, and what I've learned about life, I think we can do something if we get together." He felt that I could hold up the musical end, and he could watch out for all the other stuff.

We slowly started working. He's an ideas guy, he's playing three chess games at once in his mind. He talked his way into an audition to be the rumba band at one of the Catskill hotels. But there was no band—it was just me and him. We didn't even have a car at that time. We took trains and busses. We recruited Joey, Bang Bang, Pellé and his friend Carlos, got a little group together and improvised at the audition. At that time, Bobby played the guitar.

We got our musical foundation working at the Jewish Catskills. We got a lot of old Cuban recordings and between playing a little and partying a lot, we were able to create a musical personality that was to be our group. We took two to three years up there and during that time we were picking out what would be the songs for our first LP.

Fonseca Records was on Smith Street, a block away from my house. Mr. Fonseca was good friends with Bobby. A few people began with him, Bobby Valentín, some *jíbaro* singers and us. Fonseca was a *jíbaro* himself who didn't know from beans, but he would get an idea in his head and he would get behind it. He felt if we wanted to get a record on the radio, let's go. "What've we gotta do? Who have we gotta kill?" We got into payola, we'd meet the DJs and bring them women, whiskey, and drugs. After we got things rolling we started a fan club. At one point we had about 500 people with membership cards and pictures. We'd get the word out and everybody would call and barrage the stations with calls for our songs.

Most of our albums were all our original songs. Since I am a Nuyorican and we were working with a totally Hispanic market, and Bobby had a better command of Spanish, it was up to Bobby to come up with the lyrics. A creative guy, he came up with a lot of word ideas. Some of the ideas came from things in life that would pop up, then we'd say, "Let's write a song about this." Naturally, I would do the technical part of the arranging, but Bobby could get an idea for a song and sing me the intro. He could sing me the mambo or the ending. So he would also get the musical ideas and I could orchestrate them. We really worked together.

Back then, bands used the same musicians all the time. I used to kill those guys, since I could practice 8 hours a day of classical music. I used to come up with a lot of intricate weird stuff and we were able to do it because we rehearsed a lot. So we would rehearse a

Most of our albums were all our original songs. Since I am a Nuyorican and we were working with a totally Hispanic market, and Bobby had a better command of Spanish, it was up to Bobby to come up with the lyrics. A creative guy, he came up with a lot of word ideas.

Richie **Ray**
Bobby **Cruz**

song Bobby and I put together and at rehearsals, it would grow arms and legs and get ironed out.

Today you get a gig and you put a band together for the gig, because who can afford to have a bunch of guys on salary? Today an arrangement is made and taken right to the studio to record. Then everybody learns it the way it came out on the record. But we did it the other way around. That's why when we played it sounded as good as the record.

THE MOVE TO ALEGRE

We recorded five or six records with Fonseca and we were feeling like we were outgrowing him. He couldn't do what we wanted. A guy named Catalino Rolón, who was associated with the Palladium, would book the bands for the Latin dancing. Catalino hooked me up with Alegre and the person that I signed and dealt with was Pancho Cristal. His real name was Morrie Pelsman, a Cuban Jewish fellow, but in the industry he was known as Pancho Cristal. He was the producer and he had a good idea of what could sell. When we recorded he would give us a little input here and there. Pancho instituted the jam sessions at the Village Gate. The stuff that Al Santiago had done with the Alegre All Stars was recorded in the studio. But the Village Gate recordings were done live in concert. And it was all the best singers, the best bandleaders, the best musicians... and you get this homogenization starting to happen. All the musicians started to mesh together and mix ideas.

When Richie Ray and Bobby Cruz came into the story, the Latin picture was a tight situation. You had Tito Puente, Tito Rodríguez, Eddie Palmieri, Machito... monster bands, something tremendous. Those guys could literally blow you away. Joe Cuba, they were six guys, but man, they would take over.

So Bobby and I sat down and systematically, we had to figure out, "OK, how are we going to crack this? How are we going to get anybody to even pay attention to us?" So we started toying around with the idea that we had to be versatile. We're gonna mix things up, we're going to do things that nobody has ever done.

FROM JALA JALA TO FANIA

We had a gig at the Basin Street East. I remember Orquesta Broadway played, then we came on and we noticed that when we played a medium type of rhythm like a *guajira*, or *son montuno*, some people were dancing a step that we had never seen before. It didn't look Latin so we started asking around, and were told, "That's the boogaloo," and it works great with the *son montuno* beat. Where did it come from? Chubby Checker, the guy who invented the twist, invented it and it was a new thing he was pushing. So we jumped on the boogaloo. It was different. We could take *guajira*, add a couple of blues notes, and it became a boogaloo. A few different notes gave it a different feeling, funkier, groovier. We went full speed ahead and recorded a bunch of boogaloos. It caught on so much that everybody jumped on it and even went ahead of us. The biggest boogaloos were *I Like It Like That* by Pete Rodríguez, and *Bang Bang* by Joe Cuba.

We were known for boogaloo, but so were a bunch of other people. So we started fooling around looking for another rhythm. I noticed that El Gran Combo had recorded a rhythm on the cowbell called *jala jala*, invented by Roberto Roena, which was a big hit on Alegre. Tito Puente recorded pretty much the same song and it was also a hit. So we played with that idea, "This is a rhythm we can do something with." And we came up with a concept of

jala jala and boogaloo. Richie Ray is a pianist. So if Richie Ray is going to play *Jala Jala*, then rather than the cowbell, the piano has to announce the rhythm. And that was our smash hit.

While this was going on, Pancho Cristal was doing the descarga at the Village Gate, and all these groups were meshing. And Jerry Masucci had studied at the Police Academy at the same time as Bobby Cruz. After Jerry graduated from the Academy, he decided to become a lawyer. He hooked up with Johnny Pacheco and they started to put the Fania label together. Then they approached me; we had done two or three records with Alegre. When we opened the door with the boogaloo thing, a lot of groups came in. You get Joe Bataan, Joey Pastrana, Johnny Colón, and Willie Colón. Now Jerry had a lot of labels and a new label that he came up with was Vaya, and ours was its first record; we did *Sonido Bestial*. This is possibly our most famous song and to me it's classic salsa with Afro-Cuban rhythm, guaguancó, jazz, classical…all kinds of stuff. That's what eventually developed into salsa.

SALSA Y CONTROL

The name *salsa* was born around Richie Ray and Bobby Cruz. I'll explain how that happened. We were in Venezuela at a radio show with a guy named Fidias Danilo Escalona. He says to us, "Your music. People say I'm crazy, but that music is crazier than I. What is that?" I was weaker in Spanish at that time, so I said, "That's ketchup." I'm explaining to him that our music is like a salad with this sauce. So he turns around and says, "Well, friends, now you know. Richie Ray and Bobby Cruz's music is salsa!"

There's a magazine called *Farándula* owned by Fernando Hevia. In an editorial he called us "The assassins of Latin music," because he felt that we were adulterating Latin music by bringing in all these other elements. But we saw it as a positive. I've always felt that when you combine different cultures together, you get more richness. But there is a lot of traditionalism, *Guaguancó* has to be played in a certain way, and you can't cross the clave.

In Venezuela, when we played the carnivals after that radio interview, everybody would say, "Richie, Bobby, play salsa." Bobbie and I looked at each other and said, "This little word seems like it's going to be big." A record was coming out called *Richie Ray and Bobby Cruz, Los Durísimos*. We called the record label, "Can we include the word *salsa* on the cover?" "We've got 100,000 printed and we can't throw them out," they responded. So we made a big fuss and they finally agreed. In a space where there was nothing, they laid down *Salsa y Control*, then *Richie Ray y Bobby Cruz, Los Durísimos*. You can look back and see that there is no other reference to salsa in our Latin music before that. Then, of course, Masucci jumped on the word. He made a movie called *Salsa*, Izzy Sanabria made a salsa logo, and it went from there. We are not claiming we invented salsa. A lot of people know this story and that it is a fact.

We had a song called *Juan En La Ciudad*. It seemed like this album was not going to happen, because they put out one single and it was so so. They put out another single and it was so so. Some DJ in the boondocks on the island (Puerto Rico), started playing *Juan En La Ciudad*. He would play the song, go to commercial, then play the song again. "Now we'll go to news," then he'd play the song again. He wouldn't make any comment about it, but the only music that was coming out of there was that song. Everybody started calling the station. Next thing you know, other stations are getting called about it and they play the song because they

don't want to be left behind. That became possibly the biggest hit of all times.

Latin music, before the salsa phenomenon, was "legalistic," there was a lot of tradition. I was in the Musicians Union in Manhattan when musicians went there in the afternoons. That's where you'd get gigs. The place was full of cigarette and cigar smoke. They would sit around and talk about *La Clave* and how the rhythm had to be played. And they had certain patterns for the conga and for the bongos. Bobby and I would hang there, but we couldn't really take it too much because there was a big cultural gap. We used to say, "These guys are really big on their tradition." We caught the second half of Elvis, the Beatles, the Rolling Stones, the whole rock 'n roll revolution, so it was inevitable that it had an effect on us.

Salsa music is in a process of going back to the roots. We always look for the roots, which to me is clave, the basic Afro-Cuban clave rhythm and the basis of salsa. Black with Cuban, that is the basis, the foundation. But that is not all. What makes it salsa to me is what we did on top of that, and I'm one of the guys that have been there from the time salsa was born. I'll use chords that were a little more like English pop music. When you hear it, you say, "That is a Spanish song, but there's something about it that's different." It's a pop thing. I remember the chords to *Jala Jala*. When we first come in, the voices are singing about El Gran Combo and Puerto Rico, but it's like a rock 'n roll song, chord-wise. We tried to make it so that the structure of the song was not the same old thing.

SALSA, TRUMPETS, AND CLASSICAL

What could we do to freshen it up? All music has an intro. After you sing for a while, the instruments play a part. When we first started, Herb Alpert and the

Tijuana Brass was big. We've got lots of stuff that has trumpets because my brother was a trumpet player. We have a song called *Danzón Boogaloo* which sounds like something Herb Alpert might have done. We would listen to what was going on in the main market and every once in a while, borrow little ideas. Plus I had the classical background.

Bobby told me one day, "Let's do something classical." We have a song called *Cabo É*. I originally heard it by Celia Cruz sung with a group called Celina y Reutilio. This is not radio music. But I didn't know that. It is religious Santería music for worship. People thought we were into Santería. We had no idea. I just had some records and I liked that stuff. So I took *Cabo É*, which is an eerie African thing and we made a salsa arrangement. Since it was so powerful, I put these majestic trumpets because it talks about *La Reina del Guaguancó*. It sounded like a king or the queen would add these trumpets. We added what the song called for. We had another tune called *Adasa*. At that time there was a lot of talk about a queen and spirits and Changó. People that were into that religion would come to the dances, so we felt, "We're feeding the culture." But we didn't believe. That song had a kind of Arabian, Indian feeling to it, because *Adasa* was the Queen of the Desert. And I was very much into bebop. I would listen to Art Blakey and The Jazz Messengers, Charlie Parker, so I used to borrow little things and put it into the music.

I began in the world of salsa when I ended my education and I still had all this Tchaikovsky and Bach in my mind. On my own, I would have never dared to mess with putting the classical into this pop stuff. We didn't set out to do this. But the combination of me and Bobby with his open mind…well that changed things. The one that became most famous was *Sonido Bestial*, where I put a section of a piece by Chopin. It's a piano study called the *Revolutionary Étude, for Piano in C Minor*, for the left hand of the piano. So smack in the middle of a song comes this classical piano. Right after that comes a jazz part by itself. Nobody had ever done anything like that. The principle was a basis of *guaguancó* because it had to have what we call *mazacote*. *Mazacote* is a good rhythm percolating underneath, then over that, some interesting musical ideas. To me, that's true salsa. Today you get people like Marc Anthony and Ricky Martin and you have all the gringos saying, "Oh, yes, salsa, salsa." But what they're hearing is Latin pop, without an Afro-Cuban basis. It's more R&B, or rock 'n roll or something else. So salsa has become something else that's not salsa.

To me, it wasn't good for our music to stay in one place. But it's also possible to go so far that it stops being what it is. The good stuff is somewhere in the middle. And the good thing about that is where you have our rhythm, our personality, and our Latin culture. But you can't help it today. Our world became small, it became one. All of our cultures are intermixing now.

THE HOLY GOD: THE CLAVE

When we were first starting, it was like you were in the presence of the holy god: The Clave. The clave is the pulse that's behind the music. Some songs begin on the three part, which is: *One, two, three…one, two*. Other songs begin on the two part: *One, two…one, two, three*. Wherever it starts, it has to continue the same way, otherwise it's what they call *montao* (*montado*), it climbs on top of itself. I believe that the clave is so much a part of the DNA of the music, that it really has to be there. Otherwise, it stops being Latin music.

For a while, we tried to do it right, but eventually our musical ideas started to get complex. There are a few places in our music where, whether we want to or not, we'll cross the clave. And I'm sure those guys at the Union spent hours saying, "Did you see? They crossed the clave on such and such a song. They don't know what they're doing." In *Jala Jala*, there is a point where the music comes to a stop. By the time you come in, the clave is backwards from where it's supposed to be. You don't notice it, because everything stops and when you start again, it's backwards, but you don't realize it.

The piano in salsa is a combination—it is partly a musical instrument and partly a percussion instrument. Same with the bass. Each instrument's little patterns have to come into place properly for it to swing. When you play salsa, the clave has to be in place, but it all depends on the musicians being proficient.

The conga is a very difficult instrument. Those who play conga sacrifice their hands on the altar of the conga or they're not going to be very good conga players. The player must first learn the music. Percussion players are constantly jamming to get really polished. It has to become second nature. They have to get calloused; they have to cure the hands. Also a conga player can't be a guy with tuberculosis. He's got to be like a gorilla to beat that thing.

So what will make the music swing? First of all, if it is constructed properly so that the clave is where it should be. Then all the players have to be proficient at playing their patterns. Especially when you get into hard swinging, where you get a lot of soloing, *descarga*. The guys have to be able to last to the end. One of the reasons I do great is because I studied classical piano. I break keys on pianos because I have the muscles developed. If I have to play for a long time on a stiff piano, I can do that, because I have the training. A guy that plays the güiro has to be trained and developed physically. He has to know how to play it well enough so that he can be there for quite a while and not slow down, not lose the timing, because when you start getting tired, the rhythmic pattern doesn't come out the right way and you start to lose the swing. Years of playing creates the ability to dominate that beat and that music.

The faster it is, the softer you have to play. If you try to play real loud and fast, you're going against yourself. So it's not only that the clave be in place, it's also that the pattern be constructed the right way. The most swinging groups are ones that play together all the time, because you grow into each other—"I know where you're going, you know where I'm going and we play off each other." It's a beautiful relationship. While people love spontaneity and descarga, the way you get good music is you break your behind. First you burn your eyebrows practicing, individually and together until it becomes second nature. Only then can you interpret.

From the time we started in 1963 until our religious transition was about 10 to 11 years. Our people love *mano-a-mano*, like a big boxing match. In 1974, there was a contest in Puerto Rico at Roberto Clemente Stadium, to find out who was the *King of Salsa (Rey de la Salsa)*. I didn't want to be involved because there were new groups competing. My feeling was, people always go with the underdog. We were well established, we were doing great. I didn't want to lose out to a newly established band. But the distributors, Pacheco and Masucci insisted.

We had just recorded the album *Jamming Live,* so we came up with this song called *La Safra* where

> *The conga is a very difficult instrument. Those who play conga sacrifice their hands on the altar of the conga or they're not going to be very good conga players.*

Bobby did a song about the harvest of the sugarcane, and it talks about the wagon and the Negro working in the sugar cane plantation (cañaveral). Culturally, everybody could relate to it. We combined that with the rhythmic instruments of the mouth, like the Cuban group called Los Papines. When the song comes in, I would do the bass, "Toot, toot, toot, toot." Then Bobby would come in and sing, "Eh, eh, la safra ya comenzó." He's singing and instead of it being a bass, it's all with the mouth. So we played that song at the contest. Our LP hadn't come out yet so when we did that we blew everybody away. I was a little nervous because Ralphy Levitt's group was really popular and one of their guys had died in an accident and they had a song about him. I thought, "That song about the guy that died might kill us." But the innovative thing of "the mouths" made us the winners of *Los Reyes de la Salsa*. They gave us a big van, bought us uniforms, made us music stands….

IN A TAILSPIN

Along the way, we moved from New York to Puerto Rico. A lot of people criticized us over that, thought we were stepping backwards. While still in New York, we played a dance at a Catholic church at a youth activity. We weren't a Christian band, just a salsa band. While there, we met a girl who was a novice, who had been in a convent and had come to the city to sign some papers. She came over and asked me about the cowbell and I noticed that she was Nuyorican because she spoke Spanish with a strong English accent. Alice was cute, but I thought, "These girls don't do anything." Bobby talked to her about our next gig, and next thing you know, these nuns were in the van going to the other gig with us. It was the Dominican Independence Day and Johnny Ventura was playing with us. Well, we never got to play. A fight broke out. Tables flew, chairs flew, knives, and thank God we got out of there alive with the nuns. We thought, "God punished us for taking these girls to the dance with Johnny Ventura."

But we started a relationship and we would talk on the phone. Months later, Alice decided to leave the convent and she landed in our lap. The first few days, we took a room for her in the St. Georges Hotel. She became like our sister, our friend. "This is the little angel that God gave us." Later on all these things would fall into place. I confided in her my discomfort about winning the contest and concern for poor Ralphy Levitt's group. She told me, "Richie, you're feeling what people see is your success, becoming the Kings of Salsa. But you're still feeling empty, because there's a place in a person's heart that only God can fill. You can have all the money in the world, you can have fame, but if you don't have God, you still have that emptiness." She would always talk to us and we'd say, "Yeah, yeah, Alice."

A few years went by and we traveled all over. Alice made lots of money with us as back-up singer. If she liked a dress or a pair of shoes, she could get them in every color. We wouldn't let her drink with anyone. Only with us. We wouldn't let her do drugs with anybody…but us. We always said, "Our music is our life." We were always either working hard or playing hard. Meantime, I was struggling. I was feeling emptiness. It all started that day at the contest. I was thinking, "I've got a bunch of gold records, all kinds of money, I have five cars, a couple of homes. Maybe I need a relationship. I've never been married, I've never had kids." So I got into a relationship with another girl that liked to sing. Suddenly the girl started backing out until we broke up all together. I lost it. I felt like *Pagliacci* the clown, famous for making everybody laugh, but then he goes home at night and cries because he's empty and miserable.

I tried to get a hold of myself, but in my mind that girl's rejection was killing me. I started drinking more, doing more drugs, acting wilder. Bobby and I had different girls every day. Suddenly for the first time I decided to sacrifice and narrow it down to one, and she rejected me. In addition, we bought a nightclub; we didn't know it, but we inherited the mafia. There were bookkeeping problems, people stealing and we were losing the profits in the club. I was stressed out.

I was spiraling downhill and in the midst of it, I had this experience. I started feeling a presence in my house. Things happened and it opened my mind to the idea that God could be real, that there could be contact between God and me. That He could influence my life. One day, I felt that the presence was talking to me, "Richie, you're thinking about things which are not good. That's not what I want you to do. I love you and I have a plan for your life. I have a new song for you." I didn't react like I was being converted—I thought I was going crazy. In the middle of all this, Alice the nun said, "Richie, there's a house around the corner where they have these services. I'd like you to go with me because I'm curious, but I'm scared."

> *I was spiraling downhill and in the midst of it, I had this experience. I started feeling a presence in my house. Things happened and it opened my mind to the idea that God could be real, that there could be contact between God and me.*

THE ROAD TO REDEMPTION

I went that day and met a bunch of old ladies and one gentleman. That gentleman had been a pop singer and he spoke about how he became a Christian. It was tailor-made because a lot of the things he had thought and felt related to me. It made me feel like I had a problem. "I wish I can have the peace these people have." All of a sudden, this guy says, "Would you like us to pray for you?" So I said, "It can't hurt. I'm not doing so good." All the misery and suffering that I had been feeling for months climaxed at that moment. I started crying. I remember the old ladies saying, "That's OK. It's Jesus. He loves you. Put your life in His hands. He wants to help you. He wants to give you a new life."

I slept really well that night. I didn't know how to pray, but I said, "Hey, if these guys are right, I'm willing to get to know You. If You're there, reveal Yourself to me. Show me. I'm open." And God stepped into my life that night.

The next day, I woke up thinking that all I knew how to do was play salsa, and church people are not into salsa. So I freaked, "I hope nobody knows what happened last night and let's get back to normal." But I did do that prayer, and God was already in the picture. I was becoming very sensitive, "Oh, my God. That is so beautiful. The whole world looks different." And I literally started experiencing what the bible calls, "Being born again." I went to a four-day crusade by an evangelist named Nicky Cruz.

It was a very slow, drawn out process. God put people along the way. Mentors, good Christian people sat with me, explaining things to me. At the time, I was back at the Conservatory of Music of Puerto Rico to study some more, maybe take a position teaching. But I called the school and cancelled. I felt I needed the word of God and I knew it was going to take me a while to take it in.

MAKING MUSIC WITH GOD IN OUR LIVES

Meanwhile, all hell broke loose in my office. Fania thought I went off the deep end. Bobby was pissed off. He was studying Karate and he started breaking doors and walls. He thought I was throwing everything

out the window. I got saved, but I didn't know enough to share it with anyone else. But Bobby was just observing, and after months it started to work on him. Then he started his own search. Bobby's conversion was even more drastic than mine. We're two different personalities. I'm a very cautious person. When Bobby accepted the Lord it was a tremendous change. But he's a straight up-and-down guy. The Lord came and knocked him off his horse.

I didn't know what was going to happen, "Now I'm going to be in some little church in the middle of the island someplace playing a tambourine in the back seat." I could not figure our music together with Christianity. I thought that our music was offensive. Nicky Cruz gave us a little input, and then I remember one day Bobby said to me, "I think we can devote our music, our talent and the gift that we've been given to the service of God." We used to have a song about drinking called *Traigo de Todo*. "*Traigo de todo, caramba, yo traigo de todo. Traigo ron, traigo cerveza. Traigo los discos de Richie Ray. Y lo unico que falta es un poquito de coca-cola.*" There are songs about cheating, adultery, fornication and all kinds of bad things. So we thought, maybe we can sing stuff that would be more positive to people.

From the beginning, we said we don't want to do religious stuff. We don't want to be holier than thou. We love our people, but we want to let them know that it's possible to have a new life in Christ the Lord and still enjoy your salsa and enjoy a good life. God invented salsa. God invented *guaguancó*. Our new way of looking at things brought us persecution because there's a whole element in the church that was very strict and legalistic. So for many years and still today there are a lot of people in the church that think that Richie Ray and Bobby Cruz are of the devil because we play that paganistic salsa music from hell.

We'd dedicated our music to the Lord, but the church rejected us. They thought we were looking for another way to make money. We went to the Iris Chacón Show and told the audience what happened to us. The next day, that's all they talked about on all the christian radio shows, how we went into the Devil's Den. They took it the wrong way. But a friend of ours, a famous evangelist called Yiye Avila, responded, "The Lord has me preaching against the evil that's on TV. But if the Lord sends you to TV to preach, then that's what you've got to do."

Masucci and everybody tried to talk us out of this. When they saw it wouldn't go away, God bless Masucci, he says, "Guys, can you give me some good salsa? If you want to include your message, just don't say God or Jesus too much." He did two great things. One, we started doing Christian salsa, with Fania. That's when that song *Juan En La Ciudad* was born, which has been possibly our best seller of all time. We cannot go anywhere and not play that song.

Two, we wanted to record Christian stuff so we asked Jerry, "Can we start our own little label and do some Christian recording for the church?" He said, "By all means. I'll help you." So we used his credit, all his contacts and he helped us one hundred percent. He even gave us $10,000.00 as an offering, and he's not a Christian. Just before Jerry died, Bobby went to Medellín, Colombia for the Fania All Star Concert, and Bobby was able to pray with him. Masucci reaffirmed his belief and his faith in Jesus Christ. So we know that he's with Jesus up there. The same open mind that helped salsa to be born and grow had an open view about us and we are very grateful to him. We did about 15 Christian salsa albums with Fania. We stopped doing dances, became Pastors, started opening churches—about 70 churches around the world that we've been involved in getting started.

We slowly moved away from the center stage. During that time, salsa evolved to salsa sofisticada, salsa romántica, and then it became salsa erótica. Now you have a mish-mosh of salsa pop. It took a whole different direction. Music is an art and art will always grow arms and legs.

In 1999, José Pabón, a promoter, said, "You are in the four walls of the church and you are well-protected, while the young people are being lost. What do you need to get so we can do a concert?" Bobby and I looked at my wife Angie, and she says, "The guys will be more than happy to do the concert for so much." And José responds, "When do we sign the contract?" It turned out to be a tremendous concert. We did it at the Rubén Rodríguez venue in Bayamón in July, 1999. And it was recorded—we were able to take it to our studio to finish it our own way. It was a live double CD; the record became the benchmark, the standard for live recordings and Universal picked it up. Now we are working on *Disco Número 100,* of our fortieth anniversary concert.

THE THIRTY YEAR MARK

When I first got saved it interrupted our career. I threw away tuxedos and a bunch of stuff. It's been almost thirty years. I understand now that it's a lot simpler than what I had thought and I see that the outward appearance is not that important. At first we refused to play any of our songs. We only played Christian songs. Now we realize that God picked Richie Ray and Bobby Cruz so that we could call people's attention, give them a great concert and let them know that Jesus loves them. Now, we're having a good run. But of course, this business is not easy. You've got to be on top of it. You've got to be good. We're not as young as we used to be. Bobby just had his 65th birthday, but he's singing the same as before because we've been healthy. We don't drink, we don't do drugs anymore. And Bobby works out at the gym four times a week. We have a tour coming up and we're doing a few countries in Europe. I'm having my first piano album with a Christian company.

When we first got saved, we changed the words a lot. Bible stories inspired us. *Juan en La Ciudad* is the story of the prodigal son, a chapter right out of the bible. What we try to do now are real subjects. We have a song now about a lady called Catalina. In our culture, in the small pueblos, everybody is aware of what's going on. So everybody's got their eye on Doña Catalina. Everybody's noticed that she's looking happy. And there's talk that she's got a new love. You get the idea that maybe she was divorced and that now she has a new family and there's a guy too. The thing is that she got saved—now she's in the community of the church and there's people she can relate to. We're trying to do just good music, because we are serious musicians and our conviction is that we're Christian, and that's going to shine through whatever we do.

When we got saved, we purposefully destroyed our salsa because we got saved in a strict atmosphere, *El Pueblo Pentecostal.* Originally they had a very strict, almost primitive outlook on things, "If the music makes you move your foot, you've got to be careful, because before you know it, you'll be having an orgy." But over these thirty years we've understood how to strike a better balance. We want to get back to doing music with the vision that we originally had, with that good beat, great musical ideas and all the variety we always did. So we're getting back to the subject-matter that anybody can relate to. Our belief will shine through, and not in a preachy way. ∎

Pete "El Rodrigue

In the army, I met Eddie Rodríguez. He was playing bongos with a band and he told me, "Why don't you come and sing with the band?" There was a song that Pellín Rodríguez from Puerto Rico sang that said, "El tiempo será testigo de que yo no me equivoco. Si tu piensas que estoy loco, oye bien lo que te digo," and since they knew that number, I sang it.

"Conde"
rí
z

Pete "El Conde" Rodríguez

Born in 1933 in Ponce, Puerto Rico. Sonero-salsa singer, As a Fania All Star, Pete became the perfect combination with Johnny Pacheco, recording memorable hits.

b. Jan. 31, 1933
d. Dec. 2, 2000

Chapter 31

IN SEARCH OF A CULTURAL HERITAGE

As a child, I was too young to realize how Puerto Rican I was. But when I came to New York alone, I became more Puerto Rican. I knew about the roots of Puerto Rico, its earth, its rivers, and the bountiful fish in those rivers. I was there. You find beautiful woods in the United States too, but in Puerto Rico, even in the city, you can hear the birds sing.

My father was a carpenter and my mother wasn't an educated woman, but she found work to clothe me and teach me how to act with different people. Although my father was poor, he used to sing and had a little quartet called Gondolero or Gondolier, like in Venice. I played bongos with my father when I was five years old. He had no trumpets. He had guitars and something that takes the place of a bass, called *marímbula*. It has a hole in the center and steel tongs.

I grew up on the main street of a *barrio* that no longer exists called El Ligao in Ponce, Puerto Rico. But I always say that I come from La Cantera, because that is the place that everybody knows. We used to play dances during the Christmas holidays and the festivities of the Three Kings. There were no computers at that time, so I used my imagination. I felt like an Indian, living with and knowing all the insects and the birds that were around me.

My father got sick with tuberculosis, a disease that was killing everybody during the thirties and forties. I saw my father wither away and there was no antidote, especially in poor places like Puerto Rico. There was a bad depression. When my father was alive, I was learning how to play trumpet, but when he died, there was nobody to pay for my classes. It was a bad time for me because I needed him. He died in 1945, the same year Franklin Delano Roosevelt died. I was about twelve.

My mother had a vision, so she sent me to New York to live with my aunt. The day I arrived, nobody went to pick me up at the airport. They gave me a little note with the address written on it. The taxi driver took me to 100th street between First and Second Avenue. At that time, First Avenue was mostly Italians. You couldn't go on that side because you'd get beaten up by the Italians. That first year was very hard and I remember being beaten up by four black Americans in front of the teacher and the teacher didn't do anything.

I didn't have an overcoat and in 1947 we suffered one of the biggest snowstorms ever. Maybe because I was a little kid, but the mounds of snow on the sidewalk seemed huge and I had to walk from First Avenue to Fifth Avenue to get to school. I forgot about music because I was trying to survive. And I didn't know one word of English. It was very hard, but that didn't stop me.

I rebelled against learning English. That is why I have my accent. I graduated from Patrick Henry High and I studied to be a printer at the New York School of Printing. I used to do four-color process work for magazines and although I was very good in printing, I couldn't get into the union because the union was for white people. Then I was drafted. By that time, I understood a lot of English.

I was inducted into the army in New Jersey. Then I was sent to Fort Campbell, Kentucky. The regular army had uniforms which were baggy and sloppy looking. Then I saw a platoon of paratroopers marching past me in tailored clothes and I said, "Wow, they look sharp. I want to join them." To be accepted as a paratrooper, I had to sign for an additional year.

I wasn't used to the prejudice, but I was young. When I finished basic training, they sent me to Fort

Pete "El Conde" **Rodríguez**

Pete 'El Conde' **Rodríguez**

303

Bennings, Georgia and racism was worse there. You couldn't eat with whites in restaurants. If you went to JC Penney to buy clothes, you couldn't use the bathrooms or the water fountains. So I used to spend most of my time in the Fort. I wouldn't go out in the city because I didn't want to get into trouble. Once, on a three-day pass to New York, I saw a candy store and I hesitated to go in. I thought I was still in the southern part of the United States.

After paratrooper training, I was sent to Fort Bragg, North Carolina. The nearest town was Fayetteville. My Puerto Rican friends were white, so when we got to town on leave, everybody had to go separate ways. I used to cross the train tracks to where the black restaurants were and would eat with the poor blacks. So I decided not to go to Fayetteville either. I was stationed in the southern part of the United States for three years and four months. It was a very trying time for me, because an inferiority complex was creeping into my heart. I was very proud to be a paratrooper, but I was discouraged because of the racism.

In the army, I met Eddie Rodríguez. He was playing bongos with a band and he told me, "Why don't you come and sing with the band?" There was a song that Pellín Rodríguez from Puerto Rico sang that said, "*El tiempo será testigo de que yo no me equivoco. Si tu piensas que estoy loco, oye bien lo que te digo,*" and since they knew that number, I sang it. I was also a good dancer because I used to go to the Palladium during the Mambo craze.

When I got out of the army in 1956, I went back to the Bronx and I looked up Eddie Rodríguez. I started playing drums with his band, the Oriental

My Puerto Rican friends were white, so when we got to town on leave, everybody had to go different ways. I used to cross the train tracks to where the black restaurants were and would eat with the poor blacks.

Cubana, but I wasn't going any place because it was a mediocre band. I decided to leave that band and went with another called Jóvenes Estrellas de Cuba. I sang with them for about three weeks and got fired.

I wasn't what you'd call an experienced singer and I guess they wanted a different style. They wanted a bolero singer, with a different voice. My voice was for a *sonero*. But that didn't get my morale down. I had to take a lot of humiliation, but I kept on. Hector Ceno had a charanga band with violins and flutes, called La Novel. I sang with the band for a while. After that, I started singing in a small cabaret in the Bronx, La Campana. That was in 1959 or 1960.

I was acquiring experience. I listened to a lot of Cuban music, charanga style, so I knew most of the songs. Then, I went to the club Los Panchos. The leader of the band was Johnny Soler, a piano player. I used to sing and play congas, timbales and tumbadoras. Johnny Pacheco was having trouble with his two singers who were Rudy Calzado and Elio Romero. So he went to see me at Los Panchos Club. When Pacheco asked me to join his band, Soler got mad because he didn't want to let me go. There was a show in England called *Broadway Goes Latin*, with Edmundo Ross from Venezuela. So Pacheco said, "I have to go to England to play. We're starting on June 5th." When I started with Pacheco, he was getting famous because he had *El Güiro de Macorina*.

When he came back, they gave the repertoire to Vitín López and me. We used to sing in unison, not duet, unison, the same key. People thought Pacheco's group was going to lose popularity because his other singers were good. But we brought something they didn't have. We were young and we knew how to dance. The people liked the band very much.

Pacheco knew that the charanga fad was disappearing, so in 1964 he decided to reorganize the band. He changed from charanga to conjunto. We played at the World's Fair in the Caribbean Pavilion for six months. From there, we went to Africa. In Africa, some countries liked the charanga and in Abidjan they liked the conjunto sound with trumpets, Sonora Mantancera style.

SALSA'S POPULARITY IN AFRICA

The first bands that went to Africa came from Cuban soil. Since we were playing Cuban music, we became very popular. Even though I wasn't popular in New York, I was popular in Africa. I saw African musicians play folkloric music. Seven drums played together, what a beautiful sound.

When I came back, we made the Sonora conjunto and I signed with Johnny. I left Johnny in 1965 because Monguito, another sonero, came from Cuba and there was friction. He was supposed to be a big hot shot, but he couldn't get along with anybody. Pacheco liked him because he sounded like the singer Miguelito Cuní. He would get the arrangement, and then record it exactly like Miguelito Cuní sang it with the same inspirations. To me, that's copying. But he hit a few numbers and then I guess he got too big for his britches and he left Pacheco.

So Pacheco needed somebody to go to Africa again and he called me. He didn't have anybody else who knew the *típico* style. We went to Abidjan the capital of the Ivory Coast, which was colonized by the French. We played in a big theater. There was a multitude of people there, and they announced, "Le chanteur Pete 'Conde' Rodríguez with *Pilareño*."

And when the music started, everybody rose. The whole audience started clapping. Pacheco said, "Man, I got goose pimples." Me too. That was beautiful.

When I came back from Africa, I recorded a number named *Fania Funche*. I guess they took the Fania name from that song. Fania, Faní-a are the same, only the pronunciation is different. A Cuban group had recorded it in Cuba, but since the music of Cuba was not reaching the US, Pacheco recorded it again. By that time, Pacheco had started Fania Records with Jerry Masucci and he started uniting different bandleaders with their singers. Since I hit with Pacheco, they signed me for the Fania All Stars.

In 1968, Fania played at the Red Garter in the Village. They had Tito Puente, Monguito, and they made a record. I didn't sing much on that album. After we made the movie *Our Latin Thing* at the Cheetah, we went to Puerto Rico and the theaters were packed. Latinos felt this film, this music belonged to them, it spoke about them. At that moment, Pacheco took the leadership of the Fania All Stars. That gave him a lot of prestige.

After that, we went all over the world. We took salsa to the highest peak, to South America and Europe. It got very big for a while. Little by little, from the Cheetah we went to a lot of places we never dreamed of. We played at Yankee Stadium where a multitude of people ran onto the stadium and messed up the grass. Also, Larry Harlow wrote an opera called *Hommy*, which we performed at Carnegie Hall. I continued singing with Pacheco until 1974. But all of a sudden, Fania started losing its push. They started recording jazzy music and some albums didn't make it.

From 1979 to 1980, we had the opportunity to go to Cuba during a cultural festival. We did the album called *The Havana Jam* and we played at Varadero, a beautiful beach resort. I went to Havana not because I liked the Fidel Castro regime, but because I wanted to see my idols before they died. Miguelito Cuní, the singer, and Chappottín, the trumpet player, were still alive and I met them. In fact, they died six months later, one after the other. I met Tito Gómez, the singer from the Riverside Orchestra, who already had white hair. I met a lot of people that I wanted to see, Pello El Afrocán, Irakere, Los Van Van. I don't think I did anything wrong going there and I don't regret it because Cuban music has been a very important influence in salsa.

WHAT HAPPENED TO THE FANIA KINGDOM?

A lot of the musicians were spoiled. There was too much ego. Some of the musicians were a pain in the neck, arrived very late, caused trouble and they got better treatment than guys that were punctual. I think it started going downhill when we went to South America in 1982-83. In Bogotá, there was a mutiny in the audience, because we got to the stadium late. It wasn't our fault, it was due to bad organization. Bogotá is a plateau, at a high altitude and it's very cold, so the people were waiting for hours. They started throwing rocks and damaged the stadium.

When we went to Venezuela, the same thing happened. Now that I think about it, it was like a premonition. Why should it also happen in Venezuela? We had to run like hell, the bass player didn't know where to go, and these guys shouted,

"Huevón, get out of the way." It was as if somebody cast a voodoo curse.

I became independent in 1974, but I still traveled with Fania when they called me to go out of the country. They also included one of the songs I sang, *Catalina La O* in their repertoire and they added trombones to the Fania orchestra. I would sing it in all the concerts because it was a hit. But I got tired of singing the same song every time they called us. Salsa is not explosive like it used to be.

NEW YORK, NEW YORK

I wasn't a singer in Puerto Rico, so I got all my experience in New York. But I used to hear the music of Puerto Rico when I was young, and I kept all that in my memory bank. I knew a lot of romantic songs and all the popular singers of the thirties, forties and fifties. But then I had to learn what was happening in New York, because most of the Puerto Ricans emigrated. It was here where the word *salsa* started. It developed here more than in any other place. Most of the musicians born in different places dream of coming to play in New York. Even the Japanese want to play salsa here, because you have a lot of competition and a lot of creativity in salsa. New York is a central point where everybody gets together. The musicians forget about racism and prejudice and just play together as one. But you have to give a lot of credit to the South Americans that kept salsa going, because they love it, especially in Colombia, Venezuela, Panama, and Peru. ∎

Pete "El Conde" **Rodríguez**

I DESCRIBE MY SALSA AS AGGRESSIVE ROMANTIC. THE AUDIENCE CAN SIT DOWN AND LISTEN TO THE LYRICS AND MUSIC OF VICTOR MANUELLE WHILE THE DANCER CAN FEEL SATISFIED DANCING SOME SWINGING SALSA. I ATTRACT A YOUNG AUDIENCE AND A LARGE PERCENTAGE OF MY FANS ARE FEMALES WHO COME UP AND ASK ME, "WHEN ARE YOU GOING TO IMPROVISE?"

Victor Manue

alle

VICTOR
MANUELLE

ONE OF SALSA'S
TOP YOUNG
SONEROS AND
COMPOSERS,
VICTOR
MANUELLE
PERFORMS
ROMANTIC SALSA
WITH A FIERY
APPROACH.

CHAPTER 32

Victor Manuelle

HONING MY CRAFT

I was born Victor Manuel Rúiz Velázquez on September 27, 1970, in New York City by accident. My mother was pregnant when she left to visit some relatives, and she extended her visit. Then my dad decided to try his luck in New York and started to work there. A year-and-a-half later, my parents went back to Puerto Rico and settled in Isabela. I grew up, developed, studied and began all my musical inclinations in Isabela, on the western coast of Puerto Rico. I belonged to the state-sponsored Young People's Orchestra of Isabela. I played trumpet, but when I was about 14 years old, I started singing, which is what I do professionally.

I was raised in a humble family with a lot of sacrifice. My mother is Juanita Velázquez. My father, Victor Manuel Rúiz was a baker for 30 years and I witnessed to the sacrifice and hard work that a father had to endure to support his children. He didn't have a profession that allowed him to shower us with luxury, but we always had the warmth and love of the family and the sense of responsibility, respect for work, and knowledge that you had to earn what you wanted.

When I entered middle school in Isabela, I started taking music lessons with Professor Rabaza. I started playing trumpet, studying solfege and learning how to read music. Although I never had the opportunity to take singing lessons, I realized I always wanted to sing. It was innate, it became my profession and I have been perfecting ever since.

I was lucky to have a salsa fanatic for a father. I started listening to salsa when I was very young, Hector Lavoe, Cheo Feliciano, the Fania All Stars, Justo Betancourt, and Ismael Rivera. My father's musical taste varied because he also enjoyed Puerto Rican typical music, what we play at Christmas. My dad loved to go caroling (parrandas). When I was old enough to have my own taste, I leaned towards salsa. I loved salsa, I felt fulfilled by it and I started learning about it and studying it unconsciously. I listened to all types of music, but the genre that moved me the most was salsa.

A CHANCE MEETING

I started with a group from my town Isabela when I was about 14 or 15. I belonged to my cousin Ramón's orchestra. He plays trombone and had started a band. I participated in several small local groups before I got out of high school. When I was about 17 or 18, I had the opportunity to meet Gilberto Santa Rosa, who discovered me.

I was at a graduation dance and Gilberto was performing there. Friends from my town, knowing that I like to sing, told Gilberto, "There is a young man who sings and improvises. Ask him to come up and sing." That evening, I had the audacity to climb up on the bandstand and sing with him. We began to improvise and that's when Gilberto first approached me. I then started to work as a professional, but not as a solo artist. The first person that approached me was Andy Montañez's musical director Don Periñon. I recorded two albums with Don Periñon where I shared vocal responsibilities with Luisito Carrión and a singer from Puerto Rico named Miguel Méndez. From that moment on, I had the opportunity to accompany many artists doing *coro*. I was a freelance backup singer doing *coro* work for Cheo Feliciano, Ismael Miranda, Mario Ortiz, Cano Estremera, Rey Ruiz, Puppy Santiago and Domingo Quiñones. From there, Gilberto Santa Rosa introduced me to the people at Sony and in 1993 he produced my first album.

I always admired the soneros, the improvisers. At home, I loved playing the music of the different bands, like the Fania All Stars or Hector Lavoe, and I would challenge myself to invent improvisations that were different from the ones on the album. Later on, when I had the opportunity to belong to budding bands, I started trying to improvise and to do different things that challenged me. I loved it.

When I started my career as lead singer, my dream and my passion became my work. I began searching for my own identity. We all want a "trademark" sound. Something that sets you apart and that the audience knows... you are a salsa artist. When I came on that music scene, our genre was under a lot of criticism: there were many pre-fabricated singers, and there was a need for improvisers. And I thought to myself, "I have the ability to improvise. The Lord granted me that gift which I have cultivated." I thought that I could create a modern salsa in the romantic vein, for the new generation. It could be aggressive and it had to give me the opportunity to show my ability to improvise within those modern arrangements. And that is what we tried to create: a style that I cannot describe as traditional, because it is modern, but that maintains the essence of what traditional salsa is all about from the interpretative angle, with the *coros* and improvisation. It changes to different *coros* within the same song, which gives the singer the opportunity to develop a theme, to improvise. That is what I have tried to retain from traditional salsa: the montuno (vamp) and catchy improvisations so that I have the opportunity as a singer to express what I am feeling at that moment.

My first album, *Justo a Tiempo*, gave me my first shot at getting to be known. My backup singers on that production included top-notch people like Adalberto Santiago, Tito Allen, Tony Vega and numerous talented Puerto Rican musicians and arrangers.

The album was not a resounding success in sales or commercially, but it opened the doors for fans to know that a young man wanted to be heard within that musical genre. From then on, I appeared as a lead singer.

After *Justo a Tiempo* I recorded *Sólo Contigo*, produced by Ramón Sánchez, where for the first time, one of the tunes hit internationally, which was *Apiádate de Mí*. It was a hit in Colombia, it played in Panama, in Santo Domingo and it introduced Victor Manuelle as a salsa singer. That's when my career took off.

SERGIO AND ME

On my third musical production, we established the combination of Sergio George and Victor Manuelle that created the style I'm known for today: an urban, modern salsa. At the same time, we recovered the essence of the traditional improviser; the catchy *coro* phrases, the piano vamps, the conjunto style, mixing it with the modern salsa. With Sergio, we experimented until we found the most appropriate style so that I could showcase my trademark contribution to the genre.

The chemistry emerged immediately, because when we sat down to talk, Sergio had already hit with Marc and India's productions. He was very conscious that my style of interpreting was different from theirs, more of the street improviser, the small town improviser. He knew that he had to create another style with me, and I knew what I wanted as well. I told him, "I like that chorus section," and he then created another vamp, and between the two of us, we created the style of that compact disc. The

I always admired the soneros, the improvisers. At home, I loved playing the music of the different bands, like the Fania All Stars or Hector Lavoe, and I would challenge myself to invent improvisations that were different from the ones on the album.

resulting music was very modern and didn't sound like anything that he was working on to that moment. Sergio contributed a lot to what became my musical style, but I also had a lot of ideas in mind and between the two of us, we produced a very powerful combination.

MY STYLE

In my salsa, I try to create a style that is modern and danceable. My intention is never to imitate the past, because I think I am serving a purpose within this genre. While there are people I admire greatly, I want them to remember me for my own style, for what I am trying to create during this stage and this genre of music that I am living. A salsa that is romantic, aggressive, danceable; a salsa which in spite of its romantic content, is not salsa monga, fluffy salsa or weak salsa, lacking in improvisation or swing; because it contains both without sounding like 60s or 70s salsa, yet retains an essence that the dancer can enjoy.

I describe my salsa as aggressive romantic. The audience can sit down and listen to the lyrics and music of Victor Manuelle while the dancer can feel satisfied dancing some swinging salsa. I attract a young audience and a large percentage of my fans are females who come up and ask me, "When are you going to improvise?" That means that they know that within this musical genre, there is this person who can improvise and stray from the recording and do things they are interested in. They request it.

Improvisation allows me to do many things. Some days, improvising is a little more difficult; other days, it flows with greater ease. But this is a skill that comes pretty naturally to me, it flows from within my talent that the Lord granted me and I work on it every day, perfecting it.

My favorite improvisers are Ismael Rivera, Cheo Feliciano, Justo Betancourt, Hector Lavoe and Chamaco Rivera. I have many favorites and each one for a different reason. Ismael Rivera, for his rhythmic capacity to play with the clave, the phrasing, the way he repeats one word many times in one improvisation with a different and unique charm. Cheo Feliciano for the way he paces himself; for his thoughtfulness and quick wit, for the rhythmic and flavorful renditions. Chamaco Rivera is a streetwise improviser, he is an urban improviser that transmits the urban sentiment of the moment; he embodies the salsa of his times, the urban-ness of the Latino. I like Justo Betancourt for his melodious-ness. He could improvise and he could borrow lyrics from other songs for his improvisation as well as steal melodies and adapt them to what he was singing. From these soneros and many others, I have taken a little from here and there, and I've tried to project it within my own style.

This is a difficult job that demands a lot of responsibility towards the audience. It's not what you see from afar, which is all the glitz of being up on stage. To achieve respect, it's the same as any other profession: it requires sacrifice, a sense of responsibility, and doing what it takes to earn the respect from the fans. I also have a commitment with my culture and my land which is Puerto Rico. If I stick with it, I will earn the support of the people.

I think the Latin market is going through some difficult moments. With regards to our salsa genre, which has evolved through the years, and has gone through these ups-and-downs before and recovered, I think this genre is going to continue to thrive and it is going to continue to be a favorite with audiences everywhere. Newer generations of salseros are going to come and we will have to allow them to interpret and express it the way they see fit. Each generation of salseros, from the 1940s to the 1990s, adapted the music to his generation and added other elements. The goal is to produce quality salsa.

At the time I came on the scene, they were airing some sharp criticism towards the salsa singers: that they weren't prepared, that they didn't know how to sing salsa. You have to study the roots before you can innovate. I felt a personal commitment to know. I have it in my blood. You can talk to me not only about Franky Ruiz and Gilberto Santa Rosa who are from my generation, but also about Hector Lavoe and Ismael Rivera because I know what contributions they each have made to the genre. And I can also talk about Orlando "Cascarita" Guerra who sang with the Casino de la Playa Orchestra in Cuba. In other words, my credibility as a salsa artist comes across in other ways, not just through my performance on stage.

I do not believe that you have to be a sonero/improviser to be an excellent salsa singer. Not all salsa artists are improvisers and they are still great interpreters. Many of them are superstars within our genre. I do believe that the ability to improvise gives me an added edge.

I had the opportunity to share the stage with Oscar D'León at SOBs (Sounds of Brazil) in New York. I was the opening act for Oscar and at the end of my act, I sang an improvisation in which I expressed my admiration for Oscar as an artist and an improviser. Oscar had not gotten there yet, but his musicians told him about it. I stayed to see his show and when he saw me, since he is an improviser, he said, "You were thanking me a moment ago. Now it's my turn to thank you, so please climb up on stage because I want to hear you sing." And that's when we began to improvise back and forth, which is one of the loveliest moments in my life, because one never stops being a fan. At that moment, it was a duel of compliments. I sang about how much I admired him, he answered that he admired my short career. I answered back and that was one of the loveliest experiences I had at the beginning of my career, to sing with Oscar D'León.

One always has a role model and mine was Gilberto Santa Rosa, within my generation, because I was too young to follow the career of Hector Lavoe or Ismael Rivera. Gilberto is the person I admire the most. He has a coherence and an incredible rhythmic sense. He is an example to follow not only musically on stage, but also because of how seriously he has taken his work. He has tapped into the musical taste of this new generation without losing the essence of a good and coherent improvisation. I believe that within this generation, Gilberto is one of this generation's most consistent improvisers. He can stick to a topic, dance around it and find so many beautiful words without losing his way, all with a rhythmic ability that falls within the clave. He knows the genre well and I admire him for that.

I hold a deep respect for the people that opened the doors for us in this genre. When I get up on the bandstand with an Oscar D'León, or a Gilberto Santa Rosa, who have that gift of improvisation, I never go with the intention of competing with their improvisations. When I do it, I do it with a friendly spirit because I believe it is not necessary to get cutthroat. Even though people love these controversies and duels trying to see who is the better improviser, I feel quite satisfied with what I do and I don't feel the need to prove myself to anyone. I only ask the audience to accept my work and understand that I do it with a lot of respect. ■

Photo courtesy of Victor Manuelle

We used to burn and smash the guitars. Every time I went to a rock show, I would see something and I'd bring it back. They loved it 'cause they never went to rock shows. We had smoke, and fire crackers. And at the end of the show, "And now the Fania All Stars." and BOOM! They were big productions.

Jerry Masuc

Jerry **Masucci**

FANIA IS BORN

It all started at a party. I was the divorce lawyer for Johnny Pacheco and he was with Alegre Records at the time. He was unhappy with them and he said, "Let's start a record company." So we became partners. I got the yellow pages out and called a recording studio, an album jacket place and label place, and we made a record. The first album was *Cañonazo*, with Johnny Pacheco. It was a medium success. And then we made another record, and then another record... Then we found new guys. It just grew. All of a sudden... Bingo!

I would say promotion was a major factor in making it happen. First of all, we made two movies. The first one put the artists into another perspective. They went from a stage to a big screen. The second movie we called *Salsa*. It turned the business from a small Spanish record label into a major force. Salsa became important, it became known. They're very talented people, and they also have a backlog of hits. After all, Chubby Checker is still working with one song, *Let's do the Twist*, for thirty years. Most of these guys have many hits under their belt.

We spent lots of money promoting it. We did big concerts and we spent lots in the studio to make sure things were correct. We let the artists experiment, which costs money. You've got guys like Marty Sheller that charge a lot, and we pay them, you know what I mean? And then we also had the good artists.

It was new, it was interesting, it was exciting, and it was fun. It was my first involvement in Latin music, in any kind of music. But I went to school in Mexico and I worked in Havana. I always had a feeling for Latin things. And it all just came together.

THE FIRST FANIA ALL STARS RECORDING

I was on vacation with Symphony Sid in Acapulco, fishing and we got a call from Jack Hooke. He was running concerts at the Red Garter in the Village. There had been an all star group called the Alegre All Stars. So we said, "Why don't we have a Fania All Star night? We have a young company." He said, "That sounds like a good idea." We made some calls, and got the people together. We recorded a two volume set *Live at the Red Garter*.

Except for a few guest stars, we just used everybody we had. The artists were Johnny Pacheco, Willie Colón, Bobby Valentín, I think Hector Lavoe, Larry Harlow, Monguito, and Louie Ramírez. We had guest stars Eddie Palmieri and I think Tito Puente. That's all we had. It was a mediocre success. And we just kept going. (See the Chapter Salsa Is Born.)

YOU GOTTA HAVE A GIMMICK

For the concerts, I used to get all the gimmicks from the Rolling Stones. For Papo Lucca, we had a piano that went up and turned and went down. It was a fake piano at Madison Square Garden. So as Papo was playing, the piano would do a somersault. And we had Hector Lavoe swinging from the rafters, singing, "Mi gente..." And we had Roberto Roena in a cherry picker, playing his bongos.

We used to burn and smash the guitars. Every time I went to a rock show, I would see something I'd bring back. They loved it because they never went to rock shows. We had smoke and fire crackers. And at the climax of the fireworks, "And now the Fania All Stars..." and BOOM! They were big productions.

They had more energy than any group I ever saw. I used to get tired just watching them. But they were the best, all playing together and trying to help and outdo each other. We introduced them one at a time. "And now singing from Puerto Rico or New York…" and then we'd get everybody together and we'd introduce the director, Johnny Pacheco.

All of a sudden the announcer would say, "And now the world's greatest Latin musicians…" POW! The explosion would go off, the smoke would go out, and the place would go totally wild. We had a bass player with no wires going through the audience, and then he'd come back and smash that bass. Forget about it. The best time of our lives.

We used to fight the people off in the bull rings in Venezuela. We had to knock them off the stage. They'd climb up, and we'd have to throw them off. The salsa audience is fantastic. It's like a religion. They live and die by their music.

And then, we'd go collect the money from the promoters, and the guys would say we'd lost money. They used to steal. One time, we went to Curaçao, we did all the shows. A big fat guy took us to his house for dinner and he was supposed to pay the excess baggage, so he drove me and Johnny to the airport. He said, "I'm gonna park my car." He disappeared and left us all stranded.

Usually it wasn't so bad because we generally took care of our own things and Ralphy Mercado usually took care of getting the money. He had that down pretty well. After Yankee Stadium (See Three Concerts, Chapter 48), we worked with Ralphy on all of the gigs.

Hector Lavoe was always late. One time we were going to Caracas and he missed the plane, as usual. That was normal. And then we got to Caracas a day ahead of time. We called him. Coming? No problem, he said. Didn't show up. Then we called all the airlines and tried to figure out all the alternative routes. He didn't show up.

We decided there was no possible way Hector could make the show. So we started, and in the middle of the show he comes running down. He flew to Peru, and from Peru to who knows where. He got there and went on and sang.

The funniest thing was when everybody fought to kick Izzy Sanabria off the stage. We used to have to throw Izzy off physically. And then he'd come up another way and start going on and dancing around. He's a great guy but he's a ham. He was part of the whole thing. Without Izzy it wouldn't be the same. He did a lot for the groups, writing about them.

WILLIE COLÓN

Willie Colón had recorded for Al Santiago, the guy who started Alegre Records. Al was in a studio down the block, called Belltone, and he recorded Willie Colón. But Al didn't have the money to take the tapes out of the studio. Our engineer, Irving Greenbaum called us, "We have some tapes that are pretty good." They sent them over and I thought they were really good. Johnny thought they were really good. We bought the tapes, we signed Willie. Johnny found Hector Lavoe, we put them together and the rest is history.

At the beginning it was fun. The musicians were enthusiastic, young. But with time, they became very difficult. It's normal. As they get bigger and more important, they start to break chops.

We also had our own radio program in the afternoon: *Jerry Masucci presents Salsa*. We used to play whatever we wanted. I just played the records. I wouldn't say it was a monopoly because there were lots of other companies around. It appeared like a monopoly because we had all the hits. But it just

The salsa audience is fantastic. It's like a religion. They live and die by their music.

became too much work. You know when you get burned out? I decided, "That's it!" Take a break.

FANIA WINDS DOWN

We went from 1964 to 1980, that's a long time. What music lasts for 16 years? The same artists… This guy would get mad and he'd quit, and he'd want more money. Then we'd get another one, then they'd want to come back. It was difficult. It was the hardest thing. You have to be willing to work 24 hours a day. You have to be in the office. You have to go to the clubs at night, because that's when they play. It's fun as long as you like the nightlife. But when you get tired of it, it's not fun anymore.

I decided it wasn't worth it any more.

My all-time favorite tune? *Quítate Tu.* That was just a song that happened that first night. It was all ad-libbed.

Larry Harlow found Ismael Miranda. Miranda had a great personality and was very easy to work with. He used to work in a dry cleaning store. So I would call him and say, "We've gotta sing." He'd close the store up.

RUBÉN BLADES

Rubén sent me a letter, a crazy letter. I wish I'd saved it to this day. I received a letter that he was a songwriter, was graduating law school, and he wanted to come to New York to be a singer. Then I think I got a call from Richie Ray and Bobby Cruz who had met him. They said, "You've got to see this guy." I don't remember if I sent him a ticket, but I know he showed up in the office. I also let him stay at a little apartment I had on 79th street.

I gave Rubén a job in the office as a clerk in the mailroom. He had to do it to eat. That was the best job he had at the time, let's put it that way. That was his ticket to New York. He had recorded another album with another company, but it never happened. He had come and gone. Also he had recorded one song with Willie Colón on *The Good,*

the Bad and the Ugly, I think. And he had recorded one song with Larry Harlow. We groomed him and started recording some of his songs with other groups.

We kept pushing him and he kept pushing himself pretty good. He's a bright guy. He's probably the most organized hard worker of all. First I put him with Ray Barretto, and then with Willie Colón. He and Willie started fighting, they didn't want to work together, ever since the beginning. Egos, I guess. And in the final lineup, they broke up.

This is my recollection: I remember having a three hour meeting with them at a Chinese restaurant on 57th St. and fighting with them, telling them, "You've got to get together (or stay together)." I don't remember if it was a get together or stay together.

I paired them together because Hector Lavoe had gone out on his own and I thought Rubén and Willie were the best two. They were young, they were good-looking. Willie was a great producer, and Rubén was a great songwriter and a great singer and it seemed like a normal thing to me. It made sense. No other reason. That was always my thing, putting people together.

I gave Rubén his first chance to be an actor when I made *The Last Fight,* a feature film with Willie Colón. I always thought Rubén was going to be a good actor.

We used all our singers on the background vocals on all our albums. We recorded about fifty albums a year. So it was a lot of work.

Larry Harlow found Ismael Miranda. Miranda had a great personality and was very easy to work with. He used to work in a dry cleaning store. So I would call him and say, "We've gotta sing." He'd close the store up. So he got fired for that. He was very helpful when we made *Our Latin Thing.* He was a very astute kind of business guy. He found locations.

It was always a very up, happy group. It was tough to get them together and they would all bitch. But once they got together, they always had a good time together. Very few internal problems. It was like going back to a high school reunion. ■

Jerry displays the poster of the historic Cheetah concert

IF THE STRUCTURES ARE NOT CORRECT, ONE NEVER REACHES THE CLIMAX IN ANY WORK OF ART. PARTICULARLY MUSIC. IT'S LIKE A RELAY. IT'S NOT A QUESTION OF SOUND ITSELF, BUT OF THAT RHYTHMIC SYNCHRONIZATION AND HAVING THE PROPER MEN ON THOSE POSITIONS. THOSE MINDS ARE SO UNITED THAT THE STRENGTH IS UNBEARABLE. WE STRIVE FOR THAT CLIMAX EVERY NIGHT.

Eddie

Palmie

EDDIE PALMIERI

Born in 1936 in New York City. Bandleader, imaginative pianist, composer, arranger, a musician's musician. Eddie has received seven Grammy Awards and has remained true to his vision.

Chapter 34

LATIN ROOTS

My mother arrived in New York in 1925 when she was about 16 years old. Her parents wanted to get her away from my father who followed her a year later. In 1926, they were married. My mother came prepared as a seamstress from Puerto Rico. My father, an electrician and genius at handicraft, carpentry and plumbing, opened his Bronx Radio Lab with a partner.

I was born in Manhattan. Since my brother Charlie was 9 years older, he was my main influence. We lived at 60 E 112th street, between Madison and Park. The numbers are fresh in my mind. I can remember falling on the stoop of our house when I was a young man. I still have the scar on my forehead to remind me.

We moved to the Bronx when I was five. My dad and my grandparents bought an old candy store from an elderly gentleman and my father made it into a modern luncheonette. It was called El Mambo. I took care of the jukebox, supplying it with hit records, and I carried the soda pop bottles up from the basement. That was my job. I was about 14. He later opened Charlie's Radio Store again, which he kept until he left for California. He repaired radios and TVs.

I left high school before the Dean threw me out and tried night school over at Taft High School. On my first night there my friend Harry Gibbs told me, "Man, your father came and took my momma's TV for a long time. He finally brought it back, he charged a lot of money, and when my momma went to turn the TV on, it blew up." I went into hysterics and I couldn't even tell the teacher my name. I looked to the back of the room and saw another friend, Jimmy Ortiz, reenacting the explosion. I burst into laughter and walked out. Never went back to school, never got my diploma, and from then on, it was the faculty of my music that completed my education.

MUSICAL EDUCATION

I started to play the piano when I was eight. I was able to have great teachers because of my brother, Charlie, but by the time I was 11, Charlie got married. I studied with his teacher, Miss Margaret Bonds, a concert pianist and teacher at Carnegie Recital Halls. She left such an incredible impression on me that I played Chopin and Bach in the recital hall of Carnegie Hall when I was about 12 years old.

Then I met Claudio Saavedra, classical concert pianist and a superb technician at the Brooklyn Conservatory. He put me through trills that very few pianists go through to control muscular movements independent of the arm and independent of each finger. I was preparing to adapt to any technique. It was typical of Cuban music to have their hands spread out where you're using the long flexors, and for playing the piano, the way I was taught is the worst.

By age 13, I didn't want to play the piano any more. I wanted to play timbales. So I started playing timbales with my uncle Chino Gueits (pronounced "Gates") and his *Tropical Soul Band: Chino Gueits y su Alma Tropical*. My first job was in a Mexican club. We worked late nights. When I dozed off, my uncle would smack me on the head, "Come on, get up ya lousy bum!" I'd start playing again, and at the end of the night, he'd pay me a dollar twenty-five, wow! I had a girlfriend, so the next day I'd take her to the movies.

My mother intentionally bought me the heaviest drum case she could find and when I complained I was leaning towards a genuine hernia, she would point out, "See how beautiful your brother looks, all dressed up, not carrying anything?" I realized Mom was right. I got back on the piano when I was 15, and since then, never got off it. Unfortunately, I lost a lot of time. So I'm catching up and enjoying it more than ever.

When I was 15, my brother started recommending me to different orchestras. First I went into a band called Eddie Forestier, then I started with an orchestra called Robertito Santiago and Ray Almo. Then my brother recommended me to Johnny Segui and I played with the Wilito Sanabria band. They recorded the music coming from Cuba before the umbilical cord between the motherland in Cuba and its New York baby got cut.

In that group, there was an old piano and a Cuban guy called Pancho Rompeteclas. Rompeteclas means "break the keys," but he used to kick the keys. Then I came in and because I played hard, I got fired. But it was the best thing that could happen, because my brother recommended me to Vicentico Valdés, one of the greatest singers of Latin music, who was starting a conjunto.

When Vicentico landed with Tito Puente, he had an incredible impact on everyone. Then he went on his own. When the conjunto started, the pianist was Ray Cohen. René Hernández, the pianist of the Machito Orchestra, did the arrangements. They did incredible work together. When Ray Cohen left, I got the job, but the tail end of the orchestra did not have the impact of when they started. I stayed with Vicentico for two years.

My brother recommended me to go with Tito Rodríguez. Tito was from the "Tuxedo Company After Six." He was the most immaculate dresser we ever saw. You always thought he had on a brand

> *My mother intentionally bought me the heaviest drum case she could find and when I complained I was leaning towards a genuine hernia, she would point out, "See how beautiful your brother looks, all dressed up, not carrying anything?"*

new shirt, but it was the way his Japanese wife ironed his clothes. In the daytime, she wet the shirts, wrapped them up in aluminum foil and put them in the refrigerator. She took them out later and ironed them.

The night Tito was going to work, he would shine his own shoes. As soon as he started shining those shoes, his personal character changed drastically. On the bandstand, he didn't care who you were. He could care less for anything but your performance at that moment. That was what he demanded and that's how he behaved throughout his career. Unreal! Yet, he was the greatest típico vocalist, the best típico conjunto that we've ever had, and a swinger.

He thought only of stardom on that stage. I learned by watching him. In the form of dress code, he was my main influence when I started my orchestra. He eventually did ballads and blew everybody away. With a new technique that he utilized from a singer coming out of Cuba, he was able to phrase the music differently, as if he were singing a song rhythmically, and the timbre of his voice was unique. He was the only orchestra leader in our category that ever made money and lived well until his death.

TROMBONES IN SALSA

When I first I started, I grabbed weddings, bar mitzvahs and anything I could get my hands on. What I really wanted was a conjunto: four trumpets and a rhythm section. Cuban style! That's what I loved. But economically, I couldn't pull it off. A friend of mine owned a club called the Tritons. Johnny Pacheco was running these jam sessions on Tuesdays, and when I walked in, I met Barry Rogers. I saw him playing his trombone, and asked, "You know, I play here once in a while. Can I call you?"

I was always working with the rhythm section, and I had a flute player from another orchestra who played with me when there was enough money. Eventually, I had to use two trumpets instead of four. I tried everything I could think of, any combination, just to get jobs.

I met vocalist Ismael Quintana years before while doing an audition. I never forgot his face and when I was starting my Conjunto La Perfecta, I tracked him down. Now I had a vocalist, a rhythm section and a flute player. The flute was hot because of the pachanga. One night, the trombone played without the flute. On another night, when we had the money, the flute and trombone played. And I said, that's the sound!

We had seven men, and what we did for La Perfecta was to add one more trombone, José Rodríguez. When Barry and José got together, it became unique. The two-trombone sound in La Perfecta came about accidentally. In my first album, *La Perfecta,* you hear four trumpets alone in certain selections, and in four other cuts, you hear one flute and one trombone alone. The company kept telling me there was less and less money, so I kept cutting the men. And sure enough I ended up with the sound I wanted.

After 1961, La Perfecta took off. If we played a bad night, one that could cause heartburn and require a dose of Pepto-Bismol, even then, we were on par with any orchestra. But when we were on we reached that spiritual level due to the unification of minds, and there was no one that could even get close to us. It was our greatest musical moment. I was able to reach that musical orgasm with my orchestra mainly because of Barry Rogers, Manny Oquendo and Tommy López, the conga player. They were the original rhythm section in the Vicentito

Valdés Band. We could destroy any band on the scene from 1962 to 1968.

When I changed the band I was looking for a different sound. At that time, I thought I was Rubirosa, Errol Flynn and Charles Boyer all wrapped up in one, but without any dinero. This cannot have any wonderful or healthy results. Everything fell apart. The only thing that saved me was my teacher, Bob Bianco. Since 1965, he's been my personal guru. Every time I have gone through those lows in my mind because of the lack of knowledge of my instrument and my music, I have gone to him and he perks me up again.

On the bandstand, I display anything I want. My ego, anything. The quality of my music speaks for itself and if anyone wants to challenge that, then let's have it out on the bandstand. That's what I say to any orchestra leader that has any contention with me. Because when we play, I'm going to blow him out of there, and it's only because he's not devoted to the sacred structure of the clave. I'm sworn to the structures that guarantee to never fail me. They're always there but one must know how to utilize them, and how to protect them and how to cherish them. It's been very rewarding for me and for my presentations musically. And it can only get better. When I'm off the bandstand, that's a different story.

SACRED STRUCTURES OF THE MUSIC

If the structures are not correct, one never reaches the climax in any work of art. Particularly music. It's like a relay. It's not a question of sound itself, but of that rhythmic synchronization and having the proper men on those positions. Those minds are so united that the strength is unbearable. We strive for that climax every night. So listen for it, 'cause you'll never hear it again. The only thing you can do to these structures, the base that comes from Cuban music, is apply the harmonic approach. The harmonic approach is the overcoat, the arrangement that goes to that composition, which comes from the world of jazz. That's all I do. I utilize jazz phrasings because I comprehend the rhythmical patterns, because I'm a percussionist, and not a frustrated percussionist, because a piano is a percussive instrument. The hammers hit the string. So I use the modern harmonies on top of those visible patterns and the result is unique.

Blacks have been very important to my career. It has to do with the jazz harmonics and jazz phrasing that I utilize. The blacks are weaned on it. When I played at the Palladium on Sundays, it was an all black night and they knew that the only dance band that they got their jollies off on, besides Tito Puente's, was mine. I was their favorite. That comes because of the phrasing and harmonic structures they hear. A rock orchestra can hear it.

I have experimented in different recordings that are respected for their content, but have not been financial hits. One was called *Harlem River Drive*, from 1971, and *Lucumi, Macumba, Voodoo*, recorded for CBS in 1978.

I love variations. I grab a theme and use it in a dance tempo. But I play a piano solo on it, first. Before I record, I doodle with it. Once that arrangement starts, we do the embellishments on it, we start using it harmonically and taking it out so that we let anyone who knows music know that we are thinking music, we're approaching it with the musical thought in mind.

> *The quality of my music speaks for itself and if anyone wants to challenge that, then let's have it out on the bandstand. That's what I say to any orchestra leader that has any contention with me.*

The audience is my enemy. I told Brian Lynch, the trumpet player when we were playing in Canada, "Brian, do you realize that sitting outside is the enemy? We must destroy the enemy!" And sure enough, we get out there and POW! It's the dancer and me.

I have worked very hard on the independence not only of the hands, but also of the fingers. And I have been blessed that I'm left handed. So was my brother. That's where my strength is. And I control that orchestra. Wherever they go, I give them the foundation. The vamps and the form of my playing are the essence of where that orchestra is going.

I compose my own music. I've become a hermit in my own world, only concerned with my music and how I present my orchestra. That has shunned me from other things, but it has fortified me in my main quest, which is "How am I going to excite that audience every time I appear?" When I have the right personnel, I don't miss. There's no guesswork. You're gonna love it one way or another.

EPITAPH

One last thing. I asked Victor Paz, the great trumpet player, "Victor, when I die, and they come over to you to ask you about me, do you think it's going to be a lot of pages? What are you gonna say about me?"

He said, "No, one page. One word. Eddie Palmieri—Complications." ∎

Eddie at Lehman College, Bronx, NY

Santi*Al*

THERE'S A CONTROVERSY ABOUT WHO WAS THE
FIRST BAND TO FEATURE TWO TROMBONES,
EXCLUDING SAXOPHONES AND TRUMPETS.
BARRY ROGERS INSISTED THAT EDDIE
PALMIERI'S WAS THE FIRST TROMBONE BAND,
BUT THE FIRST BAND FEATURING THREE
TROMBONES WAS THE MON RIVERA BAND.
IT WAS MY IDEA TO FORM A TROMBONE BAND.

go

AL SANTIAGO

AN INNOVATOR,
A&R MAN
EXTRAORDINAIRE,
PRODUCER,
PROMOTER,
ARRANGER,
CONDUCTOR AND
MASTER
STORYTELLER, AL
JUMP-STARTED THE
CAREERS OF SALSA
LEGENDS JOHNNY
PACHECO, EDDIE
PALMIERI AND
CHARLIE PALMIERI.

B. FEB. 23, 1932
D. DEC. 9, 1996

CHAPTER 35

"GIVE ME A CHORD AND I'LL TAKE A SOLO

I opened my Casalegre record shop in 1955. We had put out forty-four singles but none of them had hit. We were able to break even on the 78 RPMs and 45s, but we didn't make any money. Alegre Records had no expenses because my retail store paid all the expenses.

In 1959, timbalero Mikey Collazo's brother, Harold, told me, "Ya gotta go to the Tritons. Ya gotta hear Pacheco." The Tritons was a one floor walk-up club in the Bronx and they were presenting a lot of relatively unknown Latin bands. That's the first time I heard Johnny Pacheco's name.

I went to the Tritons and after the first eight bars, I said, "I'm recording this group." I recorded Johnny Pacheco's first five albums.

I was a charanga freak before Pacheco. Pacheco used to play tambores with Dioris Valladares, who was the merengue king. Then he joined Charlie Palmieri, playing either timbales or conga or bongos, and eventually Johnny started to teach himself how to play the flute.

Charlie and Johnny formed a charanga, Orquesta Duboney, but Charlie was into more harmony and a medium tempo and Johnny was into going *embalao* at a very fast tempo. Johnny was also into simplicity and he proved himself to be right. Charlie was into intricate arrangements, counterpoint and harmony. So they split.

This is how the *pachanga* was created. Somebody took out a handkerchief, they invented a dance and the people started following them. It's Johnny's creation. Now Johnny had to give it a name. We called a meeting. I remember most of the people that were there: two people from Southern

Charlie and Johnny formed a charanga, Orquesta Duboney, but Charlie was into more harmony and a medium tempo and Johnny was into embalao, very fast tempo. Johnny was also into simplicity and he proved himself to be right. Charlie was into intricate arrangements, counterpoint and harmony. So they split.

Music Peer International, Jorge Garcia, Peter Rodríguez, Buddy (Rodríguez's manager), Federico Pagani, Charlie, Johnny and myself. We had this meeting with seven or eight people on a weekday afternoon, and the agenda was, what were we going to call this new dance? The famous dance promoter Federico Pagani said, "Let's call this new dance the pachanga." Most people went for *la pachanga*. So I was out-voted. I knew this was going to cause problems for music history.

Cubans have always said the *pachanga* came from Cuba. Cuban Edouardo Davidson, librettist, composer, singer, and genius, recorded a tune called *La Pachanga*, but it was a merengue. A few years later, Davidson, who wrote *La Pachanga* and Johnny Pacheco were at a radio station interview. On live radio, Johnny said, "I guess you have to admit I'm the father of the pachanga." So as talented as Davidson was, he came out of the closet and answered, "If you're the father of the pachanga, I'm the mother."

There's a controversy about who was the first band to feature two trombones, excluding saxophones and trumpets. Barry Rogers insisted that Eddie Palmieri's was the first trombone band, but the first band featuring three trombones was the Mon Rivera Band. It was my idea to form a trombone band. Both Palmieri and Mon were under contract to me at the time so I didn't have to play favorites. Mon Rivera's was Alegre LP catalog number 823. In Eddie's first album, catalog number 817, there's three instrumentations. The instrumentation for the first four numbers was a four-trumpet conjunto. The second instrumentation was four trumpets, a flute and Barry Rogers on the trombone. The third instrumentation was only flute and one trombone. That's the instrumentation Eddie used for his first year or two. When we did Eddie's second album, catalog number 824, he started using two trombones, and three on a couple of tracks.

In 1964, I had finished about 25 albums of the Alegre catalogue. Under the Alegre wing, we had Charlie Palmieri, Eddie Palmieri, Johnny Pacheco, Mon Rivera, Cesar Concepción, Dioris Valladares, Orlando Marín and Willie Rosario. I had ten bands under contract.

My wife thought I was faithful, and I got away with it for twelve years with excuses like, "I'm going to a recording," or "I'm going to a rehearsal." One holiday, she went through the credit card files and found a motel receipt. She told me, "I don't love you anymore." That caused my first manic flight.

After 1964, in one of my manic stages, I went to Puerto Rico and I blew a lot of money. Eddie Palmieri hit on his third album. When Eddie told me he needed $5,000 for a down payment on a house, I didn't have it. A few weeks later he told me, "Tico-Roulette is offering me $5,000 if I sign with them." I tore up his contract and told Eddie, "Go get your five grand."

I cut my nose to spite my face. I let go of one of the hottest artists in town because I didn't have five grand. Eddie was so happy that when he signed with Tico, he told them I had an album in the can. Then he told me, "When you get your bucks together, we'll do an album." I thought, "Let me wait for them to promote the shit out of that album and then we'll put it out." That was a wonderful thing Eddie did.

In the early sixties, Federico Pagani was managing the International Club, one block away from my store. I used to see him get off the subway and walk to the nightclub. Eventually, we became buddies. He encouraged many orchestras to come on my label while he would book the bands. He was some character. He couldn't speak English or Spanish correctly. He couldn't even speak Spanglish correctly.

TICO-ALEGRE

After our four-year association, Federico told me, "There's a price on your head. Tico Records put out a hit on you." Tico was the number one Latin label. They had Machito, Tito Puente and Tito Rodríguez, but we were selling more records. So I went down to Tico Records and introduced myself, "Al Santiago. I heard you were looking for me." The owner, Morris Levy hugs me, he sticks out his hand and says, "You've got balls. I like you." We became friends.

Tico and Alegre were subsidiary labels of Roulette Records. Roulette was the big jazz label. They had Count Basie, Maynard Ferguson, Frankie Lymon and the Teenagers. In the late sixties, when Tico heard I was in trouble for money, they came to me. I sold Alegre Records to Tico and eventually I went to work for them. I sold the company for $75,000. When Tico gave me all that money, all I did was pay my bills. After paying all our debts, my partner and I ended up with $1,500 total. We had $750 each, which is funny because that's what we started the record company with. So my partner, Ned Perlman gave me his $750 and says, "Start another company. If we started Alegre with $750, we've now got $1,500."

That's when I recorded Willie Colón at Beltone. With the initial $1500 I paid the musicians, made labels and took people out to dinner... but I didn't have enough to pay the studio, and they were not going to give me the tapes until I paid them. So I tried to raise the money, but before I did, Irv Greenbaum, who was working there at the time, made Jerry Masucci aware of the music we were recording. Jerry went and bought the tapes from the studio. He paid for them because I owed the studio

In the late sixties, when Tico heard I was in trouble for money, they came to me. I sold Alegre Records to Tico and eventually I went to work for them.

money. Technically, the studio should have made me aware, "Look. You owe the studio X amount of money. If you don't pay the studio by X day, we're going to sell it." But they never went through the formality of it. And you can't sue when you're not in a financial position to sue. Willie knew I didn't have the bucks and Fania was starting to take off so it was to Willie's benefit. I think they redid the record just so they wouldn't have to give me producer credit. Jerry has always tried to make out like I don't exist. He has reissued albums I did and dropped my producer credits. He went around saying that he introduced Hector to Willie. I did that. But I did release a single, a 45-RPM titled *Con Willie Colón Se Baila Mejor* on the Futura label.

Willie and Hector were both hanging around my store. Hector had gotten a couple of tuxedos and had hooked up with Tito Puente through a guardian angel named Francis. So he would sing a couple of numbers with Tito without getting paid. He just did it for the exposure. Francis and I were good friends and that's how I met Lavoe. Anyway, Willie was working in my store. He was very bright and we'd go into the store when it was closed and I'd have him put stock away while I prepared my orders for the next day.

I remember back then Willie had another singer who was on that first 45 RPM I put out. I remember the day I told Hector Lavoe, "Come on, I want to introduce you to somebody that you'll eventually end up singing with." It was at the Caravana Club which Federico Pagani was running. I introduced them and eventually Hector started singing with Willie. That was around 1966. But that's no big deal because I've done this so many times. It wouldn't bother me if it was forgotten and not mentioned. But it bothered me when Masucci claimed credit for it. But that's too gossipy.

Lucho Gatica was very big at that time. A Cuban Sephardic Jew named Pancho Cristal was Gatica's manager, and he was also managing the Cuban flutist José Fajardo. Pancho spoke both languages well, he dressed well and since he was a beer salesman in Cuba, he knew a lot of people in the business. Morris Levy liked him because he was a good salesman, so he offered him a job in public relations.

While I was at the Tico office, I told Levy, "One of our biggest artists, Ismael Rivera, is in jail in Lexington, Kentucky on a drug bust. We should let the authorities know that when he gets out, he's got a job." Suddenly, they were releasing Ismael Rivera on Levy's recognizance. Morris asked me to go for Ismael Rivera. I couldn't because I was running my record shop on the side, so he sent Pancho Cristal. Then Levy told me Pancho was going to be Ismael's producer. And he added, "I want you and Pancho to record the Tico-Alegre All Stars."

Pancho booked the Village Gate for a rehearsal and didn't call me. Morris asked, "You guys can't get along?" I told him, "The guy is a liar, a cheat, and a crook. Either he goes or I go." Now, I was making the hits. I was at the zenith of my producer of the year business. Well, Levy said, "Al, you're going to have to go." I was stunned. I went to work for Musicor Records.

My predecessors were two. Ralph Pérez, who formed Ansonia Records and Gabriel Oller, of SMC Records, who recorded Machito, Tito Puente, Marcelino Guerra, Olga Guillot, Chano Pozo, and Noro Morales in the forties and fifties.

Cuban music is the main inspiration within the New York sound. Salsa is the term that has been in use for the last fifteen years for what we call the Latin New York sound, which is a combination of Africa, Cuba, Puerto Rico and New York, plus the jazz influence.

Gabriel was the first one who recorded the New York sound, but he didn't specialize in it. I specialized in highlighting that authentic Latin rhythm section. In the forties, our bands had trumpet and sax sections. But when the conjunto came in with Puente and Rodríguez, they eliminated saxophones to economize. The bass and piano play the saxophone parts. Then the trumpets do their counterpoint.

WHAT IS SALSA?

Cuban music is the main inspiration within the New York sound. Salsa is the term that has been in use for the last fifteen years for what we call the Latin New York sound, which is a combination of Africa, Cuba, Puerto Rico and New York, plus the jazz influence.

When I was recording, the term salsa did not exist. I put out Charlie's third album, called *Salsa Na' Ma'*, but I didn't go around telling people that I had used the term before because everybody had used the term. Salsa was just another word like groovy or *guajeo* or vamp or montuno. But Izzy Sanabria with his magazine was able to make everyone fall in line with his decision to call our music salsa.

In the sixties, I started putting my name on every label: Produced by Al Santiago. I came up with good experimentations. The three-trombone sound was my idea, the *Saxofobia* was my idea, the Alegre All Star experimentation… weird as hell: flute, trombone and tenor sax… all my ideas. The bandleaders got the credit for a lot of things that were mine because I owned the company. I didn't figure I had to give myself credit. I was making money. But when I sold the record company, I regretted it. Only the musicians know what my contributions are.

I didn't realize that I was contributing to our culture. I didn't realize that I was changing things in music. I did it because I was enjoying what I was doing. And although I recorded mostly up tempos, I recorded a lot of Latin jazz. I did more Latin jazz than anyone probably, with the exception of Machito, as one band.

I liked to innovate. My structure was not to have a structure and just say, "Let's do something." That is why you read those instructions that I gave the arrangers for *Saxofobia*. I said, "I don't want no four bar ideas. I want sixteen bar ideas."

Izzy Sanabria was doing the Alegre All Star cover for *Way Out*. So Izzy made a drawing of the Alegre All Stars with me tied to a rocket like an umbilical chord. I showed it to my mother. She suggested, "Put Al on the moon sleeping with Napoleon's hat." That became my logo. So they sang, "Alberto is always in the moon." Everybody thought I was nuts. So what? It was a lot of fun. In the Indian culture, if you're crazy, people are afraid of you and they respect you. Well, my craziness may have saved my life a couple of times.

In 1973, '74 and '75, Casalegre was burglarized and I was behind on my taxes. So they were going to put a lock on my door. I sold the store and paid off all my debts. I walked away from the store after twenty years with two dollars in my pocket. Two bucks. But I don't regret it all. I could have died when I was thirty-nine because I never thought I would reach forty anyway. I've traveled, I've had plenty of women, I've eaten in good restaurants, I've stayed in great hotels. I've had a wonderful time. ■

At 14 I made my first album with Mario Ortiz's band. When I joined Tommy Olivencia's band during my third professional experience, Elias López, one of Puerto Rico's top trumpet players, took me by the hand. He said, "Try to look for the roots." Then I became a fan of the roots of our music. Roots are roots, but it is essential for the tree to grow and to blossom.

Gilber

Sant

Ro

GILBERTO SANTA ROSA

BORN IN 1962 IN
SANTURCE, PUERTO RICO,
GILBERTO IS CONSIDERED
ONE OF THE BEST
CONTEMPORARY SONEROS.
"EL CABALLERO DE LA
SALSA" (THE GENTLEMAN
OF SALSA) PERFORMED
WITH THE WILLIE
ROSARIO ORCHESTRA
FOR FIVE YEARS.

CHAPTER 36

Gilberto Santa Rosa

THE LEGACY

In Puerto Rico, the orchestras were television personalities, in particular Orquesta Panamericana with bandleader Lito Peña and El Gran Combo de Puerto Rico, my number one source of inspiration. Tito Rodríguez also had a television program where he presented Vicentico Valdés, Machito and Tito Puente. That was my first introduction to the music. I was four or five.

At home we listened to plenty of music, but there was a certain preference towards El Gran Combo. During those years Tito Rodríguez was singing *boleros* and my mom was crazy about him.

I took my first musical steps as a fan in the mid-seventies during the salsa boom that came out of New York, during the revolution Rubén Blades originated. My influence came from all the Fania people, the singers that formed the New York cast of performers. Later on, I learned that Cheo Feliciano had started out with Joe Cuba and that Ismael Rivera came from Cortijo Y Su Combo.

At 14 I made my first album with Mario Ortiz's band. When I joined Tommy Olivencia's band during my third professional experience, Elias López, one of Puerto Rico's top trumpet players, took me by the hand. He said, "Try to look for the roots." Then I became a fan of the roots of our music. Roots are roots, but it is essential for the tree to grow and to blossom.

I consider myself a sonero. It gives me a lot of satisfaction to do inspirations. The first thing I discovered was my ability to express an idea in rhyme, rhythmically. That is what sets salsa singers apart from other singers. Later, I started developing the malice to attack the vamp, to do something interesting with the montuno (the call and response section). Then it dawned on me, "I've got to respect

Gilberto **Santa Rosa**

the theme." When I started out, I was too wordy and the message didn't come across. I'd say an inspiration that could be funny, but no one laughed. Luckily I surrounded myself with people that knew the genre and they gave me advice. I think I am a good student.

I felt very comfortable singing in Willy Rosario's Orchestra. That's where I got the opportunity to mature. Any singer that joins Willy's band finds ample schooling to polish his act. That was the first band where they gave me the opportunity to sing a ballad. In Willy's orchestra, everybody had to give their best. You couldn't perform below the standard set by the group. Those of us who sang had to improvise a lot. I sang with Willy for five years.

Willy got his training during the mambo era of the fifties. He's a big fan of Tito Puente, Machito, Tito Rodríguez, and all of that movement. Although his band consists of four trumpets and a baritone, the sound is big band style, the arrangements are very aggressive. We recorded many versions of tunes that were hits in the fifties.

Physically speaking, my voice has changed. My interpretation has also matured. I am no longer singing or performing the same music that I did with Willy, but I try to strike a balance. The salsa we do is essentially romantic. We don't do erotic salsa because I don't feel comfortable singing erotic songs. Nevertheless, we try to keep the spark, the essence of the music. Now and then, we do a tune with more aggressive arrangements, seventies style. I have the ability to do a coherent and intelligent inspiration and I have the rhythm in my favor.

I am pretty traditional in the way I produce music, but I believe in evolution. And I do not like an arrangement that is overloaded, where the message is lost because there is too much music; like a suit

Gilberto and Cheo Feliciano exchange soneos at the Sonero Concert, Madison Square Garden

Gilberto **Santa Rosa**

that fits too tight or too loose. I am neither a musician nor an arranger, but I've surrounded myself with people that understand my line of thinking and know how to translate that into music. Simplicity has its purpose, as do complex things.

Songs play a very interesting psychological game. Since most people don't sing or produce records, we end up saying what they would like to say. I like to verbalize what many people want to say.

I am the product of salsa directly. For me, to talk about salsa is as natural as it is for maestro Tito Puente to talk about mambo. When I was born, this music was already called salsa. I understand that it is a commercial name for the rhythm we play. Cuba left its roots. In time, the rest of the countries added their touch. That is why the name is meaningful, because everybody tacked on their spices. The essence of the word has served its purpose.

It is easier to tell a Japanese person he's listening to salsa when he is listening to a Caribbean rhythm than to explain, "That is a son montuno, this is a cha cha cha, this is a mambo, this is a guaracha…"

I was born in a barrio in Puerto Rico. I spent my childhood in a small village. It was a very happy, musical village. That to me is positive. I understand that our music is popular music, but we don't have to equate what is popular with negative things. It is not right to blame the barrio for crime and drug problems and then turn around and blame the music.

This is basically dance music. Wherever you hear a drumbeat, which is the essence of it all, people's feet are going to move. People ask, "Why do the singers have to dance?" Because dancing is a natural reaction, a natural response from the body. Latin Jazz is a listening genre. You listen, but when you ask a jazz soloist to improvise on top of a mambo, your feet are going to move.

When I started my band, people didn't know me. Singer Frankie Ruíz had a hit song in the salsa world with *Desnúdate Mujer*. A promoter contracted me for a carnival in Puerto Rico and all afternoon long he was asking me to sing *Desnúdate Mujer*. From his table he made signs to me, "When are you gonna sing my song?" "It's coming right up," I said. He had hired me because he thought I was that singer. After the gig, I told him I was not Frankie Ruíz.

I consider myself a privileged person because I have had the opportunity to share the stage with almost all the people I admire in my field. It is beautiful to see how life gives you that opportunity. The album I recorded with Cheo Feliciano is a reward. I was also able to share music with Ismael Rivera, Pellín Rodríguez, Andy Montañez, Yayo el Indio, Tito Puente and Charlie Palmieri. It's a great feeling to have performed with those legendary artists and now to be a bandleader making my own contributions to the genre. ∎

I am the product of salsa directly. For me, to talk about salsa is as natural as it is for maestro Tito Puente to talk about mambo. When I was born, this music was already called salsa.

Shel

In the forties and early fifties, a lot of jazz musicians, feeling that they weren't being appreciated properly here in their own country, migrated and there was a big jazz community in Europe. The music started to be appreciated. In Europe the musicians were considered musicians, not jazz musicians or Latin musicians, but musicians. And if you were a virtuoso or at the top of your field, you were ranked with the top in the field of classical music. And they all came back telling the stories of how wonderful it was.

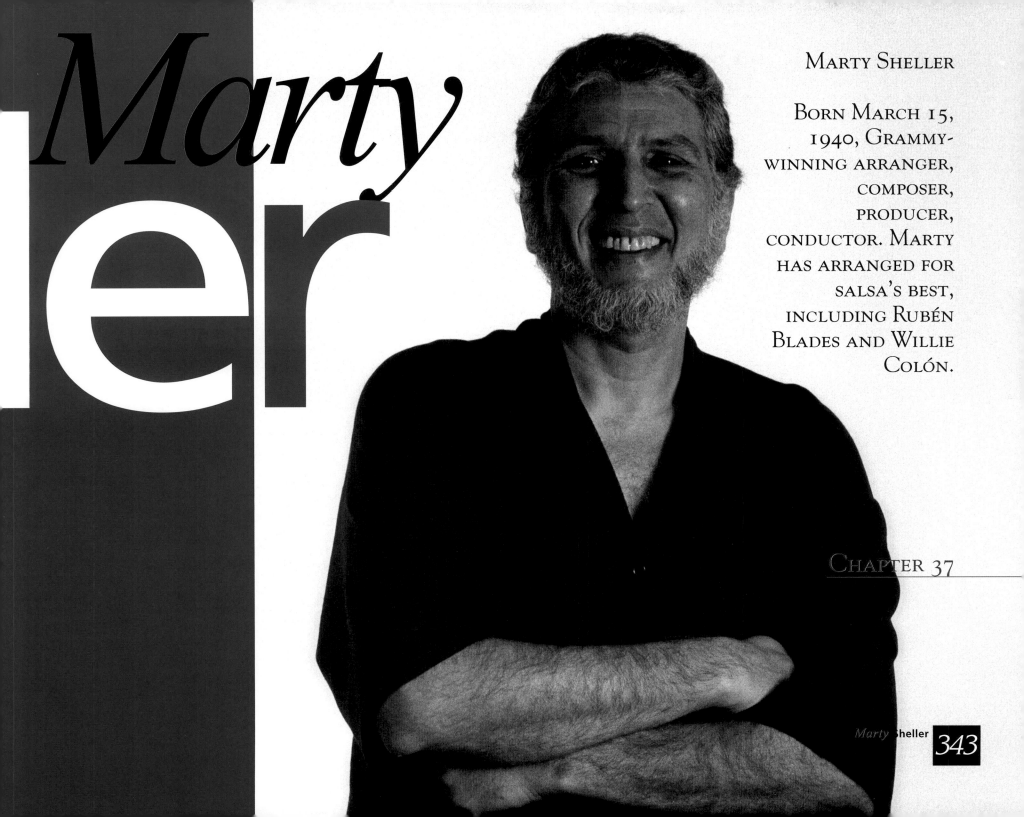

Marty
ler

MARTY SHELLER

BORN MARCH 15, 1940, GRAMMY-WINNING ARRANGER, COMPOSER, PRODUCER, CONDUCTOR. MARTY HAS ARRANGED FOR SALSA'S BEST, INCLUDING RUBÉN BLADES AND WILLIE COLÓN.

CHAPTER 37

SALSA REVISITED

The key to appreciating music: Don't judge music by what it's not. Judge it by what it is. Don't say, "But it doesn't fall on the one!" Don't judge it by that because those guys are swinging the hell out of the music.

Salsa music is like jazz used to be in the 1940s and 1950s before it gained a measure of respectability. Jazz is being taught in colleges now and musicians have a lot of work all over the world. And the same is beginning to happen with salsa. People want to find out about the music. For at least ten years now, salsa musicians have been coming back from tours in Japan and Europe saying that there is more interest and knowledge about the music there than here.

In the 1940s and early 50s, a lot of jazz musicians migrated because they felt they weren't appreciated properly here in their own country, and there was a big jazz community in Europe. In Europe the musicians were considered musicians, not jazz musicians or Latin musicians, but musicians. And if you were a virtuoso or at the top of your field, you were ranked with the top in the field of classical music. And musicians all came back telling the stories of how wonderful it was.

That same kind of interest that happened with jazz twenty, thirty years ago is now happening with salsa music. Right now there is as much interest in salsa as there is in jazz in European countries. Racism has a lot to do with it. Jazz was considered music of black people. The white establishment used it if they found famous white players playing that kind of style. Now, since jazz has gained more respectability, the next lower rung on the ladder are the Latinos.

"It's unsophisticated," you hear things like that. Some of the most rhythmically sophisticated music in the world is Latin music based on African rhythms. And when musicians who have no knowledge of that are made aware of it, you can see it in their eyes. I've seen that in many people's faces when I've explained some of the complexities of the rhythm. All of a sudden it's not considered what it was before.

I've always been involved with bands, either as a trumpet player or as an arranger. I also do arrangements for a lot of the bands like Mongo Santamaría's or Tito Puente's band that are playing a combination of jazz and Latin music. My own personal taste is in a jazz context. Because of my interest in that area, I started doing a lot of work in salsa music and built a career on it without setting out to do so. Most of my work is in that field.

I'm originally from Newark, New Jersey. I came into New York in 1957 to go to school. The Musicians Union at that time was located in the Roseland Ballroom on 52nd street and 8th Avenue. Every Monday and especially Wednesday and Friday from noon till 3 PM, musicians went to try to get work. I was a trumpet player at the time and there were a lot of Latin bands that exclusively used trumpets. Now you'll find trombones and saxes.

At the Union, the jazz musicians congregated where you first walked in. The Latin musicians congregated to the right of them, and in the middle which was the main ballroom floor, were what we called the Morrises and the Irvings. These are the guys who did the weddings and bar mitzvahs and the club dates. They had been booked for months in advance. The Latin musicians and the jazz musicians were trying to get a gig for Friday night.

As a result of my hanging out in the jazz area, especially on Fridays, I'd find bandleaders who needed musicians for that night, Saturday or Sunday night. And very often the word traveled across into the jazz section that somebody needed a trumpet player. I was brought up in the strictly American musical scene where the only Latin music I heard was at a wedding where they played a rhumba, the *Miami Beach Rhumba*, or a club date song. I had no concept of what authentic Latin music was. So I was really taken in by it.

The first band I started playing with was Louie Ramírez. Through Louie, I met Frankie Malabé, who was playing conga with the band. They introduced me to the different records. And that was the greatest introduction because these guys really knew. Since I was interested in jazz, Louie Ramírez gave me a couple of records by Cachao.

The bass player Cachao had done some Cuban jam session records. On these albums, the producers had gathered the best jazz-oriented Cuban musicians, put them in a jam session setting, provided a basic structure and said, "Okay, we're gonna play this song." Everybody knew that song. Then they gave out the solos, discussed the basic structure, how they would start, who would come in when. That was very easy to pick up on.

What intrigued me was that Frankie Malabé kept giving me records that were very strongly rhythmically influenced. I thought I knew what was going on, no problem. Each step of the way was a little more sophisticated, until the most sophisticated rhythmically are the African drum records with the bata drums, because there are a lot of rhythms that are going on top of each other. That's how I found out about *guaguancó* records and African records with the batá drums.

The first time Frankie played me one of those records, I felt like a little kid, back to square one. Where's the one? There's nobody saying "One, two, three, four, boom, tapa tapa tapa, boom." It wasn't like that at all. It's a learning experience.

What Frankie did with me was really great. He would sit and put his hands on my knees and say, "I'm gonna play what this drummer is playing." He would play what it is, and behind that I could hear what he was doing. Then he'd say, "The other guy is playing this." And where's the one, Frankie? "It's right here." Well, it finally fits in and then you say, how could I not have heard that? I was very lucky to be introduced to the music by those two very knowledgeable guys.

After a while, the word started to spread about an American trumpet player who could sight-read and solo. Then I met a couple of the guys playing in Mongo's band at the time. They needed a trumpet player. I joined Mongo's band in 1962.

SECRETS OF THE MUSIC

When you're first learning you tend to be swept away by the rhythms. In American music, the bass is always playing on the beat. One, two, three, four, boom, boom, boom, boom. So the one, the first note of the bar is always heard. In Latin music, it's not heard, it's one two, three four, one, poom poom — poom poom, and there's a big open space on the one.

They would give a cue for us to come in and I was so used to hearing a different kind of bass pattern that I would not hear where that ONE was. In order to play your part right you've got to know where the first beat of the measure is. A couple of

The first time Frankie played me one of those records, I felt like a little kid, back to square one. Where's the one? There's nobody saying "One, two, three, four, boom, tapa tapa tapa, boom." It wasn't like that at all. It's a learning experience.

times I was shocked by it, but by the end of the night I realized what was happening and I reached the conclusion that it's okay for the bass not to play on the ONE, and that there's a nice groove to the way it falls.

The trumpet parts are written the same as parts in a jazz band. In a jazz context, the solos usually have more chord changes, whereas in a Latin band, often the solos are based on a four bar, two bar, or an eight bar pattern that is just repeated over and over. The variety is more in the rhythmic end. That's why I got very interested in Latin jazz, because there you've got the combination. You have the rhythmic complexity of the Latin music, but you're playing jazz-based songs with jazz chord changes.

What they call the New York Sound is a much more rugged and ferocious approach. It's hard to say that any group of instruments constitute the New York sound. Now you find trombones in a lot of orchestras, but there's mixtures of trumpets and trombones.

MUSICAL INNOVATIONS

There are no rules. There's no saying you can't do this, you can't do that, because somebody is going to do it, and then it's monkey see, monkey do. Somebody gets a hit using a certain style, the other company says, yeah, let's do something like that.

In the 1960s, when the Beatles were really popular, the bass guitar came into prominence. Latin musicians used what they called the baby bass. It was an upright bass but much slimmer. Since it was electric, you plugged it in so the bass could be heard. Up until that time, bass players played wooden acoustic basses and would take the house mike and put it down in the bottom. So if the guy taps his foot, you also hear boom, boom, boom.

Latin musicians felt you shouldn't use electric bass. It was for rock 'n roll, it wasn't right for salsa music—until Eddie "Guagua" Rivera appeared. He was a young Latino brought up in New York, but he loved rock music. He learned the bass guitar first, and then started to learn the upright bass. But his real love was the bass guitar in rock 'n roll. As he got to be 16 or 17, he got interested in Latin music. His first job was with Charlie Palmieri. Charlie showed him the ropes. All of a sudden people started talking, "Did you hear this bass player? He's playing the bass guitar." Now in all the Latin bands it's all bass guitar.

Barry Rogers was a trombone player who played with Eddie Palmieri in the 1960s when I was working with Mongo's band. Barry was an old friend of mine. I remember people saying, "Trombone? In salsa?" Barry was the first in Eddie Palmieri's band to make people aware of the fact that trombone was possible in Latin music. Willie Colón, who's known for the New York sound, was trained as a trumpet player, but picked up the trombone because he was so knocked out with what he heard from Barry Rogers.

What they call the New York Sound is a much more rugged and ferocious approach. It's hard to say that any group of instruments constitute the New York sound. Now you find trombones in a lot of orchestras, but there's mixtures of trumpets and trombones. The bands in Puerto Rico and in Miami are playing the same kind of music. It is difficult to listen to one of their records and say, "That was recorded in Puerto Rico," or "That was recorded in New York."

THE FANIA LEGACY

Fania started very simply. Jerry Masucci was an Italian lawyer who studied law in Mexico City, learned to speak Spanish and liked the music. When he came to New York, he went around the club scene because he enjoyed the music, with the idea of doing something business-wise. Then he met Johnny Pacheco. Jerry was the lawyer and the money behind it, and Johnny was the musician and the artistic director. The first album they did was a classic album. At that time, the *charanga* bands were very popular in New York.

The first band in New York that was popular with that style was Charlie Palmieri's with Johnny Pacheco playing flute. This opportunity came up, so Johnny made his own album. I remember it very well, because the cover was an all yellow cover with a black stick figure, like a round head of a guy playing a flute. It sold like crazy and Fania Records began because there was enough money to do another album with Johnny Pacheco and to sign another artist. I think it was Larry Harlow. He did an album and it hit.

The first person I worked for at Fania was Larry Harlow. He was one of the original artists that was signed with the company and I did some arrangements for him. As they signed more artists I started doing more. That's how I started. Fania Records made it because they had the right people together at the right time, in the right place. They got a group of arrangers who were doing arranging for different groups: Louie Cruz, Louie Ramírez and myself.

Hommy was an opera style like *Tommy* but about the Latin world. I think it was the first concept album done in Latin music where there was a theme that ran through the whole record. After that, Willie Colón and Rubén did *Maestra Vida*, an album which had a theme. But Harlow's *Hommy* was like an All Star event, with Celia Cruz and different singers each playing a role. I did a few arrangements.

After the arrangements were done, I was given the job of writing interludes because they wanted music to go on constantly. They wanted music that would lead from the end of one song into the beginning of the next song. Louie Ramírez did an arrangement and at the end of his arrangement I had thirty seconds of music to compose and arrange that went from the key and mood of the end of that arrangement, and led into the key and mood of the next arrangement.

In every arrangement that I do, there's usually one part, whether it's one chord or one bar or one section, that I personally will sit back, listen to and say, "Yeah, that's the one I liked." So what I enjoyed about the Harlow project was writing those interludes.

Willie Colón, one of the first ones to sign on, was a 16 or 17 year old kid with a hit band from the Bronx. Willie did his own arranging when he started his band. When there's a hit record, a record company wants to get another record out there, and it took Willie a long time to write all the parts out. So Masucci suggested, "Let me hook you up with a good musician that you can just tell what you want. That'll save you a whole bunch of time." That's how I first met him.

Even though he was a teenager and a big hit, he never got that big a head. He was always interested in hearing new things. He told me the first two arrangements part by part. "Give this to the bass. Give this to the trombone and we're going to harmonize like this." During the course of those arrangements, we became pretty friendly. The third one was not quite as complete. He had the ideas together, but he wasn't quite sure and I offered some possibilities. I could see in his eyes the way he reacted, "Can you show me what that is?"

Now, I'm a sucker for that, because that's the way I learned. I was trained formally as a trumpet player, not as an arranger. Whatever I learned as an arranger was by trial and error and by asking questions. To this day, if I hear a piano player play something that I like, but can't duplicate, I'm not embarrassed to walk over and say, "Could you show me?" I'll get a pencil and paper and write five lines quick and write down the notes. So I feel an obligation to return that to younger people.

When I saw Willie was interested in what I was saying, that started a musical relationship. He started learning and picking up very fast. At the same time, his musical scope was expanding. He was listening to Brazilian music and other kinds of music, not strictly salsa. That's how his music started to change. I was a witness to it. He caught hell from the company. They did not support him and you can quote me on this, even if Jerry Masucci gets bugged.

When Willie decided to make an album with different music and instrumentation, he got the standard, "You've got a hit combination with the two trombone sound. Don't change anything."

RUBÉN BLADES

Rubén came to this country as an unknown in the musical field. He was a lawyer in Panama and wanted to get into the music business. He came to New York when Fania was hot, worked as a stock boy carrying records around. He introduced himself to me and told me he'd listened to a lot of things I'd done, that he had some songs he'd composed and would Mongo be interested? Most of his songs were lyrics, but he had some that might be good.

When a talent like that gives you a cassette tape and you listen to it, you say, "Wow, he sings great, he composes great, he played guitar on it. He's obviously a good musician. Let's record one of his songs." Then somebody said, "Forget about

recording his song. Let's use him in the band." He was a singer in Ray Barretto's band. Ray hooked him up. When Hector Lavoe left Willie Colón's band, Willie needed a singer and there was Rubén.

Willie had a reputation as a really swinging band, but most of the songs were the standard thing, "Let's swing, we can dance all night. We can groove and party. Me and you, baby." When Rubén came on the scene the level went up because Rubén is a very socially conscious guy, and his writing material fits perfectly within the musical context that Willie's band was into. So now you've got the best of both worlds. You've got a really swinging band with a terrific singer, which they had with Hector Lavoe, but with some songs that are much more significant, and have a lot more meat to them, lyrically and poetically. It was a terrific combination.

He and Rubén were the first guys to start using synthesizers in Latin music. Rubén caught hell in the same way. He was one of their main artists and you would think that he should get all the encouragement, but he didn't. He has the best revenge now, because he's got hit records and a great reputation doing exactly what he wants or pretty close to it.

But when you have two very strong musical personalities that work out, it's not going to last forever. Because of the way they are, they're always looking for a different thing. Rubén felt that it was time to move on. Although he didn't realize it at the time, that was the beginning of Willie's new career as a vocalist. He always had a good voice, but never considered being a lead singer. After Rubén left, Willie decided he was going to give it a shot. Again he caught hell, "Don't do anything different." And when you're dealing with creative people, that's not their nature. Their nature is to change everything.

Both of them are politically conscious. Willie told me he made a conscious effort to avoid that kind of thing because he didn't want to alienate people. Rubén had some bad experiences. I love him for it. He wrote a song called *Tiburón*, or Shark, and it was the story of a shark swimming in the Caribbean, eating up all these little things. It was a story about the United States and their Latin American policy. He went to do a concert in Miami, where there is a big Cuban population. Among that population, you say one word against the United States and you're a communist.

He did the concert and did that song. The next day, nobody played his records on the radio stations there. And the records were not being sold in the stores. That did not make him stop what he was doing. Rubén was more political.

Willie saw those kinds of things and he didn't want to go up against that. But as he got older and matured a bit, it got to the point of him saying, "I've got some things to say." They may not be as overtly political, but it's the same kind of approach.

WHAT IS SALSA?

Salsa is what Tito Puente said, "It's ketchup." Salsa is a name that was given to music that was basically Cuban music played by the original people who came here, and it was done strictly Cuban style. That's the nature of immigration. People go to a country and want to hear some of their music. When they make enough money to be able to afford it, they bring some of the bands over.

The influence of jazz and the Cuban style merged along with popular music, and arrangers arranging American style big bands as opposed to Latin started to change the music. In the fifties they called it Latin music. As the influences started to change the music, the younger generation needed a way of making it different. The word salsa came about and they hooked on to it. A lot of the older musicians rebelled against it. "Do these young punks think they created something new? It's Cuban music. All they did was to put a little jazz on top of it."

It was Cuban-based music. The youngsters growing up in this country are listening to New York radio that has everything from rock 'n roll to jazz to salsa. And young people don't want to hear what their parents heard. When they start playing and arranging, their influences are not the same as the original music from the old country. So the parents say, "That's not the real music. That's a bastardized version."

The reason I had problems with that kind of thought is that they are judging things by what it's not. It's not Cuban, it's not this or that… Well judge it for what it is. That's how the name got popular. It's not as closely aligned to the original Cuban music as it used to be.

When you listen to the most modern of the salsa bands, if you take out everything except the drummers, leave the timbales, leave the conga, leave the bongos, they're playing basically the same thing that you hear in records from the 1930s or 1940s. It's not that different rhythmically. It's different harmonically and melodically. Instead of having the traditional kinds of melodies, they're influenced by American music. Harmonically as well.

Nowadays a lot of the bands are adding synthesizers. They have a piano player and another keyboard player to play the strings parts. When you have string parts, it's not the standard Latin style strings. It's the American style, a big lush string section playing beautiful chords.

A lot of the older musicians rebelled against it. "Do these young punks think they created something new? It's Cuban music. All they did was to put a little jazz on top of it."

The only time violins were used in salsa music, in swinging up-tempo music, were in the *charanga* bands, the violin and flute bands. In those bands the violin took on the role of the piano. They were playing very rhythmic and simple harmonies. In a jazz group, you usually hear the piano player play chord style. In a Latin band, it's melodic in the sense that it's following a chord pattern, but it's a very rhythmic kind of an approach.

POINTERS FROM AN ARRANGER

The best arrangements come from people who do their homework. They come to me with definite ideas of what they want. They suggest solos, maybe a trombone solo at this point or a musical part that goes in this direction so that we can go to here. A lot of times people ask me to do an arrangement and give me total freedom. Those come out good too. But the most satisfying musically had a lot of input on the part of the musician.

Willie Colón and Rubén Blades, in the salsa field, are well prepared. When they give an arranger a piece of music, they give you a cassette of the song and then get together with you to discuss it. Usually they have a very good idea of what they want. They may have musical ideas suggesting a certain kind of bass line. Rubén plays guitar very well, so he plays and sings the tune for you. That makes it very easy because you hear the vocalist, the key it's going to be done in, and the approach. Even though Willie is a trombone player, he plays enough piano to come up with certain ideas. Then it's your job to "put the meat on top of the bones."

Few people take the time to make sure that it's the right song for them. Lyrically, it should say what they want and melodically it should be the song they want. They next need to figure out the ideas they want on it, and get the right arranger who can express those ideas musically.

It's very difficult for an artist to produce him or herself. Willie and Rubén are among the few who have done it well. Most of the time you need somebody to say, "I don't think that's the right song for you."

But record companies don't want to pay a producer, and if they do, it's so small they can't get somebody who's qualified to do it. So they get the piano player in the band, or someone who's a good musician, and they put him in charge. At least there won't be any wrong notes on the tape. But there's a lot more to it. Suppose you pick a certain song, and someone says, "When it gets to this point, even though it's a mambo, we should go into a samba. That'll really work, I can hear it." Willie has said things like that. And those special things make people go back and listen again. ∎

Patato Valdés

I MADE A FILM WITH BRIDGET BARDOT CALLED GOD CREATED WOMAN. I CHOREOGRAPHED THE DANCE FOR HER. I REHEARSED HER IN PARIS. IN THE MOVIE SHE WORE A LEOTARD, BUT I REHEARSED HER IN THE NUDE IN VADIM'S STUDIO. IN THE SCENE SHE TAKES A BATH AND I AM PLAYING IN THE BACKGROUND.

PATATO VALDÉS

BORN IN HAVANA, CUBA, NOV. 4, 1926. THIS BEETHOVEN OF THE CONGA IS AT HIS BEST WHEN HIS INSTINCTIVE CREATIVITY IS GIVEN FREE REIGN. A FEW NAMES BEAR WITNESS TO HIS VARIED CAREER: ERROLL GARNER, HERBIE MANN, AND SEX GODDESS BRIGITTE BARDOT.

CHAPTER 38

THE CUBAN POTATO CHIP

I learned to play the tres from my father, who played in the Sexteto Habanero. I learned to play the tres with him. I played the bass and I was a dancer and a boxer. When I was 12, I started playing the *marímbula*, a wooden box that began as an old bass. I played drums on two cans of ham. My dad taught me to play with a banjo. He removed the arm and he played rumba on the skin. Then I made a wooden box that had a hole on the side, and I put the guitar strings inside the box. It was made of mahogany, cedar and white pine.

I used to play and dance in street carnivals with a conga drum hanging from my waist. I was already crazy. I always I had my tres guitar and my conga, till the day a piano arrived. The first one that came was Arsenio Rodríguez's and he hired pianist Lino Frías in the conjunto. So they replaced the tres with the piano.

In jest, they'd call me "El Niño Rivera," alluding to the father of the tres guitar players. He was the most modern tres player, tres players today play like him. I had some of his ways and never realized it. After I saw the real El Niño, I never wanted to play tres again. Then I took up the conga.

I joined La Sonora Matancera at the same time as Bienvenido Granda and Lino Frías, when Valentín Cané was director. Pedro Knight, who later married Celia, had just joined. Calixto Leicea was first trumpet and Pedro was second. La Sonora always had two trumpets, but they sounded like three.

I went with Celia when she was entertaining at parties for the Popular Socialists. We played at the parks and buildings. We used to sing at the Fausto Theater, where the mambo dance originated in Cuba. Celia Cruz and Olga Guillot sang. Celia sang without a microphone. She would enter from the back, "Mi capu de tamarindo..." I would jump up at the sound of the rumba dances, with the quinto (conga), to accompany the dancers. I was eighteen.

From La Sonora I went to Conjunto Kubavana. We worked at the Zombie Club where I taught quite a few *rumberas* (women that dance rumba) how to dance. With Conjunto Casino, I invented the penguin dance. I was supposed to come to New York in 1947, but my father wouldn't sign my permission to leave. Chano Pozo came to New York in my place.

I played one conga as if they were two, then I started with two. I use three, four or five congas and I tune them like a bass: G, B flat, C, F, D. That is a harmony of notes (acorde). When the bass takes a solo, I am the bassist. Now everyone plays the tuning I invented. People used to tune to the piano and bass. When the timbale, conga and bongo play swinging rhythmic phrasings, it is called *masacote*. Percussion in true Latin music is the conga drum, timbale, bongo and bass.

I played with Machito from 1956 to 1959. Then I joined Herbie Mann and his Afro-Cuban Jazz group for nine years. Herbie Mann and Johnny Ray entered my name in the Encyclopedia of Jazz. I've recorded with Dizzy Gillespie, Quincy Jones and Billy Eckstein. In 1958, I went to Africa with Billy and my group called Afrojazziac with Herbie Mann. I played a number called *Cuban Potato Chip*. I also recorded *Monday Night at the Village Gate* with Herbie Mann.

SO YOU READ MUSIC

I can't even read the Saturday funnies. I know the notes by ear and through the tres guitar. There were 22 tunes in *Los Rituales del Diablo* with Lenny Rich. He'd show me, "Patato, let's start here." And I couldn't read. I'd lock myself in the bathroom and listen to the rehearsal. "Where's Patato?" I always pretended I was reading, because otherwise, they'd replace me with someone who could. But I was adding what wasn't there. When he realized it, Lenny asked, "You reading the chart?" No. Then he said, "Put it on the floor, motherfucker."

My hearing is extremely good. When it's cold, the sound is like a crystal glass. But humidity kills the tone of the conga. In our music, it's all about percussion—without it you ain't got nothing. Tito Puente's playing sounds like horses leaving the gate. Tito tunes, sees me playing, then looks at me out of the corner of his eye. I speak through the congas. I go, "Say... pih pih, I want you to catch my drift. I'm not going to say it twice. You hear me? Ki ki. Kan kan kan kan kan kan? Kan kan ki kan ki ki kin. Kan Kan?" My drums sing. One ahead, the other behind.

THE MARIO BAUZA CONNECTION

I played with Mario Bauzá and Graciela most. I also played in *Quitate Tu Pa' Ponerme Yo* with Fania at the Cheetah, but they edited me out.

I have not stopped playing and hopefully never will. It has given me the elixir of youth. If I get too old to play, I'll die. During concert solos, I climb up on the congas, dance on the congas, throw myself on the floor and dance.

I made a film with Bridget Bardot called *God Created Woman*. I choreographed the dance for her. I rehearsed her in Paris. In the movie she wore a leotard, but I rehearsed her in the nude in Vadim's studio. In the scene she takes a bath and I am playing in the background. Then she goes out to weigh herself in a towel and there are five drums.

I love the impossible. If it can't be done, I like it. It is more delicious to me like that. I'm gonna win you over, even if you don't want me to. ∎

My goal was to be a band leader. After Joe Quijano, I played trumpet with Willie Rosario and Charlie Palmieri. I learned arranging on my own, I studied bass on my own and I played bass with Ray Barretto when he did the charanga. I formed my group at the end of 1965, as a trumpet player. When I moved to Puerto Rico in 1969, it was hard for me to find a bass player. I always liked the bass, so I switched. I hung up my trumpet and haven't played it since.

Bobby **Valent**

ín

Born in Puerto Rico in 1941. Bassist, arranger, bandleader, Fania All Star. He founded Bronco Records in 1975, and continues to tour with the Fania All Stars when they get together.

Chapter 39

AN ARRANGER AT HEART

I was born in Puerto Rico in a village called Orocovis on June 9, 1941. My mother, Carmen Fred, died when I was around six. She worked in the school cafeterias of Puerto Rico. My father, Albertano Valentín, was a farmer and played the typical Puerto Rican cuatro as a hobby. That is where I inherited my little music thing. He died eleven years ago.

I started playing guitar at seven. When we had visitors in the house, my father would wake me up and say, "Come down and play guitar with me." He used to give me a nickel and I would play guitar. Then I'd fall asleep on top of my guitar.

In those years, I listened to Trio San Juan, Johnny Rodríguez and his Trio, boleros, trio music and typical music from Puerto Rico. I moved to Coamo and started to play trumpet when I was about ten. In Puerto Rico, we had Cortijo y Su Combo, Orquesta Panamericana and my friend had Machito, Tito Rodríguez, Tito Puente and all those big band records from New York City. I started to like tropical dance music.

In 1956, I moved to New York. I studied with teachers and read a lot of books. I started going to the Palladium. I used to stand right in front of the bandstand till 3, 4 o'clock in the morning. Professionally, I began playing trumpet in Joe Quijano's group in 1958-59. Then I started to write music.

I worked as a trumpet player with Tito Rodríguez for about a year in 1963. I learned discipline, how to direct, how to nicely tell a musician, "Play like this, be on time, dress neatly." I applied what I learned. People say he was a dictator, but you have to be that way in order to be somebody in the future.

My goal was to be a bandleader. After Joe Quijano, I played trumpet with Willie Rosario and Charlie Palmieri. I learned arranging and I studied bass on my own. I played bass with Ray Barretto when he did *charanga*. I formed my group at the end of 1965, as a trumpet player. When I moved to Puerto Rico in 1969, it was hard for me to find a bass player and since I always liked the bass, I switched. I hung up my trumpet and haven't played it since.

My type of arranging was Latin and jazz. As the years went on, I got into more danceable music. I returned to Puerto Rico and started a record company. It was the greatest thing that could have happened to me.

I met Johnny Pacheco in 1960 when he was recording with Alegre Records. When he switched from *charanga* to *conjunto*, I did some of the first arrangements. I did a lot of writing for Pacheco. He had Monguito and Chivirico Dávila singing. I recorded my first album with Fonseca Records, the same label as Richie Ray and Bobby Cruz. My second album was on Fania in 1965.

I became part of the Fania All Stars in 1970 and I recorded with them for ten years. During the first recording, I played trumpet. In Puerto Rico, I got a call from Jerry Masucci when he was recording the second album. He said I had to stay in New York for at least two months. On the second recording at the Cheetah, I was a bass player.

Pacheco had the music for the Cheetah concert a week before the show, but the music wasn't right for that type of concert. Pacheco didn't like it, I didn't like it, a lot of people didn't like it. We needed more excitement, so we changed all the music in two days. Pacheco and I stayed up all night till 4 or 5 o'clock in the morning writing for the All Stars. He would throw some ideas, I would throw some ideas, if we liked them, we wrote them down. It was nice.

That recording and that Cheetah concert are still alive in me. They introduced everybody, even the recording engineer, then Jerry told Pacheco, "You forgot Bobby." That's when he said, "Oh, my God." Then he mentioned my name. The people that bought the music say it is the best thing that ever happened in music. After that, when I walked down the street, people would stop me to say, "Eh, Pacheco forgot you." Good things happened afterwards.

HE'S GOT STYLE

The first arrangement I did was *El Sordo* for Roberto Roena, which became a big hit. I did *Bemba Colorá* and *Toro Mata* for Celia Cruz, *Anacaona* for Cheo, I did *Quítate Tu* and I composed music and lyrics of *La Contraria* for Larry Harlow and Ismael Miranda. I left the Fania All Stars because I went into the record business to become a businessman and a musician. When I started my group, I would play flugelhorn as a lead instrument for certain beautiful phrases. My group included trombone, tenor sax, baritone, a percussion section, one singer, and me on trumpet. The coro was done by the musicians. I was one of the first to introduce the baritone sax into Latin music.

I created my own style. That is why I do my own writing. Eddie Palmieri writes his own things, so do Barretto and Pacheco. I learned from Pacheco who used to get music from Los Guaracheros de Oriente. I used to get a lot of old music from Colombia and típico groups Puerto Rico. I'd listen to the melody and words, then I would put it in my own style of writing. A lot of people thought it was a brand new song. I'd say, "It's about fifty or sixty years old." I've had my group for almost 27 years. I now have two trumpets, one trombone and two saxes.

Most of the bandleaders in the fifties, sixties and seventies are musicians. As musicians we think the band comes first. We have an identity. We want the musicians to stand out. That's why we chose a good singer who was at a par with the group. The sonero sang all the rhythms, the boleros, cha cha chas, merengues and what we call salsa.

Today the singer is in first place. Bands no longer have an identity. The bandleaders are all singers. You hear one of the new recordings and you can't tell who it is until the singer starts singing. But the old groups like Puente and Machito, once you heard that first beat, you could identify the band.

Tito Rodríguez was a musician. He played the guitar and percussion. Machito was a singer, but he had Mario Bauzá, who was the musical director and bandleader. And Machito was a maracas player, a percussionist. Singers like Machito and Tito Rodríguez thought like musicians. Most singers today don't play anything, not even claves or maracas. They just stand up at the microphone and sing.

The first singer I had was Marcelino Morales, a Puerto Rican. After that I had Marvin Santiago, one of the best soneros. When we got to the montuno, that was his department. He used to sing and didn't want to stop. He was with me till 1976. People used to listen to him and make requests. That's what I call a *sonero*, when you improvise about everything.

In 1976, Marvin went on his own. His drug use was affecting my group, so I spoke to Marvin and he decided to leave. I asked him if he wanted to change, but he knew he couldn't. When he got out of jail, he had some problems with his voice and he stopped singing for a while. He still has to rest a lot.

> *Singers like Machito and Tito Rodríguez thought like musicians. Most singers now don't play anything, not even claves or maracas. They just stand up at the microphone and sing.*

As I said, Marcelino was my first singer, but when I started adding more than one vocalist to the group I had Luigi, Cano Estremera and Luisito Carrion who was with me for five years. Luigi Texidor joined my band in 1976. We did one recording that was a hit, *Nací Moreno*. When Luigi Texidor left, Cano Estremera took his place. His first big hit was *La Boda de Ella* in 1977-78. The singer that was originally going to record it was Luigi Texidor, but when Luigi left, Cano sang that tune and it became a hit. When you have two or three singers, there's always one that stands out. Johnny Vásquez has been with me for fifteen years, so he's the one that has been loyal to the group, and I've got two new singers, Giovanni Lugo and Ramsi Rios.

When you go into a group as a musician, you may stay three, four, or five years and you learn something, just like I did with Tito Rodríguez. Then you go out on your own way and that's a natural thing. Well, the first time that happened to me, it was shocking, but after that, I learned that that's the way life is. ∎

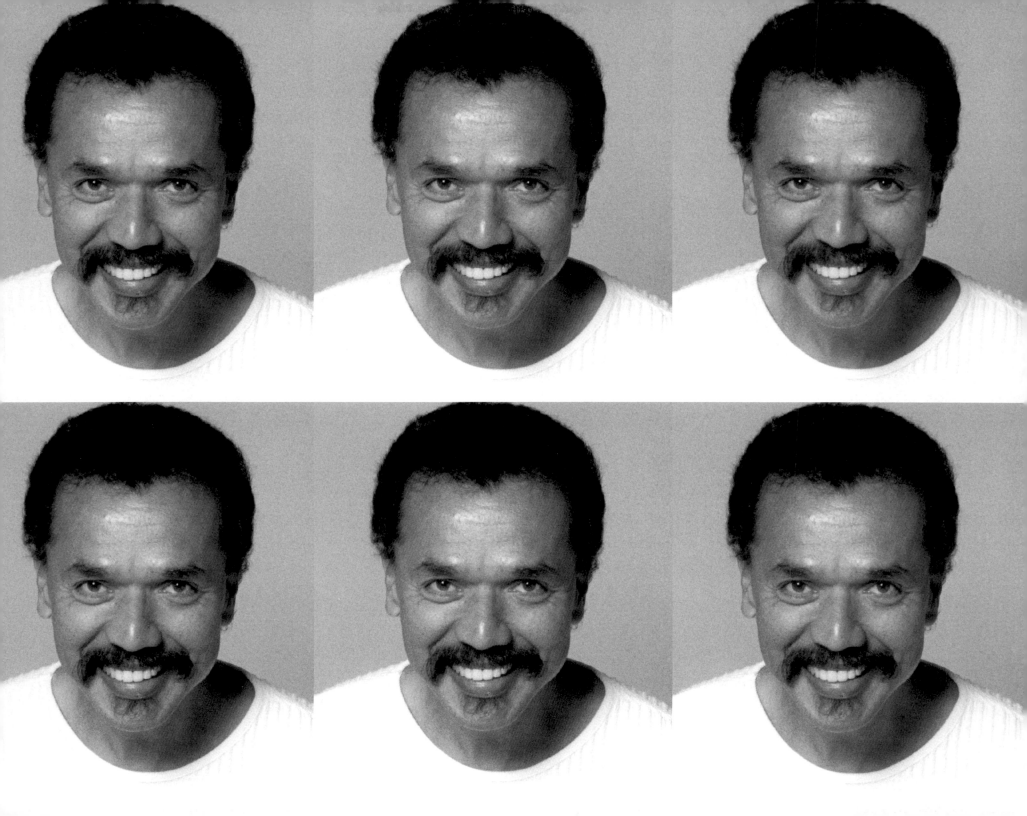

Roberto Roena

We transposed the American sound onto the Latin thing, which produced the blend. We adapted that sound to Latin music, but since we also played fifty percent American tunes, it gave us the appropriate sound. In the original Apollo Sound, there are one Latin singer and two Americans. In the first few albums, we always included two or three American songs. but this did not gel, because there was a Latino consciousness in the base.

ROBERTO IVAN
ROENA VÁSQUEZ

PERCUSSIONIST
(BONGOCERO),
BANDLEADER OF THE
APOLLO SOUND;
DANCER AND
MUSICIAN WITH
CORTIJO Y SU
COMBO, EL GRAN
COMBO, AND THE
FANIA ALL STARS.
A MULTIPLE HIT
MAKER.

CHAPTER 40

WHEN THE STUDENT IS READY, THE MASTER APPEARS

My given name is Roberto Ivan Roena Vásquez, and I was born in Mayaguez, Puerto Rico in a neighborhood called Dulces Labios January 16, 1940. My father's is Francisco José Roena Santiago and my mother is Raquel Maria Vásquez Plazas. My father is an agronomist and my mother was a seamstress.

My musical background comes from my late uncle Aníbal Vásquez, the founder of the Mambo Aces who passed in 2000. I started out as a dancer with my brother, Francisco José, who is deceased. Everybody called him Cuqui. We won an amateur contest and then became professionals. We worked as dancers on a TV program called La Taverna India. Rafael Cortijo y Su Combo with Ismael Rivera played on that program.

Cortijo's group accompanied us at all the shows and all over the island during the holidays honoring the Patron Saints. My curiosity for the music arose from hearing it so much. I used to listen to all the percussion breaks.

On one of his trips to New York, Rafael Cortijo had a problem with one of the percussionists. Cortijo called my mother to ask if I could play with him. She said, "But Roberto is a dancer." He said, "He has musical inclinations and I want your permission to let him travel. I'll take care of the rest."

He sent for me to play with him but instead, every afternoon, he gave me percussion lessons because I was a dancer. We were away for three months and I never played. The group would play at night and I'd be on stage listening. In New York, they bought me a uniform and that's when I knew I was going to be in the group. When we got back to Puerto Rico, Cortijo told me, "Next Saturday there's a dance. Wear your uniform and come with your instrument because you're going to play." I've been playing ever since.

We traveled to Venezuela and then to Panama. The band called a meeting to discuss disbanding the group. That gave rise to El Gran Combo. At that moment, I did not become a member of El Gran Combo because I didn't think it was the right way to separate from the man who had taught me. I remained with Cortijo, even though I thought the others were right—however I believe during difficult times you must come through for your friends. That's why I stayed with Cortijo.

TIME TO MOVE ON

After Cortijo moved to New York, I began to play with Mario Ortiz in Puerto Rico. Two months later, the bongo player hired by El Gran Combo left, so I joined them. That's when El Gran Combo exploded on the scene and my good times started.

In 1969, after playing with El Gran Combo for seven or eight years, I got the urge to start my group, which became the Apollo Sound. The first rehearsal coincided with the launching of the spaceship Apollo One. We thought, "The spaceship Apollo, and there's twelve of us. Let's call ourselves Apollo 12." Then I thought, they are on the first mission and we're already on 12? What if they launch Apollo 13? We'd be obsolete. We thought of twenty alternatives before I decided, "Let's call it The Apollo Sound."

Everyone said I was crazy. I was even crazier because the people I recruited were stars in their own right. According to all estimates, our group wouldn't last more than a month or two. The people I chose were fifty percent Latino, but they were into rock music fifty percent of the time. I didn't want anyone to think that because I came from El Gran Combo, I was going to follow Cortijo's style. I didn't want anyone to say we sounded like anyone else.

Cortijo has always been my idol in the roots and the complexity of salsa. I consider myself one of his most fortunate disciples, one of those closest to him and as a result, I was better able to assimilate his rhythmic form of thinking.

But what we did with Latin and Rock was totally different and, thank God, successful. There were marked differences in arranging. Rhythmically, I have my personal insights and I have tremendous faith in my form of thinking. Instrumentally for inspiration we based our sound on Blood Sweat & Tears and Chicago for the brass, and the orchestral sound. We copied it. Pretty strange, isn't it? As a matter of fact, the combination of the group is as follows: two trumpets, a tenor and a trombone. At that time, no other Latin group had a similar combination.

We adapted the American sound to Latin music, but since we also played fifty percent American tunes, it gave us the appropriate mix. In the original Apollo Sound, we had one Latino singer and two Americans. On the first few albums, we always included two or three American songs. However, the mixed group of Latinos and Americans didn't gel because there was a Latino consciousness in the base.

Even if I am the director, I believe that an orchestra is composed of all its members; they bond with each other more when they participate in the arrangement. The arrangement is the foundation of a building. The person who is playing an instrument has to participate. The first thing I stress to the arrangers is that the percussionist participates in the arrangement as actively as the brass, which ultimately shares that note with the percussion. I also tell the arrangers not to take it personally if an idea arises from one of the members of the group, or from me, naturally. The trick is to come up with something good. That was the source of our novelty.

FORMAL MUSICAL STUDIES?

None. Perhaps it was negligence on my part. Perhaps I should thank God for that. Maybe I would have become too methodical. I managed to give my music more feeling than technique. The personnel I chose were very advanced as musicians and very conscious individuals. They studied a lot of music. I even discussed musical arrangements and techniques with them where if I had been a little weak or insecure, I wouldn't have dared to do so. In fact, at that time, I was the first bongo player/bandleader, but I knew where I was headed.

Upon completion of our fifth or sixth album, we started to look at the rhythms of other places in the world to integrate them within the base of our Latin music called salsa. I am a fanatic of Brazilian music, so I incorporated the Brazilian air and mixture as an experiment. In a tune called, *Mi Desengaño*, I used the cüica (a Brazilian percussion instrument with a singing tone). It was perceived as a huge innovation that resulted in a greater stability of the personality of the Apollo Sound. We were one of the first, if not the first group to do that. Once the marriage was successful, we continued giving it that Brazilian tinge. That Brazilian air identified the Apollo Sound.

Fania signed my orchestra in 1971 and the Apollo Sound became part of the Fania musical movement. I was in Puerto Rico when the Fania All Stars were being taped at the Cheetah. Jerry

The first rehearsal coincided with the launching of the spaceship Apollo One. We thought, "The spaceship Apollo, and there's twelve of us. Let's call ourselves Apollo 12." Then I thought, they are on the first mission and we're already on 12? What if they launch Apollo 13? We'd be obsolete.

Masucci, the boss, asked me if I was interested in joining. "The best musicians from the company are participating and since you're the bandleader of that group, it is logical for you to be there." I told him it was a pleasure for me, an honor. Since then, I haven't missed one of their shows. If you ask my buddies in the Fania All Stars, they say I'm the biggest rascal of the group.

I am so attuned with the sound of my group that no matter how knowledgeable an arranger is, if a small note that may be correct is added, but doesn't have the Apollo sound or flavor, I won't use it, it won't make it. It is important to create a musical personality. I use the flugel horn with the flute a lot. By the time you hear four measures, you can identify us. Very few groups have that musical personality. It's like the personality of a human being.

The genre we call salsa is one that I can't quite assimilate or understand although I know the reason for its existence. To me, salsa is a condiment you add to food. I know the Cuban roots well. I have studied their rhythms very much. Naturally, I know my own rhythms better: bomba and plena. I am very interested in knowing where I'm from. Likewise I know the roots of Venezuela, Panama, Cuba and all the Caribbean countries, which are African.

I learned all those things from Cortijo. In fact, I owe him everything. It always filled me with wonder why I was chosen. It was a gigantic step for me. It's been like a dream. ∎

Roberto **Roena**

*Arturo Sandoval
at
Salsa Meets Jazz*

RENDER UNTO CAESAR

ASIDE FROM THE SPANISH LANGUAGE, AFRO-ANTILLEAN MUSIC HAS BEEN THE SINGLE MOST UNIFYING ELEMENT OF THE HISPANIC CULTURE.

SALSA TALKS PAYS TRIBUTE TO THE TALENTED MUSICIANS THAT QUENCH OUR THIRSTING PALATE, DOUSE OUR SALSA FEVER WITH THEIR SOUNDS, BEATS, AND POLYRHYTHMIC PULSATIONS. THEIR IMPECCABLE PLAYING, SINGING, AND SWINGING RHYTHMS TRANSPORT US TO ANOTHER TIME AND SPACE. IN AWE, WE SURRENDER AS THE VERY ESSENCE OF OUR BEING SWAYS AND SWINGS TO THE CLAVE BEAT.

Jimmy Bosch

e Azucar women's salsa group from Colombia

Ray Barretto

Yomo Toro

Rolando Briceño

DRUMMERS
COLLECTIVE

Tito Nieves

Bobbi Céspedes
Conjunto Céspedes

Milton Cardona

Nora
Orquesta de la Luz

Nestor Torres
at Salsa Meets Jazz

Jimmy Delgado

Hector "Bomberito" Zarzuela

Eddie Martínez

Papo Pepín, Harry Adorno
and Joe González

Eddie Santiago

Joe Arroyo

Oscar Hernandez

Marc Quiñones

Alfredo "Chocolate"
Armenteros

Bobby Allende

Frankie Ruiz

Luis Enrique

Mario Rivera

Salsagr

aphers

CHAPTER 42

IRV GREENBAUM

Irv Greenbaum, born in New York, 1924, is the legendary Fania recording engineer who has worked with all the salsa greats. Irv delivers some studio anecdotes to tickle your fancy.

IN THE BIZ

My involvement started almost 41 years ago, when I worked for a little independent studio in New York. We did a cross section of recordings, but a large part of it was Latin music. I became involved with Fania Records when they first started. They did a session at Mastertone and Johnny Pacheco and his orchestra was the act. He walked in with his partner, Jerry Masucci. They had just started a record company and this was their first album, *Cañonazo*. So as I started working, I heard Jerry say to Johnny in the background, "Hey, you sure this guy knows what he's doing?" That was my introduction to Jerry's personality.

One time, before I became Fania's official engineer, Jerry mentioned, "If you hear something fresh, let me know about it." I did a demo with Willie Colón which Al Santiago of Alegre Records hadn't paid for, annoying the heck out of the owner of the studio. He instructed, "If you find anybody that can use these tapes, let them have them." So the next time Jerry and Johnny came in, I dragged the tape out and played the song Willie recorded. It was jazzy, over five minutes long and Jerry sat there in dead silence for about 15 or 20 seconds. He finally responded with, "Play it again." So I played it again, and he said, "Okay, I'm gonna take it." I said, "What about the rest?" He replied, "Ah, you can throw that garbage away," and that was how Jerry got connected with Willie Colón.

My heart attack was mild, and in about six weeks I came back to Fania, which was now my employer. I got to Jerry's office and he asked, "Are you ready to do a recording for Eddie Palmieri?" I gulped. I was in no condition to do a recording with Eddie Palmieri, but we did two Grammy winning albums, *Palo Pa' Rumba*, and *Unfinished Masterpiece*, which Eddie did not want to accept the Grammy for. Harvey Averne and I completed it without Eddie's help. We started working on a Monday at about eleven o'clock in the morning until two o'clock the next afternoon. Harvey kept telling me, "This couldn't be done without you." At the Grammy ceremony, when Harvey came up for his acceptance speech as producer, all he said was, "They said it couldn't be done, but *I* did it."

People have said Eddie has a hearing deficiency. He loves to hear music blasting back. On one occasion I was doing a playback and he said, "Make it a little louder." I was at the top of the control, and there was practically nothing more to give. In fact the speakers were doing a cha cha, so I gave it the last quarter of an inch. By this time there was a wall of sound that you could hit with a hammer. But it wasn't enough. So Eddie put his knees up on the console and got closer and closer to the speakers. Then he was happy.

I did Larry Harlow's initial recording for Fania records and did many an album with him. Years later we were doing a recording where it required a lot of banging sounds at the end. Sure enough, when the tape was rolling, he put a packet of fire crackers into an ash tray, lit a match and they went off bang! bang! bang! I said to Larry, "This will go down as recording's finest moment." I was being sarcastic. So he got a misty look in his eyes and said, "No. I'll tell you the finest moment in recording. In Carnegie Hall when I stepped up on the podium and I started conducting *Hommy*." I got kind of misty myself.

One day, Pacheco was in the studio producing an album with Javier Vásquez as arranger. Pacheco was a very heavy cigar smoker and so was Javier and Alberto Valdés the conga player. Jerry Masucci was in the control room. I love cigars, but I don't make a habit of smoking them in the control room. But when Pacheco comes in he always offers me one of these very fine, expensive cigars. Since he was smoking, I lit mine up as well. Jerry Masucci didn't smoke. Eventually the session wound down. The conga player left, Javier Vásquez left with his cigar. Finally Pacheco left. And I'm left in the control room with Jerry Masucci. At that point he turns to me and says, "Hey! Put that thing out. It stinks."

Tito Puente and I were sitting in a Spanish restaurant on Sixth Avenue, where they had a strolling guitar player singing. This fellow broke into a song and at the end some people at the other end of the restaurant started looking at Tito and applauding him. So Tito stood up and took a bow. He said, "You know? I didn't write that song, but I figured that as long as they were applauding me, I might as well take a bow."

Ray Barretto is a perfectionist. Everything on his albums is absolutely perfect. If there is an error of any kind, it does not get through. One evening we were overdubbing three trumpets which had been left out of the initial recording. This particular song, as in a lot of Barretto's arrangements, was very complicated. They had a small rehearsal and then they made the take. They were blowing their brains out. Their faces were getting red, but it really sounded great. There were no flubs, no boo boos, it was very smooth. When the song ended, they all looked into the control room and Barretto was very excited. He says, "Fellows come here. You got to hear this. They came in panting a little red face, sweat rolling down and he said, "Fellows, that was a marvelous first effort."

JACK HOOKE

Born in New York, 1916, died 1999; Jack was the promoter behind Salsa Meets Jazz at the Village Gate and managed some of the biggest names, including Tito Puente and Celia Cruz.

MANAGER AND PROMOTER

It was 1961. I did concerts for Dick Clark Concerts, people like the Rolling Stones, Led Zeppelin, and the biggest most contemporary music acts of the time. My friend and fellow Brooklynite Symphony Sid was probably the most important jazz disc jockey in the country. I think Sid's interest in Latin music began with Machito. Sid instigated making recordings of Machito with jazz artists. He got so interested in Latin music that his show, which ran from eleven at night to five in the morning on stations like WABC, started to play an hour of Latin music a night. Well, in a year or two, that turned into four hours a night of Latin and one hour of jazz.

Sid called me one night in 1961 or 1962, "Hey, I'm running a Monday night Latin show at the Village Gate. Come on down." So I came on a Monday and this place was mobbed. Sid came over and asked, "How do you like it?" I said, "Man you have to be making a million bucks!" He says, "I'm not making any money. I'll show you the statements of the last three Mondays." On one show, he lost thirty dollars, another he made twenty dollars and I'm looking at six hundred people here. I said, "There is something

wrong, Sid." So he says, "Please Jack, come and run it for me. Be my partner."

"I can't," I told him. "I'm all over the country with Dick Clark. I don't have the time." Well, he begged me and after six drinks, I gave in. The next day I called Dick, "Hey, Richard, you know Symphony Sid is an old friend of mine. He's got this little enterprise at The Village Gate, and somebody is doing him wrong. I want to help him, but I want your permission." So he says, "As long as it doesn't interfere with what you are doing for me, go."

Sid was running one Latin band and one jazz group. So I sat down with him at the Gate and said, "That's no good, it's neither fish nor fowl. Those who like Latin music don't want to hear way out jazz; those who like jazz don't want to hear Latin. You're into Latin music, so let's do two Latin bands." Needless to say, it was successful.

The boogaloo was popular then. We started running with two Latin bands. We made good bucks, both of us. It was crowded every week. Sid was such a great salesman, he'd get on the radio and announce, "You should have been there on Monday night. Wow! Tito played this..." Man, that was the greatest hook in my life. You didn't need any commercials, just him mentioning it that way. So it became very successful and we ran from 1962 until 1972.

When Sid retired, Art D'Lugoff, the owner of the Gate, wanted to keep running the Monday Latin night. The word salsa wasn't born yet. I told him I wouldn't do it without Sid. So he tried it with different promoters and it failed. It was no good without Sid. Art D'Lugoff would call me every year or so, "Let's run that Monday Latin night," and I would say no. He kept after me for years, and in 1980, I said I'd talk to him about it.

SALSA MEETS JAZZ

We met for lunch and here is the funny switch about me telling Sid that jazz and Latin don't mix. I said, "Everybody is running a Latin night. You got to do something different." So between the two of us, we came up with a concept: to take two of the best Latin bands, and have an American jazz soloist like Dizzy Gillespie or Stan Getz take one song each set with the Latin band, unrehearsed and we'll call it *Salsa Meets Jazz*. I thought it was a great idea.

We could do it, but not without a disc jockey, someone like Sid. So I went to Ralph Mercado and Ray Aviles who are my dear friends, "I need a personality." Ralph said, "There's a guy named Roger Dawson. We don't like him, but if you can live with him, here's his phone number." He had a Sunday afternoon Latin show and he was English speaking. He knew who I was from the Symphony Sid days. So I had lunch with Roger, and he flipped for my idea.

Eddie Palmieri was the band that opened the first night in May 1980. It was an instant success. There were lines around the corner; we couldn't fit them in the place. Here I was mixing it and it worked. It was successful for about three or four years, before Roger lost his job. The station changed its format to country and business fell off. I was ready to give it up when another good friend, Paco Navarro said, "Why don't I come in with you? I'm on a big station and I can get a sponsor." So he came on and boom! It took an upswing again.

Then Paco lost his job, and his station changed format after two or three years. I was ready to give it up when I went to Ralph Mercado again. He said, "I won't let you give it up. It's an institution. Let me come in with you." So we brought it back to life.

Symphony Sid was the greatest. Sid crossed over from the pure Spanish-speaking people to American people. There is more money when you cross over into the big market, and Sid was responsible for it. I used to hear Ralphy Mercado say after Sid left, "When we run a concert, a dance, it's not like the days when Sid was here. Sid used to get on the air and say, "You got to come to the Brooklyn Stratos or the Manhattan Center." There would be 5,000 people waiting to get in. There is nobody on the air like that anymore. So we shouldn't ever lose sight of what Sid meant to the Latin music world.

RENE LOPEZ

Producer, collector and historian, René has been a fountain of inspiration, influencing many of salsa's top musicians. Here is his unique historical perspective.

THE LATIN MUSIC BUSINESS

I was born December 24, 1939, in New York City. I lived there until I turned 17 and joined the Navy. After my six-year tour in the Navy, I relocated back to metropolitan New York. My uncle, Catalino Rolón, booked bands at the Palladium Ballroom. He was Xavier Cugat's first male singer from 1936-40 and had made quite a name for himself. Then he formed his own band, and called himself the King of the Rumba. In the fifties, he abandoned that part of the music and became a promoter. So I listened to a lot of Latin music. By the way, I do not like the term Latin. I try to reject all the media hype.

A lot of musicians lived in the Bronx then. I knew them through my uncle. We couldn't help but hear about Machito because my uncle and he were friends. I knew Tito Puente since I was a kid,

because he would come to my house. Tito Rodríguez lived about seven blocks away. Although my closest friends were Puerto Rican, the neighborhood where I started hanging out was more Afro-American than Puerto Rican. We were into black music. We loved doo-wop, the music of the Harptones, the Rivaleers, the Vocaleers, the Crests, the Charms, the Solitaires, and the Flamingos.

African-Americans generally looked down on Latin music. That's a conclusion I came to when I joined the service and I had Afro-American friends. They would call it *Mira-Mira* music. I think that blacks rejected Latinos because of the language barrier. There's much more acceptance now, but in the 1960s, the guys who were into jazz didn't respect Latin music. Some musicians like Dizzy Gillespie gave it an honored place and nurtured *Caribbean People's Music*, which is what I like to call it.

I always liked the music of the countryside of Puerto Rico. I had conga fever and wanted to learn how to play conga drums. I became interested in the music my Puerto Rican cousins were listening to and began to collect music to play along with. The only Puerto Rican music that was similar to the music of New York was the music of Cortijo, who at that time was making his big push. I identified with Latino music from New York. A bass player named Fito Mercado played an Orquesta Aragón record for me and I initially didn't like it, it was so laid back I thought they were on librium. The New York bands were heavy on the rhythm. I wanted that strong sound of Pacheco and his charanga.

With time, my ear grew used to it. In the Philippines, I saw Orquesta Aragón in a catalog and sent for it. Then I started to understand the subtle thing about Aragón. I started hearing the difference

in the voices. Although Pacheco's band was one of the best that played that music, there was something I really liked about the Cuban sound.

THE CUBAN SENSIBILITY

I grew very close to my uncle Catalino, who was booking the Palladium and I helped him with whatever I could. That also provided an in for me. Through him I got to know all the musicians and that's how I met Eddie Palmieri. Eddie led the best conjunto that's ever played this music from New York—*La Perfecta*. Nobody had ever had a group with trombones before. It has a different timbre, a whole different sound than a trumpet. So Eddie changed the sound of the music. He created a new structure for playing the music, two trombones and a flute. His brother Charlie called it a *trombanga*. In addition, he respected and still respects the rhythmic patterns and the harmonic approach to the music·of the great Cuban conjuntos and big bands.

In the 1960s I noticed that Johnny Pacheco, Eddie Palmieri, Ray Barretto, Tito Rodríguez, Tito Puente and Machito were all playing Cuban music. I became aware of it because they did a lot of tunes that came from the Cuban records I had. I started comparing one to the other. I was already buying music directly from Cuba: Aragón, Orquesta Sublime, Benny Moré, Chappottín, Arsenio Rodríguez.

My collection is primarily Cuban music. There's a sensibility and a balance that I like more than the sound that comes from most of the New York groups, with the exception of Machito, Tito Puente, Eddie Palmieri and Johnny Pacheco. However, they were trying to get as close as they could to producing Cuban music, which is the music they loved. In the 1960s, most of the repertoire they were doing was in my collection. I was just a collector having fun. I always gave them the name of the composer and if the record companies didn't give the composer credit, I'd get hot.

When I started hanging out with Eddie Palmieri's band, Eddie had these young musicians and sort of gave them an assignment, "Hang out with René and listen to his collection." Influential musicians were Arsenio Rodríguez, Lily Martinez (the piano player and arranger with Arsenio's band), Arcaño y sus Maravillas, Benny Moré, and Peruchín among others. I had done a lot of interviews and gathered historical data to put the music into a historical context, so I became a friend.

They came to my house every night for a year—Andy and Jerry González, Nicky Marrero, Nelson González and Charlie Santiago. Alfredo "Chocolate" Armenteros came to my house almost every night for three years and was the person that taught me the most about Cuban music and musicians, opening an invaluable window into the philosophy and feelings of black Cubans. And he taught me how to really listen. So a tremendous exchange took place. By then I started getting invited to talk at different places about the music. During that time, the González brothers formed Conjunto Anabacóa with the idea of getting a jam session band together. I joined the band to sing coro and to have a good time. We did that for two or three gigs. During that time, I met Andy Kaufman, A&R man with Columbia. RCA was doing re-releases of old Cuban material and I told Andy, "They're putting the wrong tunes out. I've got 78s at home that they never release and I know they have the masters." So Andy tells me, "Why don't you stop complaining and give them a call?" He was in the music business, so he called them and the guy wanted to see me.

I did twelve reissues of RCA material. At that time, RCA's catalogue and the whole Latin operation were taken over by Caytronics. They didn't have most of the stuff so I provided most of the material from my 78 RPM records and photographs I had of every group. I did two Arsenios, two Arcaños; I did the only original material left of Tito Puente and Tito Rodríguez when they were members of the Curbelo Band. I did a Belisario López record, *Conjunto Kubavana*, which was the band Patato cut his teeth on and *Conjunto Modelo*, a favorite of Palmieri and Pacheco. Though Eddie was influenced by their music, he didn't use a lot of that material for his repertoire.

GRUPO FOLKLORICO

While I was working on the reissues, I got friendly with Joe Cayre of the Salsoul Record Label. I knew the real powerful stuff was the music Andy González and these guys were doing. The best stuff is always the jam sessions, it comes from the heart, it keys off what the singer is saying, what the piano player is doing, what the bass does. So Andy Kaufman and I proposed producing a record of "a group I've been working with that kicks ass compared with all the other groups on the New York scene."

I had never produced a record in my life. Of course, all the people I was using had recorded many times. Everybody was a pro. We came in with a new idea: to produce something that was real. There were no mambos written. You had to know the shit. Everything on those records was improvised. At CBS studios the recording engineers had set everything up. They knew fifteen musicians were coming. Andy and I told them to take the music stands out because we didn't have any music, and to take the separations out because we were going to do it live, except for the singers and the chorus. They thought we were crazy.

The first *Grupo Folklórico* (on Sony/Salsoul Records) is one of the best set of albums ever done, none of it sounded rehearsed. It came back to capturing the spontaneity in the music. Without spontaneity this music is dead. I was involved with the Center for Puerto Rican Studies and I had been to the American Folklife Festival. There was a big debate as to whether it's folk or not. I'm not a folklorist, but I have many friends that are. We thought this whole division between folk music and popular in our case was bullshit. Folk-popular music is what people play when they're communicating with each other, having a good time and celebrating a specific occasion. The other "popular" music becomes popular when it's industry controlled and promoted. And it has its place. Some ethnomusicologists see folk music exclusive of young people. If they don't see three eighty-year-old guys drunk under a tree with a jug, it ain't Mississippi Delta Blues. Music is not for one age group or ethnicity; it's a shared common experience.

Salsa is just a name. To repeat Tito Puente's words, the only salsa I know comes out of a bottle. I refer to it as Caribbean People's Music. To me, there's Spanish-speaking Caribbean People's Music, English-speaking people's, or French-speaking. When people say, well, this is the African rhythms and the European melodies, I say, don't give me that shit. Do you mean that European music is not rhythmic? Or that African music is not melodic?

The term salsa is not specific. This word was popularized and it gives a connotation of something Caribbean, and that's important. Is New York music different? Yes, although they play Cuban music by-and-large. It's different in the way it is sung, in the arranging, in its cadence. A New York, Puerto Rican,

Panamanian or Dominican musician that plays salsa, although they're playing Cuban music, they don't stop being Dominican or Puerto Rican. He or she brings that into the music.

The *son* is the musical genre that is the base of salsa. It was born in Cuba, but Cuba can no longer claim it exclusively because the *son* is played in most Spanish-speaking countries of the world. It has assumed the same position as jazz in the European and English-speaking world. Today, salsa, Latin jazz and jazz are played in probably every country in the world. Salsa is music of a common Caribbean experience and New York reflects that more than any other city in the world. There is a solid Caribbean oriented Spanish-speaking community. The musicians in New York are some of the most versatile and finest musicians in the world. Salsa music, like jazz and the *son* are built on improvisation.

All I know comes from the musicians directly. Most of the people I've interviewed have an agenda of their own, so I always try to see through it and put it all together.

MAX SALAZAR

Born in Spanish Harlem in 1932, Max Salazar wrote the book *Mambo Kingdom, Latin Music in New York*. This author, music critic and radio announcer looks deep inside salsa history....

TELL ME YOUR STORY

Between WBAI and WKCR at Columbia University, I was on the radio for 15 years. I've interviewed almost all the top names in Latin Music. I wanted a different show and by accident, I stumbled upon it: providing history along with the music.

Machito opened the doors for me when I started interviewing musicians. He called the guys and said,

"I have a friend, Max Salazar, and I want you to let him interview you." And Macho even gave me some ideas on what to ask them. Every week, that hour became a historical moment. In my interviews, people sometimes gave private aspects without realizing they were saying something explosive...like Tito Rodríguez's wife, who expressed a lot of bitterness towards Tito Puente and José Curbelo, because they kept her husband from working. Curbelo was the number one agent with the top bands. If you didn't belong to his stable, you weren't going to work in New York, at least not in the places that paid a decent salary. When he got mad at Tito Rodríguez, whoever hired Rodríguez wasn't going to get any of his bands. But when Tito Rodríguez recorded the million dollar seller, *Inolvidable*, all the world wanted him. Curbelo was overlooked, Tito Rodríguez was booked and in the end, Rodríguez had the last laugh on Puente and Curbelo.

I studied Chano Pozo's life story. He introduced the conga drums in jazz when he joined Dizzy Gillespie's band in 1946. In Cuba, Chano wrote 40 tunes that became hits here. But in the U.S. a sharp businessman can get his name added to a composition as co-composer. That means the five cents that the composer gets is now 2-1/2 cents. They brought in a third person, a guy called Gil Fuller. Dizzy and this guy wrote a bridge. Chano's tunes did not have any bridges and he wrote them without anybody's help. But if Chano wanted to record here, he had to include them as co-composers. So the credits on Manteca are Pozo, Gillespie and Fuller.

Today the only bandleader with any name or importance is Tito Puente. Puente is a complete musician. But the war of rivalry he had with Tito Rodríguez because of billing was uncalled for. Big deal. However, Puente made it important. Tito

Puente always had it, but he needed the right vocalist to shine. And he had a few, but when Vicentico Valdés came along in 1949, the band shot off immediately. However, when Puente and Vicentico split in 1954, there was gloom in this city. The Palladium crowd felt like they were robbed. They wanted to hear Puente and Vicentico because of all those lovely ballads they used to sing there. A lot of the fans met at the Palladium and later married inspired by the Vicentico-Puente boleros.

MAMBO WARS

Danzón Mambo was the first recorded mambo composed in 1938 by Orestes López, Cachao's brother, for Arcaño y Sus Maravillas. It was Arcaño that inspired Pérez Prado to play his mambo. Arcaño's mambo is very rich in melody in its montuno, it makes you want to dance. There were two other pianists at the time: Bebo Valdés and René Hernández. The sound that René Hernandez was looking for, inspired by the mambo, is what he gave the Machito Band in 1946 when he started adding his sax voicing. Bebo Valdés created la batanga in 1952. That rhythm was exciting, it was great to dance to, but the mambo was so hot that nobody wanted to replace it and the batanga died.

The Pérez Prado mambos didn't have the montuno that Orestes López created. But Prado wrote mambos and arranged them for sheet music, which sold for a dollar. According to Pérez Prado, Stan Kenton was the inspiration to incorporate those shrill trumpet notes in the stratosphere, with grunts and groans. People liked it. In fact, that kicked off the mambo era in 1949 with *Mambo Nº 5* and *Qué Rico Mambo*.

However, the following five years witnessed the rise of the Palladium mambo over the New York mambo at the "Home of the Mambo," the Palladium. The rhythm became the Palladium mambo and the one that is still danced to today. It was Machito's jazz arrangements that made this mambo different from the Cuban and Pérez Prado's mambos. The harmonies and the trumpet riffs were different. They forgot about Pérez Prado's mambo on the west coast because it would break and it would grunt, and it didn't have the excitement or the thrill of the Palladium mambo. The people that love to dance—Jewish people, Italian people, Irish people, Orientals—all started going to the Palladium. They started dancing with the Latin women and the non-Latin women started dancing with the Latinos. Then Latin music spread to the Jewish Alps, upstate New York, the Catskills.

THE MARK OF FANIA

Salsa started in New York. The music is Cuban, but the innovations that went along with it here, i.e. the mixture of jazz and R&B, makes it New York. When Johnny Pacheco got on the scene, he started playing something different that was a little jazzy, but more Cuban. He did things that were distinctive, that would make you say, "That's Pacheco!"

In the seventies, the Fania people were so dominant that they wiped out every other record label. Salsa is Cuban music, but the Fania people are the ones that created the mushroom cloud that spread all over the world and infected everybody. Jerry Masucci laid out hundreds of thousands of dollars to make nobodies into somebodies. So the only way he could recoup the money was to withhold the royalties. But musicians wanted the moon and the stars. If he paid them fifty, they wanted sixty. When he paid them sixty, they wanted seventy.

Not receiving royalties was the main complaint of the Fania artists. Then Machito said something in an interview about not caring if he received royalties, but he didn't want to talk about it on the record. After the interview, I asked him what he meant. He said, "If Mario and I had had a guy like Jerry Masucci looking out for us the way he looks out after his artists, we'd be retired today." I was shocked. He explained that Masucci bought airtime in Los Angeles, Chicago, Miami, and Puerto Rico. He did it all legitimately. No payola.

So I had Jerry Masucci all wrong. In my mind I had him as a villain before I realized what he had done. Look at what he did for salsa in the seventies. That's what helped get salsa established in Europe and other places—Fania Records.

THE COMPOSERS AND ARRANGERS

Great arrangers like Louie Ramírez, Marty Sheller, Bobby Valentín, Isidro Infante, René Hernández, and Anselmo Sacassas from the old Casino de la Playa have their own style and signature. It's not a New York thing, but an arranger's personality and imagination that makes these bands different. In Puerto Rico, one man has led the way: Bobby Valentín. Fania had a lot of arrangers, but the ones who turned out the most hits generating the money were Louie Ramírez, Marty Sheller and Bobby Valentín. Now Papo Lucca is arranging for La Sonora Ponceña and for other artists.

The music of blind Cuban composer and *tres* player Arsenio Rodríguez is the beginning of salsa. In Cuba, they took up a collection called Rayo de Luz (Ray of Light) so Arsenio would have money to pay Dr. Castro Viejo, a renowned eye surgeon. Arsenio came to New York in 1947 with the money. Everybody in Cuba was praying that something could be done to restore this genius's eyesight. Castro Viejo told him he would never see again. Arsenio went home, went to sleep, then woke up, called his brother Quique and said, "Grab a pencil and piece of paper." Then he dictated a tune called *La Vida Es Un Sueño*. The words were based on that day's experience. "What does it matter, one more heartbreak. The reality of life is to live and die." This is how songs are born.

Most of the money that Fania derived was made off Arsenio's tunes. The younger bands have recorded that funk created by Arsenio and it has a natural swing. Arsenio's *son montunos*, of which there are about five hundred, are still being recorded today, and they earn money because even a bad arranger can't make Arsenio's tunes bad. The tunes composed by geniuses like Arsenio Rodríguez, Miguel Matamoros and Ignacio Piñeiro had a real feeling, a gut feeling of what Cuban music is like. And even a poor arranger couldn't have a bad recording because these tunes sell themselves.

If you listen to the sound in Puerto Rico, it's much different from the one in New York, even from the one in Cuba. It's called *salsa romántica*. They've taken ballads and salsafied them. Louie Ramírez is the one who did it when he started a group in 1983-84 and recorded *Noche Caliente*, which took off and sold like hell. People like Luis Enrique and Frankie Ruiz have come out of the ashes and given the New York guys a run for their money.

Today's salsa is experimental. In Colombia, they're doing it with the cumbia. Willie Colón and Rubén Blades did that with *Siembra*. Tito Puente calls it hick music, but it's still salsa. Though it started with the Cuban music, now it's influencing other music.

GLOBALIZATION OF SALSA

The Finns or the Swedes may start incorporating some of their own folkloric music, because they're now using their native tongue. It sounds weird, but they're in clave. Some of them are singing in phonetic Spanish, but they're also singing in Swedish and Finnish. Salsa's appeal has turned on Scandinavians and has them dancing a few nights a week in Great Britain and other northern countries, even Japan.

It was Latin jazz that made the entry into Europe through Machito—salsa snuck in. The Machito Orchestra first went to Finland and created havoc in 1974. They went on to Paris and then to Hamburg with Newport Jazz. Since the promoter was only going to pay for eight guys, Machito couldn't take his full band. Because of that, Mario Bauzá and Graciela hit the roof. Mario told him, "You're going to bomb out." But Machito didn't want to miss that opportunity. When Machito got home from Europe, there was a letter waiting for him on the table from Mario, "I love you. You're my brother, but Graciela and I are splitting." There were other reasons, but this is what precipitated their splitting. After 35 years together, jealousy reared its head, "Nobody knows who we are, but they know who he is," was Mario's complaint. Machito was always giving credit and pointing to Mario saying, "If it wasn't for him, I wouldn't be here today. He was the architect of my fame." But Mario's heart was already eaten up.

In 1979, Finland invited Machito back. He played in Finland, Denmark and Sweden before the dam burst. Finland today has eight salsa groups, and three nightclubs where Finnish salseros go. Finnish salsa is great, it's more Cuban than New York style. Sweden, Great Britain, Paris and Tokyo have their own salsa. In Japan, you've got Orquesta de la Luz, Salsamania in Finland and Hotuane in Sweden. In Italy they have salsa recordings in their jukeboxes. They always loved the cha cha cha and the mambo, but watered down, like in *La Dolce Vita* and those fifties movies. Now it's the fiery *son montunos* that have them jumping. And it's going to get better. It's spreading so there will be salseros all over the world.

SCENT OF A MUSICIAN

To be a singer or *sonero* you've got to be thin, young, good-looking and smell great. If the average bandleader doesn't have it, his singer does. Tito Rodríguez had this romantic quality that most singers didn't have. Tito made it bigger as a soloist than a bandleader. He In the late forties, when he started his band, Tito Rodríguez didn't do boleros. His songs were all up-tempo guarachas and mambos. He had great arrangers like René Hernández creating the ability to match his music with Tito Puente. Tito Rodríguez's music was equally important and just as good. Rodríguez is the kind of guy that comes along once every fifty years. He worked hard at his trade and had business acumen.

The average man, even if he's good-looking, can't compete with the musician. I'm aware of some of the musicians' sexual prowess, their drinking habits, and their drug habits. They'd tell me they became musicians solely to meet women, so they could have the groupies follow them, so they could feel like a star. Some guys can look like the Hunchback of Notre Dame and still have beautiful women because they're great singers, or they play clave and they wear a tuxedo up on a bandstand. Yes, musicians are notorious for that.

THE MEANING OF SONERO

In the twenties the *septetos* came out with the trumpet conjunto sound. The trumpeter, the *maraquero* (maraca player), the bongocero, the vocalist and the guitarist were all *soneros* because they only played *son*, the popular music of the twenties. *Sonero* was a man who specialized in performing *son, son montuno*. But the one getting the attention was the vocalist *sonero* because he had to inspire and sing about what he saw in front of him and make it rhyme. According to old-timers, there was always a rivalry. When the soneros went from town to town, they would put each other down in their singing. Then they would have *una bronca*, a disagreement, so the Governor forbade the singing of the *son*. By the twenties, they got away from insulting each other and singing about racism, so the bans were lifted.

The musicians of yesteryear became singers and trumpet players by trial and error. They used music to supplement the primary income from the day job. They'd come out of work, put on a shirt and a tie and go up to somebody's apartment to start playing guitar or singing. At that time they were earning 2 or 3 bucks a night, but it was survival. They didn't have musical training or formal education, so they had to accept whatever was given to them. Their music was ripped off and they never got royalties. Most of today's musicians are college grads. Not all of them—some have come out of reform schools and their only salvation was music, like with Joe Bataan. For some it was a way of giving them a livelihood and making them responsible citizens.

Today, the audience is not all Hispanic, they are from almost every nationality. For them, Latin music offers that sexuality, that swing, and people burst out dancing. It doesn't matter what your ethnic background is. You like it and you're gonna move to it. And once you move in clave, look out, you're going to be at the Harvest Moon Ball competing next year. The music acts as foreplay, especially a good Cuban *montuno*. It's like a cologne that emits a scent that overwhelms you and takes your breath away. When she starts dancing and making those moves, the fuses in the mind start blowing up—it makes guys want to get married. It makes you feel alive. You don't feel this at work. Why do they go to that dance? The female. And what makes that moment worthwhile is the music in the background. It's the background music of life.

IZZY SANABRIA

Izzy's *Latin New York* magazine helped project salsa's popularity to new heights. His flamboyant appearances as Master of Ceremony at salsa concerts are something to remember. Izzy claims to be the first to use the term salsa to define the music, which makes him one of the most controversial characters in the Latin music field.

ORIGIN OF THE MUSICAL TERM SALSA

A writer from Cuba said we use the word *salsa* to disguise the fact that it's really Cuban music, that we changed the name so as not to give credit to Cuba. She's right, but this was not pre-planned. I always said that it was Cuban music. But the young Puerto Ricans kept it alive and developed it. The influence of brass from this country and the musicians here developed what I started calling salsa, because of the rhythm of the city. It is charged with a highly accelerated energy.

However, the white Cubans who came to this country and became the power of the Spanish media disregarded this music. The music they listen to is the *charanga* sound played by all white musicians. Orquesta Broadway doesn't want to be categorized under salsa, well it's not. It's very rhythmic, beautiful music. It swings, but it's violin and flute, a softer swing.

The ones who kept salsa music alive were Jews like Symphony Sid, Dick Ricardo Sugar, Joe Gaines and Roger Dawson. They kept this music alive on English language radio. This music was from the ghettos, but that is where all music comes from. Soul music, R&B, and jazz—it all comes from the lower economic classes. This music is black music. The only dark-skinned salsa artist that the white Cubans exalt is Celia Cruz.

When was the first time I heard the term applied to the music? Well, I was acknowledged by the American and international press as being the first person to start defining this music with the name salsa. Salsa is what gives Hispanic cooking its flavor. Now when a band was swinging, people would say they were cooking, cocinando. When a group has all the ingredients really clicking, people say they have salsa or they have sabor (flavor, spice).

Therefore, salsa was the flavor and spice. I applied it to other things as well. If a flamenco dancer is doing a great thing, this guy has got salsa. It could have been, "He's got jalapenos, he's got spice," but I started using *salsa*. So I defy anyone to find, prior to 1973 when I had *Salsa* the television show or prior to the *1975 Latin New York Music Awards* when this term started hitting the American media, to show me where somebody defines this music as salsa. You'll find the word in an album cover, in songs, used by disc jockeys. But it wasn't defining the music. I was trying to define this music, to differentiate this music from the rest.

Musicians all rejected the term, the top guys fought it. Puente told me, "I didn't want anything to do with it, but now I find my records categorized under salsa all over the world." They didn't have the sense of publicity I had. Now salsa, like R&B or rock 'n roll or jazz or disco, has a separate category.

Willie Colón was the first one to bring Yomo Toro's Puerto Rican *jibaro* sound into his salsa, as opposed to continuing with the jazz influence like everyone else. In 1974, while we were all on a plane going to Africa, Willie slipped out of the plane and went into the studio without Johnny Pacheco looking over his shoulder. Rubén Blades told me that Willie was incredible in the booth. Colón's complex was that he was not a great musician. But he had a style and his trombone playing was unique. His early bands were disregarded completely because they were not on clave, they were not precision-on with that Cuban beat. They were creating their own sound.

Willie survived because he had ideas. Since he couldn't write music other people wrote the arrangements and the music, so he wasn't respected. The guys who arrange and are musically schooled always feel superior. It does not mean that they are the hit makers or the hit writers.

ON THE CUTTING EDGE—SPOOFING THE FBI

My involvement started as an artist designing album covers and posters. I created the whole power thing with Barretto and the Superman image, *Indestructible* as well as the Willie Colón gangster image. They called him *El Malo* because he was a tough guy in the beginning. At least he had an image, very few people had one. When he got to Panama they brought a police escort and they put

machine guns in his hands and took photographs with him and the weaponry for television.

So I came up with a whole new concept. In the sixties, during the anti-Vietnam thing, they were selling FBI WANTED posters of guys like Bobby Seal. It was not against the law because you were helping the FBI put up their posters. That's where I got the idea. I took Willie to one of these machines that took four photographs for a quarter and using, probably, the cheapest photograph ever on an album cover, I designed a WANTED poster. People were plastering the poster on walls all over, so it caused quite a scandal. The FBI stopped it—you cannot throw into the public something that gives the illusion that it is from the FBI. People were calling the FBI letting them know where Willie Colón was. Willie's grandmother almost had a heart attack.

My spoof of the FBI looked authentic. The numbers on Willie Colón's chest were his old LP numbers. In the back it's signed by J. Edgar González. And then there was a poster on the inside with Hector Lavoe handcuffed and Colón being grabbed by police officers. The first album cover said, "WANTED by the FBI." They reprinted and called it "WANTED." Jerry Masucci could have gotten great publicity by fighting the FBI. He would have lost, but the publicity would have been enormous.

HOW TO GET NOTICED

I was the Master of Ceremonies at the Cheetah, where the whole salsa thing started. I did the radio commercial for it and it got filled wall to wall. It was so hot in that place that the costume I wore shrunk completely from the heat. As MC, I wore velvet, yellow satin and red suits. That's why I became noticed. By the time we did one concert at Madison Square Garden, Jerry Masucci got everybody suits like mine, so I went out and bought a white linen suit with a white shirt and a white tie. I stayed one step ahead of the Fania All Stars. It caused resentment towards me when I got one page to myself in Gentlemen's Quarterly magazine.

One of the most memorable evenings as MC was in Japan for the Fania All Stars Concert in 1976. The Japanese in New York pronounced Spanish well and I realized the correlation between Spanish and Japanese phonetics. So I memorized a paragraph in Japanese and the audience applauded me because I had good pronunciation. When I forgot a word, I put my hand in my pocket, pulled out the cheat sheet and said that one word. They laughed.

One time the audience booed me because of some controversial stuff I wrote in Latin New York magazine. If ten percent of the people boo you in Madison Square Garden, that's two thousand boos, it's quite loud. I'm a performer, so instead of getting upset, I went out there and said, "The rest of us might as well join this minority. Let's all boo Izzy Sanabria together. One, two, three boooo!" So I walked out of there with an applause.

RESPECT FOR RALPHY

When Jerry Masucci left the music business, that left Ralph. The only one running this business is Ralph Mercado. Ralph is a damn good promoter, he's the best there is. Ralph Mercado always likes to say, "I made you a star," and I told him, "Ralph, if it wasn't for *Latin New York* magazine, people wouldn't even know what you look like." Seconds later, this girl went up to Ralph Mercado, "Excuse me. Are you Ralph Mercado?" He smiles, throws his head back and says, "Yes, I am." And I happened to say, "What made you think he's Ralph Mercado?"

She answered, "I saw his picture in *Latin New York*." It was as if I had planned it.

ROBERT FARRIS THOMPSON

Dr. Thompson received his PhD from Yale in 1965. He is Master, Timothy Dwight College, Yale University, Professor, history of art. He's devoted his life to the historical study of African and Afro-American art and music.

INTRODUCTION—MAMBO

I was in Mexico City at the height of the Pérez Prado mambo period and was totally inspired by the quality of the sound. So I started collecting mambo records. Then a friend led me to the Palladium in New York City. I lived at the Palladium between 1959 and the day it closed in 1966, when Eddie Palmieri and the late great Barry Rogers played and people didn't want to leave.

I love Afro-Cuban music and mambo was my point of entry into life. Here we are 30 years later and I am finally starting my mambo book. To study mambo, I went to Cuba, and then bam, I was confronted with Lucumi, Abakuá, Arará, Palo, four Creole African languages. So it's taken me decades. But my love for the music has been continuous. Because I grew up in the mambo age, I see it as continuous with salsa, plus that wonderful little episode, the boogaloo. Mambo-salsa is a thirty to forty-year-old New York process developing on U.S.-Spanish-speaking soil.

IS SALSA AN URBAN PHENOMENON?

When I say it's urban I don't want to factor out whatever rural richness or funkiness might be a part of salsa and all those blues equivalents, like the *plena*. On the other hand, you would have to say that yes, it's predominantly urban, even if it draws on rural roots, because the hip stuff is happening in La Habana, Cárdenas, Matanzas, San Juan, Ponce, and Loíza. The coast brims with blacks. In the interior, where you find the *jíbaros* and the *guajiros,* the music is more white.

In 1974, I wheeled back onto the scene with a vengeance. By that time, Larry Harlow's album *Salsa* was causing a sensation. I learned about Ignacio Pineiro's *Échale Salsita* and I saw the term salsa and *Soul Sauce* on an album by the late Cal Tjader. In one of those old famous *descargas* someone shouts, "Salsa," and the other term that runs parallel with it, *Ahí, na' ma'*. Plus I heard Willie Colón's *Yo Traigo La Salsa*. In 1974, bam, I'm confronted with a name, sealed and delivered. It makes sense, the same way early jazz was played by people who referred to themselves as Hot Peppers. It's a basic Afro-Atlantic metaphor for hot music.

Salsa vaporized boundaries. It is popular music because of the fact that people dance to it and it is art music. Yes, it is of the people, but it is so complex that it is automatically an art music, a music that should be taken as seriously as Brahms or Beethoven.

I teach compositions that Larry Harlow did in 1974, like the montuno in *Wampó*, every year. When in the history of music have you ever heard a tempo that slow? I played the montuno of *Wampó* for a young composer in Boston and the tempo knocked him and his operatic singing girlfriend out. It's as classical as Beethoven and probably more complex. It should be taught in every conservatory because the complexity and the history are there, because if you get into salsa you get into mambo. If you get into mambo, you get into *guaguancó*. If you get into *guaguancó*, you've got to get into *Kongo* and *Yoruba* and Iberia.

I put it into the perspective of all of the following: religion, music, dance, African studies, Latin American studies. But above all, religion, because the idea of heating up a sound to underscore the spirit is an African idea. In Nigeria, if I want to bless you, I don't bless you with a cup of coffee. I run out and get hot pepper, then I coat my tongue and say "God bless you." The belief is that all the heat has activated my tongue and given you force. That's what salsa is all about. It's Latino music coating the tongue, giving a stronger voice.

I bring in *bata* players to show the tie-in with *Lucumí* music. I bring in *bomba* players to show the tie in with the north shore of Puerto Rico. Mambo was one blend and then you blend the blend. I'm ready for SALSA III, which may even take a new name.

THE ROLE OF DANCING IN SALSA

The dancer is a barometer of how good you are. When two hundred people are hitting the offbeat on the floor with their heel, that produces a spark. They vote with their feet. Before he died, I spent two days with the great trombone player Barry Rogers. He was talking about the role of the dancer in salsa and the lift the musicians got from the turns of the dancers. The players would focus on people that were known to go crazy as the *montunos* hit. There was a culture hero of the transition from mambo to salsa. His name was Américo Valentín. Barry told me that if he wasn't getting red in the face, you knew you were in trouble. Américo had a little whistle. When the *montunos* were really hot and the mambos criss-crossed the right way, he'd get up in front of the bandstand and start doing offbeat screams on a whistle. His face would turn beet-red. I hope salsa never loses that night person flavor.

IS SALSA CUBAN MUSIC?

Tito Puente, Tito Rodríguez, Machito and all of the people who hung out at the Palladium, "mambonicks," created a constituency without which salsa couldn't have been built. If you listen to that early mambo from around 1966 on Willie Colón's first LP, announcing the new music coming, when he goes into the *montuno* on the trombone, he is playing Cuba, but he works his New York South Bronx Latino-boy-scout-bugling into the mambo. No one is going to tell Willie Colón not to play boy scout bugle music as part of his mambo. If New York were compartmentalized, incredible salsero violinist Lewis Kahn should be playing classical music or singing as a cantor, but when he gets going on his violin, suddenly, is it Mendelssohn, is it Benny Moré? It's all of the above.

Salsa has done more to identify the aesthetic genius of Puerto Ricans than just about anything. Tito Rodríguez grew up in Puerto Rico but he tuned into Cuba. His crooning voice predicted the rise of the singers of *salsa romántica*. Another thing about salsa: you can't draw lines between the U.S., Cuba, Puerto Rico and Venezuela. This music is multi-cultural in excelsis. ∎

SALSA *is* BORN

THREE CONCERTS

from the eyes of the performers

*t*he Fania All Stars—*this multi-talented superstar group of musicians, arrangers, composers, bandleaders and soneros barrelled onto the music scene with a vengeance. Working within the Fania enclave, they crafted musical masterpieces that have withstood the test of time. By 1968, Fania Records was starting to make noise. The budding record label had a few artists on its roster and wanted to showcase their talents, so they arranged the concert where salsa was born, at the Red Garter in Greenwich Village, NYC—billed for the first time as The Fania All Stars. Among the performers were favorites Ray Barretto, Willie Colón, Larry Harlow, Hector Lavoe, Ismael Miranda, Johnny Pacheco, Eddie Palmieri, Tito Puente, Louie Ramírez, Ricardo Ray, Pete "El Conde" Rodríguez, Jimmy Sabater, Adalberto Santiago, Monguito Santamaría, and Bobby Valentín. This concert associated a bevy of names with a budding record company, though few were assigned to the label. A two volume set* Live at the Red Garter *was produced from the concert.*

THE NIGHT SALSA EXPLODED
ALL OVER THE WORLD

The Red Garter concert was only moderately successful; perhaps 1968 was not right for Salsa or Salsa was not ripe for the world, but the world was clearly ready on the steamy summer night of August 26, 1971, in New York City's Cheetah nightclub. This landmark concert known as "the night Latin music exploded around the world," consolidated top Latin bandleaders and musicians as the Fania All Stars under Johnny Pacheco's leadership, and for the next 17 years, the All Star group toured the world. The All Stars and their entourage remember that special night....

LARRY HARLOW   To form the Fania All Stars we took a singer, the band leader and one sideman from each band. It was me with my singer Ismael Miranda and trumpet player Larry Spencer; Ray Barretto, Adalberto Santiago, Barretto's singer at the time, and timbales player Orestes Vilató; Johnny Pacheco, singer Pete "El Conde" Rodríguez and Hector "Bomberito" Zarzuela, Pacheco's trumpet player; Willie Colón and Hector Lavoe. Cheo Feliciano was on the Vaya label (Fania subsidiary), Santitos Colón had just signed with Fania also, coming from Puente's band. Yomo Toro was doing a lot of recordings for Fania and he was a wonderful guy. Bobby Valentín had already moved to Puerto Rico and Roberto Roena was from Puerto Rico.

What made the salsa explosion happen was *Our Latin Thing,* the first Fania movie filmed during the Cheetah concert. That was a happening night—it was never that good again. There were lines around the block. The place was packed... kids were screaming. Originally, we had wanted to do the concert in Central Park for free. But Jerry said, "What are you, crazy? You can't do Central Park for free." The Village Gate

was open, but Jerry was swinging, he wanted more people and the bands had a big following. The Filmore had just closed, so I said, "We can go to Ralphy's place," which used to be the old Palm Gardens, the Cheetah. And Ralphy was running two nights a week at that time. Meanwhile, everybody wrote charts and we rehearsed for three days.

Pacheco begged Jerry to postpone the concert because none of the music had been written. But Jerry had already contracted a film crew. So they brought in Bobby Valentín; Bobby and Johnny boarded themselves up in a hotel around the corner from the Cheetah and started brainstorming. They wrote several tunes including *Macho Cimarrón,* *Ponte Duro,* and *Quítate Tú,* a tune inspired by a narrow door that became an anthem for the Fania soneros. On the bandstand, this tune paid homage to the art of improvisation and engaged the soneros in a fraternal war of words.

JERRY MASUCCI   Larry Harlow has a friend called Leon Gast who is an academy award-winning filmmaker. In 1971, they approached me with the idea of making a film of a concert. I needed to find a big club because I anticipated a lot of people. I called everybody in town who was throwing dances at that time and no one wanted to touch it. Then I called Ralphy Mercado who I had met when he owned a club in Brooklyn around 1965. I used to rehearse the bands there before recording. He was throwing a dance on Thursday nights at the Cheetah and he wasn't too interested, but he said, "If you pay for everything and I take the door, we'll try it."

RALPH MERCADO   The Cheetah was mine; I was the promoter there every Thursday night. The original idea of getting the Fania All Stars together was mine. We had recorded the Fania All Stars for the first time at the Red Garter, so this was the second time we got the people together. It wasn't a new idea, it had been done before with All Star bands like the Tico-Alegre All Stars. At that time, Fania was starting to gain strength. But the idea to record and film the Cheetah concert was Masucci's, he saw the potential of it. I had Thursday nights and that night, we sold to four thousand people in a place that only holds two thousand. The magic that night was unforgettable.

MASUCCI   It was a tremendous success. Ralphy had never had more than 800 people at the Cheetah. And we filmed it, recorded it and then salsa took off. It was one of those once in a lifetime things. And then it never stopped for about 16 or 17 years. Ray Barretto was the conga player and Willie Colón was a young kid. Willie came in very humbly with a song he was going to record and showed it to Ray. Barretto looked at it and gave it an "Agh!" He took it and threw it on the floor. Then they almost had a big fight. I had to get in the middle. Finally we straightened things out. Then we did a rehearsal and it was a total disaster. It was terrible, so I went to get something to eat. Johnny Pacheco and Bobby Valentín knew it was a disaster, too. They went and they huddled.

MERCADO   Symphony Sid and Dick "Ricardo" Sugar were Jewish-Americans that had Latin radio programs. In the 50's and 60's, Americans were very involved in this music.

PETE "EL CONDE" RODRÍGUEZ   Symphony Sid was the MC that night with Izzy Sanabria.

   Pacheco introduced the band, calling out their nicknames one by one. He saw a face and associated it with a name. Ismael Miranda was "Pretty Boy," Cheo "Teacher's Pet," Willie Colón "El Malo," Barretto "Mano Dura" (Hard Hands), Larry Harlow "El Judío Maravilloso (The Incredible Jew)."

MASUCCI   We filmed the concert that night. Everybody was a little nervous until they saw the crowd. The capacity was about twenty two hundred people because it was a pretty big place and there were four thousand people there. It was wall to wall people and they went crazy. The concert was history. I don't know what Pacheco and Valentín did between the two of them, but everything we recorded was incredible. I sat in the recording truck with Leon Gast. The whole night was amazing, it's probably number one on their list. The feeling between the musicians never ever again happened like that. It was one of those nights that was like a baby being born. There were no egos. They were totally playing together. People were crazy. It was just perfect. The vibrations were incredible.

PETE "EL CONDE"   You couldn't even go to the bathroom because it was so packed. There was electricity in the air.

MERCADO   That night was the explosion of salsa, not only at the Cheetah, but all over the world. The musicians played better than ever and when they started to belt out, "Quítate tú pa' ponerme yo," you heard the rivalry among the singers, because each one was trying to outdo the other. They're buddies, but when it came time to do the inspirations, it was interesting. We didn't pay the artists much, it wasn't the money, it's what happened later that made them into stars.

PETE "EL CONDE"   There was a lot of improvisation, there was competition. If you said something, I answered to see who sang the best improvisation. Everybody was up to it. I was trying to make the other guys a little bit mad, "Hey man, this guy came out with a nice inspiration. Let me see if I can counter that." To me, it was one of the best performances ever and it was a lot of fun.

CHEO FELICIANO   The Cheetah happened at the very end of 1971. To that day and since then I have never seen such euphoria in the Latin world. Maybe because of where I was coming from. When I got to the Cheetah, the whole block, 52nd Street was filled with people from Eighth to Ninth Avenue. There wasn't even room for a cockroach in there. It was very hard for me to get in, they had to open space so I could get through. My heart jumped a few times when I saw the people looking at me and saying, "It's him, it's Cheo. Look at him, he looks so good. Cheo, we love you," and all this thing started flowing. I didn't think this was going to happen. When I went into drug treatment, everybody turned their backs on me. But that night, when I saw the sincerity of the people, when I felt love from my people, I flashed back to that sad moment and said to myself, they were right in turning their backs on me, because they shook my whole humanity. They made me change and now they are back. And I'm grateful to everybody.

Finally when we came on the scene, I still was a little nervous, but when I came on and I saw the faces and I felt my blood rush and I heard them yelling, "Cheo, Cheo," I knew I was home. I guess that feeling was what gave me the incentive to sing so well that night. It may be the night I've sung the best in my whole life. It was very hard for me to get over the excitement. I got the welcome from the guys, we embraced each other. I did what was right and I was never going to change.

MASUCCI   After that night, we just went back to business and kept working and looking for new artists and proving the product. All the artists were ours that night.

This photo and the title photo show Fania All Stars concerts in the 70s, most likely in Japan

OUR LATIN THING—SALSA ON THE BIG SCREEN

HARLOW *Our Latin Thing* was the first documentary film about the Salsa movement. The original budget of fifteen thousand dollars grew to a hundred and ten thousand dollars. It took about a year and half to finish because none of us were big-time filmmakers. The movie did okay in the theatres in New York and in Puerto Rico, but more importantly, it opened the doors to other countries. The film went to Venezuela. Our records had already been there, but now the people could see us. Suddenly they started playing salsa music in Venezuela. In 1975 they were playing what we were playing in 1965, ten years behind. They had to develop, they had to learn.

The movie went to Panama where the same was true. The same thing happened in Colombia, with the addition of the cumbia (Colombian coastal music) which had some swing to it; Roberto Torres started rearranging cumbias and vallenatos into more danceable salsa stuff. Then the Fania All Stars did a couple of tours, and that opened it up more. Suddenly, record sales jumped from fifteen, eighteen thousand to fifty, a hundred thousand.

YANKEE STADIUM—AUGUST 24, 1973

As the salsa audience expanded, the promoters moved the concerts to larger venues. In a chilling leap of faith, producers Johnny Pacheco and Jerry Masucci booked the entire Yankee Stadium with hopes of filling it and the concert far exceeded their expectations. Forty-five thousand people shook the beams of the venerable structure to the rhythmic passion of Johnny Pacheco's salsa anthem, *Mi Gente* (My People), dedicated to and invoking the Latino people's presence.

MASUCCI We ran a concert at Yankee Stadium, where we also made the film *Salsa*. Everyone had said, "Forget about it, who's going to come to Yankee Stadium to see salsa groups?" They thought we were crazy. But I rented the place for one night for $180,000 cash. We had to get permits from the city, put up a bond as a guarantee, because there was a baseball game the next day, so we weren't allowed on the grass. The artists had to stay on the platform and all the people had to stay up in the stands.

We decided to include El Gran Combo to bring in the Puerto Ricans and Mongo Santamaría, to bring in some Americans; and with the Fania All Stars, we'd attract them all. And we got Jorge Santana, Carlos's brother. There was a hot record at the time called *Soul Makossa* by Manu Dibango an African saxophonist, so we put him in the group.

We called all the guys and rehearsed. The night of the concert, the sound trucks and film trucks were there. There we were at Yankee Stadium. I was watching and waiting. And the stadium was empty. All of a sudden the place filled up, about forty-five thousand people. I had no idea how many till I got the count later. We introduced the artists from the dugout with a big spotlight, like an All Star Baseball game, only with musicians. "Playing first base, we have..."

CHEO The people were sitting in the bleachers and we were behind the shortstop. There was excitement going on, the noise was going up, the expressions of the people were humming "Mmmmm!" I remember one guy on the second or third balcony was waving a small Puerto Rican flag in a very excited way. He was running up and down, all over the place, till he came to the edge. In a sudden whirl, he went flying over the edge and came flying down two balconies. Everybody saw the guy falling down. There was complete silence...

the whole place was quiet. And, boom, the guy falls on this wire mesh. The stadium was deathlike. He landed on the batter's cage. All of a sudden, the guy jumped up dancing and waving the flag! "Aaah! Aaah!" From that moment on, we kept playing music.

MASUCCI   About an hour and a half into the show, Mongo Santamaría and Ray Barretto played *Congo Bongo*, a conga duo written by Larry Harlow. Right in the middle of the song, all the people got up, left their seats, landed on the field and charged the stage.

CHEO   What happened was that the bandstand was too far out into the field. We were too far away from the crowd and when we started playing again, that excitement sparked the people. What we saw was a stampede, forty thousand people running at us. It was a flow you could not stop, so we stopped playing immediately. We threw down our instruments, jumped out the back way and ran off, because we were going to get trampled. People started taking the instruments and everything for souvenirs, they went crazy. It wasn't that they were stealing the instruments, they just wanted a piece of that stage. It was hilarious.

MASUCCI   They started to take the timbales and climb on the lighting scaffold. They were all over the stage dancing. The police came, the lights went on. And that was it, so we had to stop the concert. I was almost crying because it was all ruined. ha!

CHEO   The people climbed onto the stage, the ones in the back kept on pushing and the whole bandstand crumbled down. That was the end of the concert. We had five or six tunes to go, but we couldn't play them. The whole place was destroyed. They closed Yankee Stadium for repairs after that.

MASUCCI   I went and got the film footage, landed in a cab and drove home. I put those tapes away. went out and met Ralphy at a club. Then we all got drunk. We lost the deposit, which was twenty-five thousand dollars for the grass. The concert was incredible, but I never did it again. We had enough footage to make our film. Then we went into the studio, faked a couple of things and made yet another film.

MOTHER AFRICA—SEPTEMBER 1974

The third memorable concert took place in "Mother" Africa in 1974, where the All Stars experienced first-hand the roots of their own music. They were humbled by the monumental impact salsa music has had on the African continent. It was incredible to discover that most West Africans grew up on Cuban music, Orquesta Aragón, Arsenio Rodríguez, Abelardo Barroso, Sonora Matancera and so many others.

JERRY MASUCCI   There was a guy called Stew Levine, a famous record producer, who called me up and wanted to get in touch with Manu Dibango because they were doing the Mohamed Ali vs. George Forman fight in Zaire, and they were putting on a music show. So I asked, "Why don't you take the Fania All Stars?" He said, "Come on over, we'll talk about it." I went to see him at a hotel, in his shorts with his feet up on a coffee table with a big bottle of soda. And he said, "We're gonna take the Fania All Stars to Africa."

LEON GAST   Somebody told me, "There is a fight happening in Africa. They're doing a music festival September 21 through the 23rd, and they're looking for a film director." George Foreman was the champion; Ali was going to win back the championship that he had been stripped of unjustly in 1967 or 1968. I asked around until I found out who was filming the project. They were looking for a big time mainstream director. I was a big sports fan

Johnny Pacheco in the mid 70s with composer Ramon Rodriguez

and I had done some music films. I had just finished shooting *Salsa*, so I got the job.

The Fania All Stars were invited to Africa because the people in Africa love salsa music. The music festival also slated James Brown, The Pointer Sisters, BB King, Miriam Makeba, The Spinners, Bill Withers, The Crusaders, Lloyd Price, Sister Sledge, Manu Dibango, and several African acts.

MASUCCI The plane was 8 hours late because James Brown would not leave without his equipment on board. By the time we got on the plane, Willie Colón had disappeared. He never made the flight. Everybody went there without any money (ad honorem) because they wanted to see the fight.

GAST But the day before the Fania All Stars and the rest of the acts left for Zaire, George Foreman was cut above his left eye during a sparring match. The heavyweight championship fight between George Foreman and Mohammed Ali was postponed. Everybody was really concerned, especially the artists and the people that were coming over with them.

CHEO We were there by the invitation of President Mobutu Seseseko of Zaire. He had chartered a 707 to take all the major talent of African extraction from around the world back to Africa. That was the movement "Ali's Black Back to Africa." In that chartered plane they had James Brown with his band, Ella Fitzgerald, Aretha Franklin, The Pointer sisters. Representing Africa in the Latin rhythms were the Fania All Stars, so we all mixed together. We had a ball on that flight, singing together, all kinds of rhythms.

And we landed in Kinshasa, Zaire's capital. When the plane finally got to the terminal, we saw a representation of many, if not all the tribes of Africa, from the Watusi to the Pygmies. They were all in their native costumes with the paint on their faces dancing around the plane in a big long carnival line. In the tribal differences, with the spears, they were all doing the stepping to a certain rhythm.

We couldn't hear them because we were inside the plane watching them dance from the portholes. We just wanted to know what rhythm they were dancing to. So when they opened up the plane's door, we were very much surprised. They were singing, "Caramelo, caramelo, caramelo," a little African group with a cuatro and a tres guitar and they were playing *Caramelo*, the Cuban *son* (pregón). That was great for all of us.

In Africa, they are the masters of percussion and in one of the parties that the embassies gave us there was a group of African percussionists, tall guys, big guys. They were playing congas, handmade out of solid trunks of trees. And the skins… I don't know how they could play on those skins because they were better than a quarter of an inch thick. It was like playing on wood or even harder than wood and these guys were playing them not standing or sitting, but in a half-bent position, holding the congas with the pressure of their knees, playing at a very high speed like, "Taca taca taca taca taca tacata."

There we were, Ray Barretto, Roberto Roena, all the guys from the percussion department, watching and being amazed by the speed and the stamina these guys had. They played at that speed for over an hour without stopping. We were getting tired and sweaty just watching, and these guys were still fresh, their hands were like rocks. We were amazed by their consistency, they didn't lose tempo, they didn't look tired, it looked as though they could go on for years. Meanwhile, one of the guys who knows nothing about percussion, who knows nothing about Latin music, who has no African heritage because he's an

Orthodox Jew—fell into a trance and curled up on the floor like a snake. He was Elliot Sax, Jerry Masucci's brother-in-law. Foam was flowing out of his mouth, his eyes went white, they both turned around. He went into a trance and we couldn't get him out of it. The African women had to do a tribal ritual to get him out of it.

LUIS "PERICO" ORTIZ   This was our motherland, it was awe-inspiring. They took us to visit the tribes, to see their chanting and sacrifices. The tribes performed the drums twenty four hours a day.

We were the closing act before the Ali-Forman fight. There were 80,000 people in that stadium. James Brown, Billy Cobham and the Pointer Sisters played fabulously. Then we came on. It was a challenge because we were playing to our teachers. The tribes were there with their drums.

Two cranes were holding the stage in the air three stories high and there were no barriers at the back of the stage. We were performing near the back and at all times, the security people were telling us, "Watch your back because there is no railing." Pupi Legarreta, the violin player, was very excited and during his solo he started jumping up and down, and I shouted, "Pupi watch it. Pupi watch it. Pupi watch it!" Pacheco, who was facing the stage, saw Pupi jumping and suddenly he was gone. He fell all the way down. Fortunately, he landed on some air bags. So when we looked down, Pupi was all wrapped up in cables, playing his violin. He came back, winking at us like saying, "Don't worry. Everything is fine," and he kept on playing his violin solo....

And the show goes on.... To this day, the Fania All Stars continue to play together and entertain *nuestra gente.*   ■

*At the Yankee Stadium Concert August 24, 1973
the bandstand was too far from the audience.*

Photos in this chapter © José L. Flores courtesy of Fania Records

Abakuá 1. A secret fraternal society formed in Cuba by descendants of the Calabar tribe, referred to as the Carabalí. 2. The ritual music and dance of the Abakuá sect, which has greatly influenced Cuban secular forms such as rumba.

abanico The rim shot and roll of the timbales.

Bantú The African people of Congolese origin, as they are referred to in Cuba. Perhaps one of the most influential African cultures throughout the Caribbean area.

baqueteo The rhythmic pattern played by the timbales in the Cuban style known as danzón.

batá (drums) The sacred, two-headed drums of the Yoruba people of Nigeria.

bembé (drums) A set of three drums made from hollowed palm tree logs, with nailed-on skins which are tuned with heat.

bolero A slow, lyrical ballad.

bomba 1. A barrel-shaped drum of Afro-Puerto Rican origin, similar to the Cuban tumbadora (conga drum), although shorter; 2. A style of Afro-Puerto Rican music and dance which is also commonly found in salsa repertoires.

bongos Two small drums attached by a thick piece of wood, played while held between the knees. The bongos were developed from African predecessors in Cuba's Oriente province. Originally, the bongo's drum heads (skins) were tacked-on, but later a system of tuneable hardware was attached. Bongos today are made of fiberglass as well as wood.

cajón(es) Wooden box(es) used in early interpretations of rumba, and still popular today.

canción A simple yet fundamental musical form consisting mainly of lyrics, harmony and melody, with very basic rhythmic accompaniment. The most common setting for this style is voice and guitar, and is often referred to as trova.

cencerro A cowbell (with the clapper removed), struck with a wooden stick.

cha cha cha A rhythmic style derived from the early Cuban danzón-mambo, created by violinist Enrique Jorrín (who named the style upon hearing the scraping sounds of dancers' feet). The cha cha cha eventually became a separate musical style from the danzón.

charanga A specific style of instrumentation consisting of rhythm section (contrabass, timbales, and güiro), strings (from two to four violins, or any number of violins with a cello), and one wood flute. The piano and conga drum were added in the 1940s. This term (and style of instrumentation) evolved from the charanga francesa, developed in the early 20th century.

charanga francesa The original term for what is now known as the charanga instrumentation (see above).

charanga vallenata A style of instrumentation combining elements of the Cuban charanga and conjunto styles with the Colombian vallenato style featuring the accordion.

charanguita A popular instrumentation in peasant or country music parties (called guateques), consisting of accordion, timbales and güiro.

chékere A beaded gourd instrument of African origin used in Cuban sacred music. Also referred to as güiro - for the style of music in which it is used - as well as agbe, agwe or agüe.

clave A five-note, bi-measure pattern which serves as the foundation for all of the rhythmic styles in salsa music. The clave consists of a "strong" measure containing three notes (also called the tresillo), and a "weak" measure containing two notes, resulting in patterns beginning with either measure, referrred to as "three-two" or two-three." There are two types of clave patterns associated with popular (secular) music: son clave and rumba clave. Another type of clave - 6/8 clave - originated in several styles of West African sacred music.

claves Two round, polished sticks which are used to play the clave patterns.

columbia A rural style of Cuban rumba containing many African elements in its lyrics, polyrhythmic structure and dance style.

combo An adaptation of the North American jazz combo instrumentation in Cuba during the late 1950s, generally consisting of bass, drums, piano, sax, trumpet, Cuban percussion and electric guitar.

conga (drum) A Cuban drum derived from several African predecessors - also known as the tumbadora - originating as a solid, hollowed log with a nailed-on skin. Eventually, tuneable hardware was added and today, conga drums are made out of fiberglass as well as wood.

conjunto A specific style of instrumentation developed around 1940, derived from the septeto ensemble, consisting of guitar, tres, contrabass, bongos, three vocalists (who play hand percussion such as maracas and claves), and two to four trumpets. The piano and the tumbadora were added by legendary tres player Arsenio Rodriguez.

coro "Chorus."

coro/pregón The call-and-response relationship between the lead vocal soloist, or pregonero, and the fixed choral response, or coro. In salsa song form, this takes place during the open vamp section called the montuno.

cuatro A Puerto Rican stringed instrument (similar to the Cuban tres), derived from the guitar.

cuá The principal pattern in the Puerto Rican form (and rhythm) known as bomba.

cáscara 1. The shell or sides of the timbales; 2. The pattern played on the shell or sides of the timbales.

danza A 19th century musical and dance form which serves as a precursor to the Cuban danzón.

danzón A Cuban musical and dance form developed in the late 19th century, which is derived from the European Court and Country dances, as well as the contradanza and the danza. The instrumentation which generally interprets this style is known as the charanga orchestra, featuring strings and flute with a rhythm section. The danzón form consists of: an introduction called the paseo (A), the principal flute melody (B), a repeat of the introduction (A), and the violin trio (C). Innovations by several composers led to the addition of a fourth section (D) called nuevo ritmo, later known as mambo. This section added elements of the Cuban son, and established an open vamp over which the flute, violin or piano would improvise.

descarga "Unloading" (lit.); a jam session, as well as an improvised tune. estribillo Refrain or chorus.

guaguancó One of three styles of Cuban rumba, featuring a heightened polyrhythmic structure, and danced by male-female couples (in its traditional folkloric setting). The typical instrumentation (used by all styles) includes: tumbadoras (congas) or cajones (boxes), palitos (sticks) or cucharas (spoons), claves, and marugas (shakers).

guajeo The repeated figure played by the string instruments in a particular ensemble such as the tres' vamp in a conjunto instrumentation, or the violin vamp in a charanga instrumentation. Also used to refer to repeated horn lines, such as in a layered mambo section.

guajira An arpeggiated and floral song form, derived from the Cuban son with elements of the canción form.

guaracha Traditionally a form of música campesina (peasant or country music) which developed as a form of street music, originally featuring satirical lyrics. Now generaly associated with tunes of moderate tempo.

güiro 1. A serrated gourd or calabash, scraped with a stick, which is extremely popular throughout Latin America. It has both African and indigenous American roots. 2. A term previously used to refer to the chékere.

güiro (6/8 rhythm) A rhythmic style, so-named because of its interpretation on the beaded gourds known (at first) as güiros, and later, chékeres. In addition to the chékeres, a bell and a tumbadora may be added.

güícharo Another term referring to the güiro, particularly a Puerto Rican variety, which is distinguished by thinner grooves than those of a Cuban güiro.

habanera A precursor to the Cuban danzón, derived from the contradanza and danza.

Itótele (drum, batá) The middle drum in the set of three batá drums.

iyesá (drums) A set of four sacred, cylindrical, two-headed drums of hand-carved cedar, played with sticks.

Iyá (drum, batá) The largest drum in the set of three batá drums. "Iyá" is "mother" in Yoruba.

Lucumí The term used (in Cuba) to refer to Afro-Cubans of Yoruba descent, as well as the language and religion of Yoruba tradition.

mambo (rhythm) 1. The section added to the danzón form (in the 1940s) which featured an open vamp and instrumental improvisation. 2. An up-tempo dance style, developed through the 40s and 50s, which blended several elements of North American instrumentation and harmony with elements of the Cuban son.

mambo (section) The section of an arrangement which features new material, including layered horn lines called moñas.

maracas Hand-held rattles or shakers, made from gourds, coconuts, wood or rawhide and filled with beans. Found throughout the Americas as well as Africa.

martillo The repeated pattern of the bongos, which is frequently "ad-libbed," (or, played improvisationally).

marímbula A large thumb piano-type box of Bantú (Congolese) origin, used to provide the bass in the changüi style of the Cuban son.

merengue A rhythmic style from the Dominican Republic, which is a fast two-step, and is traditionally played on tambora, güira and accordion.

montuno (piano) The repeated, syncopated vamp secton played by the piano in an ensemble.

montuno (section) The open vamp section of a song, which features the coro/pregón (call-and-response singing) and instrumental solos.

mozambique A rhythmic style created in the 1960s by Pedro Izquierdo - also known as Pello el Afrokán - which is a style of Cuban carnaval music, traditionally played only on percussion instruments. The mozambique was popularized in North American salsa music by Eddie Palmieri, and was adapted into ensemble interpretations.

moña A horn line (either written or improvised), as well as a section featuring layered, contrapuntal horn lines. Moñas may occur during a mambo secton, or during the montuno section, such as in a "shout" chorus underneath a soloist.

nuevo ritmo "New rhythm" (lit.), referring to the added section of the danzón form in the 1940s by Orestes and Israel "Cachao" López. This section later became known as mambo.

Okónkolo (drum, batá) The smallest in the set of three batá drums.

orquesta típica An instrumentation used in the interpretation of the Creole contradanza, consisting of woodwinds, brass, strings, güiro and tympani. By the late 19th century, the tympani were replaced by the Cuban pailas or timbales, and the horn section diminished.

pachanga A rhythmic style and rigourous dance (featuring skipping and jumping movements), very popular during the 1950s, and originating in the charanga instrumentation.

pailas A term for a smaller version of the Cuban timbales.

palitos "Sticks" (lit.); specifically, the sticks and pattern played by the sticks in the genre of Cuban rumba.

pandereta A hand-held drum - similar to a tambourine but without jingles - used in the interpretation of the Puerto Rican plena rhythm, often in a set of two or three.

plena An Afro-Puerto Rican rhythm, traditionally played on panderetas, which is an important form of popular music. The plena often serves as a vehicle for the expression of social and politically relevant themes.

pregón The lead, improvised vocal which alternates with the fixed choral response, or coro.

quinto The highest-pitched drum in a set of three drums used in the styles of rumba, which improvises throughout.

rumba A Cuban folkloric secular form, consisting of drumming, dancing and call-and-response singing which contains both African and Spanish roots. There are three styles of rumba: the yambú, guaguancó and columbia.

rumba flamenca The style of rumba from southern Spain, also called rumba gitana (gypsy rumba), which influenced the Cuban rumba form.

septeto A style of instrumentation formed around 1927 by the Septeto Nacional, which consisted of the addition of the trumpet to the sexteto.

sexteto A style of instrumentation founded in 1920 by the Sexteto Habanero, consisting of the tres, guitar, contrabass, bongos, maracas and claves.

son A style of popular dance music of the peasant or working-class, combining several Spanish and African elements. The son began to take shape in the latter half of the 19th century in Cuba's Oriente province, and gave birth to several hybrids including the afro-son, guajira-son, son-pregón and son-montuno. The son is perhaps the most important form at the root of today's popular salsa music.

songo A contemporary, eclectic rhythm which blends several styles, including rumba, son, conga and other Cuban secular as well as sacred styles, with elements of North American jazz and funk.

tambora A two-headed drum from the Dominican Republic, used in the style of merengue. The tambora is strapped around the neck and played with the hands and one stick, which strikes the drumhead and the wooden side of the drum.

timbales A set of two, tuneable drums created in Cuba - derived from the European tympani - mounted on a tripod and played with sticks. The set has been added onto with several accessory items such as cowbells, cymbal and woodblocks.

timbalitos A smaller version of the timbales, tuned at higher pitches, and often added to the timbales to make up a set of four.

tres A Cuban stringed instrument derived from the Spanish guitar, consisting of three doble strings and played with a pick. The tres is the signature instrument of the Cuban son.

tumbadora A Cuban version of an African drum, consisting (originally) of a hollowed, barrel-shaped log or hand-carved trunk of wood with a tacked-on rawhide head. Later, a system of tuneable hardware was added. The tumbadora is also referred to as the conga drum, and its predecessors include the tambores de conga, used in early comparsas, as well as the makuta drums of Yoruba origin.

tumbao (bass) The repeated pattern played by the bass, often accenting beats 2+ and 4. The pattern is a mixture of influences from the styles of the contradanza and the son.

tumbao (congas) The repeated pattern played by the tumbadoras (conga drums), also referred to as marcha (march), emphasizing the fourth beat of the measure, as well as beat 4+.

yambú The oldest style of rumba, dating back to Cuba's colonial period, often interpreted on cajones (boxes), and danced by male-female couples. It is the slowest style of rumba.

Yoruba The people (and language) from Nigeria, and one of the most influential African cultures throughout the Caribbean.

This is an abbreviated version of the glossary to be found in Sher Music Co.'s book, "The Salsa Guidebook" by Rebeca Mauleon. It is available from Sher Music Co. at www.shermusic.com or by calling 707/763-8134. Thanks, Rebeca!

Bibliography

Aparicio, Frances R. (1998). Listening to salsa: Gender, Latin Popular Music, and Puerto Rican Cultures. (Hanover, NH, Wesleyan University Press.) Scholarly bent.

Aparicio, F. (1989-90). Salsa, maracas, and baile: Latin popular music in the poetry of Victor Hernández Cruz. MELUS 16 (Spring): 43-58.

Baez, Juan Carlos (1983) El Vínculo es la Salsa. (Dirección de Cultura-UCV-Fondo Editorial Tropykos-Grupo Editor Derrelieve) Ccs, Venezuela.

Bergman, B., Hot Sauces. Latin and Caribbean Pop, (Quill) New York 1985. Chapter 6. Salsa and Latin Jazz by Isabelle Leymarie

Blanco, Jesus (1992). 80 años del Son y Soneros en el Caribe. Fondo Editorial Tropykos, Caracas, Venezuela.

Blanco, Tomas. (1935). Elogio de la plena. Revista del Ateneo Puerto Rico, essay 1(1): 97-106.

Bloch, Peter. (1973). La-Le-Lo-Lai: Puerto Rican music and its performers. New York, Plus Ultra.

Boggs, Vernon. W. (1992). Salsiology: Afro-Cuban music and the evolution of Salsa in New York City, Greenwood Publishing Group.

Cabrera Infante, G. (1982). Salsa para una ensalada. Literature in transition: The many voices of the caribbean area. R. S. Minc. Gaithersburg, MD, Hispamérica and Montclair State College.

Calvo Ospina, Hernando (1995) Salsa: Havana Heat, Bronx Beat. Latin American Bureau.

Campos, Carlos. (1996). Salsa & Afro Cuban Montunos for Piano, A.D.G. Productions.

Campos, Carlos. (1998). Salsa, further adventures In Afro-Cuban music for piano, A.D.G. Productions.

Campos Parsi, H. (1976). La música en Puerto Rico. Madrid, Ediciones R.

Canizares, R. J. (1994). Santeria: From Afro-Caribbean cult to world religion. Caribbean Quarterly 40(1): 59-63.

Cardona, L. A. (1995). A History of the Puerto Ricans in the United States of America: The coming of the Puerto Ricans, Carreta Press.

Carpentier, Alejo (1946). La Música en Cuba. México, Ed. Fondo de cultura económica.

Caso, F. H. (1980). Héctor Campos Parsi en la historia de la música puertorriqueña del siglo XX. San Juan, PR, Instituto de Cultura Puertorriqueña.

Colon, J. (1982). A Puerto Rican in New York, and other sketches, International Publishers.

Cortes, F., A. Falcón, et al. (1976). The cultural expression of Puerto Ricans in New York: A theoretical perspective and critical review. Latin American Perspectives 3(10): 117-152.

Crook, L. (1982). A musical analysis of the Cuban rumba. Latin American Music Review 3(1): 92-123.

Diaz Ayala, Cristobal. (1981) Musica Cubana: Del Areyto a la Nueva Trova. Editorial Cubanacan, San Juan, Puerto Rico.

Duany, J. (1983). Popular Music in Puerto Rico: Toward an anthropology of Salsa. Latin American Music Review 5: 186-216.

Duany, J. (1988). After the Revolution: The search for roots in Afro-Cuban culture. Latin American Research Review 23(1): 244-255.

Figueroa, Frank M. (1994) Encyclopedia of Latin American Music in New York. Pillar Publications, St. Petersburg, FL.

Figueroa, Frank M. (1996) Almanaque de la Música Latinoamericana. Pillar Publications, St. Petersburg, FL.

Figueroa Hernández, Rafael (1996) Salsa Mexicana: Transculturación e Identidad. ConClave, Xalapa, Mexico.

Figueroa Hernández, Rafael (1993) El Sonero Mayor. ConClave, Mexico. Instituto de Cultura Puertoriqueña, San Juan, P.R.

Figueroa Hernández, Rafael (1996) Luis Angel Silva: Melón. Xalapa, Mexico.

Figueroa, R. (1992). Salsa and related genres: A bibliographical guide, Greenwood Publishing Group.

Flores, J. (1988). Bumbún and the Beginnings of La Plena. Centro de Estudios Puertorriqueños Bulletin 2(19).

Flores, J. (1992). Cortijo's Revenge. On Edge: The crisis of contemporary Latin American culture. G. Yúdice, J. Franco and J.

Flores. Minneapolis, University of Minnesota Press: 187-205.

Flores, J. (1993). Divided Borders: Essays on Puerto Rican identity. Houston, TX, Arte Público Press.

Gerard, Charlie with Sheller, Marty. (1989). Salsa: The Rhythm of Latin Music. White Cliffs Media Co. Crown Point, IN.

Glasser, R. (1995). My Music Is My Flag: Puerto Rican musicians and their New York communities, 1917-1940. Berkeley and Los Angeles, CA, University of California Press.

González Wippler, Migene. (1975). Santeria. New York, Anchor Press/Doubleday

Hondagneu-Sotelo, P. A cultural history of salsa, and some remarks on the nature of musical and meaning, ethnic identity, hegemony and resistance. University of California at Berkeley.

López Cruz, F. (1967). La Música Folklórica de Puerto Rico. Sharon, CT, Troutman Press.

Manuel, Peter. (1990). Popular Musics of the Non-Western world: An introductory survey. Oxford University Press.

Manuel, Peter., Ed. (1992). Essays on Cuban music: North American and Cuban perspectives. University Press of America.

Manuel, Peter., K. M. Bilby, et al. (1995). Caribbean Currents: Caribbean music from rumba to reggae. Temple University Press.

Mauleón, Rebeca. (1993). Salsa guidebook for piano and ensemble, Sher Music Co. Petaluma, CA

McCoy, J. A. (1968). The Bomba and Aguinaldo of Puerto Rico as they have evolved from indigenous, African, and European cultures. Florida State University.

Mendez, Angel. (1985). Swing Latino: Gente Caribe. La Biblia de la Salsa, Caracas.

Mujica, Hector. (1982). El Inquieto Anacobero: Confesiones de Daniel Santos a Hector Mujica. Editorial Cejota, Caracas, Venezuela.

Nuñez, Maria Virtudes & Guntín, Ramón. Salsa Caribe y Otras Músicas Antillanas. (Madrid, Ediciones Cubicas, SA.1992)

Ortiz, Fernando. (1975). La Música Afrocubana. Ediciones Júcar. Madrid.

Padilla, F. M. (1990). Salsa: Puerto Rican and Latino music. Journal of Popular Culture 24 (Summer): 87-104.

Pérez Perazzo, Alberto. (1988). Ritmo Afrohispano Antillano 1865-1965 Caracas. Publicaciones Almacenadoras Caracas, C.A.

Roberts, John Storm. (1979). The Latin Tinge: The impact of Latin American music on the United States. New York, Oxford University Press.

Rodríguez S., Lil (1997). Bailando en la casa del trompo. Caracas. Euroamericana de Ediciones.

Rodríguez Juliá, Edgardo. (1983). El entierro de Cortijo. Rio Piedras, PR, Huracan.

Rondón, Cesar Miguel. (1980). El libro de la salsa: Crónica de la músic del Caribe urbano. Caracas, Venezuela, Editorial Arte.

Salloum, Trevor. (1997). Bongo Book. Mel Bay Publications. Email Trevor Salloum at tsalloum@awinc.com

Santana, Sergio. (1992). Qué Es La Salsa?: Buscando Melodia. Ediciones Salsa y Cultura, Medellin, Colombia.

Singer, R. (1982). "My music is who I am and what I do": Latin popular music and identity in NYC, Indiana University. Doctoral dissertation by someone who has worked closely with New York Latino and Jazz musicians since the 60s. Good analysis of the differences between Cuban and Salsa music as well as the values deemed important by New York artists. Gives much needed attention to the issues of hegemony, resistance, and identity and how these factor into the creation of the music. (ER)

Singer, R. L. (1983). Tradition and innovation in contemporary Latin popular music in New York City. Latin American Music Review 4(2): 183-202.

Ulloa, Alejandro (1992). La Salsa en Cali. Colombia. Colección Crónica y Periodismo. Ediciones IUniversidad del Valle.

Vega, A. L. (1983). Letra para salsa y tres soneos por encargo (Lyrics for a salsa song and three soneos by demand). Virgenes y Martires (Virgins and Martyrs). A. L. Vega and C. L. Filippi. Rio Piedras, PR, Editorial Antilles: 81-88.

Thanks to Edward Yemil Rosario for some of these entries.

Give salsa music fans a gift they will treasure! Your loved ones, friends and colleagues will enjoy this book.

CHECK YOUR
LOCAL BOOKSTORE
OR ORDER HERE

☐ Yes, I want _____ copies of Salsa Talks at $59.95 each. (See below for shipping costs.)

Florida residents, please add $4.20 sales tax per book. Foreign orders must be accompanied by a postal money order in U.S. funds or a check in U.S. funds drawn on a U.S. bank. Allow 15 days for delivery.

Name   _____

Address _____

City, State, Zip _____

My check or money order for _____ is enclosed (make payable to Digital Domain). Please include shipping and applicable sales tax.

_____Please charge my   ☐ Visa   ☐ Master Card   ☐ American Express

Account # _____Exp. Date _____

Signature _____

Name _____

Billing Address for Credit Card _____

City _____State _____Zip_____

Shipping address if different _____

City _____State _____Zip_____

Tel. _____E-Mail_____

OR CALL TOLL-FREE (800) 344-4361 OR ORDER AT WWW.SALSATALKS.COM

Send to:
Digital Domain
931 N.SR 434 - Suite 1201-168
Altamonte Springs, Fl 32714
(407) 831-0233
Fax (407) 834-1339
Email: ofcmgr@salsatalks.com

SHIPPING COSTS
Please include $8.00 U.S. postage and handling for one or two books shipped to same U.S. address. Please inquire for all other rates including foreign shipping. We ship via Priority Mail. Allow 15 days for delivery. Prices subject to change without notice.